Away for the WEEKEND®

MID-ATLANTIC

ALSO BY ELEANOR BERMAN

Away for the Weekend: Southeast
Away for the Weekend: New York
Away for the Weekend: Midwest

Away for the
WEEKEND®

MID-ATLANTIC
REVISED AND UPDATED

**Great Getaways
within 250 Miles from
Washington, D.C.
in Delaware
Maryland
Virginia
West Virginia
Pennsylvania
New Jersey**

ELEANOR BERMAN

THREE RIVERS PRESS • NEW YORK

Published by Three Rivers Press, New York, New York.
Member of the Crown Publishing Group, a division of Random House, Inc.
www.randomhouse.com

THREE RIVERS PRESS and the Tugboat design are registered trademarks
of Random House, Inc.

Originally published in paperback by Crown Publishers in 1987.

Printed in the United States of America

Library of Congress Cataloging-in-Publication Data
Berman, Eleanor, 1934–
    Mid-Atlantic : great getaways within 250 miles from Washington, D.C. /
Eleanor Berman.—6th ed., rev. and updated.
        p.   cm.
Rev. ed. of: Away for the weekend, Mid-Atlantic. New York : Crown Trade
Paperbacks, 1996.
Includes index.
    1. Washington Region—Tours.   2. Middle Atlantic States—Tours.
I. Berman, Eleanor, 1934– Away for the Weekend, Mid-Atlantic   II. Title.
    F192.3 .B47 2002
    917.404'44—dc21   2002001666

ISBN: 0-609-80905-9

10   9   8   7   6   5   4   3   2   1

Revised and Updated

Contents

Acknowledgments

My sincere thanks to all the state and local tourism offices that supplied information and guidance for this update and revision of *Away for the Weekend®: Mid-Atlantic*. And special thanks to my editor, Elizabeth Royles, for her enthusiasm and assistance.

Introduction

From the placid waters of Chesapeake Bay to the rugged mountains of West Virginia, from Virginia plantations to the silent battlefield at Gettysburg, the mid-Atlantic region is packed with weekending treasures. This is a guide to the best of the getaways, places offering a change of pace and a recharge of spirits for every mood and season.

The 52 weekend trips that follow will take you through six states, from small-town charm to city sophistication; from gardens and galleries to solitary woodlands; from festive folk celebrations to great resorts. Throughout, you will discover the rich heritage of the region where much of our nation's future was forged.

All of the trips are within 250 miles of Washington, D.C. They are also within easy reach of Philadelphia, Baltimore, Wilmington, Richmond, Trenton—in fact, much of the Eastern seaboard from Virginia to New York. Since Washington is at the heart of the mid-Atlantic, driving directions and mileage are given from the D.C. area, but major routes are noted to make it easy to plan a trip from any direction.

It should be noted from the start that this is a personal and selective guide. Instead of trying to include all the myriad possibilities for travel in Delaware, Maryland, New Jersey, Pennsylvania, Virginia, and West Virginia, I've selected what I feel are the cream of the weekend destinations. Nor is every single sightseeing attraction, lodging, and restaurant in each location included. I've limited the book to those I've visited myself or had recommended by knowledgeable local sources or frequent visitors to these areas, people whose opinions I respect.

Since many mid-Atlantic lodgings are very special places, the best are noted in each area, and a few resorts even become destinations in themselves. However, this is primarily a guide to destinations and events, not a guide to inns or resorts, so where motels are the only accommodations available, the listings reflect this.

Bed-and-breakfasts are another popular lodging option. There is sometimes confusion as to what the term means, since many small inns that serve only breakfast call themselves bed-and-breakfast inns. A listing of associations of such inns is given at the end of this section.

Also included is a listing of registry services handling mainly a different type of bed-and-breakfast—private homes that open a few rooms to guests and serve them a homemade breakfast. These are often reasonably priced and very personal accommodations offering the chance to meet local residents and get the real flavor of living in the areas where you travel. They are also a good alternative when you make last-minute plans and inns are booked.

Since different seasons often bring different events in the same areas, you will find repeat mentions of some destinations. The trips themselves are arranged by season not only because activities change with the calendar, but to give you time to read ahead about upcoming events and to reserve rooms early. This advance notice enables you to make the most of a special show or open house, planning a relaxing and leisurely weekend of sightseeing rather than a last-minute day trip.

Don't feel bound by the calendar, however. Many of these destinations are equally appealing and less crowded when nothing special is going on, and places on the ocean or on Chesapeake Bay can be a special delight on a weekend out of season when you have them almost to yourself. The information listings at the end of each chapter are appropriate to any season you make the trip.

HOW TO USE THE BOOK

Like its predecessors in this series, *Away for the Weekend: Mid-Atlantic* assumes you have a normal two-day weekend to spend, arriving on Friday night and leaving late on Sunday. Each trip suggests activities for a two-day stay, with added attractions to accommodate varying tastes and time schedules. I've included what I hope is just enough history and background to make each area more interesting without bogging you down in detail. If you become intrigued and want more detailed information, you can get it on the spot.

When there is enough to do to warrant a longer stay, a symbol at the start of each trip will tell you so. When you do have more than a weekend to spend, use these symbols as a cue, or use the maps at the back to combine nearby weekends to fill out an extended stay. Norfolk, Williamsburg, Richmond, and Charlottesville, for example, might all be combined for a mid-Virginia tour. The same is true for destinations in and around Pennsylvania Dutch country, the Shenandoah Valley, and Chesapeake Bay.

Symbols also indicate trips that seem appropriate for children, though you are the best judge of what your own family might enjoy.

A final symbol marks a few trips that can be done entirely via public transportation. There are many other destinations where excursion air-fares make it possible to extend your weekending range and to cut down on winter driving, and others where easy Amtrak connections can save you the hassle of driving out of the city in Friday night traffic.

The symbols that indicate these various categories are as follows:

        = recommended for children

 = accessible at least in part via public transportation

        = recommended for long weekends

Lodging prices indicated are for two people; dining listings indicate the cost of main courses only rather than a whole dinner, since not everyone chooses to order a three-course meal.

For lodgings:

I (inexpensive) = under $80
M (medium) = $80 to $135
E (expensive) = $135 to $200
EE (extra expensive) = over $200

When meals are included in the rates, these letters are used:

CP = continental plan (breakfast only)
MAP = modified American plan (breakfast and dinner)
AP = American plan (all three meals)

For dining, the letters are as follows:

I = most entrees under $12 per person
M = most entrees between $12 and $20
E = most entrees between $20 and $30
EE = most entrees over $30 (often means a prix fixe menu)

When prices bridge two categories, you will find two symbols.

For sightseeing attractions, the following dollar signs indicate adult admission fees.

$ = up to $2.50
$$ = $2.51 to $5
$$$ = $5.01 to $7.50
$$$$ = $7.51 to $10
$$$$$ = over $10

You can usually assume that children pay half price. Attractions where kids are admitted free are noted, and where prices are well over $10, the fees at press time are given as an indication of what to expect.

Rates frequently increase even before a book makes it from writer to bookstore. Prices for food and lodging also tend to go up as months go by. The rates and price ranges here are as accurate as could be determined at the time of publication and are included as a general indication of what to expect. Please use them just that way, as a general guide *only*, and *always* use the telephone numbers included to check for current prices when you plan your trip. It is always wise to verify current hours and holiday closings as well.

When it comes to restaurants and lodgings, remember that a new owner can make a big difference, and changes and closings cannot always be predicted. Again, use this as a general guide, and, I hope, a reasonably accurate one.

Since AAA, Mobil, and other similar guides do so well by motel listings, I've omitted motels here unless they are the only available lodgings or have a special appeal. You can get a listing of motels by contacting the local tourist office at the end of each chapter. Throughout, (800), (866), and (888) telephone numbers are toll free.

In most cases, addresses for additional information for individual destinations are included at the end of each chapter. Use these addresses to get advance information that can make your trip more enjoyable. Internet Web sites are also given for most state and local tourist offices and the national parks so that the growing number of readers with access to computers can find current information. If you don't see a Web site for a particular destination, you may be able to find information by looking into the appropriate state site.

New telephone area codes are being assigned regularly throughout the mid-Atlantic. Those given were correct at press time, but be alert for additional changes.

If you find that any information here has become seriously inaccurate or that a place has closed or gone downhill, I hope that you will let me know in care of Three Rivers Press, 299 Park Avenue, New York, NY 10171, so that the entry can be corrected. If you discover newly opened places or some appealing ones that I have missed, I hope you will let me know about them as well.

The maps in this book are simplified to highlight locations of suggested destinations. They are not necessarily reliable as road maps. One way to get excellent free maps of each state included is to contact the tourism office of that state. These offices offer many excellent free guides to their state attractions as well.

One last tip: Reserve well ahead if you want to stay in small country inns or visit beach or ski resorts in high season. Most lodgings offer refunds on deposits if you cancel with reasonable notice, so write ahead and take your pick instead of settling for leftovers. Three or four months ahead is none too soon to book.

For this New Yorker, travel in the mid-Atlantic states to research and update this book have been wonderfully rewarding experiences. Pennsylvania, New Jersey, and Delaware were familiar to me from past writing and personal weekending, yet I discover new pleasures each time I return. Maryland, Virginia, and West Virginia were new territory for me, and each visit has become a treat. I've become addicted to Virginia ham biscuits and Maryland crab cakes; acquired beautiful mountain crafts; and discovered the sparkle of Chesapeake Bay in springtime, the bounty of Delaware's beaches in summer, the glory of autumn in the Shenandoah Valley, and the stunning beauty of the West Virginia mountains cloaked in winter white. I've also had a refresher course in American history, made all the more meaningful by standing on the ground where it was made. And everywhere, I've found warm hospitality, Southern and Northern, and helpful friends to make my job easier and my travels pleasanter.

I hope that my very real enthusiasm for these places and pleasures comes through to inspire you to share my discoveries—and to make some of your own.

STATE TOURIST OFFICES

All of the offices listed below will provide maps as well as information and literature on attractions throughout their states:

Delaware Tourism Office
99 Kings Highway
Dover, DE 19901
(302) 739-4271
Toll free: (866) 284-7483
www.visitdelaware.net

Maryland Office of Tourism
217 East Redwood Street
Baltimore, MD 21202
(410) 767-3400
(800) MD-IS-FUN
www.mdisfun.org

New Jersey Travel & Tourism
P.O. Box 820
20 West State Street
4th floor, Commerce
Trenton, NJ 08625
(609) 777-0885
(800) VISIT-NJ
www.state.nj.us/travel

Pennsylvania Office of Travel and Tourism
Forum Building, Room 404
Harrisburg, PA 17120
(717) 787-5453
(800) VISIT-PA
www.experiencepa.com

Virginia Tourism Corporation
901 East Byrd Street
Richmond, VA 23219
(804) 786-2051
(800) 759-0886
www.virginia.org

West Virginia Division of Tourism
2101 Washington Street E.
State Capitol Complex
Charleston, WV 25305
(800) CALL-WVA
www.westvirginia.com

BED-AND-BREAKFAST REGISTRY SERVICES

The reservation services listed here offer many listings of individual homes offering bed-and-breakfast hospitality in the locations noted. Rates for these accommodations begin around $75 and vary greatly, depending on the size and luxury of the rooms and whether there is a private bath. You have a better chance of being happy with your lodgings if you are very specific about what you are seeking—economy or luxury, privacy or congeniality, location in town or in the country, swimming pools or any other special needs. Listings of associations of small bed-and-breakfast inns offering statewide guides follow. Many state tourist offices also keep listings for their own states; write for the latest updates.

REGIONAL

Amanda's Bed and Breakfast Reservation Service
1428 Park Avenue
Baltimore, MD 21217
(800) 899-7533
www.amandas-bbrs.com
(Maryland, Virginia, Delaware, Pennsylvania, West Virginia, and New Jersey)

DELAWARE

Bed and Breakfast of Delaware
2701 Landon Drive, Suite 200
Wilmington, DE 19810
(302) 479-9500
E-mail: bnbofde@juno.com
(entire state)

MARYLAND

Annapolis Accommodations, Inc.
41 Maryland Avenue
Annapolis, MD 21401
(410) 263-3262
(800) 715-1000
www.stayannapolis.com
(Annapolis area)

PENNSYLVANIA

Bed and Breakfast Connection of Philadelphia
P.O. Box 21
Devon, PA 19333
(610) 687-3565
(800) 448-3619 (outside PA)
www.bnbphiladelphia.com
(Philadelphia and suburbs, Lancaster County, Valley Forge, Brandywine Valley, Bucks County, Lehigh Valley)

VIRGINIA

Blue Ridge Bed & Breakfast
Rock & Rills, Route 2
2458 Castleman Road
Berryville, VA 22611
(540) 955-1246
(800) 296-1246
www.blueridgebb.com
(All Blue Ridge areas)

Guesthouses
P.O. Box 5737
Charlottesville, VA 22905
(804) 979-7264
www.va-guesthouses.com
(Charlottesville area)

BED-AND-BREAKFAST INN ASSOCIATIONS

Maryland Bed & Breakfast Association
P.O. Box 23324
Baltimore, MD 21203
(410) 235-MBBA

Bed and Breakfast Innkeepers Association of New Jersey
P.O. Box 108
Spring Lake, NJ 07762
(732) 449-3535
www.bbianj.com

Bed & Breakfast Inns of Bucks and Hunterdon Counties
Bucks County, PA; Hunterdon County, NJ
P.O. Box 215
New Hope, PA 18938
(215) 766-9332
www.bucksinns.com

Bed and Breakfast Association of Virginia
P.O. Box 1077
Stannardsville, VA 22973
(540) 672-6700
(888) 660-BBAV

Virginia Tourism Corporation Reservation Service
(800) 934-9184
(statewide free bed-and-breakfast reservation service)

Spring

Overleaf: Daffodils in bloom at Winterthur. *Photo courtesy of Winterthur Museum and Gardens, Winterthur, Delaware.*

Apple Blossom Time
in Winchester

Spring steals softly into the Shenandoah Valley, carrying her palette of pastels, and before you know it, brown hills are tinted with soft new greens, and barren branches are crowned with blossom clouds of pink and pearly white.

In Winchester, Virginia's self-proclaimed "Apple Capital," the appearance of snowy blossoms in the countryside means the renewal of the apple orchards and cause for celebration. Ever since 1927, the first weekend in May here has been set aside for the Shenandoah Apple Blossom Festival, an event that seems to grow more gala every year.

It's a festive way to greet the season, and a good reason to visit a small city with a large share of history to its credit. You can top things off with some antiquing, a visit to historic mansions and intriguing museums, and a look at the Skyline Drive aglow in its best spring finery.

Banners in spring shades of pink and white and green float from every lamppost and windowsill in Winchester for the four-day Apple Blossom extravaganza. A Friday night parade boasting the nation's largest display of firefighting equipment is a highlight, and the Saturday parade is a knockout—a three-hour spectacular featuring big-time floats and as many as 100 marching bands, plus a celebrity marshal and the newly crowned Queen Shenandoah, an honor that has been shared by show business celebrities as well as many daughters and granddaughters of presidents.

The festival features the annual Sports Breakfast with all-star guests, as well as circus acts, entertainment, and dances to keep things humming throughout the weekend. Weekend in the Park offers arts and crafts, bluegrass music, and lots of food for all.

Winchester's modern malls and motels mask the fact that this is the oldest city west of the Blue Ridge. The three major sightseeing attractions in town, all maintained by the local historical society, mark the main events in a long history, starting with the first settlements in the 1730s. One of the first settlers was a Quaker, Abraham Hollingsworth, who came to the valley from southern Maryland, buying up 532 acres from the resident Indians for a cow, a calf, and a piece of cloth. In 1754, his son Isaac built a limestone house with walls two and a half feet thick, which he named Abram's Delight. It has been authentically restored, along with a log cabin on the site, to show what life was like in the town's earliest years.

The adjacent Winchester–Frederick County Visitors Center, located in the renovated 1833 Hollingsworth Mill House, offers a free 18-minute video on the Winchester area and maps, as well as a modestly priced audio tape, "Follow the Apple Trail Tour," that will take you along highways and byways to many attractions as well as farm markets in the countryside.

Winchester proper had its beginnings in 1735, when an English colonel, James Wood, came into the Shenandoah Valley with a handful of English, Scottish, and Welsh followers to start a tiny colony that was eventually named in honor of Wood's birthplace in England.

The land Wood's followers settled, however, was not their own. It was part of a 6-million-acre tract belonging to Thomas, Lord Fairfax, who is buried in the Episcopal church courtyard at the corner of Boscawen and Washington Streets in Winchester. In 1748, Fairfax hired his 16-year-old friend George Washington to help survey his holdings. Washington returned later as a colonel of the Virginia militia in the French and Indian War, occupying an office in a log-and-stone structure at the corner of Cork and Braddock Streets while Fort Loudoun was being constructed on a high hill at the north end of town. The office has been maintained as a museum.

George Washington lived in Winchester from 1755 to 1758, and some credit him with helping to foster the planting of the apple orchards. It was from this area that Washington was first elected to the Virginia House of Burgesses.

Perhaps the most famous of the historic structures is the house where Thomas Stonewall Jackson was quartered in 1861 and 1862 while he planned the brilliant Valley Campaign, which defeated Union troops despite overwhelming odds. The Hudson River Gothic home on North Braddock Street still looks much as it did in 1861; Jackson's first-floor office and the airy upstairs bedroom that he shared with his wife are still intact. The house contains much Civil War memorabilia.

Within a few blocks of the house are Stonewall Cemetery, where the Confederate dead are buried, and National Cemetery, where thousands of Union soldiers are at rest, moving testaments to the devastation Winchester witnessed during the Civil War. The town was of great strategic importance to both sides, providing access to the crops, cattle, and mills of the Shenandoah Valley. It changed hands more than 70 times during the war, sometimes two or three times a day, and was the site of five major battles.

The Kurtz Cultural Center, housed in an 1836 warehouse and operated by the Preservation of Historic Winchester organization, serves both as a welcome center and as a Civil War information center. Exhibit galleries include Colonial as well as Civil War history, and the center also contains a salute to a contemporary Winchester native, the late country music star Patsy Cline.

Although it was left in ruins by the Civil War, Winchester was soon rebuilt and prospered once again as a commercial and industrial center of the upper valley, and as a processing center for the burgeoning local apple industry. Lately, a variety of industrial firms have moved into the area as well. Preservationists are working hard to hold on to the reminders of the town's historic past in the midst of its present growth. About 130 original eighteenth-century buildings remain, and a number of them have been rehabilitated through the efforts of the Preservation of Historic Winchester group, which is constantly adding to its roster. You can see some of their handiwork on Tater Hill on South Loudoun Street, a onetime tenement that is rapidly regaining its lost glory.

If you follow the map available at the visitor center, you'll find still more of the past in Winchester. On Amherst Street alone are three prize properties: Hawthorne, the 1765 house lived in by Governor James Wood Jr.; the 1786 home of General Daniel Morgan, a Revolutionary War hero; and James Wood's Glen Burnie, which was occupied by the family until recently and opened to the public as a museum in 1997. The historic 1794 house is exquisitely furnished with eighteenth-century American and English furniture, paintings, and porcelains. The pastoral 264-acre setting includes a working farm and formal gardens typical of an English country house of the period.

Plans have been announced for a dramatic new Museum of the Shenandoah Valley at Glen Burnie. The expansive building designed by Michael Graves will have five galleries for exhibits on the history of the valley, plus an auditorium, gift shop, reception hall, and tearoom. If all goes well, it will be completed by 2003.

The historic district encompasses a 45-square-block area, including the renovated commercial downtown. Sights here include the Red Lion Tavern at Loudoun and Cork, the restored 1840 Court House, and Logan House, from where General Philip H. Sheridan rode out to Cedar Creek in 1864 to defeat the Confederates. One of the oldest buildings still in use in Old Town Winchester is One Block West, an 1870s stable restored as a quaint cafe.

The main downtown artery, Loudoun Street, has been turned into a pedestrian shopping mall and is the site of the midway and carnival games during the festival. Many of the old stores are now interesting shops and galleries.

Shoppers should also visit two other shopping complexes. Millwood Crossing, at 381 Millwood Avenue, around the corner from Abram's Delight, is a collection of quality shops in a renovated apple-packing warehouse. Historic Logan House has taken on a new life as Kimberly's Antiques and Linens. More antiques can be found on Boscawen and Loudoun Streets in town, and if you continue south on Route 11, you will find more choice antiquing all the way to Strasburg.

For outdoor pleasure on a fine spring weekend, drive nine miles east to Boyce and the Orland E. White Arboretum, Virginia's state arboretum, 170 acres including great stands of beeches, magnolias, and maples and meadows overflowing with spring blossoms. Visitors are invited to spread a lunch on the shady picnic tables.

If you can get here on a weekday, another worthwhile detour to

Route 277 will bring you to White Post Restorations and a fascinating tour of the shop where classic antique cars are restored. Tours are given Monday to Friday. Even if you don't know a Ferrari from a Ford, you may want to come to White Post for dinner and an overnight at L'Auberge Provençale, the best French restaurant in the area.

Another very choice lodging awaits about 15 minutes south, off Route 11 between Stephens City and Middletown. The Inn at Vaucluse Spring is on a 100-acre site once occupied by a noted valley artist, John Chumley. Guests can choose elegantly furnished rooms in the restored 1785 manor house, charming rustic quarters in the log home that Chumley occupied, or very private quarters with views of the spring-fed pond in the restored millhouse that served as Chumley's studio. All rooms feature a fireplace, and many have Jacuzzis.

Winchester has its share of restaurants, but many people choose to head south or across the nearby West Virginia border for dinner. The delightful eighteenth-century Wayside Inn has been a landmark on Route 11 in Middletown since stagecoach days, and it is a favorite choice for dinner and lodging in the vicinity. The Wayside Theatre in town offers professional theater from June through December.

Route 11 Potato Chips in Middletown, a small local factory in an old feed store, is an offbeat stop. The public is invited to watch chips in the making, a task that is done by hand on Fridays and Saturdays. The chips include seasonal specialties such as sweet potatoes, beets, parsnips, purple potatoes, and taro root.

One of the area's handsomest sightseeing attractions is found just a mile south of Middletown. Beautiful Belle Grove Plantation served as General Sheridan's main headquarters during his valley battles. The stately home is now maintained by the National Trust for Historic Preservation as a working farm and a center for regional crafts and quilts. Civil War buffs will want to make a stop on the right just before the Belle Grove entrance for the Cedar Creek Battlefield Foundation; there is an exhibit on the Battle of Cedar Creek, which took place on this site, and many books for sale relating to the Valley Campaigns of 1862 and 1864.

If you continue your antiquing tour a few minutes south to Strasburg, you'll find another Civil War battlefield park off Route 11 at Hupp's Hill. Located near trenches built in 1864 is the Stonewall Jackson Museum, detailing Jackson's 1862 Valley Campaign with maps, photos, and original artifacts. A charming children's room has junior-size Civil War uniforms to try on and wooden horses for mounting. A driving map developed by the Virginia Civil War Trails organization will lead you to all of Jackson's famous battle sites in the valley, as well as the route of Lee's retreat near the end of the war.

Strasburg is well known to antiquers for its Emporium, which has one of Virginia's largest selections of antiques under one roof. More than 100 dealers occupy an old silk mill on Route 11, with 60,000 square feet crammed with almost anything you can imagine, from Victorian bedsteads to old postcards and kitchen tools. Some of it is good; some is junk-tique. In the unlikely event that you can't find anything you like, you'll find more shops just down the block.

Also on this block is a newer attraction, the Museum of American Presidents, quite a fascinating panorama of presidential portraits and memorabilia. One of the prize exhibits is a desk that belonged to James Madison. Children will find their own hands-on area, a replica one-room school with Colonial costumes for donning, toys to play with, and puzzles and coloring sheets to be completed on the antique desks.

The Strasburg Hotel, a nicely restored Victorian dating to the 1890s, is another alternative for lodging and a recommended stop for lunch or dinner in the attractive period dining room. Rooms vary from small to spacious, but all have Victorian character and antiques with modern amenities like TV and telephones, and some of the suites offer Jacuzzis.

From Strasburg, it's easy to end an apple blossom weekend by turning east on Route 55 to Front Royal and taking a spin south on the Skyline Drive. Bring the camera or the easel. Whether you drive for 2 miles or 20, the pastel panorama of dogwoods, apples, and "red buds" in bloom is worth remembering.

Area Code: 540

DRIVING DIRECTIONS   Winchester is at the intersection of I-81, and Routes 50, 7, 11, and 522. From the D.C. area, take Route 7, Route 50, or I-66 west. The approximate distance from D.C. is 75 miles.

ACCOMMODATIONS   *Best Western Lee-Jackson Motor Inn,* 711 Millwood Avenue (U.S. Route 50 and I-81), Winchester 22601, 662-4154, I • *Holiday Inn,* 1017 Millwood Pike at U.S. Route 50 and I-81 intersection, Winchester 22602, 667-3300, I–M • *L'Auberge Provençale,* Route 340, 1 mile east of Route 50, White Post 22663, 837-1375 or (800) 638-1702, 1753 manor, antiques, E, CP; suites, EE, CP; same owners operate Villa La Campagnette, a nearby 18-acre 1890 manor house with pool, E–EE, CP • *Wayside Inn,* 7783 Main Street (Route 11 and I-81, Exit 303), Middletown 22645, 869-1797, M • *Hotel Strasburg,* 201 Holiday Street, Strasburg 22657, 465-9191, M • *Battletown Inn,* 102 West Main Street, Berryville 22611, 955-4100 or (800) 282-4106, restored 1800s building, attractive period furnishings, some whirlpools, M • **Bed-and-breakfast inns:** *Inn at Vaucluse Spring,* 140 Vaucluse Spring Lane, Stephens City 22655, 869-0200, E, CP (dinner offered to inn guests only on Friday and Saturday evening), E–EE. See also Harpers Ferry, WV, pages 166–167, and Loudoun County, page 178.

DINING   *One Block West,* 25 Indian Alley, Winchester, 662-1455, American bistro fare, M • *Violino Ristorante Italiano,* 181 North

Loudoun Street, Winchester, 667-8006, music, outdoor seating on the town mall, I–M • *Cork Street Tavern,* 8 West Cork Street, Winchester, 667-3777, pub atmosphere, try the ribs, I–M • *Pargo's,* 645 East Jubal Early Drive (Apple Blossom Mall), Winchester, 678-8800, plentiful servings of American fare, M • *Cafe Sofia,* 2900 Valley Avenue, Winchester, 667-2950, change-of-pace Bulgarian cuisine, M • *L'Auberge Provençale* (see above), prix fixe, EE • *Hotel Strasburg* (see above), M • *Wayside Inn* (see above), M–E • *Battletown Inn* (see above), mix of Southern and continental fare, M • See also Harpers Ferry, WV, page 167, and Loudoun County, page 179.

SIGHT-SEEING *Shenandoah Valley Apple Blossom Festival,* 135 North Cameron Street, Winchester 22601, 662-3863, held annually the first weekend in May. Check for current dates and events • *George Washington's Office-Museum,* Cork and Braddock Streets, 662-4412. Hours: April through October, Monday to Saturday 10 A.M. to 4 P.M., Sunday noon to 4 P.M. $$ • *Stonewall Jackson's Headquarters,* 415 Braddock Street, 667-3242. Hours: April through October, Monday to Saturday 10 A.M. to 4 P.M., Sunday noon to 4 P.M.; rest of year, Friday, Saturday 10 A.M. to 4 P.M., Sunday noon to 4 P.M. $$ • **Abram's Delight,** 1340 South Pleasant Valley Road, 662-6519. April through October, Monday to Saturday 10 A.M. to 4 P.M., Sunday noon to 4 P.M. $$; combination tickets available • *Glen Burnie Historic House and Gardens,* c/o 530 Amherst Street, Winchester, 662-1473. Hours: April through October, Tuesday through Saturday 10 A.M. to 4 P.M., Sunday noon to 4 P.M. $$$$; gardens only, $$ (check on progress of the Museum of the Shenandoah Valley at this site) • *Belle Grove Plantation,* U.S. 11, Middletown, 869-2028. Hours: April through October, Monday to Saturday, 10 A.M. to 4 P.M., Sunday 1 P.M. to 5 P.M.; also weekends in November and December holiday tours, $$$ • *Orland E. White State Arboretum of Virginia,* Route 50, Boyce, 837-1758. Hours: Daily dawn to dusk, office open weekdays 9 A.M. to 5 P.M. Free. • *Cedar Creek Battlefield Visitors Center,* 8437 Valley Pike (Route 11), Middletown, 869-2064. Hours: April through October, Monday to Saturday 10 A.M. to 4 P.M., Sunday 1 P.M. to 4 P.M., $ • *Stonewall Jackson Museum at Hupp's Hill,* 33229 Old Valley Pike (Route 11, north of Strasburg), 465-5884. Hours: Monday to Saturday, 10 A.M. to 5 P.M., Sunday noon to 5 P.M. $$ • *The Museum of American Presidents,* 130 N. Massanutten Street (Route 11), Strasburg, 465-5999. Hours: Monday to Saturday 10 A.M. to 5 P.M., Sunday noon to 5 P.M. $$ • *Shenandoah Valley Civil War Trails,* free self-guiding brochure available from Virginia Civil War Trails, 550 East Marshall Street, Richmond, VA 23219, (888) CIVIL-WAR.

INFORMATION *Winchester-Frederick County Chamber of Commerce/Convention & Visitors Bureau,* 1360 South Pleasant

Valley Road, Winchester, VA 22601, 662-4135 or (800) 662-1360, www.visitwinchesterva.com • *Old Town Welcome Center, Kurtz Cultural Center,* 2 North Cameron Street, Winchester, 722-6367; www.visitthevalley.org.

Crossing the Delaware to New Jersey

When George Washington crossed the ice-clogged Delaware River in a rowboat on a frigid Christmas night back in 1776, he was headed from Pennsylvania to Trenton, New Jersey, where his troops won a battle that helped turn the tide of the Revolutionary War.

Nowadays travelers to New Jersey's Delaware Valley have more peaceful pursuits in mind, things like country inns, antiques and art, gourmet dining, bargain hunting in Flemington, and a visit to Princeton, one of America's most beautiful and historic college towns—more than enough reasons to warrant the trip. And while you're in the neighborhood, you can check out the spot where George made history.

The first happy order of business when you plan your crossing is to find a home base among the appealing small inns on the Jersey side of the valley. Lambertville, just a footbridge across the Delaware from busy New Hope, Pennsylvania, used to be a sleepy place, until it began to attract galleries and antique shops that could not afford the rents across the river. Now it is packed with shops and a destination in its own right, with a choice of winning lodgings.

The most elegant is the newly restored Lambertville House, built in 1812 and on the National Register of Historic Places. It is in the center of town, an easy walk to all the shops, as are several small, cozy inns and the Inn at Lambertville Station, a 45-room lodging offering period Victorian furnishings and hotel amenities. Chimney Hill Farm, a charming 1820 stone house high on a hill on the edge of town, is another excellent choice. Many rooms have fireplaces; the old barn on the property has been converted to suites with both fireplace and whirlpool tub. Ma Maison, a small in-town Victorian inn, is nicely decorated and has a Cordon Bleu–trained owner who gives cooking lessons.

More inviting accommodations are in neighboring towns. A Stockton standby is the Woolverton Inn, a very private, mellowed stone country house tucked away high on a hill and surrounded by lawns and gardens. The Victorian queen of the area is Hunterdon House, up the river a bit in Frenchtown, a village that has itself begun to bloom with notable dining and shops. Chestnut Hill in Milford is another very cozy Victorian charmer facing the river.

Having made your choice and settled in, you might plan Saturday for shopping or sightseeing and Sunday for the many pleasures of Princeton. Lambertville is easy to cover, since everything is within about four square blocks. One of the choicest stops is the Porkyard on Coryell Street, an attractively renovated former sausage factory, which now holds a potpourri of country furniture, paintings, and antiques. Greene and Greene on Bridge Street offers high-quality contemporary crafts and folk art, as does the A Mano Gallery on North Union. Also on North Union Street are Goldsmiths, with award-winning hand-fashioned jewelry, and the Artfull Eye, featuring Bucks County artists, along with other fine art and antiques.

Antiquers should also head to North Union Street, where the Antique Center at the People's Store has 40 shops and many affordable pieces, and Broadmoor Antiques has a large display with ten galleries filled with fine art and antiques. Also on this same street are the 5 & Dime, packed with antique and collectible toys, and Olde English Pine, featuring antique country pine furniture.

For a break, stop in at the Lambertville Trading Company on Bridge Street for an espresso or cappuccino and the chance to pick up gourmet foods.

Stockton's main attraction is a tile store featuring a wide selection of decorative tiles from Mexico, Brazil, Holland, France, and Italy. Farther upriver in Frenchtown, there are several enticing small shops and galleries along Bridge and Race Streets. The best-known dining spot in town is the four-star Frenchtown Inn, open for dinner or Sunday brunch.

Follow Route 12 west for some serious shopping among the discount bargains in Flemington. Dansk, Mikasa china, Donna Karan, Joan and David, Anne Klein, and Corningware are just a few of the dozens of brand names with their own outlet stores, many of them clustered in Liberty Village, an upscale outlet center with an eighteenth-century motif. You can pick up a complete guide at almost any of the stores in town.

If shopping is not your thing, you can hike or cycle along the towpath beside the Delaware & Raritan Canal upriver to Stockton and Frenchtown or downstream to Trenton, or paddle a canoe through the water. Howell Farm, on a lovely bucolic 126-acre setting, is a restored late-1800s farm south of Lambertville offering an authentic portrait of farm life a century ago, a best bet for families. There's a self-guiding brochure to fill you in, and special weekend events from hayrides to ice harvests.

Treasure hunters can try their luck at the Lambertville Antique Market, where there are indoor shops and a big outdoor flea market held every Wednesday, Friday, Saturday, and Sunday one and a half miles south of town on Route 29.

Or you might choose to visit Washington Crossing State Park, several miles south on the Delaware. The park, commemorating the famous crossing, runs along both sides of the river. The New Jersey half includes the Ferry House, a restored Colonial inn where Washington and his men spent the night; the Nelson House, a small museum with historical exhibits and crafts demonstrations in summer; a nature center offering guided walks; and a visitors center with exhibits on the 1776 period. In summer, entertainment is offered at an outdoor theater.

Across the river are the McConkey Ferry Inn, where Washington held his final meeting before the crossing; replicas of the boats rowed by his men; and Bowman's Hill and Tower, the observation site used by the army. (It is 121 steps up for the view.) Should you be in the neighborhood on Christmas Day, you can watch the annual re-creation of the stormy crossing.

But there is more than military history to lure you across the river. The restored and operating Thompson Grist Mill and its barn are interesting examples of nineteenth-century life. And what could be nicer on a fine spring day than a ramble through the 100-acre wildflower preserve?

To see where Washington's daring raid surprised the British Hessian troops, continue south to New Jersey's capital city of Trenton. The Old Barracks Museum here is the finest remaining example of a Colonial barracks. Guides in period costumes will show you the re-created soldiers' squad room and point out the best of the museum's furniture and decorative arts collections. It is interesting to see the difference in quarters for the officers and enlisted men. New Jersey's excellent State Museum and one of the nation's oldest state capitol buildings are other local attractions.

Come Sunday, different kinds of pleasures await. If Hollywood were to construct a set for the world's most perfect college town, it would probably look like Princeton, New Jersey. Not only does Princeton boast the fine campus and cultural facilities of an outstanding university, but it is also a town of historic importance and outstanding architecture.

Stop at Maclean House, to the right just inside the university's main campus gate, where you can sign up for one of the free hour-long guided tours, or pick up literature for your own stroll around the Princeton campus. Either way, the place to begin is where Princeton began—at Nassau Hall, which constituted the entire college for some 50 years beginning in 1756. Nassau Hall was one of the largest buildings in the colonies and played an important part in the nation's history, serving as home of the Continental Congress for six months in 1783. George Washington, who routed the British here in 1777, returned six years later to receive the thanks of that congress.

Aside from its history, the Georgian-style hall can be appreciated for its beauty. Some say the vines climbing up its brick walls inspired the term "Ivy League," though a few New England campuses might dispute that claim. The faculty room, modeled after the British House of Commons, contains some interesting paintings, including one of George Washington at the Battle of Princeton by Charles Willson Peale.

The next stop is Firestone Library, where students need road maps and compass points on the floor to find their way around the 5 million volumes on the shelves. The library contains many rare manuscripts and usually has a special exhibit on display on the main floor.

Two eighteenth-century undergraduates who honed their debating skills at Princeton were James Madison and Aaron Burr. Whig and Clio Halls, twin Greek temples west of the library, are reminders of the societies where they competed.

University Chapel, just south of the library, is one of the most magnificent to be found on any college campus. The 1928 building is modeled after the chapel of King's College, Cambridge, England. The glowing stained-glass windows, oak pews, and sixteenth-century pulpit were brought from France. It took 100 men one year to carve the chancels, which are made of wood from England's Sherwood Forest.

To see some of the vast Princeton art collection, you need only stroll the campus past the many stunning outdoor sculptures by the likes of Nevelson, Moore, Calder, Lipchitz, and Noguchi. A Picasso sculpture, *Head of a Woman,* stands at the entrance to the University Art Museum, which houses a vast collection ranging from Egyptian sculptures to modern art. Chinese paintings and prints and drawings are among the museum's special strengths.

Save time for some of Princeton's many off-campus sights, including Rockingham, George Washington's onetime headquarters; Morven, the former official residence of the governor of New Jersey; and Drumthwacket, the present governor's mansion. Then there are the homes of Woodrow Wilson, Albert Einstein, and Aaron Burr, and literally hundreds of fine eighteenth- and nineteenth-century homes to be found on Nassau Street and the surrounding side streets, such as Alexander, Mercer, and Stockton.

The traditional inn in Princeton is the Nassau Inn on Palmer Square, across from the campus. It isn't as old as you might expect, having been built in 1937 to replace the original inn, which was torn down to make way for the new square. Nevertheless, the beamed ceilings, paneled lobby, and enormous fireplace seem right for the town. Best bet here is informal fare at the pub. There are other popular choices in town, including a splurge at a couple of rather elegant French restaurants. Whatever your pleasure, it's a fine way to end a visit to the ivied halls of Nassau.

Area Code: 609

DRIVING DIRECTIONS From the south, take I-95 north to Yardley, PA. Cross the Delaware River here and proceed north on New

Jersey Route 29 to Lambertville. The approximate distance from D.C. is 180 miles. Route 29 also intersects with Routes 78 and 202 from the north and I-95 from the east.

PUBLIC TRANSPORTATION Amtrak and bus service to Trenton; air service to Trenton/Princeton's Mercer County Airport.

ACCOMMODATIONS Lambertville: *Lambertville House,* 32 Bridge Street, Lambertville 08530, 397-0200 or (888) 867-8859, E–EE, CP • *Chimney Hill Farm Estate and Ol' Barn Inn,* Goat Hill Road, Lambertville 08530, 397-1516 or (800) 211-4667, M–EE, CP; 0l' Barn Suites, E–EE, CP • *York Street House,* 42 York Street, Lambertville 08530, 397-3007, Colonial-style 1909 mansion turned small in-town inn, M–E, CP • *Ma Maison Bed & Breakfast,* 44 Coryell Street, Lambertville 06590, 397-8292, "painted lady" Victorian in town, M–E, CP • *Bridgestreet House,* 75 Bridge Street, Lambertville 08530, 397-2503, on the busy main street, but cozy and reasonable, especially midweek, M–E, CP • *The Inn at Lambertville Station,* 397-4400 or (800) 524-1091, modern inn behind the old station, with antiques giving the feel of a country inn, M–E, CP • **Upriver:** *Woolverton Inn,* 6 Woolverton Road, Stockton 08559, 397-0802 or (888) 264-6648, M–EE, CP • *Hunterdon House,* 12 Bridge Street, Frenchtown 08825, (908) 996-3632 or (800) 382-0375, M–E, CP • *Chestnut Hill,* 63 Church Street, Milford 08848, (908) 995-9761, M–E, CP • **Princeton:** *Doral Forrestal Hotel and Conference Center,* 100 College Road East, Princeton Forrestal Center, Princeton 08540, 452-7800 or (800) 222-1131, contemporary-style conference center during the week, fine facilities for weekenders, indoor pool, tennis, trails, M–E • *Peacock Inn,* 20 Bayard Lane, Princeton 08540, 924-1707, 1775 Georgian home, antiques, M–E, CP • *Nassau Inn,* 10 Palmer Square, Princeton 08542, 921-7500 or (800) 627-7286, Colonial atmosphere, E–EE.

DINING Lambertville: *Hamilton's Grill Room,* 8 Coryell Street, 397-4343, grill specialties in a charming setting, one of the town's best, M–E • *Anton's at the Swan,* 43 South Main Street, 397-1960, creative chef, a standby for fine dining for over a decade, E–EE; bar with light food and drinks, M • *Manon,* 19 North Union Street, Lambertville, 397-2596, country French, whimsical decor, M–E • *De Anna's,* 18 South Main Street, Lambertville, 397-8957, tiny and cozy Italian cafe, M; Festival Cafe next door serves lunch, light fare, I • *The Fish House,* 2 Canal Street, 397-6477, lively mix of seafood restaurant with open kitchen, raw bar, two-story waterfall, and food market in a converted canal-side factory, unique, M–E • *Church Street Bistro,* 11½ Church Street, 397-4383, hidden gem for country French bistro fare, patio for warm evenings, M–E • **Nearby choices:** *Stockton Inn,* 1 Main Street, Stockton, 397-1250, the original "small hotel with a wishing well," charming setting for traditional fare, M–E • *Miel's Restaurant,* Bridge and Main Streets, Stockton, 397-8033, good old American home cooking, breakfast and lunch, I; dinner, M–E • *Frenchtown Inn,* Bridge Street, Frenchtown, (908) 996-3300, gourmet continental fare, elegant setting, fine Sunday brunch, E • *Ryland Inn,* Route 22 West, Whitehouse, (908) 534-4011, worth a drive for highly rated regional French, E–EE • **Princeton:** *Yankee Doodle Tap Room,* Nassau Inn, Princeton (see above), traditional American fare, known for its Norman Rockwell mural, M • *Le Plumet Royal,* Peacock Inn (see above), cozy, California/French, E–EE • *Lahiere's,* 5 Witherspoon Street, Princeton, 921-2798, formal French, E • *Mediterra,* 29 Hulfish Street, Palmer Square, 252-9680, fun spot with international fare, from tapas to Turkish specialties, M • *Acacia,* 2637 Main Street (Route 206), Lawrenceville (south of Princeton), 895-9885, top reviews for innovative nouveau American in the old post office, M–E.

SIGHT-SEEING *Howell Living History Farm,* 101 Hunter Road (off Valley Road from Route 29 south of Lambertville), 737-3299. Hours: February through November, Tuesday to Saturday 10 A.M. to 4 P.M., Sunday noon to 4 P.M. Free • *Princeton University,* guided tours from Maclean House, 73 Nassau Street, 258-3603. Hours: Monday to Saturday 10 A.M., 11 A.M., 1:30 P.M., 3:30 P.M.; Sunday 1:30 P.M. and 3:30 P.M. Free • *Washington Crossing State Park,* 355 Washington Crossing–Pennington Road, Titusville, 737-0623. Visitors Center, Route 29, 737-9304. Hours: Park open daily, 8 A.M. to 8 P.M. Visitors Center, Wednesday to Sunday 9 A.M. to 4 P.M. Hours for park buildings vary with seasons; check with Visitors Center. $$ per in summer, free rest of year • **Trenton:** *Old Barracks Museum,* South Barrack Street, Trenton, 396-1776. Hours: Daily 10 A.M. to 5 P.M. $$$ • *New Jersey State Museum,* New Jersey Cultural Center, 205 West State Street, Trenton, 292-6464. Hours: Tuesday to Saturday 9 A.M. to 4:45 P.M., Sunday noon to 5 P.M. Free • *New Jersey State House,* West State Street, Trenton, 633-2709. Hours: Building open 7 A.M. to 6 P.M. Guided tours September to June, Tuesday, Wednesday, Friday 10 A.M. to 3 P.M., Saturday noon to 3 P.M. Free.

INFORMATION *Lambertville Chamber of Commerce,* 239 North Union Street, Lambertville, NJ 08530, 397-0055; www.lambertville.org • *Princeton Area Chamber of Commerce,* 216 Rockingham Row, Princeton Forrestal Village, Princeton, NJ 08540, 520-1776.

Garden Hopping in Virginia

Historic Garden Week is a longtime Virginia tradition, a once-a-year event that opens many private doors to visitors throughout the state. But nowhere are more hidden treasures awaiting than on the little-explored peninsula known as the Eastern Shore.

Insulated from the world by water on three sides, this peaceable world of farmers and fishers has been slow to give in to change. Even if you've lived your entire life on the narrow 70-mile stretch between the Atlantic Ocean and Chesapeake Bay, you're still considered a "come here" by the natives unless your family goes back at least a generation.

The Eastern Shore was even more isolated until 1964, when the completion of the remarkable 17.6-mile Chesapeake Bay Bridge-Tunnel provided a link to Norfolk and Virginia Beach. Now Eastern seaboard motorists travel through, but few get beyond Route 13, the boring main highway, unless they are anglers or nature lovers bound for Chincoteague Island's beaches and wildlife preserves.

That's a shame, for on the main road, all you'll see mainly are fast-food outlets, an occasional motel or seafood restaurant, and tourist stops selling Virginia ham or fireworks.

Venture off onto the back roads, however, and you will discover an area rich in history and rustic charm. Along the bountiful creeks and streams that weave through the countryside and out to sea are fine old homes dating back to the early eighteenth century; some have been in the same family for generations. Distinctive in their architecture and delightful in their settings, many have a look all their own—multileveled, steep-roofed frame structures with dormer windows and two or more chimneys. A typical Eastern Shore home is one room deep and might have four different roof levels for the "big house," "little house," colonnade, and kitchen.

A selection of these privately owned and often secluded properties is opened to visitors just once each year for Historic Garden Week, and it is well worth a trip to see them. The selection changes with the years, but a recent roster gives a typical sampling: a stately brick home dating from 1818 offering the chance to see a restoration in progress; a late-eighteenth-century plantation with gardens that have been rejuvenated by dedicated master gardeners; a home circa 1722, set high on a high bluff overlooking Occahannock Creek; and a classic seaside property, a Virginia Historic Landmark that has been a residence for some 210 years, with a boxwood garden and a 1750 hand-pegged barn.

A perennial on the tour is Eyre Hall, built in 1735 and recognized as one of the great houses of the Eastern Shore. It has been home to ten successive generations of the Eyre family. The gardens are open year round, but the house is open only during Garden Week. Located on

Cherrystone Creek, the white frame home boasts fine woodwork and paneling, early French wallpapers, and heirloom furnishings, including Queen Anne, Chippendale, Hepplewhite, and Chinese export pieces. Outside, mellow brick walls enclose a magnificent boxwood garden, one of the oldest in the country, with ancient plantings of yew, crepe myrtle, holly, magnolia, and laurel. The garden is enhanced by more than 300 feet of colorful English-style mixed borders, including spring bulbs and flowering trees. Nearby, through a garden gate, is the family cemetery.

Kerr Place, located in the old port town of Onancock, is another home always included on the tour and the only one that you can count on seeing anytime you are in the area. A late-eighteenth-century Federal brick mansion, it was purchased by the Eastern Shore of Virginia Historical Society and beautifully restored and furnished with choice antiques and Oriental rugs. Based on extensive recent paint analysis, three of the first-floor rooms have been painted to appear as they did in 1801, with faux finishes representing mahogany and marble adding elegance to the doors and baseboards. Among the features are an 1803 bedchamber exhibit and the recently opened cellar for temporary exhibits. The gardens are based on an eighteenth-century garden plan and contain plants that would have been growing on the Eastern Shore circa 1799.

The landscaping of the grounds was a Garden Club of Virginia restoration project, one of many the Garden Club has funded through its annual spring tours.

Take time in Onancock for a look at Hopkins & Brothers Store, a restored functioning general store dating back to 1842 that still retains its old-fashioned air, original shelving and counters, and antique cash register. The store includes a town visitor center, as well as provisions for boaters, snacks and ice cream, bicycle and kayak rentals, and the Eastern Shore Steamboat Co. Restaurant, serving breakfast, lunch, and dinner on the waterfront. The second-floor dining room has a fine view of the creek bending its way to the bay.

The store is also ticket headquarters for summer excursion boats to Tangier Island, an oystering enclave where life has changed little over the past three centuries.

With all of this plus a small cache of antique shops, a couple of attractive bed-and-breakfast inns, and more good restaurants, Onancock makes a convenient home base for an Eastern Shore visit.

As you drive from house to house on the Garden Week tour, you'll find other interesting sights tucked away in the smaller villages of the Eastern Shore. The Eastville Courthouse has the oldest continuous set of records in the country, dating from 1632. The old courthouse, built in 1731, is part of a complex that includes a 1731 clerk's office and an 1814 debtors' prison. Eastville is also home to one of the area's best restaurants, Eastville Manor, an 1886 Victorian with fine gardens.

Another debtors' prison, circa 1782, can be found in Accomac, and historic white-spired churches dot the area. Some that date back to the eighteenth century are Hungars Episcopal (1742) in Bridgetown, St. George's Episcopal (1738) in Pungoteague, and Cokesbury (1784) in Onancock.

Even the Greek Revival St. James Episcopal Church in Accomac has a history much older than the façade might lead you to believe. The bricks in the building come from the original church built on this site in 1767, paid for with taxes levied in pounds of tobacco. Of special interest is the handsome trompe l'oeil interior, with a mural of columns and an archway that covers the ceiling and four walls. The church has been named a National Historic Landmark.

Take a drive to the picturesque harbor at tiny Willis Wharf to see a vintage general store with a highly recommended cafe. In early spring or mid-fall (the "r" months) you can visit the oyster house and observe the art of shucking this seafood delicacy.

A popular attraction for railroad buffs is the Eastern Shore Railway Museum in Parksley, comprising the restored 1906 station plus vintage railroad cars, a maintenance shed, and a host of artifacts and memorabilia from trains that have operated on the Delmarva Peninsula since the mid-1800s. Nostalgia rides aboard the old trains are offered occasionally; check the current schedule.

The Chincoteague Wildlife Refuge, with its wild ponies and many species of birds, is a well-known attraction up in the northern corner of the area and definitely merits a driving tour. Chincoteague is one of a whole chain of barrier islands on the Atlantic side of the Eastern Shore, an untouched world said to have the richest assortment of bird life in the mid-Atlantic. An annual Eastern Shore Birding Festival in early October features exhibits and photos, workshops on bird identification, and a number of trips to wildlife refuges and conservation areas. Other barrier island tours are held by the Virginia Coast Reserve, part of the Nature Conservancy.

If you come back inspired to take home a wildlife sculpture, the Turner Gallery in Onley will oblige. The foundry that makes the gallery's bronze artworks is here also. For art, try the Painter Gallery in Painter, which includes the working studio of a local artist, Dr. Joseph D. Adams. The gallery is open Wednesday through Saturday, 4 P.M. to 8 P.M., from mid-May to early August.

Should you want to take a break from sight-seeing, there are public tennis courts at many local schools along the peninsula and golf at the Northampton County course in Cape Charles. Fishing is superb, and charter boats go out from many local docks, including the Wachapreague Marina and Kings Creek Marina in Cape Charles.

Virginia's newest state park, Kiptopeke, opened in 1992 on 375 acres along Chesapeake Bay at the southernmost tip of the peninsula. Still being developed, the park offers beaches, hiking, and fishing. If you return in the fall, you can watch volunteers at work in the bird banding station, where hawks, kestrels, osprey, and other birds of prey are observed and banded from September to early November. The park is also headquarters for the fall Birding Festival.

Spring is also a prime bird-watching period, with more than 250 species spotted at this favorite spot along the Atlantic Flyway. Birding tours are available from the Wachapreague Hotel, a motel in this busy fishing village. There is also a half-mile interpretive trail at the Eastern Shore of Virginia National Wildlife Refuge in Cape Charles with panoramic views of marshes, barrier islands, bays, and inlets.

The growing number of bed-and-breakfast homes on the Eastern Shore provide some very pleasant choices for visitors. 76 Market Street and the folksy Spinning Wheel are the picks in Onancock, and the Gladstone House offers gracious hospitality in Exmore, a convenient location midpeninsula. To experience the authentic ambience of a fishing village, check into the Burton House or Hart's Harbor House in Wachapreague. Or find out how it feels to live in one of those secluded waterside homes at the Evergreen Inn, an eighteenth-century Georgian manor house on 25 acres on Chesapeake Bay, or the Bay View, an old Eastern Shore home buit in "big house, little house" style, with a pool and expansive water views.

Cape Charles, at the southern end of the peninsula, is a rough-edged town now being spruced up a bit, with several new bed-and-breakfast inns. One of the choicest inns on the Eastern Shore is the Garden and the Sea in New Church, all the way north almost to the Maryland border. Here you'll enjoy spacious rooms with stylish French country furnishings, pleasant porches, and what many consider the area's best restaurant.

With a couple of notable exceptions, dining is far from fancy in this area, but more restaurants are opening all the time, the seafood is deliciously fresh, and the prices refreshingly reasonable—another bonus for those who take the time to explore the hidden treasures of Virginia's Eastern Shore.

Area Code: 757

DRIVING DIRECTIONS   Route 13 runs the length of the Delmarva Peninsula, from Delaware and Maryland through the Eastern Shore, connecting to the Chesapeake Bay Bridge-Tunnel to Norfolk at the southern tip of Virginia. From D.C., take Route 50/301 east toward Annapolis, cross the Chesapeake Bay Bridge, follow Route 50 to Salisbury, and connect to Route 13 South. Total distance to Onancock (approximately midway on the shore) from D.C. is 185 miles.

ACCOMMODATIONS   *The Garden and the Sea Inn,* 4188 Nelson Road, P.O. Box 275, New Church 23415, (800) 824-0672, M–E, CP •

76 Market Street, at that address, P.O. Box 376, Onancock 23417, 787-7600 or (888) 751-7600, M, CP • *The Spinning Wheel,* 31 North Street, Onancock 23417, 787-7311, modest 1890s Victorian furnished with many folk antiques, including a spinning wheel in each room, I–M, CP • *Gladstone House,* 12108 Lincoln Avenue, Exmore 23350, 442-4614 or (800) BNB-GUEST, I–M, CP • *Bay View,* 35350 Copes Drive, Belle Haven 23306, 442-6963 or (800) 442-6966, recommended, screened porch with view, outdoor pool, M, CP • *Evergreen Inn,* 3230 Muir's Path, Pungoteague 23422, 442-3375, M, CP • *The Burton House and Hart's Harbor House,* 9–11 Brooklyn Street, Wachapreague 23480, 787-4560, M, CP • *Cape Charles House,* 645 Tazewell Avenue, Cape Charles 23310, 331-4920, gracious, well furnished, M, CP • *Wilson-Lee House,* 403 Tazewell Avenue, Cape Charles 13310, 331-1954, comfortable amenities, lavishly decorated, M, CP • *Picketts Harbor B&B,* 28288 Goffigon Lane, Cape Charles 23310, 331-2212 overlooking the bay, M, CP • *Comfort Inn,* 2497 Lankford Highway (Route 13), Onley 23418, 787-7787, conveniently located modern motel, I–M. See also Chincoteague, page 113.

DINING *Eastville Manor,* 6058 Willow Oak Road, Eastville, 678-7378, attractive Victorian home, creative dishes, one of the area's very best, I–M • *The Garden and the Sea Inn* (see above), fine dining, M–E • *Hopkins & Brothers Eastern Shore Steamboat Co. Restaurant,* 2 Market Street, Onancock, 787-3100, seafood in great surroundings, water views from the deck, I–M • *Armando's,* 10 North Street, Onancock, 787-8044, Italian, generous portions, very popular, I–M • *Market Street Inn,* 47 Market Street, Onancock, 787-2626, pleasant cafe for all three meals, I–M • *Wright's Seafood Restaurant,* Route 766, Atlantic, 424-4012, I–M • *Island House,* 15 Atlantic Avenue (Route 180), Wachapreague, 787-4242, modest quarters for good fresh seafood, I–M • *The Trawler,* Route 13, Exmore, 442-2092, standard seafood fare in a convenient highway location, I–M.

SIGHT-SEEING *Historic Garden Week on the Eastern Shore of Virginia,* usually held the last Saturday in April. Hours: 10 A.M. to 5 P.M. Information for the current year is available from the Tourism Commission. Because sight-seeing sites are small and hours may change, it's best to check on them also. • *Kerr Place,* 69 Market Street, Onancock, 787-8012. Hours: March through December, Tuesday to Saturday 10 A.M. to 4 P.M. $$ • *Eastern Shore Railway Museum,* 18468 Dunne Avenue, Parksley, 665-RAIL. Monday to Saturday 10 A.M. to 4 P.M., Sunday 1 P.M. to 4 P.M. $ • *Kiptopeke State Park,* 3450 Kiptopeke Drive, Cape Charles, 331-2267. Hours: Daily, daylight hours; office open 8 A.M. to 4:30 P.M. Admission per car: $$ • *Tangier Island cruises,* 891-2240, late May through mid-October, daily 10 A.M. from Onancock wharf. $$$$$ • **Wildlife and birding tours:** Check all for current schedules and rates. ***Chincoteague National Wildlife Refuge***, 336-6122 • ***Eastern Shore of Virginia National Wildlife Refuge***, Cape Charles, 331-2760 • **Island Cruises,** Chincoteague, 336-5593 • *Nature Conservancy/Virginia Coast Reserve*, 442-3049.

INFORMATION *Eastern Shore of Virginia Tourism Commission*, P.O. Box 460, Melfa, VA 23410, 787-2460; www.esvatourism.org.

Back to Bach in Bethlehem

"Its pianissimos are worth going miles to hear and when it cuts loose in a forte the very firmament trembles."

H. L. Mencken wrote those words in 1928 after hearing the Bach Choir of Bethlehem, Pennsylvania, and thousands of music lovers who throng to Bethlehem's Bach Festival each May affirm that they are still true.

Calling itself the oldest Bach choir in the world, the group traces its origins back to Bethlehem's original Moravian settlers, who brought with them a strong musical heritage when they came to the New World in 1741.

Their Collegium Musicum gave the first full American performance of Haydn's *Creation* back in 1811. A newly formed choir continued to make musical history in the late nineteenth century with firsts of two of Bach's "Passions" and in 1900 gave the first rendering in this country of the composer's formidable *Mass in B Minor,* a work that has been repeated and hailed in the major concert halls of the world. The *Mass* is the highlight of the annual Bach Festival, held for two weekends in May. It is sung in the inspired setting of the Packer Memorial Church at Lehigh University, an occasion that is a perennial sellout.

The present Bach Choir, more than 100 voices strong, has been going for more than 100 years. It is made up of devoted amateurs who sing only for the love of Bach, and they have reached a level of perfection many a professional chorus might envy. A fine accompanying orchestra that includes many professional musicians adds richness to the performances, and the reverent surroundings of a beautiful church are absolutely right.

Order your tickets early, and you will have not only a musical treat in store, but the chance to discover a community rich in history and Old World charm, with many atmospheric eighteenth- and nineteenth-century buildings and interesting museums waiting to be explored.

The Bach Festival, which marks its 95th season in 2002, begins on Thursday evening with a selection of highlights of the festival, followed

Friday with late afternoon and evening concerts of cantatas and other choral works that change each year. The *Mass* is always sung on Saturday afternoon in two parts, with a long intermission that provides a welcome chance to take a stroll or sit beneath a shady tree and admire the grounds of the Lehigh campus, resplendent in spring blooms.

All of Bethlehem, in fact, is abloom during the Bach weekends, with the pinks and lilacs of azaleas softening the gray stone of historic buildings. The town bustles with activity, as local church ladies serve lunches for music lovers, showing off their best culinary skills, and special events such as sidewalk art shows brighten the streets. The Moravian Book Shop on Main Street continues its longtime tradition of providing free Moravian sugar cake and coffee to all comers on Saturday morning. Many historic sites also have a special welcome mat out for visitors.

The sites are reminders that Bethlehem was one of early America's most interesting communities. The best way to see it is on a walking tour leaving every afternoon from the Visitors Center. A film is shown here that provides an introduction to early Bethlehem. On your own, pick up a map that will guide you on a walking tour into the city's past.

The Moravians, who settled the town, were a deeply religious Protestant denomination determined to spread the Gospel to the Indians as well as to their nonaffiliated neighbors. As the first of their New World colonies, Bethlehem was planned as an ideal community devoted to the church. Everyone was expected to work at the "general economy," a plan to make Bethlehem a center of trade and industry, with profits that would not only support the town but also fund missionary work.

Eventually 32 different crafts, trades, and industries were established along the banks of Monocacy Creek in the 1700s, producing goods of such high quality that buyers were attracted from miles around. Historic Bethlehem, a group devoted to preserving the town's unique past, is working hard to restore the industrial sites. The 1764 Spring House, the Luckenbach Grist Mill, and the 1761 Tannery have been completed, along with the 1762 Waterworks. The huge wooden wheels of the Waterworks turn once again to demonstrate how the first municipal pumped-water system in the colonies delivered water 95 feet uphill through wooden pipes to serve the town.

On the first floor of the Luckenbach Mill is History Works!, an interactive learning center gallery for children where they can hammer out a nail, grind corn, and dress like a Moravian child did 250 years ago.

Another interesting building that has been restored in town is the once-famous Sun Inn on Main Street, a lodging whose guest list included George Washington, John Adams, and General Lafayette. It is open for tours as well as for lunch and dinner in historic surroundings. Confetti Cafe and the Moravian Book Shop Deli on Main Street are convenient for a light lunch.

The Moravian church still thrives in Bethlehem. The early buildings erected by the first Moravian settlers have never needed restoration because they have been put to continual use since the 1700s. Many are now used by the Moravian Academy, a day school founded in 1856, and by Moravian College. Check before you visit; weekend hours are irregular.

Residents in early Bethlehem lived in communal "choirs" divided according to age, sex, and marital status. A walking tour takes you past the Widows', Sisters', and Brethren's Houses; the Bell House, where married couples lived; and the Gemein House, the oldest remaining structure in town. Even in God's Acre, the cemetery where the early settlers are buried, the plain stone markers divide them according to their earthly choirs.

Gemein House is now the site of the Moravian Museum, filled with mementos of the original settlement, and the splendid domed Central Moravian Church, built in 1803, still holds services. The first presentation of Bach's *Mass in B Minor* was given here.

Two other local museums are also of interest. The Kemerer Museum of Decorative Arts preserves the best furnishings of the early days, many of them owned by the museum founder, a lifetime collector of antiques. The 1810 Federal-style Goundie House was the home of a prominent Moravian brewer and includes period rooms as well as Historic Bethlehem's Shop, filled with quilts and Colonial crafts.

When you've seen the sights, take a drive across the Lehigh River to get the full impact of the striking campus of Lehigh University, 700 acres and 70 buildings running uphill to the crest of South Mountain, where there are several observation points offering a commanding view of the Lehigh Valley. There are many fine residences in this area as well, running the architectural gamut from Greek Revival and Gothic Revival to Victorian. More Victorian mansions can be found back in town on East Market from New to Linden Streets.

Not far away on the former site of the Bethlehem Steel Works, a new project called Bethlehem Works is planned. When completed it will offer family recreation, a new hotel, an ice skating center, the Iron and Steel Showcase demonstrating how steel is made, and a new National Museum of Industrial History affiliated with the Smithsonian Institution, featuring industrial artifacts of the nineteenth and twentieth centuries. The plan is to retain the original blast furnaces on the site.

If you can't make it to Bethlehem in May, you may want to mark it down for the annual August Musikfest, when the town is filled with all kinds of music and the Bach Choir usually gives a special performance. Or go at Christmas, when crowds always descend for now-legendary candlelight tours, and the choir offers special holiday concerts.

If you come for these family-oriented events, you may want to make a stop at the Discovery Center, Bethlehem's hands-on science and technology center for for kids. By all means take a 15-minute drive to Easton and the Crayola Factory, where you will see demonstrations of how crayons and markers are made, and the kids can exercise their artistic talents in the Creative Studio, an imaginative supervised activity area.

Bethlehem is a special place whenever you choose to visit, but for those who love music, there's really nothing to match the rare duet of May in bloom and Bach in Bethlehem.

Area Code: 610

DRIVING DIRECTIONS   Bethlehem is on Route 378 south, off Route 22. From D.C., take I-95 north to I-476 northeast, the northeast extension of the Pennsylvania Turnpike. Get off onto U.S. Route 22 east, then exit at Route 378 south to Bethlehem. The approximate distance from D.C. is 201 miles.

ACCOMMODATIONS   Inns: *Sayre Mansion Inn,* 250 Wyandotte Street, 18015, 882-2100, restored Victorian mansion near Lehigh campus, M–E, CP • *The Bethlehem Inn,* 476 North New Street, 18018, 867-4985, 1845 bed and breakfast, M, CP • *Wydnor Hall,* 3612 Old Philadelphia Pike, 18015, 867-6851 or (800) 839-0020, elegantly furnished restored manor house south of town, M–E, CP • **Hotels/motels:** *Radisson Hotel Bethlehem,* 437 Main Street, Bethlehem 18018, 625-5000, recently restored downtown hotel, M–E. • *Comfort Suites,* 120 West Third Street, 18015, 882-9700, M–E, CP • *Fairfield Inn by Marriott,* 2140 Motel Drive, 867-8681, I–M. Write to Tourism Authority for full motel list.

DINING   *Sun Inn,* 564 Main Street, 974-9451, lunch and dinner, great Colonial ambience, lunch, I; dinner, M–E • *Apollo Grill,* 85 West Broad Steet, 865-9600, American bistro, M • *Main Street Depot,* Main and Lehigh Streets, 868-7123, restored train station, M–E • *Candlelight Inn,* 4431 Easton Avenue, Bethlehem, 691-7777, casual, contemporary setting, continental menu, M • *Inn of the Falcon,* 1740 Seidersville Road, 868-6505, 1800s Colonial country inn, M–E • *The Cafe,* 221 West Broad Street, 866-1686, combination bakery shop and continental restaurant, lunch, I; dinner, M • *Confetti Cafe,* 462 Main Street, 861-7484, homemade soups, salads, pasta, I–M • *Moravian Book Shop,* 428 Main Street, 691-6619, soups, salads, sandwiches, desserts, I • *Bocelli's,* 91 West Broad Street, 997-8681, Italian, I–M • *Bethlehem Brew Works,* 569 Main Street. 992-1300, restaurant serving handcrafted ales in view of brewery; brewery tours available, I–M.

SIGHT-SEEING   *Bach Choir of Bethlehem,* 423 Heckewelder Place, Bethlehem 18018, 866-4382 or (888) 743-3100, www.bach.org.

Annual Bach Festival, two weekends in mid-May. General ticket sales begin March 1; check for current dates and prices and order early • *Colonial Industrial Quarter,* 459 Old York Road, access via Union Boulevard, 691-0603. Hours: self-guided tours, daily 8:30 A.M. to 5 P.M. (hours may vary; best to check) $$; History Works, 882-0450. Saturday, Sunday noon to 4 P.M. $$ • *Moravian Museum,* 66 West Church Street, 867-0173. Hours: Tuesday to Sunday, noon to 4 P.M. Closed January. $$ • *Kemerer Museum of Decorative Arts,* 427 North New Street, 868-6868. Hours: Tuesday to Sunday noon to 5 P.M. Closed January. $$ • *Sun Inn,* 564 Main Street, 866-1758. Hours: Tours available Monday to Saturday 11:30 A.M. to 8 P.M. $ • *Guided Walking Tours,* from Moravian Museum, Saturdays, 2:30 P.M., advance reservations required. Check current schedules. $$$ • *Discovery Center,* 522 East Third Street, 865-5010. Hours: Saturday only, 9:30 A.M. to 4:30 P.M., Sunday noon to 4:30 P.M. $$ • *Crayola Factory,* Two Rivers Landing, Easton, 515-8000. Hours: September through June, Tuesday to Saturday 9:30 A.M. to 5 P.M., Sunday noon to 5 P.M.; July and August, Monday to Saturday 9:30 A.M. to 6 P.M., Sunday 11 A.M. to 6 P.M. $$$$.

INFORMATION *Bethlehem Tourism Authority and Visitors Center,* 52 West Broad Street, Bethlehem, PA 18018, 868-1513 or (800) 360-8687; www.bethtour.org. Hours: Daily 9 A.M. to 5 P.M. • *Lehigh Valley Convention & Visitors Bureau,* P.O. Box 20785, Lehigh Valley, PA 18002, 882-9200 or (800) 747-0561. Internet; www.lehighvalley pa.org.

Rich Remembrances in Richmond

Old times here are not forgotten.

It isn't that time has stood still in Richmond. Just take a look along the James River at the building boom, a virtual renaissance that is changing the face of downtown and transforming the riverfront into an urban park. Or check out the shops and lively cafes blooming in former warehouses along Shockoe Slip.

But even as it moves ahead, the capital of the Old South has held fast to her heritage. It is the chance to relive a bit of the past while enjoying the good times of the present that makes a visit to Richmond so rewarding—especially in springtime, when this city of 200,000 trees is aglow with dogwoods and azaleas in bloom. There's so much to see, you may want to schedule a long weekend.

To see how the past is being beautifully preserved here, check into the magnificently restored Jefferson Hotel, over a century old, but with its fabulous Palm Court and staircase as grand as ever. The hotel's Lemaire Restaurant is the city's most elegant. Not far away, a series of brick-columned nineteenth-century row houses have become the Linden Row Inn, a delightful smaller in-town lodging. Up on Church Hill, near the church where Patrick Henry once made history, two 1800s town houses, the William Catlin House and Mr. Patrick Henry's Inn, have become inviting bed-and-breakfast inns, and the Emmanuel Hutzler House puts you right on Monument Avenue, near several top attractions.

When you've settled into properly historic quarters, the first stop must be Court End, a remarkable six-block area containing seven National Historic Landmarks and 12 buildings on the National Register of Historic Places. It shows in a nutshell why the city has good reason to take pride in its past.

Most imposing is the graceful columned Virginia State Capitol building, constructed in 1785. The Virginia Legislature, America's oldest continuous English-speaking legislative body, still meets here. The design was chosen by Thomas Jefferson based on the Maison Carrée, a Roman-style temple he considered a perfect example of classical style. The building includes a remarkable rotunda dome placed 20 feet below the roof so as not to spoil the outside roofline.

Inside are tributes to two beloved native sons, a life-size statue of George Washington (the only one he ever posed for and said to be the nation's most valuable piece of marble art) and a warm bronze likeness of Robert E. Lee, placed on the spot where Lee stood in 1861 while accepting command of the Confederate forces. Busts placed around the rotunda portray the other seven Virginia-born presidents.

More statues of Virginia heroes can be found in the shady park surrounding the capitol, including Edgar Allan Poe, who grew up in Richmond. The grounds were laid out in 1816, the wrought-iron fence added in 1819 to keep out cattle and pigs. Picnickers are welcome on the lawn. To the east is the gracious white executive mansion, the residence for Virginia's governors since 1813.

From here, Civil War buffs will want to head directly to the Museum of the Confederacy, which contains the nation's largest collection of Confederate memorabilia, including the gray frock coat Jefferson Davis wore when he was taken prisoner toward the end of the war, Jeb Stuart's boots, and the sword of surrender and gold-braided uniform General Lee wore at Appomattox. Changing exhibits highlight various facets of the war.

Richmond Battlefield Park, site of seven Civil War battles, can also be visited on a short drive from the city center. It is maintained by the National Park Service. Civil War buffs can follow other nearby battles with self-driving tour brochures available from Virginia Civil War Trails, an organization based in Richmond.

Next to the Museum of the Confederacy is the Confederate White House, the 1818 John Brockenbrogh home. Interior restoration has returned the house to its authentic 1861 appearance. Also nearby is the John Marshall House, built by the Chief Justice in 1790 when he was a young lawyer and filled with Marshall family furnishings and mementos.

Take time for a look at the neoclassical Wickham Valentine House, built in 1812 by Richmond's wealthiest resident. It is now a museum showing the history of the city and noted for its fine furnishings and period costume collection.

For more about the rich history of all of the state, drive west on Franklin Street, which turns into Richmond's grandest road, Monument Avenue, canopied by sugar maples and studded with statues of five Confederate heroes. In 1996, a new statue was unveiled honoring a modern-day hero, tennis great Arthur Ashe, who was a Richmond native.

Turn left at Boulevard to the Center for Virginia History at the Virginia Historical Society, where four centuries of local life are traced through books, maps, photos, memorabilia, and portraits. It is worth a visit just to see the magnificent murals by Charles Hoffbauer depicting the "Seasons of the Confederacy," the changing seasons tracing the fate of the South. Changing exhibits are a continuing panorama of state history.

One of Richmond's modern claims to fame is almost next door on Boulevard. The Virginia Museum of Fine Arts, the largest art museum in the Southeast, is widely known for its fabulous collection of Russian imperial jewels, including some of the famous Fabergé Easter eggs. The striking West Wing, the most recent addition, houses two major private collections. Five hundred nineteenth- and twentieth-century masterpieces, including sporting prints and works by Manet, Monet, Renoir, Van Gogh, Cézanne, Picasso, Homer, and Eakins, are the donation of Mr. and Mrs. Paul Mellon, and contemporary works by Johns, de Kooning, Lichtenstein, and Rauschenberg are the stars of the Sydney and Frances Lewis collection.

Visiting the museum and the Historical Society takes you to the Fan, a gracious neighborhood of streets that literally fan out between Monument Avenue and West Main Street. Pick any of the side streets for a delightful drive to admire the gracious Victorian homes that make Richmond a fine place to live as well as to visit, and check out West Main Street for some of the trendy new shops and cafes that are bringing new life to this area. Nearby Carytown offers more of the same.

From its earliest days, Richmond's history has revolved around the James River. Rejuvenation is taking place all along the riverfront, where the city's new office towers are located, with walking and bicycle trails in place, and footbridges to river islands with open meadows, all easily adjacent to downtown.

The first phase of a long-term 32-acre project was completed in

1998, stretching along a one-mile corridor from the historic Tredegar Iron Works site at Fifth Street to Seventeenth Street. It includes the opening of the George Washington Canal, designed by George Washington in 1787 in the hope of linking the James River and Kanawha Canal into the nation's first canal system. His dream was never fully realized in his time, but now that the canals and locks have been restored, picnickers and strollers are welcome. Narrated cruises are available, or you can rent an electric boat on Brown's Island and navigate the Haxall Canal on your own. Rafting excursions are also available on the James, offering the chance to challenge the only class IV rapids within an American city.

Like many cities, downtown Richmond is losing shoppers to the suburbs, and some of its major stores have closed. One attempt to stem the tide is the 6th Street Marketplace, stretching three blocks in the heart of downtown, with a variety of small shops and a food court. The complex is near both the Richmond Coliseum and the Carpenter Center for the Performing Arts, tying downtown's main attractions into a convenient package.

Shockoe Slip, the old cobblestoned warehouse district running uphill here from the James, has received its own renovation, adding still more fine shops, galleries, and restaurants to an area that was already a center for nightlife in the city. Also blooming is the Shockoe Bottom area, now protected from the river by a new flood wall built by the Army Corps of Engineers.

If you want to learn more about the city's past and future, join one of the Sunday afternoon walking tours offered by Historic Richmond from the Valentine Museum.

On Sunday you can pick and choose your pleasures in Richmond. Up on Church Hill, you can visit St. John's, the little white church where Patrick Henry made his impassioned "Give me liberty or give me death" speech, an event reenacted on Sunday afternoons in the summer. You'll find yourself in the midst of a charming nineteenth-century residential area now blooming anew with more than 300 restored homes.

The Jackson Ward Historic District was home to many prominent blacks and is a treasure trove of nineteenth-century building styles adorned with intricate cast-iron work. Open for touring is the home of Maggie L. Walker, a pioneering businesswoman who owned a newspaper and a bank, which continues today as Consolidated Bank and Trust, the oldest surviving black-operated bank in the United States. The house is a National Historic Site.

Learn more about the history of black Virginians from 1691 to the present at the Black History Museum and Cultural Center of Virginia, which opened in 1990 and is still growing.

A different kind of history showcase in Richmond is the Beth Ahabah Museum and Archives, telling the story of the Jewish population in the city over the centuries.

Historic homes abound in Richmond, but Maymont is the queen, the ultimate Victorian mansion, set amid a vast park that includes extensive formal gardens, a children's zoo, and a museum of antique carriages. Carriage rides are one of the highlights of a visit.

Wilton House, a stately 1750 Georgian brick mansion, was built by William Randolph III, descendant of one of the great families of Virginia. The parlor is included in a book featuring the hundred most beautiful rooms in America.

Two homes next door to each other on Sulgrave Road are something of a surprise. Both Agecroft and the Virginia House are fifteenth-century timbered Renaissance homes that were dismantled and transplanted alongside the James River. They are unique, and well worth a visit, especially for those who want to stroll their beautiful English gardens overlooking the James.

The Lewis Ginter Botanical Garden is another place to see a variety of gardens, especially prize ivy, tulips, peonies, azaleas, and rhododendrons in spring, and daylilies in summer. The 80-acre grounds include a nature trail, children's garden, three-acre perennial garden, and greenhouses.

The drive to neighboring Hanover is an interesting excursion for a tour of Hanover Courthouse and Jail and a brief history of the 1723 Hanover Tavern. You'll learn that Patrick Henry, who grew up nearby, married the innkeeper's daughter and spent three years here helping tend bar and arguing his first cases in the local courthouse.

Another short drive outside of town will take you to Patrick Henry's Scotchtown, one of Virginia's oldest plantation houses. The house was also the childhood home of Dolley Payne, who married James Madison. Tuckahoe Plantation, the boyhood home of Thomas Jefferson, is another historic home that can be visited by appointment.

For "Raven" fans, there is the Edgar Allan Poe Museum, a complex including the Old Stone House, the oldest in Richmond, furnished with mid-eighteenth-century pieces and with the Raven Room, containing 43 illustrations for the poem.

If children are along, the top-notch Science Museum of Virginia, handsomely housed in a spacious vintage railroad station, has an IMAX theater and more than 250 hands-on exhibits. On ground level, a spin tunnel illustrates how NASA scientists test future aircraft, and flight simulators put visitors at the controls. Electriworks has many changing participatory exhibits, such as a laser oscilloscope that creates giant laser "waves" through voice and hand commands. The museum also oversees the Virginia Aviation Museum, located at the Richmond Airport, a stroll through aviation history including open-cockpit mail planes, World War I and II aircraft, and a special exhibit dedicated to Virginia's own Admiral Richard E. Byrd.

Richmond also has its own Children's Museum, expressly for children under age 12. The kids, of course, will also love a visit to the water slides, roller coasters, and other thrill rides at Paramount Kings Dominion, Richmond's big amusement park, where Volcano, the Blast Coaster is the latest of ten big roller coasters. Nickelodeon Splat City, featuring messy entertainment from the TV network, is another favorite lure.

A perfect end to a Richmond visit is a twilight cruise on the paddle wheeler *Annabel Lee,* sailing down the James River, where it all began. There's no better way to see the contrast of old and new and to appreciate the dual spirit of a city maintaining pride in yesterday while facing squarely toward tomorrow.

Area Code: 804

DRIVING DIRECTIONS   Richmond is at the intersection of Routes 95 and 64. From D.C. and points north, take I-95 south into town. The approximate distance from D.C. is 111 miles.

PUBLIC TRANSPORTATION   Excellent Amtrak connections, Greyhound buses, and many airlines serve Richmond. A downtown trolley makes it easy to get around to the important sights for 25 cents.

ACCOMMODATIONS   Ask about weekend packages. *Jefferson Hotel,* Franklin and Adams Streets, 23220, 788-8000 or (800) 424-8014, historic treasure, E–EE • *Linden Row Inn,* 100 East Franklin Street, 23219, 783-7000 or (800) 348-7424, 1840 town houses, M–E, CP • *The Berkeley Hotel,* 1200 Cary Street, 23219, 780-1300, classy small downtown hotel on Shockoe Slip, E, CP • **Bed-and-breakfast inns:** *William Catlin House,* 2304 East Broad Street, 23223, 780-3746, M, CP • *Mr. Patrick Henry's Inn,* 2300–02 East Broad Street, Richmond 23223, 644-1322, M, CP • *Emmanuel Hutzler House,* 2036 Monument Avenue, 23220, 355-4885, small attractive bed-and-breakfast home near choice sightseeing, M–E, CP.

DINING   Downtown: *Lemaire,* Jefferson Hotel (see above), continental with a Southern accent, the city's elegant best, M–E • *P. T. Beauregard's Thai Room,* 103 East Cary Street, 644-2328, change-of-pace Thai menu, I–M • **Shockoe Slip and Shockoe Bottom:** *The Frog and the Redneck,* 1423 E. Cary Street, 648-3764, chic bistro with inventive Southern fare, M–E • *The Dining Room,* Berkeley Hotel (see above), fine dining, continental, E–EE• *Tobacco Company,* 1201 East Cary Street, 782-9431, restored warehouse and local landmark, lively, music, M–E • *None Such Place,* 1721 East Franklin Street, 644-0832, creative variations on traditional Virginia cuisine, housed in Richmond's oldest commercial building, M–E • *Sam Miller's Warehouse,* 1210 East Cary Street, 643-1301, old-timer for seafood and beef, M–E • *River City Diner,* 1712 East Main Street, 644-9418, 1950s-style diner complete with jukebox, I • **Fan District and nearby Carytown:** *Avalon,* 2619 West Main Street, 353-9709, varied global menu, cozy, M • *Davis & Main,* 2501 West Main Street, 353-6641, sophisticated setting, grill specialties, M • *Southern Culture,* 2229 West Main Street, 355-6939, Cajun, Southern, Tex-Mex, very popular, I–M • *Zeus Gallery Cafe,* 201 North Belmont Avenue, 359-3219, eclectic, original cuisine, intimate setting, E • *Strawberry Street Cafe,* 421 North Strawberry Street, 353-6860, casual, salad bar, a local favorite for lunch, I, and dinner, I–M • *Nacho Mama's,* 3449 West Cary Street, 358-6262, casual cantina for Mexican fare, I • **Church Hill:** *Millie's Diner,* 2603 East Main Street, 643-5512, creative trendy dishes, funky diner decor, M, terrific breakfasts on weekends, I • *Mr. Patrick Henry's Restaurant* (see inn above), townhouse ambience, M–E.

SIGHT-SEEING   Ask at downtown attractions, hotels, or Richmond Visitors Center about the Richmond Pass, good at your choice of five attractions at substantial savings. *Agecroft Hall,* 4305 Sulgrave Road, 353-4241. Hours: Tuesday to Saturday 10 A.M. to 4 P.M.; Sunday 12:30 P.M. to 5 P.M. $$ • *Beth Ahabah Museum & Archives,* 1109 West Franklin Street, 353-2668. Hours: Sunday to Thursday 10 A.M. to 3 P.M. $$ • *Black History Museum and Cultural Center of Virginia,* Clay Street between First and Adams, 780-9093. Hours: Tuesday to Saturday 10 A.M. to 5 P.M. but may vary; best to phone for current hours. $ • *Children's Museum of Richmond,* 2626 West Broad Street, 788-4949. Hours: Monday to Saturday 9 A.M. to 5 P.M., Sunday noon to 5 P.M. $$ • *Lewis Ginter Botanical Garden,* 1800 Lakeside Avenue, 262-9887. Daily 9 A.M. to 5 P.M. $$ • *John Marshall House,* 818 East Marshall Street, 648-7988. Hours: April through September, Tuesday to Saturday 10 A.M. to 5 P.M., October through December to 4:30 P.M. $$ • *Maymont,* 1700 Hampton Street at Pennsylvania Avenue, 358-7166. Grounds and gardens open daily April through October, 10 A.M. to 5 P.M.; indoor exhibits, Tuesday to Sunday noon to 5 P.M. $$ • Carriage rides: April through October, Sunday noon to 5 P.M. $$ • *Museum and White House of the Confederacy,* 1201 East Clay Street, 649-1861. Hours: Monday to Saturday 10 A.M. to 5 P.M.; Sunday noon to 5 P.M. $$$ • *Edgar Allan Poe Museum,* 1914 East Main Street, 648-5523. Hours: Tuesday to Saturday 10 A.M. to 4 P.M.; Sunday, Monday noon to 4 P.M. $$ • *Richmond National Battlefield Park,* 3215 East Broad Street, 226-1981. Hours: Daily 9 A.M. to 5 P.M. Free • *St. John's Episcopal Church,* 2401 East Broad Street, 648-5015. Guided tours: Monday to Saturday 10 A.M. to 4 P.M.; Sunday 1 P.M. to 4 P.M. $$ • *Science Museum of Virginia,* 2500 West Broad Street, 367-6552. Hours: September to May, Monday to Saturday 9:30 A.M. to 5 P.M., Sunday 11:30 A.M. to 5 P.M. Memorial Day to Labor Day, open Friday and Saturday to 7 P.M. $$ Additional charge for IMAX films or planetarium •

Scotchtown, Scotchtown Road, Ashland 227-3500. Hours: May through October, Tuesday to Saturday 10 A.M. to 4:30 P.M.; Sunday 1:30 P.M. to 4:30 P.M., April open weekends only. $$ • *Tuckahoe Plantation,* 12601 River Road, 364-1151. Grounds open daily, house visit by appointment only • *Valentine Museum,* 1015 East Clay Street, 649-0711. Hours: Monday to Saturday 10 A.M. to 5 P.M., Sunday noon to 5 P.M. $$ • *Virginia Aviation Museum,* 5701 Huntsman Road, Richmond International Airport (I-64 exit 197), 236-3622. Hours: Daily 9:30 A.M. to 5 P.M. $$ • *Virginia House,* 4301 Sulgrave Road, 353-4251. Hours: Friday, Saturday 10 A.M. to 4 P.M.; Sunday 12:30 P.M. to 5 P.M. $$ • *Virginia Museum of Fine Arts,* 2800 Grove Avenue, 367-0844. Hours: Tuesday to Sunday 11 A.M. to 5 P.M., Thursday to 8 P.M. $$ • *Virginia State Capitol,* Capitol Square, 9th and Grace Streets, 786-4344. Hours: April to November, daily 9 A.M. to 5 P.M.; rest of year, Monday to Saturday 9 A.M. to 5 P.M., Sunday 1 P.M. to 5 P.M. Free • *Virginia Historical Society,* 428 North Boulevard at Kensington, 342-4901. Hours: Monday to Saturday 10 A.M. to 5 P.M., Sunday 1 P.M. to 5 P.M. $$ • *Maggie L. Walker National Historic Site,* 600 North 2nd Street, 771-2017. Hours: Tours every half hour, Wedneday to Sunday 9 A.M. to 5 P.M. Free • *Paramount Kings Dominion,* 16000 Theme Park Way, off Route 30, Doswell (exit off I-95, 20 miles north of Richmond), 876-5000. Hours: April to early October, daily Memorial Day to Labor Day, weekends before and after. Hours change with seasons; phone for current times. Admission: $33.99; parking, $$$ • **River Excursions:** Phone for current offerings and rates. *Richmond Raft Company,* City Docks, 4400 East Main Street, 222-7238, rafting trips on the James. • *Annabel Lee,* 3011 Dock Street, 644-5700. Varied riverboat cruise offerings, including local outings and plantation tours • *James River and Kanawha Canal Cruises,* Turning Basin at Canal and Virginia streets, Shockoe Slip, 649-2800. **Walking tours:** Phone for current schedules. *Historic Walking Tours,* 649-0711; *Richmond Walks,* 673-WALK.

INFORMATION *Metropolitan Richmond Convention and Visitors Bureau,* 401 North Third Street, Richmond, VA 23219, 782-2777 or (888) 742-6666; www.richmondva.org.

House Hunting in Old New Castle

You can always spot a first-time visitor to New Castle, Delaware. Openmouthed oohs of delight are easy clues that someone new has discovered Delaware's first capital, a tiny riverside charmer whose brick sidewalks, white cupolas, Georgian town houses, and Colonial gardens have hardly changed a whit in appearance in 200 years.

Normally, New Castle is almost a chance discovery, for though a handful of buildings are open to the public, this is not a museum piece but very much a living town. For more than 60 years, however, New Castle has held an annual open house, known as A Day in Old Newcastle, when the public is invited in for one day only, the third Saturday in May, to view the exceptional homes and gardens. It's a gala day that includes Colonial-era reenactments, period music, and horse-drawn carriage rides.

There is no better time to become acquainted with this extraordinary pocket of history, followed on Sunday by the discovery of some other little-heralded Delaware gems, including the present capital city of Dover.

In its earlier years, as the seat of government of the "three lower counties" of Pennsylvania, which eventually became the state of Delaware, New Castle was a center of trade and travel, and its leading citizens were lawyers, judges, and government officials, people of taste and distinction whose homes reflected their wealth and position.

But fate took the spotlight away from New Castle. In 1777 the capital was moved inland to Dover, safer from the guns of the British fleet. By the mid-1800s Wilmington had overshadowed New Castle as a railroad and commercial center, and in 1881 even the county offices and court were removed, leaving the town to settle into mellow obscurity.

The whims of fate and the resulting relative poverty of New Castle's residents kept building alterations to a minimum, leaving the town much the way earlier generations had known it. Today, a walk through the streets is a rare journey back in time. *The New Castle Heritage Trail,* a brochure available at the courthouse and in many shops, is an excellent guide, along with the annual house tour program.

Flags of the Netherlands, Sweden, Great Britain, and the United States are still displayed on the balcony of the New Castle Court House to honor the history of the town, which was founded by the Dutch back in 1651 at a strategic point on the edge of the New World. It changed hands five times and had four names over the next 30 years. When William Penn claimed it as part of his land grant in 1682, it became a Colonial capital.

New Castle streets boast examples of Dutch, Colonial, French, Georgian, Federal, and Empire architecture. Some buildings are made of clapboard, stone, or stucco, but the look of the town is predominantly Georgian- and Federal-style red brick. The homes on the tour vary each year, but you can count on seeing fine mantels, paneling, staircases, and fireplaces, as well as woodwork and flooring of note, and rare and beautiful examples of the Colonial furniture maker's art.

The gardens tucked behind the homes are long and narrow and represent a charming variety of formal and informal. Dressed in their mid-May colors, they make a happy addition to the day's touring.

In all, there are more than 50 sights on the open-house roster each year, including the historic public buildings and spaces that are customarily open to everyone. If you can't make it for the house tour, the public buildings are worth seeing anytime.

Chief among them is the beautiful 1732 New Castle Court House, whose cupola is a town landmark. Delaware's original state capitol before the government center was moved to Dover has been restored with its courtroom, judge's bench, and witness stand as they were in the town's early days.

The town green, according to local tradition, was pegged out as common land by Peter Stuyvesant back in 1655. The Market Place was used for trade as early as 1682, and the Old Town Hall, built in 1823 with a unique arch connecting Delaware Street with the Market Place, has served as both firehouse and federal courthouse during its long life.

A small building with an impressive history is the 1832 ticket office of the New Castle–Frenchtown Railroad, one of the nation's first steam railroads, which brought many prominent passengers to New Castle before the Civil War.

Immanuel Episcopal Church, the sponsor of the annual Day in Old New Castle, originally was built on the town green in 1703. When the building burned in 1980, it was reconstructed with the remaining original wall materials. George Read, a signer of the Declaration of Independence, and other prominent Delaware statesmen are buried in the graveyard here.

A few lovely historic homes also are open to the public. The Old Dutch House, the oldest brick dwelling in the state, was built before 1700. The 1730 Amstel House had the honor of George Washington's presence as a guest at a wedding held in the home in 1784. The George Read II House, an outstanding Georgian mansion with a handsome formal garden, has been restored to its early splendor by the Historical Society of Delaware.

Stroll down Delaware Street to see the fine home of Senator Nicholas Van Dyke at number 400 and, at number 300, the home where the Marquis de Lafayette attended the wedding of Dorcas Van Dyke and Charles I. du Pont in 1824. Near the end of the street is the spot where William Penn first set foot on New World soil in 1682.

The Strand, along the Delaware River, is also lined with many fine residences.

To fortify you during the annual house tour, sidewalk vendors offer snacks, and high tea is served in the historic Immanuel Parish House. Or take a picnic to Battery Park, on the water adjoining the historic area.

New Castle lodgings help maintain the spirit of the past. The nicely restored Armitage Inn is a 1732 residence facing the Delaware River, and the William Penn Guest House and the Terry House are tiny, elegantly furnished Federal-era town houses. Fox Lodge is a change of mood, a Gothic Revival mansion turned bed-and-breakfast just outside the center of town.

You can dine in historic surroundings at the Arsenal on the Green, once an actual arsenal, located just behind the courthouse. A hearty Sunday brunch is served beginning at 11 A.M.

Following brunch, having spent Saturday under the Colonial spell of Old New Castle, you can move south on Sunday for some further early Delaware charm in the little historic cluster known as Odessa, and then on to Dover, the state capital.

Located midway between Wilmington and Dover, Odessa was once a thriving commercial center. Today it is a small village remarkable for its aura of that earlier time and for its rich architecture. Two of the finest homes, the Corbit-Sharp House and the Wilson-Warner House, are under the auspices of the Winterthur Museum and are maintained by this noted institution as examples of eighteenth-century elegance. The Collins-Sharp House, one of the earliest structures still standing in Delaware, is used for open-hearth cooking demonstrations on Fridays and Saturdays from March through October. The 1822 Brick Hotel has been restored as a gallery with changing exhibits.

It is 26 miles farther to Dover, a town of broad tree-lined avenues and many fine homes. The expansive lawns of Capital Square and the original Town Green, lined with red brick government buildings, give the center of town more the look of a Colonial college campus than a government seat.

Stop at the Visitors Bureau on Federal Street for a printed tour to guide your wanderings, or make advance arrangements with the Dover Heritage Trail for a guided walking tour. You'll be pleased to see that most of the attractions in the state capital are free.

From your brochure, you'll learn that Dover, the center of Kent County, was formally laid out in 1717 according to a plan set forth by William Penn shortly after he arrived in America. He named the town after Dover in Kent, England.

A bit of early American history was made here when Caesar Rodney, a favorite Delaware hero, galloped off to Philadelphia to sign his name to the Declaration of Independence, ensuring his state's adoption of the document. It was also from Kent County that the famous Delaware Battalion marched to join Washington's main army, winning the respect of all Americans and the nickname "Blue Hen Chickens" for the spirited fighting cocks the men carried with them to war. The Blue Hen became the state bird, perhaps an omen that one day the Delmarva Peninsula would become the heart of the nation's chicken-raising industry.

Among the major sights in Dover is the Georgian Revival State House on the Green, one of the nation's oldest. It is now used only for ceremonial occasions, and its courtrooms, legislative chambers, and governor's office have been nicely restored. A larger-than-life 1802 portrait of George Washington hangs in the senate chamber.

Also open to visitors is the eighteenth-century Meeting House and Gallery I and II complex, whose diverse exhibits include an 1880 gallery of turn-of-the-century crafts and commercial shops; the Johnson Memorial Building, which highlights the men, machines, and music of the golden age of the American phonograph; and the Meeting House Gallery. The last is actually the restored 1790 Presbyterian church and is of interest for its circular stair and belfry and changing displays of local history.

Another important Dover attraction is the Samuel C. Biggs Museum of American Art, a private nonprofit institution. In 1990 the Delaware General Assembly funded a modern addition to the brick and cast-iron 1858 Kent County Levy Court House to house both the Biggs collection and the Delaware State Visitors Center. The museum includes paintings spanning 200 years, from Colonial portraits to twentieth-century Impressionism. Gilbert Stuart, Charles Willson Peale, Albert Bierstadt, and Thomas Cole are some of the well-known early American artists represented. One gallery is devoted to the works of Wilmington illustrator Frank Schoonover, and another to watercolors. The impressive furniture and silver collections represent some of the best Delaware and Philadelphia craftsmen of the eighteenth and early nineteenth centuries, with a notable collection of tall clocks.

Dover is rightfully proud of its historic homes. Many dating from the eighteenth century are clustered on South State Street near the Green. The nineteenth-century Victorian homes are farther north on South State and on South Bradford. Many of them are open for Old Dover Days early in May. The governor's lovely 1790 Georgian home on Kings Highway is also sometimes open for tours. Check for current schedules.

Dover's other showplace is the John Dickinson Mansion, a 1740 residence that was the boyhood home of one of the state's foremost early patriots, the man known as the "Penman of the Revolution" for his many political pamphlets and articles. The seat of a 5,000-acre plantation, the mansion faces the St. Jones River across the fields and is a fine sight in its rural setting. A fire in 1804 destroyed much of the original woodwork, but the interior has been restored with comparable period paneling.

One final attraction in Dover recommended for children is the little Delaware Agricultural Museum, where farm equipment is displayed and exhibits illustrate the evolution of the state's dairy and poultry industries. (You won't need to be told it is across the street from Dover Downs when you hear the roar of the stock-car racers.) Beside the main building there are village buildings, including a one-room schoolhouse, a gristmill, a sawmill, a blacksmith shop, and a typical farmhouse with outbuildings. The buildings and their contents show farm life in the late nineteenth century. It's another part of the past in a little state with a big share of history.

Area Code: 302

DRIVING DIRECTIONS   New Castle is on Routes 9 and 141, both exits off I-95 a few miles southeast of Wilmington. From D.C., take I-95 north, turning off at Route 141 east. The approximate distance from D.C. is 110 miles.

PUBLIC TRANSPORTATION   Amtrak to Wilmington, bus service to Wilmington and Dover. SEPTA trains also connect Wilmington with Philadelphia.

ACCOMMODATIONS   All New Castle zip codes are 19720. *Armitage Inn,* 2 The Strand, 328-6618, best in town, M–E, CP • *William Penn Guest House,* 206 Delaware Street, 328-7736, shared baths; I–M, CP • *Terry House,* 130 Delaware Street, 322-2505, M, CP • *Fox Lodge,* 123 West 7th Street, New Castle, 328-0768, M–E, CP • *Rodeway Inn,* 111 South du Pont Highway, 328-6246, motel alternative if inns are full, I, CP • *Sheraton Dover Hotel,* 1370 North du Pont Highway (U.S. 13), Dover 19901, 678-8500, indoor pool, M. Also see Wilmington, page 46.

DINING   **New Castle:** *Arsenal on the Green,* 30 Market Street (behind the courthouse), 328-1798, period ambience, M–E • *Jessop's Tavern,* 114 Delaware Street, 322-6111, casual, microbrewed beer and pub menu, M • *The Cellar Gourmet,* 208 Delaware Street, 323-0999, light fare for lunch, I • *Lynnhaven Inn,* 154 North du Pont Highway (U.S. 13), 328-2041, early American decor, varied menu, M–E • *Air Transport Command Restaurant,* 143 North du Pont Highway (U.S. 13), 328-3527, features WWII planes and ambience, M–E • *Opera House Victorian Tea Room,* 308 Delaware Street, 326-1211, stop in on weekends, 11 A.M. to 5 P.M., for a proper high tea, with scones, tea sandwiches, and pastries, I • **Dover:** *Blue Coat Inn,* 800 North State Street, north of town, Dover, 674-1776, seafood and colonial recipes, M–E • *Tango's Bistro,* Sheraton Dover Hotel (see above), California cuisine in a pleasant setting, M–E • *Plaza Nine,* 9 East Lockerman

Street, Treadway Towers, Dover, 736-9990, overlooking a lake, out-door dining, M–E.

SIGHT-SEEING *A Day in Old New Castle,* c/o Immanuel Church, P.O. Box 166, New Castle, 19720, 322-5774. Held annually third Saturday in May, $$$$ • *George Read II House,* 42 The Strand, New Castle, 322-8411. Hours: March through December, Tuesday to Saturday 10 A.M. to 4 P.M.; Sunday noon to 4 P.M.; January, February weekends only or by appointment. $$ • *Amstel House Museum,* 2 East 4th Street at Delaware Street, New Castle, 322-2794. Hours: March through December, Tuesday to Saturday 11 A.M. to 4 P.M.; Sunday 1 P.M. to 4 P.M., January, February weekends only, $; combination ticket with Old Dutch House, $$ • *Old Dutch House,* 32 East 3rd Street, 322-2794. Hours: same as Amstel House. $ • *New Castle Court House,* 211 Delaware Street, New Castle, 323-4453. Hours: Tuesday to Saturday 10 A.M. to 3:30 P.M.; Sunday 1:30 P.M. to 4:30 P.M. Free • *Historic Houses of Odessa,* Corbit-Sharp House, Collins-Sharp House, Wilson-Warner House, and Brick Hotel Gallery, off Route 13, Odessa, 378-4069. Hours: March through December, Tuesday to Saturday 10 A.M. to 4 P.M.; Sunday 1 P.M. to 4 P.M. $$ for one building, combination tickets for two or three houses.

Dover: *Delaware State House,* the Green at South State Street, 739-4266. Hours: Tuesday to Saturday 10 A.M. to 4:30 P.M., Sunday 1:30 P.M. to 4:30 P.M. Free • *Meeting House and Gallery I and II,* 316 South Governors Avenue, 739-4266. Hours: Tuesday to Saturday 10 A.M. to 3:30 P.M. Free • *Sewell C. Biggs Museum of American Art,* 406 Federal Street, 674-2111. Hours: Wednesday to Saturday, 10 A.M. to 4 P.M., Sunday 1:30 P.M. to 4:30 P.M. Free • *John Dickinson Plantation,* Kitts Hummock Road, south of Dover, 739-3277. Hours: Tuesday to Saturday 10 A.M. to 3:30 P.M., Sunday 1:30 P.M. to 4:30 P.M. Closed Sundays in January and February. Free • *Delaware Agricultural Museum and Village,* 866 North du Pont Highway, junction of U.S. 13 and Alt. U.S. 13, Dover, 734-1618. Hours: April through December, Tuesday to Saturday 10 A.M. to 4 P.M.; Sunday 1 P.M. to 4 P.M.; rest of year closed weekends. $$ • *Dover Heritage Trail Walking Tours,* P.O. Box 1628, Dover, DE 19903, 678-2040.

INFORMATION *New Castle Visitors Bureau,* P.O. Box 465, New Castle, DE 19720, 322-8411 or (800) 758-1550; www.visitnewcastle. com; *Delaware Visitor Center,* 406 Federal Street, Dover, DE 19901, 739-4266.

A Taste of Little Washington in Virginia

There are 28 towns named for "the father of our country," but this hamlet was the first, perhaps because it was George himself who was responsible for the original plan for Washington, Virginia. He was a 17-year-old surveyor for Lord Fairfax when his 1797 journal recorded "in the Blue Ridge Mountains I laid off a town." Romantic legend has it that Gay Street, one of the town's two main streets, may have been named by George to please the lovely Gay Fairfax.

The layout hasn't changed much in all this time, still just five blocks long by two blocks wide, and the population is just 170, but this tiny village cradled by the Blue Ridge Mountains looms large when it comes to weekend pleasures.

It began with the amazing success story of the Inn at Little Washington. The Inn opened in an unpromising location in 1977, on the site of a onetime auto-repair shop in a run-down, little-known hamlet. It went on to become one of the most lauded and luxurious inns and restaurants in the country.

The attention has triggered a total transformation in Washington. Quaint eighteenth- and nineteenth-century village houses of clapboards and logs now house intriguing shops with art, gifts, crafts, and antiques of high quality. Antebellum homes and vintage farmsteads have become charming bed-and-breakfasts. And those who can't afford the original inn's quite hefty tab can enjoy excellent cuisine at a variety of good restaurants that have opened in recent years.

There's more to do in neighboring Sperryville, home to a giant antique cooperative and known as the "Little Apple" for its abundant orchards, which are in full blossom in spring. Continue west on Route 211 a few miles past Sperryville and you've reached the Skyline Drive, Virginia's magnificent mountaintop roadway, also resplendent in spring blooms. The combination is hard to beat.

Washington shopping is unique because of the uniformly high quality of the shops housed in historic quarters and the presence of artists and artisans in many of their shops and galleries. They are clustered along the two principal streets of the town, Main and Gay.

Strolling along Main Street, visitors will find that one unusual stop is the log cabin at number 322, which is now home to jeweler Edmund Kavanagh, whose specialty is repoussé, the delicate art of raising gold and silver in relief. His ceremonial pieces have included the Prince Philip Henley Regatta Trophy and an 18-karat bowl presented to President Dwight Eisenhower.

Across the street, there's more fine jewelry in Chris's Shop, number

349, where jewelry artist Christopher Goodine displays his unusual silver and gold pieces in a distinctive wavy pattern. Rare Finds at number 371 has a variety of attractive gifts and accessories as well as a few antiques, and Pockerknockers' at number 423, another restored eighteenth-century building, is an appropriate setting for elegant reproduction period lighting.

Two stops for art lovers are found next to the Inn at Little Washington on Middle Street, a short street that runs between Main and Gay. The Middle Street Gallery is an artists' cooperative, and artist Peter Garon is usually present at his attractive upstairs contemporary studio and showroom.

Turning down Gay Street, you'll find the Sunnyside Farm Market, with produce from local farms and gourmet specialty foods. The Washington Arts Building at 311 holds the Talk of the Town, a shop with regional handmade gifts, and the workshop of cabinetmaker Peter Kramer, who creates one-of-a-kind handcrafted furniture. Craftsmen can often be seen at work here.

On Gay, you'll also pass the Rappahannock County Court House, built in 1835, the impressive 1873 Washington Baptist Church, and the Rappahannock Historical Society, circa 1830, where you can learn more about local history. The Theatre at Washington, at 291 Gay, a small cultural center, has interesting offerings that range from plays and a Friday night film series to concerts by jazz greats and a regular Smithsonian series of chamber music. Ask for the current schedule.

The Inn at Little Washington calls itself "America's most celebrated country inn," and who's to argue when the rooms are sumptuous and every critic goes into ecstasies over the dining room. Things are even more luxurious since a recent $2.5 million kitchen and bedroom addition.

More modest but quite appealing inns are found on Main Street. My picks would be the stately, elegant Middleton Inn, an 1850 mansion, and the Foster Harris House, a charming small in-town Victorian, furnished with taste and boasting mountain views from some rooms. Each is an easy walk to all the shops.

Two inns just outside town offer spectacular mountain views. Fairlea Farm, a fieldstone farmhouse just a five-minute stroll from the shops, is a warm, friendly, informal inn on 40 acres dotted with sheep and cattle, with bucolic views across the pastures. For drama, it's Sycamore Hill, a stunning contemporary home set atop Menefee Mountain at 1,043 feet, with a huge round glass window and a 65-foot veranda to savor the showstopping views. The grounds, covering several hundred acres, include lovely gardens and a National Wildlife Habitat.

The award-winning prix fixe dinners at the Inn at Little Washington run more than $100 on weekends. The only alternative in town is the Country Cafe, a family restaurant open for all three meals. But fine dining with a smaller tab can be found north of town in Flint Hill, where two former Inn chefs have created a pretty little storefront cafe called Four and Twenty Blackbirds that is widely praised for its eclectic menu. The Flint Hill Public House serves a varied contemporary menu in a 1903 schoolhouse converted to a restaurant and pub. Just south of town is the Bleu Rock Inn, known for its French-American cuisine.

Driving south from Washington on Route 211, watch for the sign on the right and head to the top of the hill for Sunset Hills Farm, where the apple and peach blossoms are in bloom in spring, and products like brandied peaches and peach and apple butter made from the crops are for sale in the farm store. The mountain views are amazing. Guest rooms are available in the Frank Lloyd Wright–inspired home.

Just before you get to Sperryville, look for the signs pointing left to the Sperryville Antique Market, an old apple barn filled with wares from dozens of dealers. There's a little bit of everything, rare books to furniture, and the quality is high.

Those who admire the country clothing and goods in the Faith Mountain catalog will want to stop at the big Faith Mountain store just outside Sperryville, where there are some good buys on catalog merchandise. Many additional shops are found in town and along Route 211, the highway leading to the Skyline Drive.

Two fine country retreats can be found a few miles south of Sperryville on the road toward Culpepper. The antique-filled Conyers House has retained its eighteenth-century ambience. Saddles hung on the porch tell you that riding is important here, and guided trail rides are offered by the riding-enthusiast hostess. Belle Meade Inn, an airy, bright Victorian farmhouse on 137 hilltop acres, has mountain views and a pool and hot tub. There's a New Age ambiance here, and guests can enjoy massages at the inn.

Little Sperryville has a potpourri of small shops in town, and more on Route 211 heading toward the Skyline Drive. A worthwhile stop on the highway is the Glassworks Studio and Gallery, where you can often see glassblowers at work.

There are many fruit stands on the road, with offerings like jellies and jams and a few local crafts, but they won't be in full swing with fresh fruit until apple season arrives.

You won't have to wait, however, to see the Skyline Drive, dressed in the soft pastels of springtime. The show begins in March with red maple, service berry, and hepatica in bloom; wildflowers appear during April and May, and pink azaleas arrive in late May, followed by mountain laurel in June. Whenever you arrive, it's a vista to treasure.

Area Code: 540

DRIVING DIRECTIONS From Washington, D.C., take Route 66 west to Gainesville, then Route 29 south to Warrenton, connecting to Route 211 west into Washington, VA, about 60 miles.

ACCOMMODATIONS   Washington: *The Inn at Little Washington,* Middle and Main Streets, 22747, 675-3800, super-luxurious and super-expensive, EE, CP • *Middleton Inn,* 176 Main Street, 22747, 675-2020 or (800) 816-8157, EE, CP • *Sycamore Hill House,* 110 Menefee Mountain Lane, 22747, 675-3046, M–EE, CP • *Fairlea Farm,* Mt. Salem Avenue, 22747, 675-3679, M, CP • *Foster Harris House,* 189 Main Street, 22747, 675-3757 or (800) 666-0153, M, CP; suite, E, CP • *Heritage House,* Main Street, 22747, 675-3207, small 1837 home in town, antiques and lace, M, CP • *Sunset Hill Farm,* 105 Christmas Tree Lane, Jenkins Mountain 22747, (800) 980-2580, E–EE, CP • **Sperryville:** *Conyers House,* 3131 Slate Mills Road, 22740, 987-8025, E–EE, CP • *Belle Meade Inn,* 353 F.T. Valley Road (Route 231), 22740, 987-9748, M–E, CP.

DINING   *Inn at Little Washington,* perennial raves, prix fixe, expect to spend $100 or more per person • *Country Cafe,* 3889-A Main Street, Washington, 675-1066, family-style restaurant serving all three meals, I–M • *Bleu Rock Inn,* 12567 Lee Highway (Route 211), Washington, 987-3190, M–E • *Four and Twenty Blackbirds,* Routes 522 and 647, Flint Hill, 675-1111, top reviews, M–E • *Flint Hill Public House,* Route 522, Flint Hill, M.

SIGHT-SEEING   *The Theatre at Washington,* 291 Gay Street, 675-1253. Check current schedule for movies, jazz, Smithsonian chamber concerts, plays.

INFORMATION   *Washington Business Council,* P.O. Box 393, Washington, VA 22747, 675-3128. Sperryville information:www.sperryville.com.

Having a Fling at Fair Hill

Highland Games are a Scottish tradition that have been around as long as anyone can remember. The bagpipes, nimble dancing, and unique sporting competitions that mark these events are loved by Scots no matter where they live—which is lucky for all of us, because the tradition is kept alive in Fair Hill, Maryland, and everyone is invited to watch.

Fair Hill has hosted the Colonial Highland Gathering each May for more than 35 years. The same grounds that hold some of the top steeplechase racing events each year make an ideal backdrop for the gathering, with fields of tall grass waving in the wind, lending a far-away feeling to it all.

Attending the Colonial Highland Gathering makes an ideal family outing. You can round out the weekend by visiting the nearby famous gardens of the Brandywine Valley, or by getting acquainted with the many attractions even closer in Wilmington, Delaware.

The only problem you face at the Highland Games is where to look first, for this day-long event boasts more attractions than a three-ring circus. Some of the most diverting activities are the athletic competitions. According to legend, the Highland Games began as a kind of informal athletic test allowing kings and clan chiefs to pick the best men available for their forces. It still takes a mighty man to prevail! The Highland Heptathlon is actually seven events that demand great strength and endurance. During the course of the action, participants lift and throw at least 1,000 pounds as they compete at weight, stone, and hammer tosses. The various missiles weigh anywhere from 16 to 56 pounds.

But all the preliminaries pale before the incredible "tossing of the caber." A caber looks much like a telephone pole, measuring 16 feet in length and weighing more than 150 pounds. Heaving the heavy pole end over end is a feat that tries even the halest; and some contestants find they can hardly lift the caber, much less toss it anywhere. Yet each year a few stout lads emerge who seem to have inherited the prowess of their ancestors and manage to give the king-size missile a prodigious toss that sets off wild cheering from the sidelines.

Far different but equally fascinating are the sheepdog herding demonstrations, in which uncannily clever canines herd a flock of five sheep through and around a far-flung obstacle course of fences and into a pen. All that these carefully trained border collies have to guide them are the distant whistles of their masters, which they recognize as signals to go right, left, forward, or back. To see these wonderfully bright animals steering their charges around the course at top speed is nothing less than mesmerizing.

When you've had your fill of the flocks, seat yourself back in the bleachers to watch yet another kind of competition, a parade of fair lads and lassies clad in bright kilts, tunics, and plaid kneesocks nimbly performing classic dances such as the Highland Fling, the Sailor's Hornpipe, and the Sword Dance while the judges rate their skill at executing the carefully prescribed steps of each dance. You'll appreciate the dancers' grace even more when you learn that Highland dancing also originated as an athletic event, and dancers still must be in top physical shape to perform the vigorous dances. In the past, dancing was used by Scottish regiments as a regular drill to develop stamina, agility, and endurance. The youngest contenders start in the morning, followed by big brothers and sisters and finally by the adults.

Throughout the day, all around the grounds, pipers and drummers in full regalia are vying, first individually and then as bands, in the bagpipe competitions. The contestants, in colorful plaids, come from throughout the mid-Atlantic states.

There are even more diversions along the sidelines. Two teams of spinners and weavers are at work producing shawls that will be auctioned off to the highest bidder. Depending on the varying entertainment planned each year, you might see mock warriors in armor reenacting a medieval sword fight or demonstrations by magnificent Clydesdale horse teams. Food booths tempt with Scottish specialties from scones to meat pies to fish and chips. A whole rainbow of tartan plaids are for sale, by the yard or as kilts or tams, along with Scottish jewelry and music. Over at the Tea Barn, you can sit back and enjoy traditional Scottish music and learn Scottish dance steps from members of the Royal Scottish Country Dance Society.

During the midday ceremonies and later when the awards are announced, everything else stops for the most colorful event of them all, the massed pipe bands parading the field in an unforgettable splash of color and sound.

The games continue all day, and on Sunday there are many diversions to fill out your weekend. Fair Hill is in the very northeastern corner of the state, just a few miles from the Delaware–Pennsylvania border. It's an easy drive to Longwood Gardens, the most outstanding floral attraction in the Northeast, or to Winterthur, the house-museum famed as the site of the foremost collection of early American antiques and furnishings. In spring, the 64-acre gardens are a woodland wonderland of rare azaleas, rhododendrons, and other prize plants. For more on these two exceptional sites, see "Dropping in on the du Ponts of Delaware," page 180.

Or you might choose to stay in Wilmington and take the opportunity to explore a pleasant small city that is often overlooked because of the many top attractions around it. Wilmington has many new attractions, and special appeal for families. Take a walk on Market Street Mall to see how the city has carefully preserved its past. Willingtown Square at the 500 block on the mall was a preservation effort that saved six of the city's historic homes from the late eighteenth and early nineteenth centuries, moving them to this site. Now used as offices, the houses border a grassy area perfect for picnic lunches. Bordering the square is the 1798 Old Town Hall, now headquarters for the Historical Society of Delaware, which features changing exhibits on Delaware history in the main hall. Kids love the old jail cells in the basement and the displays of old children's toys.

Adjacent is the Delaware History Museum, in what was a 1940s art-deco-style Woolworth's. The Discovery Center, open on Saturday for the kids, includes Grandma's Attic, a place to play dress-up and play with toys from the past. The "Distinctively Delaware" interactive exhibit is an excellent overview of Delaware history for both adults and children.

One of the prize restorations on the mall is the Grand Opera House at Eighth Street. The state's most important Victorian landmark, it has been returned to its early grandeur and now serves as Delaware's Center for the Performing Arts, featuring many live theater and musical performances as well as a series of classic films.

A long walk or a drive farther on Market toward the Brandywine Creek brings you to a picturesque neighborhood known as Old Brandywine Village, once a prosperous milling center and now the site of many handsomely restored stone houses that were the homes of mill owners.

A lovely 80-acre park designed by Frederick Law Olmsted along the meandering Brandywine Creek is a welcome oasis of green in the midst of the city. Here's where you will find the Brandywine Zoo, nicely set on 180 acres.

Wilmington is unusually rich in museums. Besides Winterthur, Longwood, and the many other du Pont properties detailed beginning on page 180, the fine small Delaware Art Museum boasts the country's largest collection of English Pre-Raphaelite art, as well as works by American artists from Thomas Eakins to Winslow Homer and Robert Indiana, and illustrations by the famous Brandywine School of artists, which included N.C. Wyeth, Frank Schoonover, and Howard Pyle. A special feature is a window of 18 spectacular "Persian Flowers" by the noted contemporaroy glass artist Dale Chihuly. The Children's Participatory Gallery allows youngsters to use different media to create their own unique designs. And don't overlook the excellent Museum Shop.

Children will also enjoy the Discovery Room at the Delaware Museum of Natural History, with its games, experiments, microscopes, skeletons, and fossils. Besides displays of Delaware fauna, dioramas and exhibits here include a visit to an African waterhole, a walk over the Great Barrier Reef, a 500-pound clam, and the largest bird egg in the world. On selected "Make It–Take It" Sunday and Monday afternoons, children with a parent can make a craft to take home.

Collectors and children alike will find the Delaware Toy & Miniature Museum of interest. The private collection of miniature vases is said to be the largest in the world, dating as early as 600 B.C. and representing 18 countries. The kids will like the antique dollhouses, dolls, and toys.

Those who favor modern art will find it at the Delaware Center for the Contemporary Arts. Located near the Christina Riverwalk, the DCCA is a showcase for new and experimental work. It includes seven exhibit galleries and 26 studios for professional artists.

Be sure to check on any current offerings at the new First USA Riverfront Arts Center, a building specifically designed to house "blockbuster" art exhibits. The Center is a main part of the redevelompent of the Christina Riverfront, with lovely parks, a 2.3-mile landscaped and lighted Riverwalk, restaurants, nightspots and outlet stores that include L.L. Bean and Coldwater Creek. During warm months, water taxis ply the river, picking up and discharging passengers at nine designated stops. You can also take in an inexpensive baseball game at the handsome 6,500-seat stadium built for the Wilmington Blue Rocks baseball team, a farm team of the Kansas City Royals.

It is interesting to see the activity at the busy Port of Wilmington at the bottom of Christina and Terminal Avenues, the closest Delaware River port to the sea. Along the Christina River near Old Swedes Church (1698) and the Hendrickson House (1690) is the Kalmar Nyckel Shipyard, where the first ship to land in Delaware has been meticulously restored. The Shipyard is near Christina Park, the site of that first landing in 1638. When the *Kalmar Nyckel* isn't off serving as a sailing goodwill ambassador for the state of Delaware, the 130-foot vessel can be boarded to see the handsome woodwork, intricate rigging, six working cannons and enormous masts that reach ten stories above the waterline.

Admirers of Victoriana will want to visit the Rockwood Museum, a nineteenth-century country estate with an 1851 manor house and conservatory, many original outbuildings, and a garden landscaped in the Romantic style.

Another pleasant local family diversion is a nostalgic ride on the Wilmington and Western Steam Railroad, located on Route 41 in Greenbank Park. In continuous operation since 1872, the train offers a ride into the countryside with scenic views of the Red Clay Valley. Adjacent to the railroad is the Greenbank Mill, a 300-year-old operating grist and textile mill. The 18-foot waterwheel, farm site, and resident Merino sheep are favorites with families.

In season, a short drive out of Wilmington to nearby Delaware Park will add thoroughbred racing to your agenda. Families can picnic in the picnic grove of the park, which is set on 500 acres of meadows and woodlands. If you are feeling lucky, slot machines, video poker, and blackjack are now available at the track in a Victorian-styled Slots Parlor.

Downtown Wilmington lodgings run the gamut, from the landmark, lavish Hotel du Pont to a thrifty Courtyard by Marriott. Bed-and-breakfast fans will find a pleasant haven on the edge of Brandywine Park. The Boulevard Bed & Breakfast, a spacious restored city mansion circa 1913, is listed on the National Register of Historic Places. The home is within a walk of downtown.

A little farther into the leafy countryside is another historic landmark, the unique Inn at Montchanin Village. This is a nineteenth-century hamlet of hillside homes that once housed workers at the du Pont powder mills, now restored to hold 37 guest units. The rooms and suites vary in size, but all are luxuriously furnished and come with lavish marble baths.

Dining is equally varied, with the bonus of no tax on meals in Delaware. Depending on the season, evening entertainment might include the Three Little Bakers Dinner Theater; drama, music, or dance at the Grand Opera House; drama by the Delaware Theatre Company; or Broadway shows at the Playhouse at the Hotel Du Pont, often with big name stars.

You'll find more than enough to do in and around Wilmington to fill out a weekend, an ideal complement to a Fair Hill fling.

Area Codes: Fair Hill, MD, 410; Wilmington, DE, 302

DRIVING DIRECTIONS   Fair Hill, MD, is 13 miles west of Wilmington, DE, at the intersection of Routes 213 and 273. Take I-95 north toward Wilmington. From I-95, follow Route 273 west to Fair Hill; from Wilmington follow Route 2. To reach Longwood Gardens from Fair Hill, take Route 841 north and turn right on Route 1 to Kennett Square, PA. For Winterthur, follow Route 2 east to Wilmington and turn left on Route 52 headed northwest. Continue on Route 52 to intersect with Route 1 at Kennett Square. The approximate distance from D.C. is 106 miles.

PUBLIC TRANSPORTATION   Amtrak has excellent service to Wilmington's train station, bus transportation is available via Greyhound, and there is a regular shuttle service to Wilmington from Philadelphia International Airport. Many downtown hotels offer free pickup from the Amtrak station. DART buses go to some museums and points of interest. Check with the Delaware Transportation Store in the Amtrak station.

ACCOMMODATIONS   Newark: The closest lodgings to Fair Hill are in Newark, the attractive home of the University of Delaware. *Christiana Hilton,* 100 Continental Drive, Newark 19713, 454-1500, E–EE • *Residence Inn by Marriott,* 240 Chapman Road (Route 273), Newark 19702, 453-9200, all suites, good for families, M–E • *Hampton Inn,* 3 Concord Lane, Newark 19713, 737-3900, M • *Holiday Inn-Newark,* 1203 Christina Road, Newark 19713, 737-2700, M • *Comfort Inn,* 1120 College Avenue, Newark 19713, 368-8715, I.

Wilmington: Ask about weekend packages including sightseeing. *Hotel du Pont,* Rodney Square, 11th and Market Streets, Wilmington 19801, 594-3125, E–EE • *Wyndham Garden Hotel,* 700 King Street, 19801, 655-0400, M–E • *Brandywine Suites Hotel,* 707 King Street, Wilmington 19801, 656-9300, all suites, M–E, CP • *Sheraton Suites,* 422 Delaware Avenue, Wilmington 19806, 654-8300, indoor pool, M–E, • *Courtyard by Marriott/Downtown,* 1102 West Street, Wilmington 19801, 429-7600, M–E, I–M on weekends • **Bed-and-breakfast inns**: *The Inn at Montchanin Village,* Route 100 and Kirk Road, Montchanin 19710, 888-2133 or (800) COW-BIRD, E–EE, CP • *The Boulevard Bed & Breakfast,* 1909 Baynard Boulevard, Wilmington 10902, 656-9700, I–M, CP. See also Brandywine Valley listings, pages 231–232.

DINING **Fair Hill and Newark:** *Fair Hill Inn,* Routes 273 and 213, Fair Hill, (410) 398-4187, historic home, continental fare, M–E • *Klondike Kate's,* 158 East Main Street, 737-6100, varied informal fare in a Victorian setting, I–M • *Le Chameleon,* Christiana Hilton (see above), fine dining, M–EE.

Wilmington: *Green Room,* Hotel du Pont (see above), old-world elegance, E–EE; lavish Sunday brunch, E • *Brandywine Room,* Hotel du Pont (see above), intimate, handsome walnut paneling, a million dollars worth of Wyeths on the walls, M–EE • *Krazy Kat's,* The Inn at Montchanin Village (see above), light hearted decor and serious cuisine, lunch, M-E, dinner, E • **Restaurant 821,** 821 Market Street, 652-8821, across from the Grand Opera House, Mediterranean menu, one of the city's best, E • **Deep Blue Bar and Grill**, 111 West 11th Street, 777-2040, excellent seafood, M–E • **Vault—The Steakhouse,** 1000 West Street, 421-9988, wood-fired grill, live entertainment, in a former bank, E • *The Silk Purse,* 1307 North Street, Wilmington, 654-7666, fine dining, M–E, also casual dining upstairs at *The Sow's Ear,* M • *Positano,* 2401 Pennsylvania Avenue, 656-6788, French/Italian, widely praised, E–EE • *Sienna,* 1616 Delaware Avenue, 652-0653, bright, appealing setting, interesting Mediterranean menu, cigar bar upstairs, M–E • *Carucci,* 606 Greenhill Avenue, Wilmington, 654-2333, opera-singing waiters, Northern Italian food, M • *Toscana Kitchen + Bar,* Rockford Shops, 1412 North du Pont Street, Wilmington, 654-8001, a local favorite for Tuscan dining, M–E • *Buckley's Tavern,* 5812 Kennett Pike, Centreville, DE (just outside Wilmington), 656-9776, comfortable country tavern, convenient for Winterthur, lunch, I–M, dinner, M • *Harry's Savoy Grill,* 2020 Naamans Road, 475-3000, traditional decor and American menu, M–E • *Columbus Inn,* 2216 Pennsylvania Avenue, Wilmington, 571-1492, old-timer, Colonial flavor in historic building, M–E • *Waterworks Cafe,* 16th & French Streets, 652-6022, old waterworks on the Brandywine River, outdoor dining in season, lunch, I–M; dinner, M–E.

SIGHT-SEEING *Colonial Highland Gathering,* Fair Hill Race Track, Routes 273 and 213, Fair Hill, MD, usually third Saturday in May, 9 A.M. to 5 P.M. For current date and admission fees, Scottish Games, 9 Bowman Way, Newark, DE 91711, (302) 453-8998, www.fairhillscottishgames.org, or contact the Cecil County Chamber of Commerce (see below) • *Brandywine Zoo,* North Park Drive, Brandywine Park, Wilmington, 571-7747. Hours: daily 10 A.M. to 4 P.M. $$; November to March, Free • *Delaware Art Museum,* 2301 Kentmere Parkway, Wilmington, 571-9590. Hours: Tuesday to Saturday 9 A.M. to 4 P.M.; Sunday 10 A.M. to 4 P.M. Open Wednesday to 9 P.M. $$ • *Delaware Center for the Contemporary Arts,* 200 South Madison Street, 656-6466. Hours: Tuesday to Friday 10 A.M. to 6 P.M.; Wednesday to 8 P.M., Saturday 10 A.M. to 5 P.M., Sunday 1 P.M. to 5 P.M. Free • *Delaware Park Race Course,* Route 7 off I-95 exit 4B, Stanton (south of Wilmington), 994-2521. Hours: Racing season mid-April through early November, Tuesday, Wednesday, Saturday, and Sunday. Post time, 12:45 P.M.; Clubhouse restaurant, betting, slots, and blackjack open year-round. • *Delaware History Museum,* 504 Market Street, 656-0637. Hours: Monday to Friday noon to 4 P.M., Saturday 10 A.M. to 4 P.M. $$ (includes Old Town Hall); Discovery Center, Saturday 10 A.M. to 4 P.M. children $, adults free • *Delaware Museum of Natural History,* Kennett Pike (Route 52) five miles northwest of Wilmington, 652-9111. Hours: Monday to Saturday 9:30 A.M. to 4:30 P.M., Sunday noon to 5 P.M. $$ • *Delaware Toy & Miniature Museum,* Route 141, Wilmington, 427-8697. Hours: Tuesday to Saturday, 10 A.M. to 4 P.M., Sunday noon to 4 P.M. $$ • *First USA Riverfront Arts Center,* 800 South Madison Street, 277-1600 or (888) 395-0005. Phone for current offerings • **Greenbank Mill,** 500 Greenbank Road, 999-9001. Hours: Friday, Saturday, 10 A.M. to 4 P.M. $$ • *Kalmar Nyckel Foundation,* 1124 East 7th Street, 429-7447. Hours: Monday to Saturday, 10 A.M. to 4 P.M., Sunday noon to 4 P.M. $$$ • *Rockwood Museum,* 610 Shipley Road, 761-4340. Hours: Tuesday to Saturday 11 A.M. to 4 P.M. $$; grounds are free • **Town Hall Museum,** 512 Market Street, Wilmington, 655-7161. Hours: Vary. Best to phone • **Wilmington & Western Railroad,** Greenbank Station, Route 41, 998-1930. Hours: March through December, varying days and hours depending on the season; best to phone. $$$ • **Wilmington Theater Companies:** Phone for current offerings. *Delaware Theater Company,* 200 Water Street, 594-1100 • *Three Little Bakers Dinner Theatre,* 3540 Foxcroft Drive, Pike Creek Valley, 368-1616; *Playhouse Theatre,* du Pont Building, 10th and Market Streets, 656-4401. For additional Wilmington attractions, see page 180, "Dropping in on the du Ponts of Delaware."

INFORMATION *Greater Wilmington Convention & Visitors Bureau,* 100 West 10th Street, Suite 20, Wilmington, DE 19801, 652-4088 or (800) 422-1181; www.visitwilmingtonde.com • **Cecil County Chamber of Commerce,** 135 East Main Street, Elkton, MD 21921, (410) 392-3833 or (800) 232-4595.

Down to the Sea in Solomons

Will success spoil Solomons Island? That was the question that worried the locals. The word is out about this miniature fishing village in southern Maryland, a quaint dot on Chesapeake Bay joined to the mainland by a bridge built on a bed of oyster shells. The tourists and yachtsmen are coming faster every year.

But so far, there is no need for concern. Things have changed, but development has been done in the most tasteful way, and the spirit of Solomons is intact. With Chesapeake Bay, the Patuxent River, and an inlet known as Back Creek hugging the town with water on three sides, this is still a special getaway. If anything, it looks better than ever with the Riverwalk, a boardwalk installed along the Patuxent, and a picnic area and fishing pier near the bridge leading into town. When motels went up, they were placed away from the center of town, leaving the quaint look intact.

You can still come down on a fine day in May or June and feel a million miles away from the city, sniffing the salt air, watching the boats go by, and savoring a seafood dinner on an outdoor deck facing the water. And you can learn a good bit about the bay at the fine Calvert Marine Museum, which keeps expanding and getting better.

To add to the weekend's fun, there's the chance to scout for fossils, stroll beneath tall cypress trees, explore archaeology, and enjoy some pretty, peaceful nature preserves and beaches by the bay in nearby Calvert County parks. Solomons is equally fine as a romantic getaway or a family outing. Families will especially appreciate that most admissions are moderate or free.

If you rent a boat or sign on for a charter or a fishing cruise at one of the many marinas, you'll need no further guidance as to how to spend your time. If you are a landlubber, there is just enough to do on Solomons to keep things interesting when you tire of gazing out to sea.

The place to start is the Marine Museum, whose Drum Point Lighthouse is Solomons's landmark. The 1883 structure, moved here in 1975 for restoration, is one of only three octagonal cottage-type lights remaining of 45 that served Chesapeake Bay waters at the turn of the century. You can take a tour, see the keeper's quarters, go out on the deck, and climb up top to see the Fresnel lens that beamed the light out to sea.

In the museum building, galleries deal with three themes: boat building and maritime history; the plant and animal life of Chesapeake Bay and its Patuxent River arm; and the rich fossil deposits that lie at nearby Calvert Cliffs. Among the favorite displays are the aquarium, where you can see the fish and plant life beneath the waters around you, including Maryland's famous blue crabs, and the river otters, everybody's favorite clowns, who are seen in a naturalistic setting that serves as an introduction to the museum's outdoor walkways. Along the shores of salt and freshwater marshes, you can observe a variety of birds, crabs, fish, and plants.

All kinds of wonderful boats are on display indoors, both real and models. The model-making and wood-carving shop often has artisans at work, demonstrating their crafts.

At the J. C. Lore Oyster House annex in town, about half a mile south of the museum complex, exhibits tell the story of the fishing, clamming, crabbing, and oystering industries that once were the island's mainstay. Among them are re-created settings of a fisherman's shanty and a clam house. You can touch the tools and gear used by local watermen and step up to the tables where workers shucked Patuxent River oysters.

And if all the talk of boats makes you want to get out to sea, you can take a cruise around the harbor and the Patuxent River on the museum's 60-foot 1899 bugeye, the *William B. Tennison,* the oldest licensed passenger vessel on Chesapeake Bay.

The museum also manages the area's newest attraction, the Cove Point Lighthouse, built with funds appropriated by Congress in 1825 to mark the entrance to the Patuxent River.

A complete tour of the rest of Solomons on land will take you about 5 minutes by car and 15 on foot, that's how compact things are. The island took its name from one Isaac Solomon, who established a large oyster-packing operation here. It was also headquarters for several shipyards that developed to support the fishing fleet, known best for bugeye sailing craft, like the *William B. Tennison,* that were built here in the nineteenth century. The deep, protected harbor has been a busy marine center ever since, though most of the industry today is pleasure boating.

Most of the sights are concentrated along Patuxent Avenue, where one side is now the Riverwalk and the other is shops and restaurants quartered in some of the town's quaint old homes. Harmon House is a complex of several shops with wares from gifts to antiques to Christmas ornaments. Next door is Solomons Style with some interesting beachwear.

The most upscale shops are in a new building called Avondale Center, where the tenants include Fine Things, with many attractive decorating ideas, and Solomons Mines with fine jewelry. Down the street is Carmen's Gallery, displaying a variety of art.

Plan a drive to take in the fine view from Sandy Point, where the Patuxent River and the bay converge, and to admire the views from the many marinas, where boats can be chartered for sailing and fishing.

Over in Dowell, the settlement opposite Solomons on the other side of Back Creek, Annmarie Garden, a promising sculpture garden, is taking shape on 30 acres of trees and gardens along a creek. It is especially beautiful in spring, when over 400 azaleas are in bloom. It is the scene of a week-long Gardenfest in spring, and an Artsfest that features over 250 juried artisans. Garden in Lights is an annual attraction in December.

If you while away a lazy Saturday in Solomons and want a change of scene on Sunday, you'll find much more to see and do nearby. Follow the graceful arching bridge over the Patuxent, and you can explore some of the history in neighboring St. Mary's County, including Sotterley, an eighteenth-century plantation, and St. Mary's City, a re-creation of Maryland's earliest settlement (see page 91).

Heading back toward Washington along Route 2/4 brings you to Calvert Cliffs State Park, 1,460 wooded acres leading to the majestic cliffs on the western side of Chesapeake Bay. The high cliffs here, some dating back as much as 15 million years, were formed from ancient sea floors by winds and waves. The cliffs are famous for their Miocene fossils, and you may want to join the scouters looking for fossils along the open beach. No digging is allowed, but if your eagle eye spots a find, it's yours. In season, naturalists conduct guided fossil talks. It is about a 45-minute walk to reach the shore, a pleasant little hike, and there are also 13 miles of hiking trails in the park.

The visitors center at the neighboring Calvert Cliffs Nuclear Power Plant is located in a nineteenth-century tobacco barn, with tobacco still hanging from the rafters. It offers an interesting look at the agricultural and archaeological evolution of the area, with emphasis on the fossils in the nearby cliffs. As you would expect, there are also interactive exhibits explaining how nuclear power works.

Further along Route 2/4, take a detour down Route 264 to Route 265, Mackall Road, to Jefferson Patterson Park for another interesting look at the past. The 512-acre park is the site of 52 identified archaeological sites, some dating back to 7500 B.C. Some of the finds are on view in the visitors center in a display called "12,000 Years in the Chesapeake," chronicling the lifestyle changes in the region over the centuries. A special children's room has some fascinating exhibits, like teeth of mastodons and mammoths, and games that let youngsters try to match animals with their tracks. A barn-exhibit complex on the grounds is being developed into a museum of farm life, and you can see the restoration techniques that are being used to preserve old tools and farm equipment. Demonstration gardens showing typical plants grown in different eras are being planted as well. Walking the Archaeology Trail allows you to visit the places where generations of Indians and colonists settled along the Patuxent River.

The drive along Mackall Road is a lovely one, showing the placid farmland of Calvert County at its best, with many picturesque tobacco barns along the way. A 1989 county survey counted more than 150 of these barns, half of them built before 1900. The barns come in several styles, and it is fun to drive along and watch for the different shapes.

Battle Creek Cypress Swamp Sanctuary is a 100-acre preserve for nature lovers who want to walk among the tall trees in the northernmost natural stand of bald cypress in America. The trees are unique, standing from 70 to 100 feet tall and having surrealistic "knees" for roots that stand as high as four feet. The knees help to stabilize the trees. The park has been certified as a natural landmark. An elevated boardwalk makes for a pleasant shady stroll.

Another fine place for a stroll is Flag Ponds Nature Park, a 327-acre preserve with three miles of gentle trails leading past all manner of flora and fauna. In spring, the rare blue flag iris is one of many wild-flowers that flourish in the park. The park also features a wetlands boardwalk with observation platforms overlooking two ponds and a visitors center with wildlife exhibits, plus a nice little beach and fishing pier on the bay. The beach here also may yield fossils if you have a keen eye.

If beaches are your pleasure, you should know about two little towns further north off Route 2. Chesapeake Beach is an old resort that is coming back to life, with a new water park and lots of spiffy new construction on the waterfront. The adjacent town of North Beach, until recently a rather down-at-the-heels community, is also looking a lot better, with a boardwalk along the extensive waterfront. Stop into the restored train station in Chesapeake Beach for intriguing photos and displays from the days when folks from Washington used to flock here by train. If you decide to give this undiscovered region a try, you can take advantage of the very nice public beach nearby at Breezy Point, which is maintained by Calvert County.

You can have a last seafood dinner in Chesapeake Beach, or you might want to wind things up with a traditional Sunday dinner at the Old Field Inn in Prince Frederick, located in a lovely historic home that is guaranteed to end the weekend on a gracious note.

Area Code: 410

DRIVING DIRECTIONS Solomons is at the southern tip of Routes 2 and 4. From D.C., follow Route 4 (the Pennsylvania Avenue extension) east until it becomes Route 2/4 south. The approximate distance from D.C. is 67 miles. From Baltimore and points north, take Route 97 to Annapolis, then Route 2 south.

ACCOMMODATIONS Solomons inns are quite small, so reserve early. *Back Creek Inn,* Calvert and A Streets, 20688, 326-2022, prime spot on the water, lovely gardens, and a hot tub, M, CP; private cottage with porch and fireplace, E • *By the Bay Bed & Breakfast,* 14374 Calvert Street, P.O. Box 504, 20688, 326-3428, Victorian ambience beside Back Creek, M, CP • *Solomons Victorian Inn,* 125 Charles Street, 20688, 326-4811, a Victorian charmer with water views, a prize aerie with whirlpool on the third floor, and carriage house suites with harbor views, M, CP; suites, E, CP • *Holiday Inn Select Solomons,* P.O. Box 1099, 20688, 326-6311, not the usual motel, a resort with a big pool, tennis, and an attractive waterside setting, M; some efficiencies, M–E • *Comfort Inn Beacon Marina,* P.O. Box 869, 20688, 326-6303, standard motel with pool, some rooms with water views, M, CP.

DINING Most Solomons restaurants specialize in seafood and water views; reservations are recommended on weekends. *Dry Dock,* C Street at Back Creek, 326-4817, best in town, M–E • *Lighthouse Inn,* Patuxent Avenue, 326-2444, also well regarded locally, M–E • *Solomons Pier,* Routes 2/4, 326-2424, prize location on the Riverwalk, M–E • *Captain's Table,* 275 Lore Road, 326-2772, hidden gem for all three meals, all-you-can-eat breakfast bar, deck overlooking Back Creek, M • *C.D. Cafe,* Avondale Center, 326-3877, casual, varied menu, excellent desserts, I–M • *Stoney's Seafood House,* 3939 Oyster House Road, Broomes Island (take Route 264), 586-1888, informal waterfront location with the best crab cakes in southern Maryland, I–M; second location, same crab cakes without the view: 545 Solomons Island Road North, Fox Run Shopping Center, Prince Frederick, 535-1888 • *Vera's White Sands,* White Sands Drive (off Route 4), Lusby, 586-1182, Hawaii by the bay, thatched huts, carvings, palm trees, and all; you have to see this to believe it, M • *Rod 'n Reel,* Route 261 and Mears Avenue, Chesapeake Beach, 257-2735, waterfront, standard seafood menu, M–E • *Smokey Joe's Grill,* Route 261 and Mears Avenue, Chesapeake Beach, 257-2427, lively old-timer on the marina, known for ribs, steamed crabs, M • *The Old Field Inn,* Main Street, Prince Frederick, 535-1054, M–E. For cocktails, you can't beat the Holiday Inn (see above) for water views and generous free hors d'oeuvres.

SIGHT-SEEING *Calvert Marine Museum,* 14200 Solomons Island Road (Route 2/4), P.O. Box 97, 326-2042. Hours: Daily 10 A.M. to 5 P.M. $$; *William B. Tennison* boat cruises. Hours: May through October, one-hour cruise, Wednesday to Sunday 2 P.M. $$ • *Annmarie Garden,* Dowell Road, Solomons, 326-4640. Hours: Daily 10 A.M. to 4 P.M. Free • *Calvert Cliffs State Park,* Route 765, Lusby (301) 872-5688. Hours: Daily sunrise to sunset. $ donation • *Jefferson Patterson Park and Museum,* 10515 Mackall Road (Route 265), St. Leonard, 586-8500. Hours: Mid-April to mid-October, Wednesday to Sunday 10 A.M. to 5 P.M. Free • *Battle Creek Cypress Swamp Sanctuary,* Grays Road off Route 506, Prince Frederick, 535-5327. Hours: April through September, Tuesday to Saturday 10 A.M. to 5 P.M., Sunday 1 P.M. to 5 P.M.; October to March until 4:30 P.M. Free • *Flag Ponds Nature Park,* Solomons Island Road North (Route 2/4), 10 miles south of Prince Frederick, 586-1477. Hours: Memorial Day through Labor Day, Monday to Friday 9 A.M. to 6 P.M., Saturday, Sunday 9 A.M. to 8 P.M.; rest of year, Saturday, Sunday only 9 A.M. to 6 P.M. $$$ per car • *Calvert Cliffs Nuclear Power Plant Visitors Center,* 1650 Calvert Cliffs Parkway, Lusby, 495-4673. Hours: Daily 10 A.M. to 4 P.M. Free • *Chesapeake Beach Railway Museum,* State Road 261, Chesapeake Beach, 257-3892. Hours: May through September daily 1 P.M. to 4 P.M.; weekends in April and October. Free • *Breezy Point Beach,* Breezy Point Road off Route 261, south of Chesapeake Beach, c/o Calvert County Division of Parks, 535-1600. Hours: Memorial Day to Labor Day, 6 A.M. to dusk, $$.

INFORMATION   *Calvert County Tourism,* Courthouse, Prince Frederick, MD 20678, 535-4583 or 800-331-9771; www.co.cal.md.us/cced.

Saluting the Generals in Lexington

The horse-drawn carriages trotting tourists around town seem perfectly at home on the quaint streets of Lexington, Virginia.

The town is growing fast on the outskirts, but the feel of the past remains strong in the center, among brick sidewalks, nineteenth-century façades, and gracious college greens. Wherever you go, you find yourself following the paths of four great American generals, George Washington, Robert E. Lee, Thomas J. "Stonewall" Jackson, and George C. Marshall.

Thanks to the exploits of those generals, Lexington, a town of 7,000, attracts visitors from all over the country, here to tour the home of Stonewall Jackson and the picture-book campuses of Washington and Lee University and the Virginia Military Institute (VMI), where these leaders played important roles.

Yet there's more than history to lure you to Lexington in the spring. There is the lush beauty of the lower Shenandoah Valley, cradled by the Blue Ridge and Allegheny Mountains, and locals will tell you it's at its loveliest in May, when the laurels burst into bloom along the Maury River.

The carriages leaving across from the Historic Lexington Visitor Center are a fine way to get the lay of the land and learn some of the local lore, or you can do it on your own with the walking tour provided by the Visitor Center. Either will take you past some two dozen fine nineteenth-century homes along Washington Street and Lee and Jackson Avenues, then to the red brick buildings and white colonnades of Washington and Lee, and finally to the austere buff-colored neo-Gothic stone façades of VMI, "the West Point of the South."

Washington and Lee, the nation's sixth-oldest college and the oldest one established inland, was an impoverished school when George Washington saved it in 1796 with a gift of $50,000 in stock. Grateful trustees immediately renamed the school Washington Academy.

It became Washington and Lee after Robert E. Lee assumed the presidency after the Civil War, with the goal of transforming a classical academy into a university that could prepare its graduates for the formidable task of rebuilding the ravaged South. Lee turned the school into a university of national prominence. He made many advances in the curriculum, adding a school of law, introducing courses in science and engineering, laying plans for a school of commerce, and initiating the first course in journalism at an American college. His presence attracted outstanding teachers and endowments from prominent citizens, such as inventor Cyrus H. McCormick, whose farm was north of Lexington. Lee's name was added by the school in appreciation after his death.

Many of the campus landmarks are due to Robert E. Lee as well. The beautiful red brick Lee Chapel, where he attended daily services with his students, was designed and built under his supervision in 1867. Lee's onetime office is now a museum whose most famous exhibit is Edward Valentine's remarkable recumbent statue of Lee. The noted Washington-Custis-Lee portrait collection is also here. Recent renovations have added new state-of-the-art displays and a new storyline. In the chapel itself are the famous Charles Willson Peale portrait of George Washington as a colonel in the British Army and a Pine portrait of Lee in Confederate uniform. The general and his family are buried in the crypt on the museum level.

Lee's office remains, preserved just as he left it for the last time on September 28, 1870, with papers in disarray on the desk. His faithful horse, Traveller, rests in a marked plot just outside.

By extraordinary coincidence, the Lee-Jackson House was the residence of both these Southern heroes at different times. Jackson lived in the east wing before the Civil War while he was married to Elinor Junkin, daughter of the college president. She died in childbirth, and he later remarried and moved into town.

Lee lived in the house while the President's House was being built, with a wraparound veranda where his wheelchair-bound wife could enjoy the outdoors, and a stable for Traveller. The presidents of Washington and Lee continue to live in this home.

Both the chapel and the front campus of Washington and Lee have been declared National Historic Landmarks. The long colonnade, with its statue of George Washington, tempts almost everyone to whip out a camera. The statue is usually white, but has been known to take on a brighter hue after a nocturnal raid by cadets from rival VMI next door.

It is Stonewall Jackson whose statue stands on the parade ground at VMI. Founded in 1839, this is the oldest state-supported military college in the nation, and the entire campus around the 12-acre parade grounds has been named a National Historic District. The dress parades held usually on Fridays are a treat to see; check the visitor center for the current schedule.

It was here that General Jackson taught philosophy, physics, and artillery tactics for ten years before he went off to defend his beloved Shenandoah Valley and enter the annals of America's greatest military heroes. In those days, he was known only as a stern teacher and a devout man who started a local Sunday school for blacks.

A few decades later, George C. Marshall, VMI class of 1901, began a remarkable career in Lexington that culminated in the Marshall Plan to rebuild World War II–torn Europe, making him the only professional soldier ever to earn the Nobel peace prize.

The VMI Museum in Jackson Memorial Hall holds exhibits of cadet life past and present, a kind of minihistory of the nation's past. One of the most fascinating exhibits is a replica of the cramped barracks rooms, where cadets' mattresses are rolled almost as compactly as their neatly folded socks. Uniforms and weapons as they changed over the years are also featured, and there is an explanation of the venerable VMI honor code, which inspired the old movie *Brother Rat,* starring actor Ronald Reagan.

Two small butternut jackets in the museum suggest the youthfulness of the "boy soldiers" who in 1864 marched from VMI some 80 miles north to New Market to help General Breckenridge defend the Shenandoah Valley. Ten of them lost their lives. The Cadet Chapel in Jackson Hall features a striking oil painting depicting the brave cadet charge.

Prize exhibits in the museum are the uniform coat worn by Stonewall Jackson as a professor, as well as the bullet-pierced raincoat he was wearing when he was fatally wounded at Chancellorsville. His horse, Little Sorrel, also has been mounted as a museum display.

Jackson's exploits in the Shenandoah Valley against overwhelming odds are among the legendary chapters of American military history. Jackson's home—the only one he ever owned—has been restored as it was when he lived here just before the Civil War. It still contains many of his personal possessions. In 1857 the young widower married Mary Anna Morrison and purchased this modest house on Washington Street. They decorated it with the latest in furniture, woodstoves, and carpeting purchased on summer trips to New York and Philadelphia from 1858 to 1860. In 1861 Jackson marched off to war, never to return to the home he loved. An Edward Valentine statue of the hero stands over his grave in Stonewall Jackson Memorial Cemetery.

VMI's George C. Marshall Museum and Library uses photo murals and displays to tell the story of the man who served his country so well. Marshall reached the highest cadet rank of first captain at VMI, served as an aide to General John J. Pershing in World War I, then was army chief of staff in World War II. He was also ambassador to China, secretary of state, and secretary of defense, as well as architect of the plan that brought new life and hope to battered Europe after World War II. A 25-minute electric map presentation tracing the course of World War II shows the progress of the conflict the way the chief of staff might have viewed it.

Take time for a stroll in Lexington to admire the arts and crafts at Artists in Cahoots, a cooperative gallery for local artists and artisans at One West Washington Street, and sample the homemade ice cream at Sweet Things. The Lexington Historic Shop has a wealth of used books, antiques, and Confederate materials.

The Virginia Horse Center on Route 39 is a big draw for horse lovers, with a busy schedule of shows all year, thanks to the excellent indoor arena. The Lenfest Center for the Performing Arts at Washington and Lee offers a full schedule of dance, opera, music, and drama from September to May; and the Lime Kiln Theater offers concerts and plays from Memorial Day through Labor Day in a remarkable outdoor setting, an old kiln with a stage of stone. One of their traditions each year is a series of performances of *Stonewall Country,* reliving the general's times with original music, battle scenes, and vivid portraits of Civil War heroes.

One of the greatest pleasures of Lexington is the opportunity it affords to alternate history with scenery. A few miles south of town is the natural wonder known as Natural Bridge, whose 215-foot-high stone arch, on property once owned by Thomas Jefferson, is more imposing than its pictures convey. The Natural Bridge complex has other attractions, including underground caverns, a wax museum and the most recent addition, the Monacan Indian Living History Village, where visitors can learn about and assist Monacans with canoe building, shelter construction, hide tanning, mat weaving, and other traditional activities. A separate attraction, the Virginia Safari Park, a 180-acre drive-through zoo, offers views of elk, bison, zebras, antelopes, ostriches, and other animals.

Not far to the east is the Blue Ridge Parkway, the remarkable road across the spine of the mountains connecting Virginia's Shenandoah National Park with Great Smoky Mountain National Park in North Carolina. The green hillsides along the road are brightened in spring by pink bouquets of mountain laurel and rhododendron.

A scenic circuit about 15 minutes north on Route 11 takes you to Route 606 west, Raphine Road, and the chance for wine tasting at Rockbridge Vineyard and a pleasurable visit to the Buffalo Springs Herb Farm, a series of beautiful gardens that have been featured in *Country Home* magazine. Besides the gardens, there's the Big Red Barn beside a rushing creek, offering herbal products, dried flowers, gift items, and a variety of garden books, and a Plant House stocked with herb plants and garden accessories.

Just across the fields from the farm is Wade's Mill, a working mill that has been grinding flour since 1882. The Mill's own stone-ground flours are for sale in a shop that also features pottery and baskets by Virginia artists. The Mill schedules cooking classes and other special events, and the Herb Farm holds many workshops and occasional herbal lunches, so check the schedules.

Continue heading south on Raphine Road until it blends with 252, an attractive rural drive that ends at Route 39, where a turn west will bring you to Lexington's most scenic countryside attraction, Goshen Pass. This stunning mountain gorge runs for three miles where the boulder-strewn Maury River has cut through a range of the Allegheny Mountains. On either side are woodlands filled with rhododendrons, laurels, ferns, pines, maples, and dogwoods that are lovely in spring. Besides its beauty, the river is popular for swimming in summer, canoeing, fishing, hiking, and picnicking year-round. When you turn east once again, you're only 12 miles from Lexington.

Another popular outing from Lexington is a walk along the Chessie Trail, a footpath heading east between Lexington and Buena Vista along a scenic old railroad bed beside the Maury River.

You can have a choice of lodgings, convenient to sight-seeing in town or making the most of the countryside. Within the Lexington Historic District are the historic McCampbell Inn and Alexander-Withrow House, dating from 1789 and 1809, respectively, and the Sheridan Livery Inn, a restored livery stable with hotel-style rooms. All offer amenities such as TV and telephones.

Within walking distance of the town center are two pleasant small bed-and-breakfast inns: The Keep, an 1891 brick Victorian, and the comfortable Llewellyn Lodge, owned by a native who is a wealth of information on the area, from the best fishing holes to the finest scenic drives. North of town on Route 11 is the elegant Maple Hall, a columned brick 1850 mansion.

There are several other choices in the pastoral countryside outside town. Among my favorites are Stoneridge, a secluded and stylishly decorated 1829 Federal home south of town on 36 wooded acres, and the Applewood Inn, a uniquely designed solar home on three levels, with an outdoor pool, a hot tub, and spectacular views. Hikers can enjoy the inn's 35 acres and an adjoining 900 acres of the Rockbridge Hunt, but you needn't go farther than a five-minute walk up the hill for a dazzling 360-degree mountain vista. The hosts offer a unique outing, guided llama treks.

Two of the most scenic accommodations anywhere in the valley are found just off the Blue Ridge Parkway, within a half hour's drive from Lexington. The Peaks of Otter Lodge to the south is doubly lovely since the peaks are reflected in a mountain lake; if you take the Park Service bus up to the summit of Flat Top Mountain, you'll be rewarded with soaring views.

North of Lexington, perched high on the side of the mountain with

40-mile views, is the Sugar Tree Inn, a dream retreat built of hand-hewn logs, with sophisticated rustic country decor and a lovely glass-walled dining lobby for looking out at the wildflowers and the birds. Every room has a fireplace. The inn offers a variety of nature weekends for hikers and bird and wildflower lovers.

Area Code: 540

DRIVING DIRECTIONS Lexington is at the intersection of I-81 north and south, Route 60 east, and I-64 west. From D.C., take Route 66 west, then I-81 south. The approximate distance from D.C. is 193 miles.

ACCOMMODATIONS *Historic Country Inns of Lexington,* 11 North Main Street, Lexington, 463-2044, has two town properties: Alexander-Withrow House and McCampbell Inn, both M–E, CP, and Maple Hall on Route 11, seven miles north of town, also M–E, CP • **In-town inns:** *The Keep,* 116 Lee Avenue, Lexington 24450, 463-3560, M, CP • *Llewellyn Lodge,* 603 South Main Street, Lexington 24450, 463-3235 or (800) 882-1145, I–M, CP • *Sheridan Livery Inn,* 35 North Main Street, Lexington 24450, 464-1887, M, CP • **Country inns:** *Stoneridge,* Stoneridge Lane, P.O. Box 38, Lexington 24450, 463-4090 or (800) 491-2930, four miles from town, M–E, CP • *Applewood Inn,* Buffalo Bend Road, P.O. Box 1348, Lexington 24450, 463-1962 or (800) 463-1902, five miles from town, M–E, CP • *Brierley Hill,* 985 Borden Road, RR 6, Box 21A, Lexington 24450, 464-8421 or (800) 422-4925, modern home in traditional style, mountain views, one mile from town, M–E, CP; full dinner for guests by reservation, EE, CP • *Inn at Union Run,* 325 Union Run Road, Lexington 24450, 463-9715, Victorian creekside manor, views, three miles outside town, M, CP • *Peaks of Otter Lodge,* Blue Ridge Parkway, P.O. Box 489, Bedford 24523, 586-1081 or (800) 542-5927, M • *Sugar Tree Inn,* Highway 56, Steeles Tavern 24476, 377-2197 or (800) 377-2197, very special, open April through December, M–E, CP.

DINING *Willson-Walker House,* 30 North Main Street, 463-3020, fine dining in 1820s period decor, best in town for formal dining, M–E • *Maple Hall* (see above), elegant setting, M–E • *Inn at Union Run* (see above), fine dining, steaks a specialty, M–E • *Sugar Tree Inn* (see above), by reservation, prix fixe, E • *Peaks of Otter Lodge* (see above), I–M.

SIGHT-SEEING *Stonewall Jackson House,* 8 East Washington Street, 463-2552. Hours: Monday to Saturday 9 A.M. to 5 P.M., Sunday 1 P.M. to 5 P.M. $$ • *Lee Chapel,* Washington and Lee University, 463-8768. Hours: April to October, Monday to Saturday 9 A.M. to 5 P.M. Sunday 1 P.M. to 5 P.M.; rest of year to 4 P.M. Monday to Saturday,

Sunday 2 P.M. to 5 P.M. Free • *The VMI Museum,* VMI campus, 463-6232. Hours: daily 9 A.M. to 5 P.M. Free • *George S. Marshall Museum,* VMI campus, 463-7103. Hours: Daily 9 A.M. to 5 P.M. $$ • *Lexington Carriage Company,* P.O. Box 1242, Lexington, 463-3777. Hours: April through October, daily 10 A.M. to 4:30 P.M.; June, July, and August, 9 A.M. to 5 P.M. 45-minute sight-seeing tours. $$$$$ • *Virginia Horse Center,* P.O. Box 1051, Lexington, 463-2194. Contact for horse show schedules • *Buffalo Springs Herb Farm,* Raphine Road (Route 606), Raphine, 348-1083. Hours: April through mid-December, Wednesday through Saturday 10 A.M. to 5 P.M., Sundays 1 P.M. to 5 P.M.; closed Sundays in June, July, August. Free; phone for special lunch and program information • *Wade's Mill,* 55 Kennedy Wade's Mill (off Raphine Road), Raphine, 348-1400. Hours: April through the Sunday before Christmas, Wednesday through Saturday 10 A.M. to 5 P.M., Sunday 1 P.M. to 5 P.M; closed Sundays in June, July, August. Free; phone for special event schedules • *Rockbridge Vineyard,* 30 Hillview Lane (off Raphine Road), Raphine, 377-6204. Hours: tours and tasting, May through October, Wednesday to Sunday, noon to 5 P.M. April, November, and first three weekends in December, Saturday and Sunday noon to 5 P.M. Free • *Natural Bridge of Virginia,* U.S. 11 at Route 130, Natural Bridge (800) 533-1410. Hours: Daily 8 A.M. to dark. Day pass includes nature trail and Monacan Indian Living HistoryVillage and evening show, "The Drama of Creation." Caverns and Wax Museum tickets extra. $$$$ •.*Virginia Safari Park,* 229 Safari Lane, Natural Bridge, 291-3205. Hours: April through October daily, 9 A.M. to 6 P.M., March and November, weekends, weather permitting. $$$

INFORMATION *Historic Lexington Visitor Center,* 106 East Washington Street, Lexington, VA 24450, 463-3777 or (877) 453-9822; www.lexingtonvirginia.com.

Tea and Serenity in Chestertown

People in Chestertown, Maryland, like to boast that their revolutionary tea party was far more daring than the one held in darkness by those publicity-grabbers in Boston. It was broad daylight on May 23, 1774, when a band rowed out to the brigantine *Geddes,* moored in Chestertown Harbor, and tossed the tea on board into the drink, an act that is re-created with great gusto every year on the Saturday before Memorial Day.

The whole town turns out for the fun—a morning Colonial parade complete with fife and drum corps, demonstrations of Colonial crafts from boat building to candle making, eighteenth-century country dancing, an art show, walking tours through the historic district, and all kinds of music and entertainment from puppet shows to choir concerts.

There is a lot of prize Maryland Eastern Shore eating, from fried chicken to crab cakes, and the chance to join some spirited square dancing. The big event, the reenactment, takes place at 2 P.M. on Saturday afternoon.

Chestertown is celebrating a long-ago time when this small town was a major stop on the main land route between Philadelphia and the Virginia colony, not to mention one of Maryland's most prosperous ports, with a prime location just 20 miles upriver from Chesapeake Bay. In those days, the 1746 customs house, still standing beside the Chester River, was a bustling center for cargo from around the world.

As time passed, cities like Baltimore overshadowed Chestertown as a port, and the town did not grow or change for many years. This has turned out to be a very good thing for anyone today who loves strolling picturesque brick-paved lanes lined with prize eighteenth-century architecture.

The present riverfront is a treasury of fine homes dating back to the golden days of 1730 to 1775; many of the homes are the gracious brick mansions of merchants and shipowners who grew wealthy along with the young town. The entire center of town has been declared a historic district. Bring the kids for the tea party fun, but come back to Chestertown when all is serene to experience a tranquil stroll into the past.

A self-guided walking tour map, available free in many of the shops on High Street, concentrates on Water Street and its eighteenth-century showplaces along the river. The old customs house next to the landing on Water Street was used as both business and residence, and like most of Chestertown's finest homes, it is notable for its Flemish bond brickwork with glazed headers (the ends of the bricks) forming patterns within the overall façade. Using headers meant more brick and extra expense, a kind of Colonial conspicuous consumption particularly popular here.

On the riverfront part of the year is a replica of the 1768 schooner *Sultana,* an authentically re-created tall ship that was built here as a way to teach students about Colonial maritime history. When it is not sailing to other Chesapeake Bay ports, it is moored at the town dock

On land, the local showplace is Widehall, at 101 Water Street, a Georgian beauty built in 1770 by the town's wealthiest merchant, John Smythe, with a show-off exterior of all header bricks. Along with many of the riverfront houses, Wide Hall was later embellished with lovely gardens extending to the water's edge, and porches on the rear of the house for taking in the view.

The interiors of the houses are equally impressive. At River House, built by John Smythe's son, Richard, at 107 Water Street, the wood-work in an upstairs bedroom was so beautiful, it was removed to the Winterthur Museum near Wilmington, Delaware, where it now adorns a chamber known as the Chestertown Room. All the fine homes are privately owned, but they do open a few times each year for the Candle-light Walking Tour held in the historic district in mid-September, the annual house tour in October, and Christmas tours.

The Buck Bacchus Store Museum, restored to its 1700s appearance as a residence, is only occasionally opened to tours. It displays household articles from the nineteenth and early twentieth centuries, when it also served as a general store.

One home that does welcome visitors is the Geddes Piper House, a Philadelphia-style town house restored by the Historical Society of Kent County and filled with period furnishings to show what life was like in Chestertown in the eighteenth century. Queen Street and Lawyers Row are other lanes worth exploring. The Nicholson House, at 111 Queen, home of a family of early naval heroes, is one of the few Federal-style houses in Chestertown. Picturesque Lawyers Row is a line of small Victorian buildings designed for law offices around 1840 and still used by local attorneys. There are many fine examples of later architecture such as these interspersed among the oldest buildings.

One other building of note is the Emmanuel Protestant Episcopal Church, where a 1780 convention voted to withdraw officially from the Church of England and take the Episcopal name, which was soon adopted everywhere in America.

Take a short drive to Washington College to see the only campus that George Washington personally sanctioned to use his name. Legend says that he even helped sell lottery tickets to finance the establishment of the college, which was founded in 1782 as Maryland's first institution of higher learning. The original buildings were lost to a fire in 1827, but the red brick nineteenth-century campus still merits a look.

Chestertown has a growing number of interesting shops on High and Cross Streets, including half a dozen antique shops. Twigs 'n Teacups on Cross Street is especially inviting, with a little something for everyone, gifts to books.

Two of the inns on High Street are unusual enough to merit a stop for sight-seeing. It would not be surprising if someone in Colonial garb answered the door of the White Swan Tavern, so authentic is this restoration of an early 1700s lodging. The owners ordered an archaeological dig on the site to be sure the restoration was accurate. A display case was installed downstairs to show some of the dig's finds—clay pipes, wineglasses, stoneware mugs, and ale glasses, all used on this very spot centuries ago. The authentically furnished period rooms have enormous charm, but there are only four of them and two suites, so reserve early. If you can't get a room, come for tea, served daily from 3 P.M. to 5 P.M.

Across the street, the Imperial Hotel re-creates a later period. The 1903 hotel will delight anyone who likes Victorian froufrou. The rooms are small for their tab, but beautifully furnished. You can also sample the ambience in the fancy dining rooms.

There are two more recommended small inns in town, the Widow's Walk and the Parker House, or you may choose among some very appealing lodgings in the countryside not far away.

Chestertown's environs are flat, open areas leading to the bay, ideal territory for bikers. And bird-watchers will appreciate the many species to be spotted at the Eastern Neck National Wildlife Refuge, where there is an observation boardwalk, or Chesapeake Farms, both major resting places for migratory and wintering waterfowl. October to March is peak time for the birds, but the wildlife refuge offers nature trails that are pleasant strolls year round, and rowboats are for rent just outside the entrance for fishing or crabbing in the bay. All it takes to try your hand at crabbing is a piece of string, a chicken neck, a pail, and lots of patience.

On the way to the refuge you'll pass Rock Hall, the tiny town that is the boating capital of the upper Chesapeake. This town with a population of 1,600 claims that more boats are docked here than are found in Annapolis, and Rock Hall is coming to life with new inns, and restaurants to serve its sailors. It is just the place to savor a seafood dinner by the bay, and if you want to charter a sailboat, ask at any of the dozen marinas. Kayak Canoe in Rock Hall offers guided tours of the surrounding inlets and coves, as well as lessons for beginners.

The little Waterman's Museum has displays and photos about the oystering and crabbing industries that thrive in the region, including carvings and boats.

The Shops at Oyster Court, 2671 Main Street, is the place to look for a variety of interesting shops and the America's Cup Cafe, a best bet for coffee or a light meal for lunch or dinner. For dessert stop at Durding's Store, a restored 1930s corner drugstore, for an old-fashioned ice cream soda.

For further exploring, take a drive through more of the picturesque villages that dot this upper portion of Maryland's Eastern Shore. Twenty miles to the south on Route 213 is Centreville, whose 1792 courthouse is the oldest in the state. To the north, Galena is for antiquers. Ask for the *Kent County Driving Tour* brochure, available from the Kent County Tourism Office, and you'll find a listing of area parks, including Betterton Beach, a waterfront park at the head of Chesapeake Bay with a sandy beach and boardwalk.

Then again, you might be happy never leaving Chestertown at all, just meandering down to the landing to sit awhile watching the sailboats go by and admiring the gardens behind the houses on the river, then strolling back to the White Swan, just in time for your own afternoon tea party.

Area Code: 410

DRIVING DIRECTIONS Chestertown is on Route 213. From D.C., follow Route 50/301 east across the Chesapeake Bay Bridge to Route 213 north. The approximate distance from D.C. is 80 miles. From the north, take Route 301 south to Route 213 south.

ACCOMMODATIONS *White Swan Tavern,* 231 High Street, Chestertown 21620, 778-2300, M–E, CP • *Imperial Hotel,* 208 High Street, Chestertown 21620, 778-5000, M–E, CP • *Widow's Walk Inn,* 402 High Street, Chestertown 21620, 778-6455, homey Victorian in town, M, CP • *Parker House,* 108 Spring Avenue, Chestertown 21620, 778-9041, gracious home on a quiet street just a stroll from the town center, M, CP • **Lodgings outside town:** *The Inn at Mitchell House,* 8796 Maryland Parkway, Tolchester Estates, 21620, 778-6500, an informal, homey farmhouse on ten acres overlooking a pond, M, CP • *Brampton,* 25227 Chestertown Road, Chestertown 21620, 778-1860, a beautiful 1860s mansion on nicely landscaped grounds, one mile from town, M–EE CP • *Great Oak Manor,* 10568 Cliff Road, Chestertown 21620, 778-5943 or (800) 504-3098, a 25-room mansion on 12 acres overlooking the bay, golf and tennis guest privileges at the nearby Great Oak Landing resort, eight miles from town, E–EE, CP • **Rock Hall:** *The Inn at Osprey Point,* 20786 Rock Hall Avenue, Rock Hall 21661, 639-2194, small luxury Williamsburg-style inn adjoining a yacht club, pool, M–E, CP • *Moonlight Bay Inn,* 6002 Lawton Avenue, Rock Hall 21661, 639-2660, charming old house with nice gardens, directly on the water, newer west wing has balconies with views, whirlpool tubs, M–E, CP • *Swan Haven,* 20950 Rock Hall Avenue, Rock Hall 21661, 639-2527, waterside 1898 Victorian cottage, TV in rooms; best rooms are in the Haven addition, with private balconies, M, CP.

DINING No visit to Chesapeake Bay is complete without a sampling of seafood. You'll find it in Chestertown at *Old Wharf Inn,* foot of Cannon Street, 778-3566, M • In Rock Hall, *Waterman's Crabhouse,* foot of Sharp Street, 639-6221, has a great dockside location and outside deck, I–M, • **Other dining:** *Blue Heron Cafe,* 236 Cannon Street, Chestertown, 778-0188, innovative regional American cuisine, M–E • *Imperial Hotel* (see above), elegant, continental menu, E–EE • *The Black-Eyed Susan,* 601 Washington Avenue, 778-1214, Maryland standards plus creative additions, M • *The Inn at Osprey Point* (see above), elegant setting, continental dishes plus seafood, M • *Swan Point Inn,* Rock Hall Avenue (Route 20) and Coleman Road, Rock Hall, 639-2500, prime rib is the house specialty, M–E, light menu, I–M • *America's Cup Cafe,* Shops at Oyster Court, 5761 Main Street, Rock Hall, coffeehouse and informal fare, I.

SIGHT-SEEING   *Geddes Piper House,* 101 Church Alley, 778-3499. Hours: Wednesday to Friday, 10 A.M. to 4 P.M. year-round, also Saturday, Sunday 1 P.M. to 4 P.M. May to October, $ • *Waterman's Museum,* 20880 Rock Hall Avenue (Route 20), Rock Hall, 778-6697. Hours: Daily 10 A.M. to 5 P.M. Free • *Chesapeake Farms Wildlife Habitat,* 7319 Remington Drive, off Route 20 south of Chestertown, 778-8400. Hours: February to October, daily dawn to dusk. Free • *Eastern Neck National Wildlife Refuge,* 1730 Eastern Neck Road, Rock Hall, 639-7056. Hours: Daily sunrise to sunset; visitor center open Monday to Friday 7 A.M. to 4 P.M.

INFORMATION   *Kent County Tourism Office,* 400 High Street, Chestertown, MD 21620, 778-0416; www.kentcounty.com.

Gardens and Galleries near Philadelphia

William Penn must have planted the seed in 1682 when he proclaimed his new city of Philadelphia a "greene country towne." Today, the flower-loving Philadelphia countryside boasts the largest concentration of public gardens in the country, some 30 showplaces from wooded arboretums to floral extravaganzas. Each May, the Philadelphia area stages "The World's Largest Garden Party," with special events and tours at 26 gardens, arboretums, and historic houses that are members of the Gardens Collaborative.

To make things even nicer, many of these gardens are associated with exceptional art museums and galleries. A prime example is the Barnes Foundation in Merion, where a 12-acre garden echoes the colors of the treasures inside, one of the world's outstanding private collections of Impressionist art.

You can't take in all the gardens and galleries in one visit, but you can plan a route that makes for a beautiful spring outing. The three-day Memorial Day weekend is a good choice, since many other special events are taking place, including one of the country's most prestigious and exciting horse shows.

One prize garden path takes you to the Main Line, the exclusive suburban towns running along Route 30 west of Philadelphia. That's where you'll find the Barnes Foundation in Merion, with a stunning array of more than 150 Renoirs; prize works by Picasso, Van Gogh, and Rousseau; 60 paintings by Matisse; and 61 Cézannes, more than can be found in any one place outside the Louvre.

A Barnes visit is more meaningful if you know its unique history. Albert Coombs Barnes was ahead of his time in recognizing the genius of the Impressionists, buying up canvases wholesale before the rest of the world caught on—50 Renoirs at a time, the first major purchases of Modigliani's work, and 60 Soutines at $50 per canvas. Stung by critical barbs after an early show, however, he withdrew, building his own museum and school for art appreciation, and allowing no one from the art establishment to call. Barnes's will specified that his foundation remain difficult to visit, and paintings were forbidden to be moved or changed from his own crowded arrangements.

It took a lawsuit in 1961 to bring about even limited public hours. More brouhaha and multiple suits followed in the early 1990s when a board decided to publish a catalog and send paintings on tour to raise money for badly needed renovation. This initial tour of highlights from the Barnes drew more than a million visitors in Tokyo and the largest attendance ever for a single exhibit in Paris. The building reopened late in 1995 after three years of renovations that modernized the infrastructure but left the pictures in position exactly as Barnes decreed, with small wrought-iron objects still surrounding the paintings in meticulous patterns. The number of visitors remains limited, and reservations are required to be sure of admittance to the Barnes.

It is worth the effort. The display of floor-to-ceiling and wall-to-wall paintings is all but overwhelming. Besides the most famous Impressionist works, the Barnes Foundation boasts outstanding Klees and Mirós, plus prize paintings by old masters such as El Greco, Daumier, Titian, and Tintoretto.

Many visitors never get beyond the paintings to see the formal garden and arboretum behind the house. That's a mistake, since they are filled with more than 150 varieties of plantings reputedly chosen by Albert Barnes and his wife, Laura, for their aesthetic value. A garden of some 500 roses, for example, is said to replicate the palette of some of the Impressionist paintings in the gallery. The arboretum is also used as a school for horticulture.

Not far away are two other rewarding stops, Chanticleer, a 30-acre "pleasure garden" in Wayne, on the former estate of a pharmaceutical pioneer and millionaire, Adolph Rosengarten, and the Jenkins Arboretum in Devon, providing a lovely woodland walk among spectacular prize azaleas.

Devon is also home to the country's largest outdoor horse show, an important annual equestrian event for more than 100 years. You don't have to be a horse lover to appreciate the skill of the almost 1,500 riders who compete for more than $100,000 in prizes at the Devon Horse Show. The action in the arena can be breath-stopping when the champs go through their paces, gracefully leaping high over the hurdles.

Horses are only part of this show. Billed as the Horse Show and Country Fair, the event began as a one-day fund-raiser, a genteel Main

Line affair augmenting equestrian competition with a miniature village of quaint thatched-roof cottages where you could have tea served from silver teapots and buy country-fresh fruits and vegetables. It now runs for nine days beginning Memorial Day weekend and has expanded to an 18-acre site, but many vendors are housed in the same fairy-tale pastel blue cottages built in 1919, unchanged except for modernization with wood-shingled roofs. Along with crafts and horsey equipment and souvenirs, they offer boutiques and antiques, hardly the sort of thing you'd find at an ordinary country fair. You can still find tea sandwiches at some of the food stalls, and pretty young girls vending "slurping lemon sticks," a Devon tradition. The fair is still run by volunteers for the benefit of nearby Bryn Mawr Hospital.

When you are ready for more gardens, you'll find that even the colleges along the Main Line have a green thumb. Outstanding arboretums are found on the campuses of Haverford, Bryn Mawr, Villanova, and the American College in Bryn Mawr. The sylvan plantings serve an educational purpose for the schools as well as providing enjoyment for the public. All are free.

A few minutes' drive south of the Main Line may be rewarding for home gardeners. The lovely Scott Arboretum on the campus of Swarthmore University in Swarthmore is planned to show the best trees, shrubs, and perennials recommended for growing in this region.

A drive to the Brandywine Valley at the Pennsylvania-Delaware border would yield another weekend's worth of gardens, including one of the country's floral showplaces, Longwood Gardens. Read more about this region on pages 180–185 and pages 230–231.

The Valley Forge area also has its share of gardens and galleries. Chief among its treasures is Mill Grove, the first American residence of naturalist painter John James Audubon, and a rare opportunity to see the original oversize folio *Audubon Birds of America* hand-colored prints on display.

The 175-acre grounds are a wildlife sanctuary with trails and wildflower walks along the picturesque banks of Perkiomen Creek. Some 400 species of flowering plants have been chosen to be attractive to birds. Feeding stations and nesting boxes help winged visitors to feel at home.

The Wharton Esherick Studio, surrounded by gardens of wildflowers, is a delightful discovery. This one-of-a-kind fairy-tale cottage is filled with wooden carvings and sculptural furniture created by a master who has been called the most important furniture designer of the twentieth century.

Even the Valley Forge Historical Park turns out to be a green respite. Besides its history exhibits, the park offers 3,600 acres dotted with flowering trees and wildflowers, and six miles of trails for walking or cycling. In spring, a canopy of 50,000 blooming dogwoods lights up the landscape in pink and white.

A final garden path closer to Philadelphia begins in suburban Chestnut Hill, where the Morris Arboretum of the University of Pennsylvania is a romantic and tranquil oasis. The former Victorian estate offers 92 acres of gorgeous greenery, featuring more than 7,000 kinds of trees and shrubs from around the world. Also on the grounds are a lovely rose garden, floral displays, a Japanese rock garden, a swan pond, and a graceful old-fashioned fernery under glass with waterfalls and pools. This garden's native woodlands are home to many of Philadelphia's oldest and largest trees.

When you've had your fill of flowers, Chestnut Hill is the perfect antidote. Just driving the winding wooded roads and admiring the lovely stone houses of one of Philadelphia's prime residential areas is a treat. But Chestnut Hill also offers a chic shopping area along Germantown Avenue, and the Chestnut Hill Hotel is an excellent stop for dining, as well as a recommended home base for the weekend. Other suggestions are the hotels on City Line Avenue, near Merion, or Main Line locations such as Radnor, Wayne, and Malvern.

From the Morris Arboretum, you might explore the historic homes and gardens of the Germantown neighborhood by continuing toward the city on Germantown Avenue, or visit the lively young neighborhood of Manayunk near the Schuylkill River. Both are a short drive away.

Germantown's cobblestoned, tree-lined streets and centuries-old stone houses bear witness to a community that dates back to 1683, when William Penn deeded an area six miles northwest of Philadelphia to a group of German Quaker and Mennonite settlers. It was the site of a pitched battle between Continental and British forces in 1777, and after the Revolutionary War it was developed as a rural retreat for Philadelphia's elite. The arrival of one of America's first commuter railroads transformed Germantown into the city's first modern suburb, and by the 1850s, gingerbread Victorian homes had joined the original stone architecture. The area has gone downhill, but thanks to a group known as Historic Germantown, many of the finest homes have been preserved and are open to the public.

One must is Cliveden, a superb Georgian country house built in 1763 by Benjamin Chew, chief justice of Pennsylvania. It is now maintained by the National Trust for Historic Preservation and is filled with elegant Chippendale and Federal furnishings. Early spring at Cliveden is a sea of yellow daffodils and forsythia; azaleas, dogwoods, and rhododendrons change the color scheme as the season progresses, and the perennial garden remains colorful until frost.

Wyck is one of the oldest houses in Philadelphia, dating back to 1690, and was home to one family for nine generations, until 1973. It is nationally known for its magnificent gardens of old roses, still growing in their original plan dating from the 1820s.

There are more historic houses galore. The Deshler-Morris House is the fine home where George and Martha Washington lived in 1793 and

1794, when yellow fever epidemics drove the federal government out of Philadelphia. It is said that Loudoun, a gracious Greek Revival house on a hill, would have been the U.S. capitol had the government remained in Philadelphia. Built in 1801, the house was occupied by the same family until 1939.

Grumblethorpe and Stenton Mansion are two more eighteenth-century homes, and the Ebenezer Maxwell Mansion is a Victorian change of pace, showing the evolution of life in the neighborhood. Visiting hours are quite limited for these homes. The Germantown Historical Society Museum Complex, comprising a visitor center and three 1700s homes, will tell you about the area's history and should be able to give current information on the homes.

To see one of the liveliest sections of the city, drive toward the Schuylkill River and Manayunk's funky Main Street, a growing potpourri of interesting shops and popular dining places. Antiques, crafts, home furnishings, and a thriving farmer's market are among the places for browsing, and trendy restaurants abound.

Keep heading along the Schuylkill into the city and across the river to West Philadelphia to visit 44-acre Historic Bartram's Garden, where the local planting mania began. This riverside neighborhood isn't the city's best, but here is where you can see the oldest living botanical garden in America, planted by Quaker John Bartram, who traveled the wilds of the American colonies by horseback in search of interesting seeds and plants to bring back to his farm. His goal was to document all the native flora of the New World. His work earned him the appointment of "Royal Botanist for North America" from King George III.

The farm, a National Historic Landmark, has been preserved virtually unchanged for two centuries and includes the furnished Bartram house as well as the botanical garden and a wildflower meadow with a wonderful view of the Philadelphia skyline.

If you've planned your outing for Memorial Day weekend, you may well want to stay in Philadelphia for the annual Jam, a lively festival now in its second decade of bringing New Orleans jazz, blues, gospel, and zydeco to Penn's Landing on the Delaware River. It's the city's official welcome to summer.

Area Codes: 610 for Main Line towns; 215 closer to Philadelphia

DRIVING DIRECTIONS   Main Line towns are on U.S. 30, west of Philadelphia. From D.C., take I-95 north. At Wilmington, take exit 8, Route 202 north to U.S. 30 east. The approximate distance from D.C. to Devon is 145 miles. From I-76 or I-276, the Pennsylvania Turnpike, take Route 252 south into Devon. For Merion, follow U.S. 30 east to Route 1, City Line Avenue, and turn right at 54th Street, Old Lancaster Road. Watch immediately for Latch's Lane on the left. For Germantown and Chestnut Hill, return to Route 1 heading toward Philadelphia to Wissahickon Drive, then exit at Johnson Street and bear right to Germantown Avenue, the heart of Germantown. The avenue continues running north directly into Chestnut Hill.

PUBLIC TRANSPORTATION   Amtrak, buses, and many airlines service Philadelphia.

ACCOMMODATIONS   Many hotels have offered a garden package with special rates and discounts on admissions; for current information, contact the Gardens Collaborative (see below) • *Chestnut Hill Hotel,* 8229 Germantown Avenue, Chestnut Hill, 19118, (215) 242-5905, small hotel with attractive period furnishings, M–E • **Main Line:** *Radnor Hotel,* 591 East Lancaster Avenue (Route 30), St. David's 19087, (610) 688-5800, outdoor pool, fitness center, E • *Wayne Hotel,* 139 East Lancaster Avenue (Route 30), Wayne 19087, (610) 687-5000, restored Victorian, E, CP • *Adam's Mark Hotel,* City Line Avenue and Monument Road, Philadelphia 19131, (215) 581-5000, health club, indoor/outdoor pool, M • *Holiday Inn City Line,* 4100 Presidential Boulevard (City Line Avenue at I-76), Philadelphia 19131, (215) 477-0200, indoor/outdoor pool, M. For Valley Forge area lodgings, see pages 260–261.

DINING   **Chestnut Hill (215):** *Pollo Rosso,* Chestnut Hill Hotel (see above), reasonably priced Italian, brick oven pizza, M • *Roller's,* 8705 Germantown Avenue, 242-1771, cheerful, noisy bistro, interesting menu, M • *Flying Fish,* 8142 Germantown Avenue, 247-0707, no-frills seafood, always crowded, M–E • *Cin Cin's,* 7838 Germantown Avenue, 242-3548, affiliated with Yangming (see below) and equally praised Chinese/French blend, M • **Main Line (610):** *Toscana Cucina Rustica,* 24 North Merion Avenue, 527-7700, excellent Italian, M • *Abbey Grill,* Radnor Hotel (see above), sophisticated American cuisine, gardens, dancing on Friday, nice Sunday brunch overlooking the gardens, M–E • *Yangming,* 1051 Conestoga Road, Bryn Mawr, 527-3200, the Main Line's best Chinese, with a French accent, M • *Savona,* 100 Old Gulph Road, Gulph Mills, 520-1200, highly praised, very upscale Mediterranean, E–EE • *Ristorante Primavera,* 384 Lancaster Avenue, Wayne, 254-0200, Italian, excellent pasta dishes, wood-fired oven, M • *Fourchette 110,* 110 North Wayne Avenue, 687-8333, sophisticated American grill, M–E • *Le Mas Perrier,* 503 West Lancaster Avenue (Route 30), Spread Eagle Village, Wayne, 964-2588, pleasant contemporary decor, creative French cuisine from Philadelphia's most famous chef, George Perrier, M–E • **City Line (215):** *The Marker,* Adam's Mark Hotel (see above), country French, elegant atmosphere, E–EE • **Manayunk:** *Jake's,* 4635 Main Street, Manayunk, 483-0444, informal setting for serious New American menu, very popular, outstanding brunch, E • *Kansas City Prime,* 4417 Main Street, Manayunk, 482-

3700, chic spot for steak and seafood, M–EE • *Sonoma,* 4411 Main Street, Manayunk, 483-9400, Italian with a California accent, extremely popular, M • *Manayunk Brewing Company,* 4120 Main Street, 482-8220, converted mill, great place for lunch or a brew on a riverside deck, also full restaurant menu, M • **Another option:** *Valley Green Inn,* Springfield Avenue & Wissahickon Creek, Fairmount Park, (215) 247-1730, a perfect ending to a garden weekend, good American fare in a woodsy park setting on the creek, M.

SIGHT-SEEING *Garden events:* For a guide to garden special events throughout the month of May, contact the Gardens Collaborative, 9414 Meadowbrook Avenue, Philadelphia, 19118, (215) 247-5777, ext. 175; www.libertynet.org/gardens. • *Arboretum Villanova,* Villanova University, 800 Lancaster Avenue (Route 30), Villanova, (610) 519-4426. Hours: Daily dawn to dusk. Free • *American College Arboretum,* 270 South Bryn Mawr Avenue, Bryn Mawr, (610) 526-1228. Hours: Daily dawn to dusk. Free • *Barnes Foundation,* 300 Latch's Lane, Merion, (610) 667-0290. Hours: Friday and Saturday 9:30 A.M. to 5 P.M., Sunday 12:30 P.M. to 5 P.M. Admission by reservation; phone (610) 664-7917. $$ • *Chanticleer,* 786 Church Road, Wayne, (610) 687-4163. Hours: April through October, Wednesday to Saturday 10 A.M. to 5 P.M., until 8 P.M. Fridays June through August, $$ • *Bryn Mawr College Arboretum,* 101 North Merion Avenue, Bryn Mawr, (610) 526-5000. Hours: Daily, dawn to dusk. Free • *Jenkins Arboretum,* 631 Berwyn Baptist Road, Devon, (610) 647-8879. Hours: Daily dawn to dusk. Free • *Haverford College Arboretum,* 370 Lancaster Avenue (Route 30), Haverford, (610) 896-1101. Hours: Daily dawn to dusk. Free • *Historic Bartram's Garden,* 54th Street and Lindbergh Boulevard, Philadelphia, (215) 729-5281. Hours: Grounds open daily dawn to dusk. Free. House tours, May through October, Wednesday to Sunday noon to 4 P.M. $$ • *Mill Grove,* Audubon and Pawlings Roads, Audubon (near Valley Forge), (610) 666-5593. Hours: Grounds open Tuesday to Sunday dawn to dusk. House: Tuesday to Saturday 10 A.M. to 4 P.M.; Sunday 1 P.M. to 4 P.M. Donation • *Morris Arboretum of the University of Pennsylvania,* 100 Northwestern Avenue, Chestnut Hill, (215) 247-5777. Hours: Daily 10 A.M. to 4 P.M. Guided tours, Saturday, Sunday at 2 P.M. $$$ • *Scott Arboretum,* Swarthmore College, 500 College Avenue, Swarthmore (south of Route 30, off I-476 below Route 1), (610) 328-8025. Hours: Daily dawn to dusk. Free • *Valley Forge National Historical Park,* Route 23, Valley Forge, (610) 783-1077. Hours: Daily 9 A.M. to 5 P.M. Park grounds are free; admission charged for some buildings • *Wharton Esherick Museum,* Horseshoe Trail Road, Valley Forge, (610) 644-5822. Hours: March to December, tours given on Saturday and Sunday; reservations required. $$$ • **Philadelphia area,** all (215): *Cliveden,* 6401 Germantown Avenue, (215) 848-1777. Hours: April to December, Thursday to Sunday noon to 4 P.M. $$$

• **Wyck,** 6026 Germantown Avenue, (215) 848-1690. Hours: April to December 15, Tuesday, Thursday, and Saturday 1 P.M. to 4 P.M. $$ • For information on touring other Germantown homes, contact **Germantown Historical Society,** 5501 Germantown Avenue, (215) 844-1683. Visitor Center and Museum hours: Tuesday, Thursday 10 A.M. to 4 P.M., Sunday 1 P.M. to 5 P.M. $$ • **Devon Horse Show,** P.O. Box 865, Devon, PA 19333, (610) 964-0550, nine days beginning Memorial Day weekend. General admission: Adults, $$$; additional charge for reserved seats.

INFORMATION   **Philadelphia Convention and Visitors Bureau,** 1515 Market Street, Philadelphia, PA 19102, (215) 636-1666 or (800) 90-PHILA; www.gophila.com.

Arts in Bloom in Norfolk

The Virginia Waterfront International Arts Festival grows bigger every year. An annual rite of spring, the month-long arts celebration encompasses eight cities, from Williamsburg to Virginia Beach, and features more than 60 performances, including several free outdoor events. It draws more than 1,000 world-class artists from around the globe, from the Royal Shakespeare Company of London to the Moscow Festival Ballet, from Broadway shows to symphonies.

Norfolk is the heart of things, and to make things even nicer, the dates of the arts festival often coincide with the annual Azalea Festival. A festive parade and floral displays make spring an ideal time to get to know this blooming city.

Norfolk is a town that has reinvented itself, changing from a fading navy town to a vibrant magnet for tourists. It began with the transformation of the waterfront, where the Waterside Festival Marketplace opened in 1983, an attractive and airy building modeled after the old ferry terminal it replaced. Then came Nauticus, the National Maritime Center, a science center with the latest high-tech adventures and historic ships for boarding, and the addition of the Harbor Park baseball stadium for the Norfolk Tides, the AAA farm team of the New York Mets.

The excitement spread with the opening of the $300 million MacArthur Center in 1999, an upscale shopping mecca with more than 150 shops, restaurants, and entertainment venues right in the heart of downtown Norfolk. With all these new attractions, visitors are flocking to discover a city with no end of things to see and do.

The choicest lodgings in town are the Sheraton Waterside Hotel and the Norfolk Waterside Marriott. The Sheraton is directly on the waterfront, and it is entertaining just to stroll its walkway along the Elizabeth

River. Norfolk is home port to the world's largest naval base, as well as a favorite destination for yachters. And there is almost always something to see on the water; The Marriott is a block from the harbor, adjoining the city's Waterside Convention Center, but it offers water views from the higher stories.

Here's a city where you should not miss a harbor sightseeing tour. The paddle wheeler *Carrie B* offers a close-up look at the naval shipyard, which dates back to 1767, as well as the nation's oldest dry dock and everything from nuclear subs and aircraft carriers to luxury liners. Longer cruises on the three-masted schooner *American Rover* take you to Hampton Roads harbor. And there are evening dine-and-dance cruises on a boat called the *Spirit of Norfolk.* The *Carrie B* also runs a seven-hour tour that includes the flora and fauna of the Great Dismal Swamp in nearby North Carolina.

The tour of the world's largest naval base, where some 130,000 people work, has long been a favorite activity in Norfolk, especially on weekends, when there is open house aboard some of the ships. The base is home port for more than 100 ships of the Atlantic Fleet, including 5 aircraft carriers and over 30 aircraft squadrons. The *Victory Rover,* docked at the Nauticus pier, offers two-hour cruises to the naval base.

Naval vessels also dock beside Nauticus, the National Maritime Center, the most recent being the *Wisconsin,* one of the largest battleships ever built by the U.S. Navy. Boarding the main deck is free.

The Nauticus building, which looks something like a cross between an aircraft carrier and a spaceship, is a one-of-a-kind attraction, an entertainment and education center offering imaginative and enlightening hands-on journeys through the maritime world. The chance to re-create a naval battle from the control room is just one of the adventures in this inspired environment, which is especially good for children. Many interactive exhibits on the *Wisconsin,* aquarium displays, and the free Hampton Roads Naval Museum are also part of the complex. A maritime theater shows movies about the sea.

Nauticus is just one of the discoveries in a city that also boasts an unusually long list of interesting sights having nothing to do with the sea. A town trolley tour will give you the lay of the land, or you can follow the Norfolk tour signs by car. The information center can also provide walking tours taking in the turn-of-the-century commercial buildings downtown, the city's earliest buildings in the area known as West Freemason, and the lively Ghent section, a turn-of-the-century residential area that includes some of the city's most interesting shops and restaurants.

Norfolk has a museum for every taste. The stately Chrysler Museum of Art has exhibits spanning the centuries and includes many paintings by the masters. This museum's special claim to fame is one of the world's great glass collections, with extensive displays of Tiffany, Sandwich, and French art glass.

Military history buffs can relive the past at the Douglas MacArthur Memorial, a museum housed in the city's 1850 city hall. The galleries tell the story of a remarkable general whose life is also a chronicle of modern American history. The introductory film includes original World War II news clips.

Among the historic houses in town, the Moses Myers House is the best of the lot. The oldest historic home in the United States interpreting early Jewish American life, it is an impressive Georgian mansion built by one of America's first millionaires, and it still contains most of the owner's fine original furnishings.

Other interesting attractions include the 1739 St. Paul's Church, Norfolk's oldest building, and Hunter House, a Victorian mansion on a cobblestoned block in the historic Freemason neighborhood.

At the Norfolk Botanical Garden, flower lovers can tour 155 acres of camellias, laurels, roses, holly, tulips, and rhododendrons. You can see the sights on foot on meandering walkways, by tram, or—best of all— aboard boats cruising the canals between the gardens in the summer season to see more than 20 theme gardens, including a three-and-a-half-acre rose garden and the Bristow Butterfly Garden, planned to attract colorful winged creatures.

Both flora and fauna can be seen at the Virginia Zoological Park, a 42-acre kingdom for animals, from rare white rhinos and Siberian tigers to domestic sheep, plus the Botanical Conservatory, which houses tropical and desert plants in a 1907 greenhouse.

For another pleasant outing, you can take the five-minute ride aboard the little pedestrian ferry from The Waterside across the river to Portsmouth to stroll streets lined with historic homes. The local information office near the dock will provide you with a free walking tour, or you can opt for the 45-minute trolley tour, which shows you more of the sights, including the Lightship Museum, the Virginia Sports Hall of Fame, and the Portsmouth Naval Hospital. If kids are along, don't miss a stop at the Children's Museum of Virginia, a creative space where more than 60 interactive exhibits teach children about physics, math, and science while they have fun with bubbles, mazes, optical illusions, puzzles, and experiments. The museum also includes a planetarium.

Back in Norfolk, shoppers will surely want to check out the MacArthur Center, with Nordstrom and Dillard's department stores as anchors. For unique boutiques, head for Granby Street; the Ghent neighborhood along Colley Avenue and 21st Street also offers a variety of wares, including antiques. Art lovers will want to see the d'Art Center, where some three dozen regional artists work and sell.

A lovely residential drive brings you to the Hermitage Foundation Museum, a Tudor mansion filled with the owner's Oriental art treasures. The ornate house may not be to everyone's taste, but the setting will be. Bring a picnic; you're welcome to enjoy the 12-acre grounds bordering the Lafayette River.

Come night, you'll find that Norfolk is an arts-minded community, home of the Virginia Opera, Virginia Symphony, and Virginia Stage Company, and with its own chamber music and little theater groups. The Harrison Opera House, home of the Virginia Opera, has been beautifully restored, as has the historic Wells Theatre.

The waterfront is the scene of special events and concerts from jazz to reggae throughout the warm months. A highlight is the annual Harborfest in early June, which includes a parade of sailboats, visiting tall ships, music and entertainment on three stages, and a breathtaking fireworks show on Saturday night.

You'll also discover a wealth of good eating in local restaurants, particularly delicious seafood fresh from Chesapeake Bay.

Should the weather be with you, spring is a perfect time to take the easy 15-minute drive to Virginia Beach before the summer crowds arrive. When you see the spiffy remodeled boardwalk, you may well decide to extend your stay. Be sure to pay a visit to the aquarium and exhibits at the Virginia Marine Science Museum, the most-visited museum in the state, a premiere showcase for marine science exhibits.

For yet another outstanding monument to the maritime heritage of this area, take a half-hour drive to Newport News and its lavish Mariners Museum, a wonderful story of the world's oceans and the vessels that ply them. The collections of figureheads, ship models, and carvings are unsurpassed, and you'll often see costumed interpreters making the maritime history come alive.

How to fit it all into one weekend along with the Virginia Waterfront Arts Festival? You may well decide that this is a port that deserves a return call.

Area Code: 757

DRIVING DIRECTIONS   Norfolk is at the eastern tip of I-64 and connects with Route 13 from the north via the Chesapeake Bay Bridge-Tunnel. From D.C., take I-95 south to Richmond and follow I-64 east. The approximate distance from D.C. is 200 miles.

PUBLIC TRANSPORTATION   All major airlines service the city, as do buses. Amtrak trains stop at nearby Newport News. City trolley service makes it easy to get around.

ACCOMMODATIONS   Ask about weekend packages. *Sheraton Waterside Hotel at Norfolk,* 777 Waterside Drive, 23510, 622-6664, pool, best location, M–E • *Norfolk Waterside Marriott,* 235 East Main Street, 23510, 627-4200, M–E • *Radisson Hotel Norfolk,* 700 Monticello Avenue, 23510, 627-5555, pool, M • *Doubletree Club,* 880 North Military Highway, 23502, 461-9192, pool, M • *Old Dominion Inn,* 4111 Hampton Boulevard, 23508, 440-5100, best budget choice, M,

CP • *Page House Inn,* 323 Fairfax Avenue, 23507, 625-5033 or (800) 599-7659, attractive bed-and-breakfast home in charming Ghent area, M, CP.

DINING *La Galleria,* 120 College Place, 623-3939, northern Italian, creative lighting, original artwork, M • *Freemason Abbey,* 209 West Freemason Street, 622-3966, renovated church abbey, American cuisine, I–M • *Ship's Cabin,* 4110 East Ocean View Avenue, 583-4659, a top choice for seafood, grill specialties, bay views; try the Oysters Bingo, M–E • *Todd Jurich's Bistro,* 210 West York Street, 622-3210, eclectic regional cuisine, M–E • **Ghent restaurants:** *Painted Lady,* 112 East 17th Street, 623-8872, New Orleans ambience in a restored Victorian home, M–E. • *Bobbywood Creative American Bistro,* 7515 Granby Street, 440-7515, the name says it, I–E • *No Frill Bar and Grill,* 806 Spotswood Avenue, 627-4262, wide choices, reasonable, I–M • *Magnolia,* 749 West Princess Anne Road, 625-0400, creative regional cuisine in turn-of-the-century storefront, I–E • For lunch, try *Doumar's Drive-In,* 1919 Monticello Avenue, 627-4163, serving barbecue, sandwiches, and homemade ice cream cones; they claim, in fact, to have the world's first ice cream cone maker.

SIGHT-SEEING *Virginia Arts Festival,* P.O. Box 3595, Norfolk, VA, 23514, www.virginiaartsfest.com; dozens of events, late April to late May; tickets through Ticketmaster, (757) 671-8100 • *Chrysler Museum of Art,* Olney Road at Mowbray Arch, 664-6200. Hours: Tuesday to Saturday 10 A.M. to 5 P.M., Sunday 1 P.M. to 5 P.M. $$ • *d'Art Center,* 125 College Place, 625-4211. Hours: Tuesday to Saturday 10 A.M. to 6 P.M., Sunday 1 P.M. to 5 P.M. Free • *Douglas MacArthur Memorial,* City Hall Avenue and Bank Street, 441-2965. Hours: Monday to Saturday 10 A.M. to 5 P.M., Sunday 11 A.M. to 5 P.M. Free • *Hermitage Foundation Museum,* 7637 North Shore Road, 423-2052. Hours: Monday to Saturday 10 A.M. to 5 P.M., Sunday 1 P.M. to 5 P.M. $$ • *Adam Thoroughgood House,* 1636 Parish Road, Virginia Beach. Hours: April to December, Tuesday to Saturday 10 A.M. to 5 P.M.; Sunday 1 P.M. to 5 P.M.; January to March, Tuesday to Saturday noon to 5 P.M. $$; combination ticket, $$$ • *Hunter House Victorian Museum,* 240 West Freemason Street, 623-9814. Hours: April to December, Wednesday to Saturday 10 A.M. to 3:30 P.M., Sunday 12:30 P.M. to 3:30 P.M. $$ • *Moses Myers House,* 331 Bank Street, 664-6283. Hours: Tuesday to Saturday 10 A.M. to 5 P.M., Sunday 1 P.M. to 5 P.M. $$ • *Nauticus, The National Maritime Center* (includes Hampton Roads Naval Museum), One Waterside Drive, 664-1000. Hours: Memorial Day to Labor Day, daily 10 A.M. to 6 P.M.; rest of year, Tuesday to Saturday 10 A.M. to 5 P.M., Sunday noon to 5 P.M. $$$; theaters additional • *Norfolk Botanical Garden,* Azalea Garden Road adjacent to Norfolk Airport, 441-5830. Hours: April 15 to October 15, daily 9 A.M. to 7 P.M.;

rest of year to 5 P.M. $$; tram tours, mid-March to October, boat tours April to September, both $ additional • *Norfolk Naval Station,* 9079 Hampton Boulevard, 444-7955. Hours: Guided bus tours leave from naval base tour office and from The Waterside, last 45 to 50 minutes. Phone for exact starting times. $$; ship open houses, Saturday and Sunday year round. Free • *Norfolk Trolley Tours,* 222-6000, tickets for one-hour tours from kiosk at The Waterside pickup point. Hours: Memorial Day to Labor Day, daily; check for current schedule. $ • *St. Paul's Episcopal Church,* 201 St. Paul's Boulevard, 627-4353. Hours: Tuesday to Friday, 10 A.M. to 4 P.M. Donation • *Virginia Zoological Park,* 3500 Granby Street, 441-5227. Hours: Daily 10 A.M. to 5 P.M. $$.

Cruises: Check all for current schedules and rates. *Carrie B,* Waterside dock, 393-4735, paddle wheeler harbor cruises • *Victory Rover,* Nauticus dock, 627-7406, naval base cruises • *Spirit of Norfolk,* Waterside dock, 627-7771, lunch and dinner harbor cruises • *American Rover,* Waterside dock, 627-SAIL, Two- and three-hour cruises, tall ship schooner cruises.

Nearby attractions: *Virginia Marine Science Museum,* 717 General Booth Boulevard, Virginia Beach, 425-FISH. Hours: Daily 9 A.M. to 5 P.M.; to 9 P.M. June 15 to Labor Day. $$$$ • *Mariners' Museum,* 100 Museum Drive, Newport News, 596-2222. Hours: Daily 10 A.M. to 5 P.M. $$

INFORMATION *Norfolk Convention and Visitors Bureau,* 232 East Main Street, Norfolk, VA 23510, (800) 368-3097 or 664-6620, www.norfolkcvb.com. Additional City Information Center, first floor, Nauticus. Visitor Information Center, the MacArthur Center, and at exit 273 off I-64 as you enter Norfolk, 441-1852.

Summer

Overleaf: Canoeing at Delaware Water Gap, Pennsylvania. *Photo courtesy of Pocono Mountains Vacation Bureau.*

The Washingtons and Lees of Westmoreland

You can't blame them if they like to name-drop in Westmoreland County, Virginia. This enclave between the Potomac and Rappahannock Rivers at the top of Virginia's Northern Neck has produced more statesmen than any other county in America—George Washington, James Monroe, and Robert E. Lee, to name a few.

History is impressive here, what with Stratford Hall, the magnificent ancestral home of the Lees, and Wakefield, the site of Washington's birthplace, to visit. But it isn't the only reason for a trip. Swimming and boating await on the Potomac at Westmoreland State Park, there are hiking trails at the park and several nature preserves, berries and fruits are ripe for picking at Westmoreland Berry Farm, one of Virginia's top vineyards is nearby, and the seafood is fresh and sweet at Colonial Beach.

Without doubt, Westmoreland's standout attraction is Stratford Hall, one of Virginia's most beautiful historic plantations, and worth a trip on its own. Allow plenty of time, for the house is only part of the pleasure of the visit.

Built high on a bluff above the Potomac in the 1730s by Thomas Lee, the acting governor of Virginia, Stratford spawned four generations of patriots who shaped the history of the nation. Richard Henry Lee, who introduced the motion for independence in the Continental Congress, and his brother Francis "Lightfoot" Lee, who also signed the document, lived at Stratford during their boyhood years. Years later, in 1807, Ann Carter, wife of Revolutionary War hero Harry "Light-Horse" Lee, gave birth to Robert E. Lee in the big sunlit bedroom, the one with the canopy bed, on the upper floor. He slept in the cradle that remains in place at the window.

The H-shaped Georgian manor house was built of bricks made on the site and timber cut from virgin forest. The Great Hall in the center, 29 feet square with a tray ceiling 17 feet high, filled with elaborately carved walls and doors and exquisite antiques, is considered one of the most beautiful rooms in America. All of the rooms are of interest, but the 250-year-old kitchen, with a fireplace large enough to roast an ox, holds a special reward—homemade ginger cookies are served to refresh hungry guests. A plantation lunch—a satisfying Southern menu that includes ham or fried chicken, candied sweet potatoes, and biscuits—is available on the grounds at a log-cabin dining room on the edge of the woods.

Visitors can also walk the meadows where the Lees rode and follow a trail thick with wildflowers to the "cool, sweet spring" so fondly remembered by General Lee during the hardships of the Civil War. A formal garden lined in boxwood invites a stroll along its oyster-shell paths, or you can visit the replicas of flourishing eighteenth-century vegetable and flower gardens. Eighteenth- and early-nineteenth-century coaches can be seen in the long Coach House and Stable.

Down the "rolling road" where hogsheads of tobacco used to move downhill to the Potomac, the old plantation mill has been rebuilt on its original foundations. The huge waterwheel that once served several plantations is still turning, its wooden gears powering the millstone that continues to grind corn, wheat, oats, and barley. You can buy a take-home sampling from the Stratford Store.

Stratford Hall Plantation is still managed as a farm on 1,700 of its original acres, making it one of the oldest continuing agricultural operations in the country.

Just a few miles down the road, you can get a look at life as it was on a more modest Colonial farm at the George Washington Birthplace National Monument, administered by the National Park Service.

George Washington was born here on his father's farm, located on Popes Creek off the Potomac River. He lived here for three and a half years, until the family moved to Ferry Farm near Fredericksburg. The original Popes Creek home was lost to a fire; only an outline of oyster shells marks the site. The present Tidewater house and its acres were intended to re-create the sights, sounds, and smells of eighteenth-century plantation life—the kind of life that influenced the character and development of the nation's first president. An exhibit at the visitor center tells about early life at Popes Creek, and guided tours are available every half hour explaining life in the house and kitchen.

In the fields, set off by split-rail fences, you can watch plowing, planting, hoeing, weeding, harvesting, and all the other day-to-day activities that take place on a farm during the growing season. There are demonstrations of plantation crafts such as woodworking, black-smithing, and leather working, and of the female chores of spinning and weaving. And from May to September there are special events, including sheep shearing, garden tours, Colonial music concerts, and archaeological walks, plus lots of other activities to keep things interesting.

If you want to learn more about the Lees, Washingtons, and other important phases of the rich history in this area over the past 300 years, stop at the Westmoreland County Museum in Montross.

When you've had enough history for one weekend, lighter diversions await. The 2,500-acre Ingleside Plantation, which is Virginia's largest plant nursery, is also a top winery, with 45 acres of vineyard within the grounds producing many varieties of grapes. The wines are frequent award winners. Visitors are welcome to tour the vineyard and winery and taste the wines. Ingleside puts on many special weekends, from jazz concerts to wine seminars to black-tie dinners.

Everyone is equally welcome at Westmoreland Berry Farm and Orchard along the Rappahannock River, where you are invited to come in your old clothes, pick up a basket, and head for the fields to pick your own fruit. Mid-May to mid-June means strawberries; summer brings cherries, black raspberries, blueberries, apricots, and peaches; and late summer to fall adds grapes, apples, and pumpkins to the crops available. Along the river, the farm includes the Voorhees Nature Preserve, maintained by the Nature Conservancy, with several miles of woodland trails offering observation points overlooking river and marshes.

Whether you want more walking trails or you're ready to simply relax, head for Westmoreland State Park and its 1,300 acres along the Potomac. The park facilities include camping sites and cabins; six miles of trails through marshlands, woods, and meadows; boat rentals; picnic grounds; and both the beach and a pool for swimming. Naturalists offer guided hikes and evening programs during the summer.

You'll also find a sandy strand of beach along the Potomac north a bit in the little town of Colonial Beach, as well as lots of seafood restaurants.

Lodgings are limited in the immediate area, but if all are filled, you can always settle into Fredericksburg or go farther out on the Northern Neck around Irvington, each roughly 35 miles from Stratford Hall.

Wherever you stay, even if you do nothing but visit Stratford Hall, you won't be sorry you made the trip.

Area Code: 804

DRIVING DIRECTIONS   Stratford Hall is on Route 3, reached via I-95 or Route 301 from north or south. From D.C., take I-95 south to Route 3 east. The approximate distance from D.C. is 100 miles.

ACCOMMODATIONS   *The Inn at Montross,* 21 Polk Street, Courthouse Square, Montross 22520, 493-0573, historic inn, recently renovated, M, CP • *Bell House,* 821 Irving Avenue, Colonial Beach 22443, 224-7000, landmark summer mansion of Alexander Graham Bell, facing the Potomac, M • *'Tween Rivers,* 16006 Kings Highway, Montross, 22520, 493-0692 or (800) 485-5777, M, CP • *Greenwood,* 99 Maple Street, Warsaw 22572, 333-4353, 1880s Georgian-style bed-and-breakfast home, I, CP • *Westmoreland State Park,* Route 1, Box 600, Montross 22520, (800) 933-PARK, cabin accommodations, studios to two-bedroom units, I; one-week minimum stay in summer, two-night minimum in fall • *Days Inn,* 30 Colonial Avenue, Colonial Beach 22443, 224-0404, M, CP. See also Northern Neck, pages 128–129, and Fredericksburg, page 157.

DINING   *Inn at Montross* (see above), M • *Mooring Restaurant,* Route 608, Kinsale, 472-2971, seafood on the river at at Port Kinsale Marina, I–M • *The Pilot's Wharf,* Cole's Point Plantation, near Hague, 472-4761, Potomac River views, outdoor crab deck, casual ambience, surf and turf menu, M–E • *Wilkerson's,* Route 205, Colonial Beach, 224-7117, old-timer for seafood, open March to October, I–M • *The Dockside,* Colonial Beach Yacht Club, Colonial Beach, 224-8726, on the point, M–E • *Stratford Hall* (see below), plantation lunches, I–M.

SIGHT-SEEING   *Stratford Hall,* off Route 214, Stratford, 493-8038. Hours: Daily 9 A.M. to 4:30 P.M. $$$$ • *George Washington Birthplace National Monument,* Route 204, off Route 3, George Washington's Birthplace, 224-1732. Hours: Daily 9 A.M. to 5 P.M. $; under 16, free • *Westmoreland County Museum, Library and Visitor's Center,* Montross, 493-8440. Hours: April through October, Monday through Saturday 10 A.M. to 5 P.M., rest of year to 4 P.M. Free • *Ingleside Plantation Vineyards,* Box 1038, Route 638 south of Route 3, Oak Grove, 224-8687. Hours: Monday to Saturday 10 A.M. to 5 P.M., Sunday noon to 5 P.M. Tours and tastings, free. Many special events with varying fees; best to check the current calendar • *Westmoreland Berry Farm,* Route 637, Box 1121, Oak Grove, 224-9171 or (800) 997-BERRY. Hours: In growing season, daily 8 A.M. to 7 P.M., after Labor Day to end of October, to 5 P.M. Many family-oriented special events. Free except for purchases • *Westmoreland State Park,* Route 347 off Route 3, six miles west of Montross, 493-8821. Daylight hours daily year-round; pool and restaurant open Memorial Day through Labor Day. Cars, $ • *Rappahannock River Cruises,* 453-BOAT, daily cruises from Tappahannock (on the other side of the river). Phone for current rates and schedules.

INFORMATION   *Westmoreland County Tourism Department,* P.O. Box 996, Montross, VA 22520, 453-6303 or (888) SEE-WCVA; www.westmoreland-county.org.

Combing the Beaches in Delaware

Undiscovered they're not. Worth discovering they are. There's good reason why Rehoboth and its neighboring towns on the Delaware shore have become known as "the nation's summer capital." Of all the beach areas along the mid-Atlantic, none offers so much variety as these bountiful shores.

Pick your own kind of atmosphere. You'll find seaside state parks incorporating miles and miles of unspoiled beach, your choice of relative quiet or a social scene, plenty of beachfront accommodations for sea lovers, places for families and scenes for singles, water and land sports galore, and even a bit of history to explore just in case the sun does not shine.

At the top of the Atlantic shore is Lewes, once mainly a fisherman's town, but now with a chic new look, thanks to some very pleasant inns, cafes, and many antique shops now livening up the old village. The Zwaanendael Inn and the Inn at Canal Square are small hotels with some of the most elegant rooms to be found at the shore, and the Virden House is a charming small bed-and-breakfast in the center of town. There are more bed-and-breakfasts not far from town as well. They've brought a new clientele, who patronize the boutiques and the dozen or so antique shops along Front and Second Streets.

Little Lewes also boasts a lot of history. It was the first town in the Delaware colony, a Dutch whaling outpost, known as Zwaanendael as early as 1631. Though the English supplanted the Dutch in 1664, Lewes remains proud of its earliest heritage. In celebration of the 300th anniversary of the town's founding, a replica of the step-gabled town hall in Hoorn, Holland, was built honoring David Pietersen deVries, a Hoorn native who sponsored the first settlement. The building, called the Zwaanendael Museum, is unique in this country and counts among its visitors several members of the Dutch royal family. Inside, an exhibit known as "Lewes: A Good Harbor" tells the long history of Lewes.

The museum is the starting point for the Lewes Historic Walking Tour, a rather formal title for an informal look at some interesting sights. Among them are historic homes (the oldest dating back to 1685), two 1800s churches, and a small historic complex on Shipcarpenter Street that includes the Burton-Ingram House, now the local historical society, whose cellar walls are made of ships' ballast stones and brick. Rabbit's Ferry House, a restored one-room farmhouse, and the Thompson Country Store are also part of the tour, which proceeds along Front, Second, and Third Streets between Savannah Road and Shipcarpenter Street.

Still a lure for many is the busy canal near the center of town, where anglers head out for mackerel, bass, and bluefish and compete in annual tournaments with prizes for hooking the biggest sea trout, sharks, tuna, and marlin. Those who don't like to fish can enjoy the scene and the catch at cafes along the water.

For beach lovers, Lewes is just one mile from 3,320-acre Cape Henlopen State Park. This beach and nature lover's delight at the junction where Delaware Bay opens into the Atlantic offers four miles of sandy Atlantic beachfront, plus bay shore for crabbing and fishing. It is known for its "walking" sand dunes, which shift with the winds. Walking trails lead across the lower back of the Great Dune, the tallest between Cape Hatteras and Cape Cod. The park, which shelters nesting colonies of seabirds and unusual plants, also has tennis and basketball courts, a nine-hole Frisbee golf course, a fishing pier, nature trails, and the Seaside Nature Center with an aquarium, a touch tank, and marine exhibits. There are great views from the park observation tower, and sunsets along the inner arm of the cape are highly recommended for romantics.

It's just six miles from Lewes to Rehoboth Beach, the center of shore activity in summer. This busy little town is a far cry from the Methodist camp meeting that launched it as a seaside mecca where souls could be saved by baptism in the sea. In Hebrew, the name means "one more sinner." Today Rehoboth boasts handsome residential sections that are summer retreats for numerous D.C. luminaries, and a thriving art colony revolving around the Rehoboth Art League, where exhibits and concerts are held. The league's attractive headquarters are in a complex of historic houses in Henlopen Acres, one of the town's poshest and most pleasant neighborhoods.

Rehoboth has the finest homes and the most sophisticated restaurants on the shore, yet it is at heart an old-fashioned family resort. While socialites are entertaining one another at cocktail parties around Henlopen Acres, North Shores, and Silver Lake, children are playing on the sidewalks in the older section of town, called the Pines, as their parents watch contentedly from big screened porches. Many families rent these pleasant homes by the week.

Rehoboth's boardwalk, a local landmark since 1884, was refurbished in 1992, the result of a damaging storm the year before. A bustling lineup of pizza stands, T-shirt emporiums, penny arcades, and miniature golf games makes this a hangout heaven for young people. The entire boardwalk is lined with low-rise lodgings where you can almost fall out of bed onto the beach, a real plus for ocean lovers.

This is definitely not the area to look for solitude, but it is fine for families. Teens love it, especially for the volleyball and other sports played on the lighted beach between Rehoboth and Olive Avenues each night. For little ones, there's Funland, an amusement park in miniature with bumper cars and other gentle rides guaranteed to delight the small fry.

Rehoboth runs south right into Dewey Beach, the young singles' favorite hangout. The beach is built up with low-rise motels and beach houses but lacks Rehoboth's food stands and amusements, so though there may be plenty of people socializing on the beach, you don't have the ongoing bustle of a boardwalk. Only a narrow strip about two blocks long separates the Atlantic shore from Rehoboth Bay and the Lewes-Rehoboth Canal area here, both choice spots for clamming and crabbing. And, as in Lewes, both surf and deep-sea fishing here are prime. Recently, kayaking has become popular in the bay.

Rehoboth and Dewey have a growing number of bed-and-breakfast inns. Chesapeake Landing, on the Rehoboth/Dewey border, is exceptional, a secluded, tasteful contemporary home a short walk from the beach, but with its own pool and a dock on Spring Lake with boats for guests. In Rehoboth, the spacious Victorian Sea Witch Manor is a standout, serving afternoon tea and evening dessert to guests. Though rooms are small, the unpretentious Royal Rose Inn offers attractive rates.

Bethany Beach calls itself the "quiet resort" and is a best bet for a peaceful beach getaway by the sea. If you stay in a beachside motel near Bethany's quiet, noncommercial boardwalk, you'll hardly need a car. You can walk out the door to the beach, walk only a block or so into town for meals and shops, or walk to the center of the boardwalk to the concession stand for a hot dog or an ice cream cone.

Fenwick Island also bills itself as quiet, but on the route south from Bethany toward Fenwick begins the condominium buildup that culminates eventually in the maze of hotels and honky-tonks just down the road in Ocean City, Maryland. Fenwick Island does have its own unspoiled state park, and a lot of the coastal area south of Rehoboth has been preserved from any development as part of Delaware Seashore State Park, including a section south of Dewey Beach and just north of Indian River Inlet that is a favorite for surfers.

There's plenty of opportunity to bike, play tennis, rent a sailboat, or go fishing all along the coast. A few listings follow, but you can get a current rundown by looking at the brochures put out by each town's tourist office each year.

If you want to do some shopping, Rehoboth is the best bet. Route 1 outside town has built up amazingly over the last several years and turned into outlet city, with all manner of discount stores. Rehoboth Outlets now has three centers and more than 140 stores, including such well-known names as L.L. Bean, Polo–Ralph Lauren, and Donna Karan. Shoppers enjoy an extra advantage because Delaware has no sales tax.

With the exception of one out-of-place bright pink new complex, the town has retained its old-fashioned look and has its full share of interesting smaller shops. Trendy clothes are found at boutiques like Crysti or South Moon Under. Check the little arcades off both sides of Rehoboth Avenue, such as Penny Lane or Village by the Sea, where many interesting shops for clothes and gifts are tucked away. Antiques are offered at a few spots on Route 1, but as mentioned, Lewes offers the best browsing for antiques.

Rehoboth has experienced a boom in creative restaurants in recent years, with old favorites such as Chez La Mer and Blue Moon and Back Porch joined by many newcomers. Fusion, with a creative American menu, is highly recommended by local innkeepers. However, as a sign of the pleasant mix in Rehoboth, most people still pay their annual respects to Grotto Pizza on the boardwalk, perhaps the longest-running show in town.

Don't come to the Delaware shore expecting solitude—there's too much going on here not to attract crowds. But do expect a relaxed atmosphere and enough variety to offer almost anyone a rewarding stay. And if you really long to get away, all you have to do is walk far enough from the parking lots on the state-run beaches, and you'll find it's just you and the sun and the sea.

Area Code: 302

DRIVING DIRECTIONS   Delaware Beaches are accessed from Route 1. From D.C., take Route 50/301 across the Chesapeake Bay Bridge to Route 404 east, which merges into Route 9. Follow Route 9 east into Lewes or turn south on Route 1 to Rehoboth, Dewey Beach, Bethany, or Fenwick Island. The approximate distance to Rehoboth from D.C. is 125 miles. From northern points, take Route 113 south to Route 1 south. The Cape May–Lewes Ferry makes the trip across Delaware Bay in about 70 minutes; (800) 64-FERRY for schedules, rates and information. A trolley runs from the Ferry to Rehoboth. In Rehoboth, a parking permit is required in nonmetered areas; buy a daily or weekly pass at City Hall, 229 Rehoboth Avenue; for rates and information, phone 227-6181.

ACCOMMODATIONS   Expect two- and three-night minimums in season. Rates are for high season, are less fall through spring.

Lewes: *The Inn at Canal Square,* 122 Market Street, 19958, 645-8499 or (800) 222-7902, small hotel with 19 attractively furnished rooms, most with balconies on the canal, 3 rooms on the courtyard, 2 rooms in a moored houseboat, E, CP • *Zwaanendael Inn,* 142 Second Street at Market Streets, 19958, 645-6466, 24 rooms, 2 suites, restored older hotel, M–E • *Bay Moon Bed & Breakfast,* 128 Kings Highway, 19958, 644-1802, (800) 917-2307, charming decor, walking distance to town,

E, CP • *Wild Swan Inn,* 525 Kings Highway, Lewes 19958, 645-8550, Victorian bed-and-breakfast home, pool, E, EP.

Rehoboth: Inns: *Chesapeake Landing,* 101 Chesapeake Street, 19971, exceptional, secluded contemporary, pool, E–EE, CP • *Sea Witch Manor,* 71 Lake Avenue, 19971, grand old turreted Victorian near the center of town, M–E, CP • *Royal Rose Inn,* 41 Baltimore Avenue, 19971, 226-2535, modest, comfortable small bed-and-breakfast inn, pleasant hostess, M–E, CP • *Corner Cupboard Inn,* 50 Park Avenue, Rehoboth 19971, 227-8553, cozy old-timer, simple charm, E–EE, MAP • **Motels, condos, hotels:** Many choices are available directly on the beach or bay. A few possibilities: *Boardwalk Plaza Hotel,* 2 Olive Street, Rehoboth 19971, fancy Victorian, EE, CP • *Henlopen Hotel,* Lake Avenue at Boardwalk, 19971, 227-2551, high-rise hotel, E–EE • *Star of the Sea,* 307 South Boardwalk, Rehoboth 19971, or (888) 722-6006, oceanfront condos with kitchens, balconies, pool, EE • *Admiral Motel,* 2 Baltimore Avenue, Rehoboth 19971, 227-2103 or (888) 882-4188, pool, E–EE • *Oceanus Motel,* 6 Second Street, Rehoboth 19971, 227-9436 or (800) 852-5011, pool, E–EE, CP • *Beach View Motel,* 6 Wilmington Avenue, Rehoboth 19971, 227-2999 or (800) 288-5962, pool, M–E • *Atlantic View Motel,* 2 Clayton Street, Dewey Beach 19971, 227-3878, pool, M–E • *The Bay Resort,* Bellevue Street on the Bay, Dewey Beach 19971, 227-6400, pool, M–EE • *Blue Surf Motel,* Oceanfront at Garfield Parkway, Bethany Beach 19930, 539-7531, M–E. Write each town for complete motel lists.

DINING Note that some restaurants may be closed in winter.

Lewes: *The Buttery,* New Devon Hotel (see above), 645-775, creative fare, E–EE • *Gilligan's,* 134 Market Street, 645-7866, seafood on the canal, M–E • *Kupchick's,* 3 East Bay Avenue, 645-0420, varied menu, Victorian setting, M–E • *Second Street Grille,* 15 Second Street, 644-4121, trendy, varied menu, E • *La Rosa Negra,* 128 Second Street, 645-1980, Italian, well recommended locally, M • *Rose & Crown Restaurant and Pub,* 108 Second Street, 645-2373, casual, attractive, M.

Rehoboth: *Chez la Mer,* 210 2nd Street at Wilmington Avenue, Rehoboth, 227-6494, gourmet spot, a longtime favorite, E–EE • *Fusion,* 50 Wilmington Avenue, 226-1940, eclectic American, much praised, E • *Celsius,* 5-C Wilmington Avenue, Rehoboth, 227-5767, creative chef, contemporary menu, M–E • *Yum Yum Pan Asian Bistro,* 37 Wilmington Avenue, 226-0400, mix of Asian cuisines, M–E • *Espuma,* 28 Wilmington Avenue, 227-4199, Spanish and Mediterranean, seafood paella a specialty, E • *Back Porch Cafe,* 21 Rehoboth Avenue, Rehoboth, 227-3674, imaginative menus, another old favorite, E • *Blue Moon . . . a Restaurant,* 35 Baltimore Avenue, 227-6515, trendy, good food, E • *Camel's Hump,* 21 Baltimore Avenue, 227-0947, Middle Eastern fare, M–E • *Stoney Lonen,* 208 Second Street, 227-2664, Irish pub menu and seafood, M • *The Big Fish Grill,* 4117 Highway 1, 227-9007, fresh seafood at fair prices, M • *Jake's Seafood House,* 1st Street between Baltimore and Maryland Avenues, 227-6237, casual seafood restaurant in town, I–E • *Iguana Grill,* 52 Baltimore Avenue, 227-0948, informal, Southwestern and American, I–M • *Royal Treat Breakfast and Ice Cream Parlor,* 4 Wilmington Avenue, 227-6277, favorite spot for breakfast, I.

Dewey Beach and below: *Rusty Rudder,* Route 1, Dewey Beach, 227-3888, noisy, informal, outdoor deck, a singles meeting place, M–E • *The Waterfront,* McKinley Street, Dewey Beach, 227-9292, outdoor barbecue, ribs, bay views, young crowd for late dancing, M–E • *Sedona,* 26 Pennsylvania Avenue, Bethany Beach, 539-1200, creative Southwestern cuisine, E–EE.

SIGHT-SEEING *Zwaanendael Museum,* Savannah Road and Kings Highway, Lewes, 645-9418. Hours: Tuesday to Saturday 10 A.M. to 4:30 P.M., Sunday 1:30 P.M. to 4:30 P.M. Free • *Lewes Historical Society Complex,* Shipcarpenter & Third Streets, 645-7670. Guided tours from Rabbit's Ferry House Visitor Center. Hours: Mid-June to Labor Day, Tuesday to Friday 11 A.M. to 4 P.M., Saturday 10 A.M. to 12:30 P.M. $$$ • *Rehoboth Art League,* Henlopen Acres, 227-8408, classes and exhibits. Monday to Saturday, 10 A.M. to 4 P.M., Sunday 1 P.M. to 4 P.M. Free • *Rehoboth Jolly Trolley,* transportation between Rehoboth and Dewey, with stops between. Hours: Daily in summer, weekends May and September, usually every half hour. Schedule posted on the boardwalk.

Beach programs: All state beaches have summer guided walks and nature programs; check each for the current schedules. *Cape Henlopen State Park,* Route 9, Lewes, 645-8983; *Delaware Seashore State Park,* Route 1, Rehoboth, 227-2800; *Fenwick Island State Park,* Route 1, Millville-Oceanview, 539-9060.

SPORTS **Biking:** *Bob's Bike Rentals,* 30 Maryland Avenue, Rehoboth, 227-7966 • *Lewes Cycle Sports,* Savannah Road, Lewes, (888) 800-BIKE or 645-4544 • **Boat Rentals:** *Rehoboth Bay Marina,* Dewey Beach, 226-2012 • *Rehoboth Bay Sailing Association,* Dewey Beach, 227-9008 • **Fishing:** *Fisherman's Wharf,* Lewes, 645-8862 • *Delaware Seashore State Park Marina,* Rehoboth, 227-2800 • **Kayaking:** *Coastal Kayak,* (877) 44-KAYAK or 539-7999 • **Tennis:** In Lewes, Cape Henlopen State Park, 645-8983, and city-run courts at Cape Henlopen High School, Kings Highway, 645-7777. In Rehoboth, city courts located at Rehoboth Junior High School, State Road; and

Rehoboth City Courts, on Surf Avenue between Rehoboth Beach and North Shores. In Dewey Beach, Waterfront Sports Complex, McKinley Street, 227-8534.

INFORMATION   *Lewes Chamber of Commerce & Visitors Bureau,* P.O. Box 1, Lewes, DE 19958, 645-8073; www.leweschamber.com • *Rehoboth Beach–Dewey Beach Chamber of Commerce,* P.O. Box 216, 73 Rehoboth Avenue, Rehoboth Beach, DE 19971, (800) 441-1329 or 227-2233; www.beach-fun.com • *Bethany-Fenwick Area Chamber of Commerce,* P.O. Box 1450, Bethany Beach, DE 19930, 539-2100, outside Delaware (800) 962-SURF; www.bethany-fenwick.org.

Back to the Beginning in St. Mary's

Southern Maryland is a world apart, the place where the state was born in 1634, and where the tranquility of another era still persists.

Tourists from D.C. hurrying to the Eastern Shore seem to have forgotten this closer-to-home side of Chesapeake Bay, so there's blessedly little commercialism to intrude on the placid landscape. Take a drive, and you pass miles of lush green tobacco fields and weathered barns where the big broad leaves are hung to dry, old plantation houses still standing proud, and wooded groves hiding narrow sandy strands of beach along the bay or the river.

This is the place for quiet pleasures—picnicking beside the water, hunting for wildflowers, or pushing off for a sail. For a change of pace, you can pull up beside the Amish buggies at the farmers market, pay a call on an eighteenth-century plantation, go antiquing, or walk straight back into the seventeenth century at a unique living museum.

The main attraction for history-minded visitors is the chance to retrace the footsteps of some 200 English settlers who sailed to the edge of the world three and a half centuries ago with Leonard Calvert and planted Lord Baltimore's colony in the wilderness, the first Catholic settlement in America. Only Jamestown and Plymouth have longer histories.

The settlers first landed on St. Clement's Island in the Potomac River, the spot marked today by a 40-foot cross. Accessible only by boat, the island has been preserved in its natural state.

Exhibits in the Potomac River room at the St. Clement's Island–Potomac River Museum at Colton's Point take you back to the early years on St. Clement's Island with a scaled replica of the island lighthouse and bell tower and a chance to learn about the lives of its early inhabitants from the Piscataway Indians to the Calvert family, the proprietors of the Maryland colony. Ceramics and other artifacts excavated from local archaeological sites are displayed, along with models of the *Ark of London* and the *Maryland Dove,* the ships used by Maryland colonists on their Atlantic Ocean crossing to the New World.

This museum also maintains the Piney Point Lighthouse, located about 45 minutes away. Built in 1836, it is one of only four remaining lighthouses on the Potomac River. The grounds of the lighthouse are a six-acre park, a nice spot for a picnic and a stroll along a boardwalk with exhibit panels on the history of the area.

For 60 years a tiny frontier village guided the affairs of this new colony called Maryland, and the 840-acre complex known as St. Mary's City gives you a vivid idea of what life was like in those earliest days. A National Historic Landmark, the site commemorates the efforts of Lord Baltimore to establish religious toleration in the colony.

The houses, barns, and tobacco fields of a seventeenth-century settler have been re-created at the Godiah Spray Plantation, providing a fine picture of the farm life that was the heart of early Maryland. In another section of the complex, the State House of 1676, where Lord Baltimore established laws granting religious freedom, has been reconstructed, along with a typical inn of the period, Farthing's Ordinary.

You can also board the *Maryland Dove,* a square-rigged replica of one of the two ships that arrived here in 1634, typical of those that traded on the Chesapeake coast.

This is more than a collection of buildings and a boat, however. Historic St. Mary's City comes to life from mid-March to November with living history performances that put you right in the middle of seventeenth-century life. You can visit the Spray family on their plantation and watch the chores being done, sit in on trials for pig stealing or murder in the Old State House, and hear the latest gossip and a drinking song or two at the tavern. You may even be recruited to serve on a mock jury in the courtroom or join the hunt for a runaway indentured servant.

Also on the expansive grounds of Historic St. Mary's City is the Woodland Indian Exhibit, with a re-created loghouse, showing what the land and life here were like before the colonists arrived.

Archaeological sites and excavations in progress can be seen at various points on the grounds, continually bringing more of the past back to light. In many cases, frameworks and foundations show where buildings once stood. An exhibit and slide show at the visitor center tells you more about the digs and shows you some of their finds.

The view alone is worth the trip to Sotterley Plantation near Hollywood, where you can see how well the early planters prospered. Home of an early governor of Maryland, the 1717 house commands a superb vista from a ridge overlooking the Patuxent River. It stands atop the old "rolling road," where hogsheads of tobacco once were rolled to ships waiting in the harbor. The low white house with tall chimneys is modest on the outside, but within it is a warm home filled with fine antiques and notable woodwork, especially the striking Chinese Chippendale staircase and the great shell-shaped alcoves of the drawing rooms. Though showing its age just a bit, it has a special sense of life that is lacking in some historic homes, because the present owner still arrives occasionally for a country weekend. A compound comprising tenant houses, barns, a smokehouse, a tobacco shed, and other outbuildings reflects the self-sufficient community that constituted an early Maryland plantation.

A popular present-day diversion in St. Mary's County is Point Lookout State Park at the southernmost tip of the peninsula, where Chesapeake Bay meets the Atlantic Ocean. There are beaches for sunning and swimming, campgrounds, boats for rent, hiking trails, a 700-foot lighted fishing pier, and lots of big boulders where you can perch for an unbeatable bay view. If you want a more private strip of beach for strolling by the bay, you'll find it at Elm's Beach off Route 235.

Point Lookout has its own special bit of Civil War history, told in a small museum. Back in 1862 it was the site of a Union hospital, and later it became part of a prison where more than 20,000 Confederates were confined in deplorable conditions. Many of their guards were blacks who were former slaves. More than 3,500 Southern soldiers died here.

Fishing and boating are other favorite pastimes in southern Maryland, and you'll find charter captains ready to take you out at many of the marinas in the area. Stop at the Chamber of Commerce or call the St. Mary's County Division of Tourism for a list of names and numbers.

You can board a boat at Point Lookout for a day cruise to Smith Island and a look at the unique lifestyle of the 750 hardy fisherfolk who populate this isolated isle. Many are direct descendants of the original settlers, most of whom came here from Cornwall, England, in 1657. A big Chesapeake Bay seafood lunch on the island is part of the tour.

Shopping is not a major activity in these parts, though you'll pass antique shops here and there as you wander, but a few places are worth a special stop. Cecil's Old Mill on Indian Creek Road (Route 471) off Route 5 in Great Mills is a cooperative gallery in a restored 1810 mill where artists and craftspeople are often on hand personally to demonstrate and sell their work, and the old general store across the road is now Cecil's Country Store, offering antiques and gifts .

You'll almost surely see Amish and Mennonite families who live in this area shopping at the farmers market held every Wednesday and Saturday in Charlotte Hall on Route 5.

A pocket of neat Amish farms can be seen in the countryside near Charlotte Hall in a triangle formed by Routes 5, 488, and 6. You may want to stop off along Route 236 at Kate's Variety Store, a little store located in a modest home where handmade quilts are for sale.

A good reason for a return trip in the fall is the annual St. Mary's County Oyster Festival at the Leonardtown fairgrounds. This event includes the National Oyster Shucking Championship Contest and National Oyster Cook-Off and features Chesapeake Bay oysters cooked up in just about every conceivable way. The Blessing of the Fleet in early October on St. Clement's Island is another colorful event. Check for this year's dates.

As you head back up the peninsula, Upper Marlboro is worth a stop. There are historic buildings to see and places to enjoy the outdoors as well.

Take a drive to see the 1881 County Courthouse; the 1846 Trinity Episcopal Church; and Darnall's Chance, the home of Daniel Carroll, a signer of the U.S. Constitution, and his brother John, the first American bishop of the Roman Catholic church. Built around the beginning of the nineteenth century, Darnall's Chance is the oldest building in Prince George's County.

Then, for a nature break, head for Patuxent River Park, 6,000 acres with opportunities for hiking, boating, fishing, relaxing, or renting a canoe and paddling down the river. Guided nature cruises on the river via canoe or pontoon boat are often scheduled; check in advance. Also in the park is Patuxent Village, with a rough-hewn cabin, smokehouse, hunting and trapping shed, and packing house, showing what it was like to live along the river 100 years ago. Park naturalists demonstrate pioneer skills such as scoring logs with a broadax and finishing them with an adze. If you want to see more old tools, the extensive W. Henry Duvall Memorial Tool Collection is open on Sundays from 1 P.M. to 4 P.M. Many planned activities here require advance reservations, so phone ahead.

Merkle Wildlife Sanctuary is another possibility, home to thousands of migrating Canada geese in season. There is an observation deck for watching birds and a visitor center with nature exhibits. Don't forget your binoculars.

Old Maryland Farm, with animals, gardens, and exhibits of antique farm equipment, is a good bet for families.

For the most part, dining in southern Maryland means fresh seafood at reasonable prices at no-frills marina cafes. A drive over to lively Solomons Island in Calvert County for dinner makes a nice change of pace.

As for lodgings, the Brome-Howard Inn in St. Mary's is a best bet, a nineteenth-century building on 30 riverfront acres, with a highly regarded dining room. Or you can stay amid history at one of the old manor houses offering bed-and-breakfast accommodations on the waterfront, a live-in sampling of the placid lifestyle that still marks southern Maryland.

Area Code: 301

DRIVING DIRECTIONS   St. Mary's City is on Route 5. From the D.C. Beltway (I-95), follow Route 5 south. The approximate distance from D.C. is 68 miles. From points north or south, take Route 301 and turn east on Route 5 south.

ACCOMMODATIONS *Brome-Howard Inn,* 18281 Rosecroft Road, P.O. Box 476, St. Mary's City 20686, 866-0656, M–E, CP • **Bed-and-breakfast lodgings:** *St. Michaels Manor,* Route 5, Scotland 20687, 872-4025, 1805 home on Long Neck Creek, I–M, CP • *Enfields,* 21400 Colton Point Road, Avenue, 20609, 769-4755, recently restored 1901 Victorian on 73 acres, outdoor hot tub, I, CP • **Motels:** *Best Western Lexington Park,* Route 235, Lexington Park 20653, 862-4100, small pool, tennis, I • *Days Inn,* Three Notch Road, Lexington Park 20653, 863-6666, pool, M.

DINING   *Brome-Howard Inn* (see above), modern American menu featuring regional seafood, M–E • *The Willows,* Route 5, Leonardtown, 475-6553, regional specialties, I–E • *Tavern at the Village,* Wetstone Lane, Wildewood Retirement Communitcy, California, 863-3219, fine dining, eclectic menu, E–EE • **Waterfront dining:** *Evans Seafood,* Route 249, St. George Island, Piney Point, 994-2299, I–E • *Scheible's Crabpot Restaurant,* 235 Wynne Road, Scheible's Fishing Center, Ridge, 872-5185, I–M • *Spinnaker's Restaurant,* Point Lookout Marina, Miller's Wharf Road, Ridge, 872-4340, seafood and water views, I–E • *Nicky D's,* take Route 249 and follow signs, Valley Lee, 994-1155, varied menu, outside deck, I–M. See also Solomons, page 53.

SIGHT-SEEING   *Historic St. Mary's City,* P.O. Box 39, Route 5, St. Mary's, 862-0990 or (800) SMC-1634. Hours: mid-June to mid-September, Wednesday to Sunday 10 A.M. to 5 P.M.; mid-March to mid-June, mid-September to late November, Tuesday to Sunday 10 A.M. to 5 P.M. $$$ • *St. Clements Island Potomac River Museum,* Colton's Point, end of Route 242, 769-2222. Hours: Late March through September, Monday to Friday 9 A.M. to 5 P.M., Saturday and Sunday noon to 5 P.M.; rest of year, Wednesday to Sunday noon to 4 P.M. $; children under 12, free • *Sotterley Plantation,* Hollywood (follow signs from intersection of Routes 235 and 245 near Hollywood), 373-2280. Hours: Grounds open year-round, Tuesday to Sunday 10 A.M. to 4 P.M. House tours May through October, Tuesday to Sunday 11 A.M. and 2 P.M.; grounds, $; house tour, $$ • *Point Lookout State Park,* Route 5, Scotland, 872-5688. Hours: Daylight hours daily. Park, free; beach and picnic area, $$ on summer weekends, otherwise free. *Civil War Museum,* Memorial Day to Labor Day, daily 10 A.M. to 5 P.M., weekends in May. Free • *Smith Island Tours,* Capt. Alan Tyler, Rhodes

Point, (410) 425-2771, six-hour cruise with lunch. Check current rates and schedule • *St. Mary's County Oyster Festival,* 863-5015, www.usoysterfest.com, held at Leonardtown fairgrounds the third weekend in October. Check for this year's schedule and fees. • *Patuxent River Park,* 16000 Croom Airport Road, Upper Marlboro, 627-6074. Hours: daily 8 A.M. to dusk. Free • *Merkle Wildlife Sanctuary,* 11704 Fenno Road, Upper Marlboro, 888-1410. Hours: grounds daily 7 A.M. to sunset; visitor center 10 A.M. to 4 P.M. Free • *Old Maryland Farm,* 301 Watkinds Park Drive, Upper Marlboro, 218-6770. Hours: Tuesday to Friday 10 A.M. to 2:30 P.M., Saturday 9 A.M. to 4:30 P.M., Sunday 11:30 A.M. to 4:30 P.M. Free.

INFORMATION *St. Mary's County Division of Tourism,* P.O. Box 653, 23115 Leonard Hall Drive, Leonardtown, MD 20650, (800) 327-9023 or 475-4411; www.tourism@co.saint-marys.md.us; also www.southernmdisfun.com • For Upper Marlboro, *Prince George's County Conference and Visitors Bureau, Inc.,* 9200 Basil Court, Suite 101, Largo, MD 20774, (888) 925-8300 or 925-8300; www.co.pg.md.us/visitorinfo.

A Folklore Feast in Kutztown

It all began some 50 years ago when three college professors joined forces to find a way to celebrate their heritage over a Fourth of July weekend.

Today, the Pennsylvania German Festival has grown into a nine-day extravaganza that is one of the country's most colorful exhibits of folk arts and food. In fact, there are two festivals. When a split occurred among the organizers, the original event, held for many years in Kutztown, Pennsylvania, moved farther west in 1996 to the Schuylkill County Fairgrounds in Summit Station.

However, the folks in Kutztown organized to continue their own almost identical Pennsylvania German Festival on the same dates. Kutztown University, home of the Pennsylvania German Cultural Heritage Center, became a sponsor.

The people we call Pennsylvania Dutch actually are not Dutch at all but are descended from German immigrants of the late 1600s. *Dutch* was easier to pronounce than *Deutsch,* so they were dubbed "Dutch" in the new land. Unlike the austere Amish sects to the south in Lancaster County, the settlers around Kutztown and Reading became known as the Fancy, or Gay, Dutch, famous for the brightly painted hex signs that adorn their barns "chust for nice." Their love of color, song, and dance gives this festival its lively flavor.

The grounds in Kutztown overflow each year with dozens of demonstrations of such traditional Pennsylvania German crafts as quilting, fraktur and tole painting, chair caning, silver and tin work, wood carving, crewel embroidery, hex sign painting, furniture graining, rag rug making, and glassblowing. Quilts are not only seen in the making; nearly 1,000 finished handmade quilts entered in the annual Kutztown competition go on display and are for sale at very reasonable prices.

Because farm life is such a large part of the Pennsylvania German tradition, many demonstrations show off typical farm activities, from milking and sheep shearing to making apple butter. And since cooking also has long been a specialty of these industrious folks, you can count on food galore: homemade sausage and scrapple, apple pandowdy, Schnitz und Knepp (dried apples and dumplings), and that famous molasses-flavored dessert known as shoofly pie, to name just a few of the treats.

All of this is to the tune of music, folk songs, and polka bands. Free dance instruction allows everyone to join in the "hoedown" square dances and jigs.

Despite all the music and merriment, the festival still has an educational focus. Talks are held throughout the day for those who want to learn more about the customs of the Pennsylvania Germans. Typical talks might explain the difference between the Plain and Fancy sects or detail the techniques of the crafts.

There's more than enough here to fill a happy day, plus plenty in surrounding Berks County to round out your stay. For starters, drive north from Kutztown to Old Route 22, known as the Hex Highway, a prize route for viewing barns decorated with brillant hex signs. Five covered bridges are in the area, including Kutz's Mill Bridge over Saucony Creek, near Route 737 north of Kutztown. A free map and visitor's guide will lead you to the rest.

Follow 737 farther north to Kempton and the Hawk Mountain Sanctuary, named for the birds of prey that can be sighted here in the fall. The sanctuary provides 2,400 mountaintop acres for viewing protected birds and animals, eight miles of trails, and lovely scenery. The Appalachian Trail crosses the crest of the Blue Ridge Mountains at the sanctuary's eastern edge, giving hikers unparalleled vistas of Pennsylvania Dutch farmlands.

Another interesting side trip is the Rodale Institute Research Center, reached off Route 222 east of Kutztown. Visitors are welcome at this 333-acre farm, one of the world's leading research facilities for organic horticulture. The guided tour includes the demonstration garden, where new vegetable and flower varieties are tested, as well as some of the barns, research fields, and orchards. You'll learn a lot about organic gardening, and you can visit a museum exhibit called "Food: The Essence of Life," which shows how food gets from the farm to the table. The book store where the tour begins has a fine selection of books and garden-related items, and a small cafe where sandwiches, salads, and snacks are served.

A mile south of Kutztown at 740 Noble Street a giant antique market takes place every Saturday at Renninger's, with some 200 indoor booths and another 125 dealers at the outdoor flea market. You'll also find an authentic farmers market at Renninger's on Fridays and Saturdays. Come early for the pick of the crop. There are antique shops in Kutztown and throughout the area for more collectibles.

The Pennsylvania Germans Cultural Heritage Center in Kutztown also is definitely worth a visit any time you are in the area to learn about the history and lifestyle of the early German immigrants of the area. Guided tours take you through an 1830 one-room schoolhouse, an 1810 stone farmhouse, and a nineteenth-century barn.

Any day also is a good time to head south on Route 222 to scoop up bargains in Reading, a town that proudly calls itself the "outlet capital of the world," boasting a host of major outlet centers, many in old factory buildings converted to showrooms featuring merchandise from hundreds of top manufacturers. Corning, Donna Karan, Gap, Polo–Ralph Lauren, Tommy Hilfiger, Wrangler, Capezio, Evan-Picone, Bass, Nine West, Mikasa, Calvin Klein, Vanity Fair, Reebok, and Danskin are just a few of the brands with their own stores, and more labels of all kinds await in other outlets.

While you are in Reading take a drive to the top of Mt. Penn for the soaring view from the landmark known as the Pagoda.

Two worthwhile historic sights nearby are the Daniel Boone Homestead, on Route 422 east of Reading, and Hopewell Village, a restored iron-making community dating back to 1771, located on Route 345 south of Birdsboro.

French Creek State Park, adjoining Hopewell Village, offers 6,500 scenic acres in the Blue Ridge Mountains with areas for picnicking, swimming, hiking, and boating. Blue Marsh Lake and Recreation Area offers another 6,200 acres of recreation, with a 1,100-acre lake for boating, water sports, and swimming. And almost everyone marvels at the Blue Rocks, a natural wonder that is a fossil of the Ice Age, located northeast of Reading in the mountains of northern Berks County.

There are some fine country inns near both festivals, and a host of motels near Reading, but you might also make your headquarters for the weekend to the south in Ephrata, where there are some unique attractions and two appealing lodging choices. Doneckers is one part fine restaurant, one part posh store, and one part elegant inn in a series of restored local homes dating from 1797 to 1926. Smithton is a gracious 1763 home where every guest room has a fireplace, and the four-poster beds are made up with handmade quilts and goose-down pillows. The inn even supplies nightshirts to put you in an old-fashioned mood. In summer you'll find fresh flowers in your room and breakfast served outdoors in the garden house.

As for shops in Ephrata, in addition to its original store, Doneckers operates the Artworks, a former factory transformed into four floors of some 30 shops and galleries for artists and craftspeople. Many artisans can be seen at work on their crafts. Photography, pottery, quilts, sculpture, jewelry, paperweights, handmade kaleidoscopes, photography, paintings, and whimsical folk carvings are just a few of the offerings.

Ephrata boasts one of the more unusual historic attractions in this region. Ephrata Cloister is the restored community of a monastic sect founded in 1730. You'll have to duck your head to pass through the low doorways (a reminder of humility) and go single file down the narrow halls (symbols of the straight and narrow path) to see where these dedicated people lived and the narrow wooden ledges where they slept, with eight-inch wooden blocks for pillows. There are eight surviving buildings, and they evoke an unusually vivid sense of the austere way of life practiced here. From the second Saturday in July through Labor Day weekend, the cloister presents Vorspiel, an outdoor musical drama depicting the everyday life of this spartan eighteenth-century communal society.

Historic rites a bit more festive are to be found nearby if you come over the Fourth of July, when Hopewell Village celebrates the day with a living-history pageant reenacting Colonial camp life.

But then again, no specific occasion or season is really needed to visit one of these gala Pennsylvania German events. Any day you pick is going to feel like a holiday.

Area Codes: 610; Ephrata, 717

DRIVING DIRECTIONS   Kutztown is on Route 222, off Route 78 or Route 9, the Pennsylvania Turnpike Extension. From D.C., take I-95 north to Wilmington. Exit here for Route 202 north, which turns into Route 322 north, connect to Route 100 north to Allentown, get onto Route 9 north briefly, and exit onto Route 222 west to Kutztown. The approximate distance from D.C. is 190 miles.

ACCOMMODATIONS   *Die Bauerei (The Farmhouse) Bed & Breakfast,* 187 Sharadin Road, Kutztown 19530, 894-4854, farm setting outside Kutztown, I–M, CP • *The Inn at Bally Spring Farm,* 90 Airport Road, Barto 19504, 845-8900 or (800) 845-4289, farmhouse on 95 acres, comfortable rooms and suites in the converted barn and 1734 carriage house, rooms, I–M, CP, suites; E, CP • *Glasbern Country Inn,* 2141 Pack Horse Road, Fogelsville 18051, 285-4723, attractive lodging in elegantly restored farm buildings; pool, whirlpool baths, fireplaces, E–EE, CP • *Hawk Mountain Bed and Breakfast,* 221 Stony

Run Valley Road, Kempton 19529, 756-4224, contemporary lodge, pool, views, M, CP; with whirlpool and fireplace, M–E, CP • *The House on the Canal,* 4020 River Road, Reading 19605, 921-3015, farmhouse B&B on the Schulkill River, rooms with whirlpools and TV, M, CP • *The Inn at Reading,* 1040 Park Road, Wyomissing 19610, 372-7811 or (800) 383-9713, modern motel within walking distance of Reading outlets, pool, M–E.

Ephrata: *The Guesthouses at Doneckers,* 318–324 North State Street, Ephrata 17522, 738-9502, rooms, M, CP; suites with whirlpools, some fireplaces, E–EE, CP; guest houses also include The Homestead, Gerhart House, and 1777 House nearby • *Smithton Inn,* 900 West Main Street, Ephrata 17522, 733-6094, M–E, CP • Write to the Visitors Bureau for complete list of area bed-and-breakfasts and motels.

DINING *Green Hills Inn,* 2444 Morgantown Road, Green Hills, 777-9611 (south of Reading), excellent French fare, M–E • *The Restaurant at Doneckers,* 333 North State Street, 738-9501, elegant continental menu, E, Hearthside Cafe, bistro menu, I–M • *Oley Valley Inn,* 401 Main Street, Oley, 987-6400, 1881 inn with Victorian ambiance, American cuisine, M–E • *Glasbern Country Inn* (see above), elegant French country cuisine, E–EE • *Stokesay Castle,* Hill Road and Spook Lane, Reading, 375-4588, grand castle surroundings on ten-acre setting with views, E • *New Smithville Country Inn,* 10425 Old Route 22, outside Kutztown, 285-2987, atmospheric old general store/post office building, I–M • **Family-style Pennsylvania Dutch meals:** *Haag's Hotel,* Old Route 22, Shartlesville, 488-6692, I–M • *Shartlesville Hotel,* Old Route 22, Main Street, Shartlesville, 488-0620, M.

SIGHT-SEEING *Kutztown Pennsylvania German Festival,* Kutztown Fairgrounds, (888) 674-6136, www.kutztownfestival.com, late June through early July, including Fourth of July. Hours: 9 A.M. to 6 P.M. $$$$ • *Pennsylvania German Cultural Heritage Center,* Luckenbill Road off U.S. 222, Kutztown, 683-1330. Hours: Daily 10 A.M. to noon, 1 P.M. to 4 P.M. $$, under 12, free • *The Artworks at Doneckers,* 100 North State Street, 738-9503. Monday, Tuesday, Thursday to Saturday, 10 A.M. to 5 P.M., Free • *Reading Outlet Stores:* Listings available from Berks County Visitors Bureau. Hours vary with the seasons, so it is best to check • *Ephrata Cloister,* 632 West Main Street, Ephrata, 733-6600. Hours: March to December, Monday to Saturday 9 A.M. to 5 P.M., Sunday noon to 5 P.M.; rest of year, closed Tuesday, $$$; Vorspiel performances, late June through Labor Day, Saturdays. Check current prices • *Rodale Institute Research Center,* 611 Siegfriedale Road, Kutztown, 683-1400. Hours: Daily May to October, Monday to Saturday 9 A.M. to 5 P.M., Sunday 10 A.M. to 3 P.M. Self-guided tours,

$$; guided tours at 11 A.M., $$$; November to April, closed Sunday and guided tours only by advance reservation. • *Hopewell Furnace National Historic Site,* Route 345, south of Birdsboro, 582-8773. Hours: Daily 9 A.M. to 5 P.M. $$; under 17, free • *French Creek State Park,* Route 345 south of Birdsboro, Elverson, 582-1514, daily daylight hours. Free except for boat rentals or swimming fees • *Daniel Boone Homestead,* Daniel Boone Road off U.S. 422, east of Reading, Baumstown, 582-4900. Hours: Tuesday to Saturday 9 A.M. to 5 P.M., Sunday noon to 5 P.M. $$ • *Hawk Mountain Sanctuary,* 1700 Hawk Mountain Road, Kempton, 756-6000. December to August, Daily 9 A.M. to 5 P.M., September to November, 8 A.M. to 5 P.M. $$.

INFORMATION   *Reading & Berks County Visitors Bureau,* 352 Penn Street, Reading, PA 19602, 375-4085 or (800) 443-6610; www.readingberkspa.com.

Sea Breezing at Spring Lake

Swans glide tranquilly across a mirror-smooth lake. Strollers take in the sea breeze from a pristine two-mile boardwalk, while old-timers rock gently on the porches of vintage Victorian hotels.

It's the New Jersey shore the way it used to be—and still is in Spring Lake, a perfect getaway for an old-fashioned weekend by the sea.

One of the towns along the posh oceanside stretch once known as the Gold Coast, Spring Lake seems determined to remain what it has been for a century—a gracious vacation oasis. Strict ordinances have deliberately held back the so-called progress that has afflicted so many shoreline communities in the form of video arcades, fast-food eateries, and newly built condominiums.

The heart of things remains the spring-fed lake for which the village was named and the shady green park that surrounds it, stretching for five blocks right through the center of town. Rimmed by weeping willows and spanned by a picturesque wooden footbridge, the lake is a haven for fishermen and boaters, a swimming pool for ducks and geese, and a frequent landing pad for seagulls that shuttle back and forth between its tranquil waters and the ocean, just a shell's throw away.

The first to spot the unique attraction of a shore site with its own freshwater lake was a group of Philadelphia businessmen back in 1875. They formed the Spring Lake Beach Improvement Company, acquired the 285-acre property then known as Osborn Farm, and hired engineer Frederick Anspach to plan a whole new resort town. The centerpiece of the development was the ultraelegant Monmouth House Hotel, completed in 1876 with 270 bedrooms, a dining room seating 1,000 guests, and large parlors overlooking the ocean. A success from the start, it was quickly joined by more elaborate hotels and guest houses. Soon millionaires were building mammoth "summer cottages" in Spring Lake. A fire in 1900 slowed things temporarily, but the town rebuilt and remained a thriving part of the privileged people's shore.

Some of the hotels and many of the homes were transported here by wealthy businessmen directly from the 1876 Centennial Exposition in Philadelphia. Brochures from the town historical society point you to these and many other buildings remaining from the turn of the century.

Some of the old landmarks have fared better than others as time has brought changes to Spring Lake. You'll see modern homes here and there where Victorian beauties like the the Monmouth House and the Warren Hotel once stood. The huge Essex-Sussex, where the movie *Ragtime* was filmed, retains its prize spot across from the beach but is being converted into a senior citizens residence.

But the Hewitt Wellington, now a condominium complex, has many of the newly elegant rooms available for weekend rentals. Hotels like the Breakers have been refurbished and added air-conditioning, TV, and other modern comforts like whirlpool baths. And a growing number of the old homes have become delightful bed-and-breakfast lodgings. Among the pleasantest are the Sea Crest, Normandy Inn, and Ashling Cottage.

Spring Lake acquired its nickname, the Irish Riviera, for the many Irish families who were among the earliest to establish summer mansions here. The head of one prominent family, philanthropist Martin Maloney, built the town's showplace, St. Catherine's Church, in 1901 as a memorial to his daughter, who died at the age of 17. The ornate Romanesque architecture, marble altar, and frescoed ceilings, modeled after a Vatican chapel, are proudly shown off to visitors by the natives.

One remaining sign of the Irish influence is the Irish Center, a boutique on Third Avenue, the town's main shopping street, where you will find Irish fisherman sweaters, Donegal tweeds, Celtic jewelry, walking sticks, and a wide assortment of teas, cookies, and candies—all imported from the Emerald Isle.

The three-block "downtown" of Spring Lake is more preppy than touristy, but it does make for a pleasant stroll and some interesting browsing for gifts, summer dresses, Christmas ornaments, children's clothing, or colorful beach hats.

If you want a light lunch, Who's on Third on Third Street will oblige, and Susan Murphy's Old Time Ice Cream at 601 Warren Avenue is guaranteed to satisfy your sweet tooth.

There's plenty to do by day in Spring Lake. Day passes can be bought for a fee at the beach, though many lodgings provide badges admitting their guests to the two town bathhouses, each with a salt-water pool. You can fish for the trout stocked in the local lake, play tennis in the park or golf at nearby facilities, jog along the boardwalk, or take a walk or ride a bike to look at the cupolas and gingerbread of the town's fine houses. Most of the inns will either lend you a bike or help you rent one.

All of the blocks between Ocean and Third Avenues have prize homes to be seen. Check out Coalbrook, Martin Maloney's 26-room carriage house at 105 Morris Avenue. On Monmouth Avenue, the Rolin House (circa 1888) at 207 and its neighbor at 214 are in the aptly named Spring Lake Beach Victorian style and are also worth a look (especially the latter, a gingerbread classic with carpenter Gothic shingles, floor-to-ceiling windows, and stained glass). Two survivors from the Centennial Exhibition are the Missouri State Building at 411 Ocean Road and the Portuguese Government Pavilion at 205 Atlantic Avenue.

Evenings are quiet here. Along with dancing, the larger hotels offer some entertainment; there are summer productions at the theater located in the attractive local community house, and concerts are held in the park. Younger vacationers looking for nightlife head for the pubs in Sea Girt.

But mainly this is a town for an after-dinner stroll by the lake or the sea and quiet talk on the wide porch of your inn, pleasures of a more tranquil era in a town that remains a picture book from the past. The only swingers in Spring Lake are in the gliders on the front porch.

Area Code: 732

DRIVING DIRECTIONS Spring Lake is on the Jersey shore about midway between New York and Philadelphia, at exit 98 on the Garden State Parkway. From D.C., take I-95 north, across the Delaware Memorial Bridge to the New Jersey Turnpike. At exit 7A, follow I-195 east to Route 34 south; at the traffic circle, follow Route 524 east into town. The approximate distance from D.C. is 206 miles.

PUBLIC TRANSPORTATION Connecting train service is available from Philadelphia. For information, call New Jersey Transit, (973) 762-5100.

ACCOMMODATIONS All Spring Lake zip codes are 07762. Expect minimum stays in season. Rates given are for high season, usually late May through September, and are lower the rest of the year. *Normandy Inn,* 21 Tuttle Avenue, 449-7172 or (800) 449-1888, a Victorian beauty, E–EE, CP • *Sea Crest by the Sea,* 19 Tuttle Avenue, 449-9031 or (800) 803-9031, elegantly furnished Victorian, E–EE, CP • *Ashling Cottage,* 106 Sussex Avenue, 449-3553 or (888) ASHLING, charming rooms, E–EE, CP • *La Maison,* 404 Jersey Avenue, 449-0969, stylish decor, E–EE, CP • *Hollycroft,* 506 North Boulevard, 681-2254 or (800) 679-2554, change of mood, secluded lodge with knotty pine walls, log beams, E, CP • *Victoria House,* 214 Monmouth Avenue, 974-1882 or (888) 249-6252, charming 1882 Queen Anne Victorian, E–EE, CP.

Modernized hotels: *Spring Lake Inn,* 104 Salem Avenue, 449-2010, 1888 hotel remodeled into a smaller lodging with charm, inviting porch, some ocean views, E–EE, CP • *Hewitt Wellington,* 200 Monmouth Avenue, 974-1212, one of the best of the big hotels, E–EE • *The Breakers,* 1507 Ocean Avenue, 449-7700, pool, E–EE • *The Grand Victorian Hotel,* 1505 Ocean Avenue, 449-5327, E–EE • *The Ocean House,* 102 Sussex Avenue, 449-9090 or (888) 449-9094, the 1878 Colonial Hotel, newly and nicely refurbished, E–EE • *The Sandpiper,* 7 Atlantic Avenue, 449-6060 or (800) UB-HAPPY, indoor pool, E–EE, CP. One pleasant, well-furnished motel deserves mention for its location on the park, some cooking units for families: *The Chateau,* 500 Warren Avenue, 974-2000, E–EE.

DINING *The Old Mill Inn,* Old Mill Road off Route 71, Spring Lake Heights, 449-1800, delightful ambience, good food, longtime area favorite, E–EE • *Whispers,* Hewitt Wellington (see above), 449-3330, well recommended locally, M–E • *Sisters,* 1321 Third Avenue, 449-1909, contemporary fare in a former luncheonette, walls lined with books, good bet for lunch, I, and dinner, M–E • *The Breakers* (see above), Italian and seafood, nice view, mixed reviews, M–E • *The Sandpiper* (see above), candlelit dining room, continental menu, M–E • *Who's on Third,* 1300 Third Avenue, 449-4233, all three meals, good choice for lunch or light dinner, I–M • Some nearby recommendations: *Bella Luna Bistro,* 703 Belmar Plaza, Belmar, 280-7501, excellent Mediterranean fare, outdoor dining, M–E • *Matisse,* 1400 Ocean Aveue, Belmar, 681-7680, inventive chef, eclectic menu, M–E • *Rod's Olde Irish Tavern,* 507 Washington Boulevard, Sea Girt, 449-2020, informal pub food, lively, popular, M.

INFORMATION *Greater Spring Lake Chamber of Commerce,* P.O. Box 694, Spring Lake, NJ 07762, 449-0577; www.springlake.org.

Reliving the Past in Gettysburg

The silent green countryside of Gettysburg, Pennsylvania, is a landscape peopled with ghosts.

With all the years that have passed since the famous Civil War battle was fought in 1863, it is still impossible to visit the site without feeling moved by the events that took place here long ago, when the nation's unity was saved by the bloodiest battle in its history.

The human drama and tragedy of battle become almost tangibly alive during the annual Civil War Heritage Days, held the last weekend in June and the first week in July. Flags stand at attention in long rows on every main street in town, and a reenactment of the battle brings dust and smoke to the battlefield once again.

On July 1, 2, and 3, 1863, soldiers from the North and South, Americans all, fought here in one of history's most memorable battles. Visiting Gettysburg means retracing the battle through its three-day course, and all manner of commercial enterprises are ready to help you do this, the result of the large crowds that continue to be attracted to the site each year.

The best advice is to avoid them all—the Lincoln Train Museum, the Gettysburg Battle Theater, the wax museum Hall of Presidents, even the red-white-and-blue tour bus with its recorded narration accompanied by a "cast of thousands" re-creating the sounds of battle in "living stereo sound." Instead, stick to the National Park Service offerings, where you get less sound and a more human side of a battle whose drama needs no embellishment.

As soon as you arrive in town, head for the Gettysburg National Military Park Visitor Center. The center is outdated and is slated to be replaced, but meanwhile it provides all you need to make the most of your visit. Start with the Electric Map Orientation Program, a 30-minute overview of the battle's progress displayed on a giant relief map with colored lights tracing the course of the action. The Center includes the Museum of the Civil War, the largest exhibit of objects associated with the conflict.

If you are already knowledgeable about the battle, pick up one of the printed auto guides and perhaps rent an audiocassette for your own tour of the meticulously maintained and well-marked battlegrounds.

Otherwise, sign up fast for a licensed battlefield guide. These serious battle buffs have passed stringent written and oral exams to qualify for their posts. For a reasonable fee, a guide will join you in your car for a private tour over the battleground and answer all your questions. In two hours, a knowledgeable guide can tell you more about the battle and the generals and men who decided its course than a dozen textbooks. Some of the guides are actually at work on their own books.

If you have a wait until a guide is available, you can whet your appetite at the Cyclorama Center, where you will see a film called *Gettysburg 1863* and a sound-and-light program depicting the action of Pickett's Charge displayed against Paul Philippoteaux's famous painting of the battle, a giant circular canvas 356 feet in circumference and 26 feet high.

You'll learn from the various exhibits that the first day of battle looked bad for the Union forces, who had retreated through the streets of Gettysburg to the heights outside of town. That proved to be a major break for the Northerners, whose new lines turned out to be positions of strength, especially when Lee's generals were unable to coordinate their attack on the second day.

On July 3 General Robert E. Lee made the fateful decision to assault the center of the Union line on Cemetery Ridge in the battle that went down in history as Pickett's Charge. After a thunderous two-hour artillery bombardment that completely shrouded the field in smoke, the air cleared and Union defenders looked down on an unbelievable sight—12,000 Confederate soldiers shoulder to shoulder in a line a mile wide, an ocean of an army sweeping forward, guns glinting in the sun, colors held high. The Confederates charged on, only to be mowed down by the murderous blasts of Union fire. In 50 minutes, 6,000 were dead or captured, and the tide of the Civil War turned irreversibly to the North.

The human factors that contributed to the astounding battle are fascinating, even if you have never had much interest in battles or wars. Overconfident Confederate troops who had battered Union forces in the South were making only their second foray into the North, where a third of their opponents were determined young Pennsylvania farm boys defending their home ground. The battle itself was never meant to happen; Lee was planning to fight in the cover of the mountains. It began only because a Southern scouting brigade happened upon a Union cavalry division in Gettysburg. Reinforcements for this minor skirmish came willy-nilly, without any overall plan.

According to one guide, Lee's ill-fated charge, incomprehensible to us today, was the result of using traditional battlefield tactics, which were ineffective against the high-power cannons that represented a new advance in weaponry.

The stories of brothers fighting brothers and of 12-year-old drummer boys lost in the fray are heartbreaking, and so are the neat rows of thousands of graves in the National Cemetery and the many state monuments to fallen heroes.

To add to your understanding of all these events and sites, free National Park Service ranger-guided walking tours are held at the National Cemetery and at the major action points, including Pickett's

Charge and the Valley of Death. Evening campfire programs sometimes take place at an amphitheater in the same woods where Confederate soldiers once camped.

During the weekends of Civil War Heritage Days, you can actually visit living-history encampments where volunteer participants dressed in authentic Union and Confederate uniforms set up tent camps, realistic right down to campfire cooking. Demonstrations show infantry and cavalry drills and artillery firing, and the well-informed mock soldiers answer any and all questions about the camp life of Civil War troops. During the week, lectures are held each night for those who want to learn more about the Civil War. The Fourth of July also is marked in Gettysburg by fife and drum corps and brass band concerts, and the Fireman's Festival of rides, games, and entertainment.

The highlights of the week are the battle reenactments, which take place usually the weekend before or weekend after July 4. The earth shakes with the boom of cannon and rifle fire and the charging hooves of the cavalry, smoke clouds the battlefield, and you begin to understand in a new way the horrors of war and the terror that must have been in the hearts of the valiant young men who fought here, many of them only teenagers or in their early twenties.

This is also the week for the Civil War Book Show, featuring dozens of dealers selling new and rare books, photos, and prints, and the Civil War Collectors Show, where some 250 display tables offer original Civil War accoutrements, weapons, documents, and memorabilia. Civil War buffs will find lots of shops selling memorabilia in Gettysburg year-round.

There's more history to be found on a walking tour in Gettysburg, a small town still a bit reminiscent of the way it looked in 1863. The printed tour available at the information center located in the old railway station on Carlisle Street shows you the routes where troops marched into town, where Lincoln lodged and worshiped when he came to give the Gettysburg Address, the school building that served as a hospital for wounded from both sides, and the church-turned-hospital where holes had to be drilled in the floor to allow the heavy flow of blood from the wounded to drain through.

One of the homes served for ten years following the war as an orphanage for the children whose fathers were lost in the war; another was a hotel whose liquor was "liberated" by Confederate troops; others still hold in their walls cannonballs fired more than a century ago. One favorite local tale deals with Jennie Wade, a 20-year-old woman who was the only civilian casualty of the battle, struck down by a bullet in her own kitchen. Another story tells of the tavern where a cannonball literally cleared the table of its settings and then landed in a mattress without harming anyone.

Candlelight walking tours, including a Ghosts of Gettysburg tour, are a fun way to learn the local lore.

You can visit General Lee's headquarters, the house where the general and his staff made plans for one of history's most memorable battles. The old stone house, one of the few historic houses in Gettysburg open to the public, holds a collection of Civil War relics.

Just a few blocks from the heart of town is the campus of Gettysburg College and the office where the late President Dwight D. Eisenhower worked on his memoirs after his retirement.

The lovely 495-acre Eisenhower Farm in the nearby countryside may be visited on National Park Service tours and is a vivid reminder of the spirits and personalities of the president and his wife, Mamie. Living-history interpreters and park rangers offer programs on the high points of Eisenhower's career and also lead outdoor walking tours on the farm, which is a National Historic Site.

Tour or no, a drive out of town into the rolling Pennsylvania countryside is a happy ending to a Gettysburg visit. Suggested driving routes are available at the information center. The 40-mile Historic Conewago Tour meanders through the eastern half of Adams County, crisscrossing Conewago Creek and passing farms, country churches, and picturesque villages like Victorian New Oxford, a village boasting dozens of antique shops.

The 36-mile Scenic Valley driving route loops along Route 234 past covered bridges, farms, and the famous Adams County apple orchards. The countryside is a consoling reminder that beauty transcends battles and that peace reigns supreme in the valley.

Area Code: 717

DRIVING DIRECTIONS   Gettysburg is on Route 15, roughly midway between Harrisburg, PA, and Frederick, MD. From D.C., take Route 270 north to Frederick, then Route 15 north into town. The approximate distance from D.C. is 80 miles.

PUBLIC TRANSPORTATION   Nearest major Amtrak and bus stop is Harrisburg, 28 miles away.

ACCOMMODATIONS   *Baladerry Inn,* 40 Hospital Road, Gettysburg 17325, 337-1342, quiet inn on nice grounds, some rooms with patios, near the battlefield, M, CP • *Battlefield Bed & Breakfast,* 2264 Emmitsburg Road, Gettysburg 17325, 334-8804 or (888) 766-3897, 1809 farm across from the battlefield, costumed historical presentations, M–E, CP • *Best Western Gettysburg Hotel,* One Lincoln Square, Gettysburg, 337-2000 or (800) WESTERN, recently refurbished in-town hotel, suites with whirlpool tubs, M–E • *Brafferton Inn,* 44 York Street, Gettysburg 17325, 337-3423, charmer in the historic district, M, CP • *Doubleday Inn,* 104 Doubleday Avenue, Gettysburg 17325, 334-9119, antique-filled Colonial on the battlefield, M, CP • *Farnsworth*

House Inn, 401 Baltimore Street, Gettysburg 17325, 334-8838, historic 1833 home, some rooms with fireplaces, whirlpools; sharpshooters were once housed in the garret room, M, CP • *Gaslight Inn,* 33 East Middle Street, Gettysburg 17325, 337-9100, well furnished, fireplaces, some steam showers, Jacuzzis, M–E, CP • *Keystone Inn,* 231 Hanover Street, Gettysburg 17325, 337-3888, comfortable Victorian home, five blocks from town center but away from the crowds, M, CP • There are many motels in Gettysburg; write for full list.

Inns outside town: *Antrim 1844,* 30 Trevanian Road, Taneytown, MD 21787, (410) 756-6812, historic estate 12 miles from Gettysburg, by far the most elegant in the area, E–EE, CP • *Herr Tavern Publick House,* 900 Chambersburg Road, Gettysburg 17325, 334-4332, renovated rooms, all with fireplaces, some with Jacuzzis, but note that the restaurant is popular and the road can be busy, I–E, CP • *Hickory Bridge Farm,* 96 Hickory Bridge Road, Ortanna 17353, 642-5261, nice rural location ten miles from Gettysburg, M–E, CP • *The Old Barn,* One Main Trail, Carroll Valley 17320, 642-5711, renovated 1853 barn, pool, peaceful location eight miles west of Gettysburg, M, CP.

DINING Gettysburg is often mobbed, and restaurants are, too; try to dine early or late or drive a few miles out of town. *Blue Parrot Bistro,* 35 Chambersburg Street, 337-3739, little ambience but a well-regarded chef, M • *Dobbin House,* 89 Steinwehr Avenue, 334-2100, historic, charming, M • *Farnsworth House* (see above), Southern specialties, M • **Outside Gettysburg:** *Altland House,* Route 30, Abbottstown, 259-9535, landmark village building, highly regarded chef, 15 miles east of town, M–E; also lighter fare downstairs, I–E • *Antrim 1844* (see above), fine dining, prix fixe, EE • *Herr Tavern Publick House* (see above), wide-ranging menu, M–E • *Hickory Bridge Farm,* Orrtana (see above), country dining in an old barn, home cooking served family style, M for full meal • *Historic Fairfield Inn,* Route 116, Main Street, Fairfield, 642-5410, 1757 former stagecoach stop, eight miles west of town, M.

SIGHT-SEEING *Gettysburg National Military Park,* 97 Taneytown Road, accessible from Routes 134 and 15, 334-1124 • *National Park Visitors Center and Museum of the Civil War,* Hours: Daily 8 A.M. to 5 P.M., to 6 P.M. in summer months. Park Service ranger talks and guided walks, free; private guides, $35 for two hours; Electric Map Orientation Program, $$; Cyclorama Sound and Light Program, $$ • *Eisenhower National Historic Site,* shuttle buses depart from Eisenhower Tour Information Center at the side of the National Park Service Visitor Center. Hours: April 1 to October 31, daily 9 A.M. to 4 P.M., rest of year Wednesday to Sunday, except closed earlier during January to early February, $$$ • *General Lee's Headquarters,* Route 30 (eight blocks west of Lincoln Square), 334-3141. Hours: Daily mid-March to November, 9 A.M. to 5 P.M., $$ • *Candlelight tours:* Phone for current schedules, 337-0445.

INFORMATION *Gettysburg Convention and Visitors Bureau,* 35 Carlisle Street, P.O. Box 4117, Gettysburg, PA 17325, 334-6274 or (800) 337-5-15; www.gettysburg.com.

Communing with Nature in Chincoteague

There's absolutely nothing fancy about Chincoteague, Virginia's Eastern Shore beach retreat—and that's exactly why so many people fancy the place.

This low-key, laid-back little waterman's enclave offers no kitsch, no quaintness, no frills. The condos and high-rises haven't made it here, nor will you find much in the way of nightlife or shopping or reason to dress for dinner.

What you will find is a causeway beckoning to miles of exquisite unspoiled Assateague Island National Seashore beaches—beaches so wide that a short walk will bring space all to yourself even on the busiest summer day. Add the Chincoteague National Wildlife Refuge, a part of Assateague, with the famous Chincoteague wild ponies and some of the most fascinating bird and animal life to be seen anywhere on the Atlantic seaboard, and you have a unique back-to-nature getaway.

Assateague is the northernmost of the sandy chain of barrier islands off the Eastern Shore. It stretches from just south of Ocean City, Maryland, to Chincoteague, with public entrances found only at either end. Though the island is only about 37 miles long, the drive between the two developed areas takes an hour and a half.

The Maryland section of the island includes Assateague Island National Seashore and Assateague State Park. Chincoteague National Wildlife Refuge is located on the larger Virginia section of the island. In conjunction with the refuge, the Assateague National Seashore manages a recreational portion of the beach with lifeguards and public facilities.

Snow geese, mergansers, ospreys, herons, egrets, graceful white-tailed deer, and river otters are among the hundreds of species of birds and animals found in the refuge. They can be seen on hiking and biking trails and on the Wildlife Loop, a three-and-a-quarter-mile drive that is open to hikers and bikers but closed to cars until 3 P.M. each day. A concessionaire, Assateague Island Wildlife Tours, provides a 90-minute narrated tram tour through the northern portion of the refuge, which is normally open only to hikers. Scenic boat tours circling the island are also offered.

The Refuge and the National Park Service offer many programs all summer, including guided walks, bird walks, evening slide shows, campfire programs, and activities especially for children.

Almost universally, the sight that delights visitors most is that of the free-spirited wild ponies that roam the refuge. Youngsters seem particularly taken with the ponies, especially since a children's book and movie, *Misty of Chincoteague,* caught the fancy of children everywhere.

Legend says that the ponies are descendants of mustangs that swam ashore from a wrecked Spanish galleon four centuries ago. Though their growth has been stunted by a sparse diet of marsh grasses and bayberry leaves, the shaggy, sturdy small horses nonetheless have managed to survive and thrive. At present there are two herds, a small one of about 40 horses in the Maryland part of the park and another of about 150 horses in the Virginia section, where a fence separates state and federal jurisdictions. The ponies travel in packs of from 2 to 20 horses, with the smaller horses often protected by a stallion.

The horses are bothered by mosquitoes and flies during the summer, but nature has provided them with help in the form of white cattle egrets, birds that feed on these insects. Camera shutters click furiously when the egrets perch on the ponies' backs to catch their prey. (Human visitors, not having such helpful guardians, are well advised to bring along insect repellent when they visit the refuge.)

A remarkable sight, drawing thousands of spectators, is the pony swim and sale held annually the last Wednesday and Thursday in July. The Chincoteague Volunteer Firemen round up the ponies and swim them across the channel to town, where excess young are sold at auction. The sale serves a dual purpose, keeping the herd down to a number that can be supported by the vegetation on Assateague and providing funds for the local Volunteer Fire Company.

Back on Assateague, a long, thinning tail of shoreline hooking away from the ocean shelters the waters of Tom's Cove and is the setting for beaches and many water-related activities, including clamming and surf casting. Piping plover nesting areas in this area are closed to public access mid-March through October to protect this endangered species.

Assateague has seen a growing number of visitors since 1960, when a bridge was built connecting it to the mainland. Nevertheless, Chincoteague itself remains basically a town where most of the population of 3,500 continue to make their living from oysters, clams, and crabs, just as their families have done for generations. There is no sewage treatment plant, forestalling any thought of large development, and although some handsome vacation homes are being built, the town itself is basic, not beautiful. Most of the homes and buildings are modest frame structures.

Accommodations consist of campgrounds, trailer parks, cottages, a growing number of attractive bed-and-breakfast inns, and lots of motels, making for a democratic mix, from RVs to BMWs, in local store parking lots. Among the motels, the Refuge and the Driftwood have the closest locations to Assateague. The Island Resort and Spa, which overlooks the bay, isn't really a resort but does have attractive grounds, a boardwalk overlooking the Intracoastal Waterway, and an indoor pool and hot tub.

At dinner, you can opt for the Landmark, one of the restaurants geared to tourists and boasting the island's best sunset view, or join the mix of locals and visitors at an old-timer like Don's, which offers evening entertainment. Wherever you go, you can count on a menu rich with delicious fresh clams and crabs and, in season, the special local pride, Chincoteague oysters. These famous salt oysters are cultivated on sand and rock public grounds that the oystermen seed and harvest much as landlubbers might tend a vegetable garden. The local Oyster Maritime Museum on Maddux Boulevard shows you how it is done and also gives a close-up look at oysters, crabs, starfish, and other denizens of the nearby deep. Kids love the touch tank.

You can do further exploration of the marine life in nearby marshes and inlets on nature cruises and kayak tours.

Chincoteague has one additional distinction, its wood carvers. The roster of the Chincoteague Decoy Carvers Association lists some 20 members who can be visited at their home studios, and fine decoys and bird carvings can be found in local shops as well as at the Refuge Waterfowl Museum. The museum, containing an enormous private collection, is a must for anyone who is interested in shorebird art. The Carvers Association has an annual show over Labor Day weekend, and the Easter weekend Decoy Festival also brings many knowledgeable collectors to town.

Two other out-of-season events are worth noting. One is the Oyster Festival, held over Columbus Day weekend in October, one of the months when the oysters "r" in peak season. The second is the annual Waterfowl Open House at the National Wildlife Refuge during Thanksgiving week, just in time for visitors to see thousands of migrating waterfowl in residence.

If you are in search of activity away from the beach, NASA maintains an experimental rocket program on nearby Wallops Island and offers a small museum, as well as free tours to the launch sites during the summer months. Or you might take a drive across the peninsula to Onancock and board a boat for the remote, otherworldly atmosphere of Tangier Island.

But if you get into the rhythm of things on Chincoteague, chances are you'll be happy right here, kicking off your shoes, slowing down your pace, and just enjoying unspoiled nature at its very best.

Area Code: 757

DRIVING DIRECTIONS Chincoteague is off Route 13 at the northern end of Virginia's Eastern Shore. From D.C., follow Route 50/301 across the Chesapeake Bay Bridge, and take Route 50 to Salisbury. Turn south on Route 13, then turn off at Route 175 east into town. The approximate distance from D.C. is 175 miles.

ACCOMMODATIONS *Refuge Motor Inn,* 7058 Maddox Boulevard/ Beach Road, P.O. Box 378, 23336, 336-5511, indoor/outdoor pool, M • *Driftwood Motor Lodge,* 7105 Maddox Boulevard/Beach Road, P.O. Box 575, 23336, 336-6557, M • *Island Resort and Spa,* 4391 Main Street, 23336, 336-3141, motel with views, indoor/outdoor pools, hot tub, M–E • *Assateague Inn,* 6570 Coaches Lane, 23336, 336-3738, overlooking wetlands, decks and docks on the water, I–M.

Bed-and-breakfast choices: *Cedar Gables Seaside Inn,* 6095 Hopkinds Lane, 23336, 336-1096 or (888) 491-2944, contemporary home with water views, pool, hot tub, luxury rooms with whirlpools, fireplaces, TV, E • *The Watson House,* 4240 Main Street, 23336, 336-1564 or (800) 336-6787, attractive classic Victorian, M–E, CP • *Inn at Poplar Corner,* 4248 Main Street, 23336, 336-6115 or (800) 336-6787, newly built luxury Victorian from Watson House owners, whirlpools, some water views, E, CP • *Island Manor House,* 4160 Main Street, 23336, 336-5436 or (800) 852-1505, spacious, elegantly furnished restored 1848 home, M, CP • *Miss Molly's Inn,* 4141 Main Street, 23336, 336-6686 or (800) 221-5620, cozy Victorian, M–E, CP • *Channel Bass Inn,* 6228 Church Street, 23336, 336-6148 or (800) 249-0818, same owners as Miss Molly's, some spacious rooms, tearoom open to the pubic, M–E, CP • *Year of the Horse Inn,* 3583 Main Street, 23336, 336-3221 or (800) 680-0090, casual ambience, on the water, M, CP • *Garden and the Sea Inn,* 4188 Nelson Road, New Church 23415, 824-0672, about 20 minutes away, among the best lodging and dining on Virginia's eastern shore, M–E, CP.

DINING Not surprisingly, seafood is the thing at most restaurants, and all are informal. *A.J.'s on the Creek,* 6585 Maddox Boulevard, 336-1539, pleasant atmosphere, screened porch, recommended, M–E • *Beachway,* 6455 Maddox Boulevard, 336-5590, open for all three meals, I–E • *Captain Fish's Steaming Wharf and Deck Bar,* 3865 Main Street, 336-5528, open-air deck overlooking the water, raw bar,

M–E • *Don's Seafood,* 4113 Main Street, 336-5715, old-timer serving all three meals, crab cakes are a specialty, I–M • *Garden and the Sea Inn* (see above), worth a drive, M–E • *Landmark Crabhouse,* North Main Street, Landmark Plaza, 336-5552, water views, seafood and steak, M • *Steamers,* 6251 Maddox Boulevard, 336-5478, all-you-can-eat steamed crab and shrimp specials, M • *Village Restaurant,* 6576 Maddox Boulevard, 336-5120, waterfront dining, M • *Channel Bass Tea Room,* Channel Bass Inn (see above), stop in for a civilized break, tea and scones, I.

SIGHT-SEEING *Chincoteague National Wildlife Refuge,* P.O. Box 62, Chincoteague 23336, 336-6122. Hours: May through September, 5 A.M. to 10 P.M.; April and October, 6 A.M. to 8 P.M.; November through March, 6 A.M. to 6 P.M. Seven-day pass $$ per car; no charge for walkers or bikers • *Assateague Island National Seashore—Virginia District,* same hours and fees as the refuge. Toms Cove Visitor Center, 336-6577, daily 8 A.M. to 6 P.M. in season; inquire here about guided walks and programs • *Assateague Island Wildlife Tours,* c/o Chincoteague Wildlife Refuge Visitors Center, 336-6577, check current hours and fees for tram tours and cruises • *Oyster & Maritime Museum,* 7125 Maddox Boulevard, 336-6117. Hours: Memorial Day to Labor Day, daily 10 A.M. to 5 P.M.; March 1 to late May and mid-September to November 30, weekends only. $$ • *Refuge Waterfowl Museum,* 7059 Maddox Road, 336-5800. Hours: April 1 to December, Thursday to Monday 10 A.M. to 5 P.M.; hours may vary during November and December, best to call. $$ • *NASA Visitor Center* Goddard Space Flight Center, Wallops Flight Facility, Wallops Island, Route 175, 824-1344. Hours: July 4 to Labor Day, daily 10 A.M. to 4 P.M.; rest of year, Thursday through Monday 10 A.M. to 4 P.M. Free. • **Nature cruises:** *Captain Barry's Back Bay Cruises,* 336-6508, birding and scenic cruises • *Tidewater Expeditions,* 336-3159, kayak tours • *Wildlife Expeditions,* 336-6811, more kayak options. Check all for current hours and rates.

INFORMATION *Chincoteague Island Chamber of Commerce,* P.O. Box 258, Chincoteague, VA 23336, 336-6161; www.chincoteague chamber.com.

Taking the Waters in West Virginia

Never underestimate the power of a celebrity endorsement. Even in the 1700s, a few notable investors was all it took for the world to beat a path to the waters at Berkeley Springs, West Virginia, launching America's first successful health spa.

Of course, the list of names signing up to buy property at the mineral springs was quite impressive, beginning with George Washington himself and including three signers of the Declaration of Independence, four signers of the Constitution, seven members of the Continental Congress, and five Revolutionary War generals. Small wonder that people came from as far away as Europe to try out the benefits of the baths and that Berkeley Springs became one of early America's prime resorts.

Fickle fashion moved elsewhere, and things are a bit quieter now in the mountains of West Virginia, but you can still bathe in the beneficial waters and have your tensions massaged away in the bathhouse, now part of a small state park that is on the National Register of Historic Places. As a bonus, you can enjoy another of West Virginia's most popular state parks, plus one of its most delightful resorts and spas, both located not far down the road.

The spring water that started it all comes from five main sources and many lesser ones, all within 100 yards along the base of a steep ridge rising above a narrow valley. The springs give off about 2,000 gallons of clear sparkling water per minute at the constant temperature of 74.3 degrees Fahrenheit. Long before the first white men discovered them, these warm waters were already drawing Indians all the way from Canada and the Great Lakes to the Carolinas. It was the Indians, in fact, who introduced the colonists to the springs.

George Washington was a 16-year-old accompanying another George, the teenage son of Thomas, Lord Fairfax, when in 1748 he camped here while helping to check the western boundaries of the Fairfax property, an occasion he noted in his diary. There is no proof, but a favorite legend says he relaxed for a while in the small natural stone tub at the springs, a space that never would have been adequate for his grown-up six-foot frame. What is certain is that the tub pointed out is the one that marks the main spring.

Washington helped spread the fame of the health spa. In 1776 he persuaded Lord Fairfax to give his land holdings and 50 adjacent acres to the Colony of Virginia, which at that time included what is now West Virginia, making it possible for others to enjoy the beneficial waters. The Virginia General Assembly borrowed the name of a famous resort in England and formed a town called Bath, which is still its official name. They created a board of trustees to govern the new town and began constructing bathhouses and other public buildings to take advantage of the natural springs.

When some of the nearby property went up for sale, George and his friends were first in line. The Washingtons commissioned a summer cottage here. Though there is no record of George actually living in the house, half a dozen visits by the Washington family were recorded between 1750 and 1784. In 1794, Washington and Alexander Hamilton stayed overnight in Bath on their way to quell the Whiskey Rebellion.

In Berkeley Springs State Park you can soak up the benefits of the water in two different buildings. The newer building gives a choice of a conventional bathtub or one of the Roman baths, sunken pools lined with tile and marble holding 750 gallons of water each. The more historic 1815 Roman Bath House offers private bathing chambers daily in season and on weekends the rest of the year. The museum on the second floor of the Roman Bath House has exhibits on the history and geology of the springs.

Besides the baths, the park offers various forms of physiotherapy, such as infrared heat and massage, all at state-regulated rates far below those of the average health club. And there is now an outdoor swimming pool for more athletic summer visitors. Just be sure to make your reservations well in advance, because the schedule does tend to get filled. Two weeks ahead is the earliest you can book, and it is none too soon.

The state park is in the center of the village, and right next door is the columned Country Inn. This is more hotel than inn, and bigger and busier than you might expect in a small country town, but lots of people seem to like it nevertheless. It has its own spa and fitness center. There are a few comfortable bed-and-breakfast inns in town as well.

When you emerge from the baths, the main diversions at Berkeley Springs are a few public tennis courts and antiquing. Antique centers include the Old Factory Antique Mall, between Williams and Union Streets, Heritage Trail on Washington Street, and the Berkeley Springs Antique Mall, across from the park. The Shops of Fairfax Street are smaller stores with a variety of offerings.

A former storage building in town is being turned into the Ice House Art Center, with space for galleries, concerts, and plays.

You can follow in George Washington's footsteps by driving the Washington Heritage Trail; a brochure and map available from the Berkeley Springs Visitors Center show the way. The 54-mile trail has been declared a National Scenic Byway.

Since George spent a lot of time in the area, the drive will take you to most of the prime sights, including the Panorama Overlook off Route 9. Cited by no less an authority than *National Geographic* magazine as one of America's outstanding views, the overlook takes in the Potomac and Great Cacapon valleys and the states of West Virginia, Pennsylvania, and Maryland. George often rode his horse here, no doubt enjoying the vistas.

Having admired the view, unless you plan to spend a lot of time at the baths, it's better to seek accommodations out of town that take advantage of the scenic mountain surroundings and the outdoors.

One pleasant possibility is Cacapon State Park, one of West Virginia's superb state parks that are among the true travel bargains of the world. This long, narrow preserve of 6,115 acres extends across the state's eastern panhandle almost to the Maryland border and encompasses Cacapon Mountain, whose bulk dominates the view everywhere on the broad plain below. A gravel road and hiking and bridle trails lead 1,400 feet up to the summit.

There's plenty to do here—golfing at the 18-hole Robert Trent Jones championship course, tennis, fishing, boating, swimming, sunning, horseback riding, strolling on a sandy lake beach, and hiking in the deep cool woods. The park staff also conduct guided hikes, craft workshops, and evening entertainment.

Rooms in the air-conditioned main lodge look down on the lush green golf course. The furnishings are basic motel, but you won't find a motel that touches these amenities for the price. Rustic cabins are available here as well. They go fast, and with good reason, so reserve way ahead.

The alternative to Cacapon Park is a uniquely attractive resort nearby called Coolfont, tucked in a wooded valley on 1,300 acres with two small spring-fed lakes. Lodges and alpine chalets are hidden in the trees so as not to spoil the faraway feel of the landscape, and the modernistic Treetop House Restaurant in the main lodge is at the top of a five-story main building with big, wide windows overlooking the lakefront. The restaurant is known for its emphasis on healthy, low-fat and low-calorie choices.

Classical music, art lessons, and low-key relaxation set the tone for this classy, small, health-oriented resort. Tennis, hiking, biking, boating, and swimming indoors and out are standard activities, and there are many fitness classes and wellness seminars as well as a spa with massages and other services. Special holistic spa weekend programs include tai chi and yoga, and there is a Break Free from Smoking program for those who want to kick the habit.

The yoga and the yogurt found at Coolfont are amenities that were not known in George Washington's day, but the hot tub would no doubt be right up George's alley.

Area Code: 304

DRIVING DIRECTIONS   Berkeley Springs is on Route 522 in the eastern panhandle of West Virginia. From D.C., take Route 7 west to Winchester, then Route 522 north. The approximate distance from D.C.

is 103 miles. For expressway driving, follow Route 270 north to Route 70 north to Hancock, Maryland, then take Route 522 south. Route 70 is the best route from points west and north.

PUBLIC TRANSPORTATION   Greyhound bus service to Hancock, MD, six miles from Berkeley Springs.

ACCOMMODATIONS   *The Country Inn,* 207 South Washington Street, Berkeley Springs 25411, 258-2210 or (800) 822-6630, I–M , suites, M–E • *Cacapon Lodge,* Cacapon State Park, off Route 522 south of Berkeley Springs, 25411, 258-1022, lodge, I; cabins sleeping four, I; larger cabins, M • *Coolfont Resort,* 1777 Cold Run Valley Road, off Route 9 south, Berkeley Springs 25411, 258-4500, from D.C. (800) 424-1232, E–EE, MAP.

Victorian bed-and-breakfast homes in town: *Highlawn Inn,* 304 Market Street, Berkeley Springs 25411, 258-5700, some fireplaces, whirlpools, M–E, CP • *The Manor Inn,* 415 Fairfax Street, Berkeley Springs 25411, 258-1552, M, CP • *Aaron's Acre,* 501 Johnson Mill Road, Berkeley Springs 25411, 258-4079, M, CP.

DINING   *The Country Inn* (see above), M • *Tari's Premiere Cafe,* 123 North Washington Street, Berkeley Springs, 258-1196, creative in-town cafe, I–M • *Lot 12 Public House,* 300 Warren Street, Berkeley Springs, 258-6264, upscale dining, M • *Maria's Garden,* 201 Independence Street, Berkeley Springs, 258-2021, Italian menu, I–M • *Panorama Steak House,* Route 9 West at Prospect Overlook, 258-9370, prime location and prime rib, M–E • *Cacapon Lodge* (see above), I–M • *Treetop Restaurant,* Coolfont Resort (see above), overlooking lake, M–E.

SIGHT-SEEING   *Berkeley Springs State Park,* Berkeley Springs, 258-2711 or (800) 225-5982, www.wvparks.com/berkeleysprings; warm spring baths, massages, swimming pool. Bathhouse open year-round. Hours: Daily 10 A.M. to 6 P.M. Old Roman Bath House open daily Memorial Day to Columbus Day, weekends rest of year, same hours. Reservations advised. Bath and shower, $20; bath and massage, $32. Pool open Memorial Day to Labor Day, $$. Rates may change; best to check.

INFORMATION   *Travel Berkeley Springs,* 304 Fairfax Street, Berkeley Springs, WV 25411, 258-9147 or (800) 447-8797; www.berkeleysprings.com.

Riding the Rails to Paradise

"Wait for Daddy!"

The eager six-year-old outdistancing his dad wasn't the only one who couldn't wait to climb aboard. Everyone in the station seemed excited at the prospect of hopping onto the cheerful yellow train whose steam engine was huffing and puffing in readiness for the ride from Strasburg to Paradise, Pennsylvania.

Riding the Strasburg Rail Road, the nation's oldest short-line system, is a nostalgia trip for some, a new adventure for others, and a scenic treat for all, since the route runs right through the heart of Amish farm country and affords a rare close-up view of the Plain People at work. The 45-minute round-trip train ride to Paradise is the main attraction, but it is actually only one of the railroading stops in Strasburg, a town that is paradise for anyone who is entranced with history and the romance of trains. The fine Railroad Museum of Pennsylvania, with one of the nation's most comprehensive collections of locomotives and rolling stock, the Toy Train Museum, and collectors' shops galore all are located in this railroading mecca, where you can even spend the night in a motel room that is a comfortable converted railroad caboose.

The lure of the trains brings many a camera-toting Lancaster County tourist into town, yet Strasburg has managed to withstand most of the commercialism that has hit much of Pennsylvania Dutch country. It remains a small village of great appeal whose Main Street is a historic district.

You might want to make your first stop the Railroad Museum of Pennsylvania, a comprehensive and rare collection of classic locomotives and railroad cars dating from 1831 to 1941. The new hall is reminiscent of a huge arched train shed of the late nineteenth century. Visitors can visit the old Steinman Station, enter the cab of a steam locomotive, view the stateroom of a private car and the interior of a Pullman sleeper, and actually walk under old #1187 to see what made the 62-ton locomotive go.

The museum also contains displays of old signal lanterns, bells, dishes, timetables, and paintings, providing just enough background on American railroading history to whet your appetite for boarding the train at the Strasburg Rail Road 1892 Victorian station just across the road.

This train ride has been delighting the public ever since it became a tourist operation in 1958, turning this into one of the few railroads to turn a profit on its passenger operations. Today the stock includes several steam locomotives and more than a dozen wooden coaches, all beautifully restored with green plush seats, polished wooden paneling, and oil lamps. Many passengers like to pay an extra dollar to ride on the open-sided observation car that was used in the movie *Hello, Dolly!* The parlor car Marian has a plush interior and a first-class attendant. If you like, you can have lunch or dinner in the dining car.

With a *woo-woooo* of the whistle and a clanging of the bell that absolutely delight young passengers, the train departs on its sentimental journey past immaculate white farmhouses and green fields where straw-hatted Amish farmers and their families can be seen working in the fields with mule- and horse-drawn farm equipment, much the way their fathers and grandfathers used to do it 75 to 100 years ago.

Spinning windmills, black buggies on roadways in the distance, and neat rows of sober-colored clothing flapping on the line are further evidence of the way of life among these simple people, who seem to manage just fine without such modern contrivances as clothes dryers and refrigerators, telephones and cars. The Amish do not consider modern conveniences evil in themselves, but simply temptations to a worldly life.

Nor does lack of the latest technology diminish the productivity of these lush farms. There are some 22,000 Amish currently living in Lancaster County, each with a farm averaging around 80 acres, according to our train conductor, who doubles as tour narrator. The fields outside the window are broadleaf tobacco, a lucrative crop that contributes millions annually to Pennsylvania's economy. Although farming remains the principal occupation, in recent years, many Amish have become entrepreneurs in small businesses like farm machinery, furniture making, and crafts such as quilting.

Paradise, unfortunately, has little to offer except a lumberyard and a sign warning of the end of the road. Still everyone applauds as the engine whistles past on a parallel track, on its way to be switched to the rear for the ride back to Strasburg. Many laugh as an Amtrak train roars by on an adjoining track. "You can connect here for Chicago," the good-natured narrator informs his passengers, "if you can run fast enough."

Back in the station, it's worth taking time for a quick tour of the private luxury coach owned by the president of the Reading Railroad during the heyday of train travel. It cost a whopping $100,000 back in 1916 and has separate sitting, dining, and sleeping quarters, all with cut-glass ceiling lamps, lace-curtained windows, and mahogany paneling inlaid with rosewood.

The gift shop in the station will provide you with train models, books on railroading, and caps and kerchiefs for young engineers. Collectors will find more treasures at the Strasburg Train Shop.

By now it's time for lunch, and there's no more appropriate setting than the dining car at the Red Caboose, one of the most unusual lodgings around. More than 30 old cabooses have been renovated to include one double bed at the back, four bunks up front, a bathtub and shower, and a television housed in a potbellied stove.

The Red Caboose is located just in front of the Toy Train Museum, which tends to fascinate nostalgic parents as much as the kids. The museum, which serves as national headquarters of the Train Collectors Association, houses antique toy trains that offer a miniature look at transportation progress over the years, plus a bundle of memories of holidays spent putting up toy train tracks around the Christmas tree. Five lavish working layouts include standard gauge, Lionel, and "0" gauge trains, with miniature trees, stations, homes, and churches making up realistic town settings.

Save a bit of energy for a stroll around Strasburg, which still has the look of an early Lancaster County village. It was settled in the early 1730s by a group of Swiss Mennonites who named their new home in honor of the cathedral city of Alsace. The present Main Street began as part of the Great Conestoga Road, the first westward trail from Philadelphia.

A dozen of the 29 oldest brick structures, dating back to the eighteenth and early nineteenth centuries, can be seen, including four of the oldest stone houses. And there are at least two dozen log houses still standing in the area along East and West Main and Miller and South Decatur Streets, which has been proclaimed a National Historic District. The oldest of these is the Christopher Spech House, circa 1764. If you want to know more about the homes, pick up a printed "strolling tour" from the Strasburg Heritage Society headquarters at 122 South Decatur Street.

During your walk, you'll surely want to take a break at the Strasburg Country Store and Creamery on the corner of Centre Square, restored in 1984 as an old-fashioned emporium with a potbellied stove, a player piano, and an 1890 soda fountain. Ice cream here is so rich, it reminds you why the dish was named "cream" in the first place, and the scoops are served up in big melt-in-your-mouth homemade sugar cones.

On the way out the door, you may well spy an Amish buggy sharing a red light with a group of cyclists or pulling up to the drive-in bank, the kind of contrast that makes Strasburg such a special place.

Adjoining the Creamery is the Strasburg Village Inn, the 1787 Thomas Crawford Tavern turned into an 11-room bed-and-breakfast with Colonial-style reproduction furnishings. Even more authentically restored is the Limestone Inn, a 1786 stone house that is one of the historic homes on Main Street. Also on Main is the Iron Horse Inn, a rustic restaurant that serves up good food amid railroad memorabilia.

If there's no room at the inns, Historic Strasburg Inn is a larger complex on Route 896 just outside town. It is neither historic nor a country inn, but it is a very pleasant motel complex, situated on expansive grounds that adjoin scenic farmlands, and it provides a pool and TV in the rooms to keep kids happy.

You might also consider staying at one of the nearby Mennonite farms, which could be an interesting experience for city children—or adults, for that matter. Lists of farm lodgings are available from the Mennonite Information Center or the Pennsylvania Dutch Visitors Bureau.

You may want to schedule some of the sights of Strasburg for Sunday in order to leave time on Saturday to visit one of the famous Amish farmers markets offering bountiful fresh produce, home-baked goodies (including that sticky molasses confection known as shoofly pie), all kinds of relishes, and delicious homemade apple butter. The Central Market at Penn Square in Lancaster is the biggest. Saturday markets also can be found on Route 340 in Bird-in-Hand, and farther north on Route 772 in Leola. Plan to get there early for the pick of the crop.

You can see the beautiful farmlands that mark this part of the world by driving on any of the side roads between Routes 30 and 340, or off Routed 741, 896, and 23. You'll recognize the Amish homesteads by their windmills and the absence of electric wires. Note also the distinctive additions on some of the farms. Known as "Gross Dawdis," they are an Amish solution to the generation gap. When a farmer reaches retirement age, an annex to the main house is built, allowing him to enjoy the fruits of his labor and be part of the family without getting in the way of the younger generation. Sometimes you'll see double additions, marking a three-generation home. Along the way are many one-room schools attended by Amish children through grade eight; these are a particularly winning sight when the children are outside playing ball.

The Amish worship in their own homes, but you'll pass many Mennonite meetinghouses with a covered shed providing parking for worshipers arriving in horse-drawn buggies.

If you want a guided back-roads tour, the Mennonite Information Center provides guides who will accompany you in your own car for a reasonable hourly rate.

Many frame houses along the back roads have roadside stands selling produce or homemade jams or baked goods, and you'll also see a lot of signs advertising quilts. Visiting the quilt makers can be a fascinating experience. Some women have only their own work for sale, but an entrepreneur like Emma Witmer on Route 23 in New Holland stocks more than 100 quilts in her upstairs bedrooms, all hand-stitched at home by Amish and Mennonite women. The quality varies with the intricacy of the stitching and the fineness of the colors, and so does the price.

Lovina's Stitchery is another unique stop south of Strasburg on May Post Office Road (drive south on Decatur Street, which becomes May Post Office Road). This is a small shop in a building that looks like a barn with a skylight, filled with high-quality quilts made by Amish crafters in both contemporary and traditional dark Amish patterns. You'll understand the skylight when you realize that the Amish owner observes tradition by allowing no electric lights in the shop.

Antique Amish quilts in bold dark colors have become serious collectors' items and go for many thousands of dollars. Some fine examples are displayed at the Quilt Museum in Intercourse. It is part of a complex of shops clustered around the People's Place, a center for Amish and Mennonite arts and crafts in Intercourse. There are films here on the Amish (for a fee), a courtyard gallery with free art exhibits, and a well-stocked book-and-craft shop. The associated shops across the road include the Old Country Store, with many excellent crafts and quilts, and Village Pottery, both featuring work by Mennonite artisans. Crafts of the World next door offers handcrafts from around the world, with sales benefiting artisans in Third World countries.

On Route 340 between Bird-in-Hand and Intercourse are Peace Valley Furniture and Leacock Furniture, two of several shops in Lancaster County selling country-style furniture hand-made by Amish artisans. Bird-in-Hand offers another choice lodging, Greystone Manor Bed & Breakfast, a Victorian mansion with handsome period furnishings.

Many Amish shops close on Sunday, so if shopping is in your plans, do it on Saturday.

Though most of the many Amish commercial attractions that abound in the area are more hokum than historic, you might want to visit the Amish Farm and House for the chance to see how a traditional Amish house looks inside.

If you are looking for more worldly diversions, the outlet malls on Route 30 east of Lancaster grow bigger by the year. The Strasburg Antique Market features more than 40 dealers in a restored nineteenth-century brick warehouse, about a quarter mile east of the railroad. On Sunday, antiquers may want to drive to Adamstown on Route 272 between Lancaster and Reading for the big weekly Stoudtburg Antique Mall, which draws some 500 dealers.

One final strong recommendation for families is a visit to the Landis Valley Museum, a state-operated complex that presents all facets of Pennsylvania's rural heritage in a village of old buildings representing 150 years of architectural styles. The structures are filled with more than 100,000 objects and tools, and there are demonstrations to bring the traditional crafts and skills to life.

Like riding the rails, it's a look at life the way it used to be and still is for some in this picturesque corner of America.

Area Code: 717

DRIVING DIRECTIONS Strasburg is at the intersection of routes 896 and 741, south of Lancaster. From D.C., take I-95 north to the Baltimore Beltway, I-695. Head northwest toward Towson and take exit 24, I-83 north to York, Pennsylvania, then Route 30 east through Lancaster, turning right on Route 896 to Strasburg. The approximate distance from D.C. is 116 miles.

ACCOMMODATIONS *Red Caboose Motel,* Route 741, Paradise Lane, Strasburg 17579, 687-5000, I–M • *Historic Strasburg Inn,* Route 896, Strasburg 17579, 687-7691, children under 16 free in parents' room, pool, M–E • *Strasburg Village Inn,* 1 West Main Street, Strasburg 17579, 687-0900, M–E, CP • *Limestone Inn,* 33 East Main Street, Strasburg, 687-8392 or (800) 278-8392, M, CP • *Greystone Manor,* 2658 Old Philadelphia Pike (Route 340), Bird-in-Hand 17505, five minutes from Strasburg via Route 896, 393-4233, 1833 mansion with fine Victorian furnishings, carriage house rooms with country decor, M, CP • *The King's Cottage,* 1049 East King Street, Lancaster 17602, ten minutes from Strasburg, 397-1017 or (800) 747-8717, gracious B-and-B, M–E, CP • *Gardens of Eden,* 1894 Eden Road, Lancaster 17601, 393-5179, ten minutes from Strasburg, a charmer amid wildflower gardens, M, CP. For information on farm lodgings, contact Mennonite Information Center, 2209 Millstream Road, Lancaster 17602, 299-0954 or the Pennsylvania Dutch Visitors Bureau, listed below.

DINING *Iron Horse Inn,* 135 East Main Street, Strasburg, 687-6362, rustic, railroad memorabilia, basic menu, I–M • *Red Caboose* (see above), dinner in the diner, Victorian dining coach with soundtrack and simulated motion, modest fare but great for kids, I–M • *Log Cabin,* 11 Lehoy Forest Drive, Leola, 626-1181, tops for decor and food, E • *Washington House,* Historic Strasburg Inn (see above), standard fare in large but pleasant dining room, E • *The Pressroom,* 26–28 West King Street, Lancaster, 399-5400, open kitchen, upscale casual, burgers to full dinners, I–E • *Olde Greenfield Inn,* 595 Greenfield Road, off Route 30, outside Lancaster, 393-0668, fine dining in restored farmhouse, but family-friendly, M–E • *Groff's Farm,* 650 Pinkerton Road, Mount Joy, 653-2048, out of the way but worth it for delicious Pennsylvania Dutch fare in a 1756 farmhouse (Chicken Stoltzfus here is famous), M–E • *Catacombs,* 102 North Market Street, Mount Joy, 653-2056, another Mount Joy winner, continental menu in the aging vaults of a former brewery 42 feet belowground, M–EE • **Haydn Zug's,** 1987 State Street, East Petersburg, 569-5746, Colonial decor, fine dining, family-owned, recommended locally, M–EE • To sample Pennsylvania Dutch specialties, commercial but bountiful, try *Stoltzfus Farm Restaurant,* 3718 East Newport Road, Intercourse, 768-8156; *Good and Plenty,* Route 896, Smoketown, 394-7111, M, *Plain 'n Fancy Farm and Dining Room,* 3121 Old Philadelphia Pike, Bird-in-Hand, PA 17506, 768-4400, all M, or the noncommercial bountiful spread at **Sunny Crest,** 2587 Valley View Road, Morgantown, (670) 286-5000, I.

SIGHT-SEEING *Strasburg Rail Road,* Route 741 East, Strasburg, 687-7522. Hours: daily mid-April to October, December 26-31; weekends February to early April, late October to mid-December, Check current schedules. Closed January. $$$$ • *National Toy Train Museum,* Paradise Lane off Route 741 East, Strasburg, 687-8976. Hours: May to October and December 26–31, daily 10 A.M. to 5 P.M.; weekends only April, November. $$ • *Railroad Museum of Pennsylvania,* Route 741 East, Strasburg, 687-8628. Hours: April to October, Monday to Saturday 9 A.M. to 5 P.M., Sunday noon to 5 P.M.; closed Mondays November to April. $$$ • *Landis Valley Museum,* 2451 Kissel Hill Road, off Route 272, Landis Valley, 569-0401. Hours: March to December, Monday to Saturday 9 A.M. to 5 P.M., Sunday noon to 5 P.M. $$$; November, December, March, $$ • *Amish Farm and House,* 2395 Route 30, east of Lancaster, 394-6185. Hours: June through August, daily 8:30 A.M. to 6 P.M.; April, May, September, October to 5 P.M.; rest of year to 4 P.M. $$$.

INFORMATION *Pennsylvania Dutch Visitors Bureau,* 501 Greenfield Road, Lancaster, PA 17601, 299-8901, free maps, guides, introductory film on the area. To receive visitors guide by mail, phone (800) PADUTCH; www. padutchcountry.com.

Sights and Sails on the Northern Neck

Surrounded by water, steeped in history, and serene as a perfect summer day, Virginia's Northern Neck is an escape to tranquility.

The twentieth century seems light-years away from the tip of this narrow picturesque peninsula bounded by the Potomac and Rappahannock Rivers and Chesapeake Bay. Life here is a blend of country living and saltwater tang, with fragments of the past still present on every byway. Places like Christ Church near Irvington, built in 1732, the year George Washington was born, are well worth seeing and are on a scale small enough not to tax the energy level on a hot summer day.

If you have the time and energy, there is plenty more to see and do nearby. Yorktown is only 35 minutes away, and it is less than an hour to all the sights of Williamsburg. Or you can literally sail away to the past on a boat from Reedville bound for Tangier or Smith Islands, fishermen's enclaves so remote from the rest of the world that some residents still speak with an Elizabethan accent.

Or you can be easily tempted to forget about history and just head for the water that beckons everywhere, settling into a resort and spending your time doing absolutely nothing but having fun in the sun.

One compromise plan might be to devote Saturday to relaxing and leave some of Sunday for sight-seeing. Another is to mark this down for a long weekend, with time for all the many pleasures the area holds.

The ideal place to sample resort life, Northern Neck style, is the Tides Inn in Irvington, one of Virginia's landmarks. Lots of people who can afford the tab happily spend a whole vacation at the Tides with never a thought of leaving at all. This gracious and handsome family-run resort is now into its fifth decade. Surrounded by water, water everywhere, its special claim to fame is a fleet of yachts that regularly take guests out on the Rappahannock and the bay, and up Carter's Creek for luncheon picnics or to watch the sunset over the bay with cocktail in hand. Besides the boats, the Tides offers 45 holes of golf, including the legendary Golden Eagle, as well as tennis, sailing, paddle boats, and a giant saltwater pool overlooking the water. This is a gracious, old-fashioned, genteel inn, enjoyable for young and old alike.

Golfers and families can also opt for the less formal, more modern Tides Lodge on the other side of Carters Creek. Guests have access to two and a half golf courses, three pools, six restaurants, and seven tennis courts. Water taxis and vans make it easy to enjoy both complexes.

Windmill Point is a much smaller, low-key resort with motel-variety rooms. However, the location, where the Rappahannock meets the bay, is ideal. The resort has its own pool, marina, and small beach and shares the golf course and tennis facilities of an adjoining condominium complex. The dining room offers water views.

If you prefer inn ambience, there are a growing number of appealing bed-and-breakfast inns in and around Irvington and near the ferry piers in Reedville. You won't be completely without recreation. The very pleasant Inn at Levelfields, an antebellum manor house with lovely Colonial decor, offers an important summer bonus—its own swimming pool—and there are public golf courses and tennis courts around Irvington. Belle Island State Park offers bike rentals, hiking, picnicking, and guided canoe trips on the Rappahannock. The Northern Neck is rich in bird life, from great blue herons to ruby-throated hummingbirds, and canoers often see bald eagles soaring overhead.

It will take only a little while to fit in a visit to the area's prime attraction, historic Christ Church, widely considered to be Virginia's finest example of Colonial church architecture.

Robert "King" Carter, who funded the church's construction, played a major role in state and American history as patriarch of one of Virginia's most important families. His descendants numbered eight governors of Virginia, three signers of the Declaration of Independence, two U.S. presidents, and General Robert E. Lee. Carter's generosity in replacing an earlier wooden church here stemmed partly from his desire to retain the church on the site of his parents' grave, which remains there today. The tombs of the benefactor and two of his wives are outside the church, Carter's being among the largest and most ornate of his day.

The church itself is in the form of a Latin cross, with three-foot-thick walls made of brick fired in the Carter kilns. Exterior bricks are alternated lengthwise and endwise in the Flemish bond pattern that was popular in Colonial America. The rare original three-decker walnut pulpit still stands, the original marble baptismal font remains, and the 25 pews are the only original high-backed pews left in Virginia. A reception center on the grounds offers a small museum and a narrated slide show about the church.

There are other rewarding excursions nearby. One will take you to Lancaster Green, which is surrounded by an original 1797 clerk's office, an 1819 jail, and an 1863 courthouse. The Mary Ball Washington Museum and Library on the green honors George Washington's mother, who was born in Lancaster County, and Washington family memorabilia is displayed. Epping Forest, site of the 1690 home where Mary Ball was born, is on Route 3 near Lively, but it is not open to the public. And on Route 622 you'll find St. Mary's White Chapel, the 1669 church where young Mary Ball worshiped; many of the tombstones in the churchyard bear her family name.

Reedville's Fishermen's Museum, ensconced in the town's oldest house, has displays and artifacts of the local menhaden fishing industry, the largest producer of fish oils in the United States. Reedville is also a popular departure point for charter fishing boats and for the ferries to Tangier and Smith Islands.

You'll have to allow a full day for the boat trip to either island. Choose Tangier and you'll be in the place that is called "the soft-shell crab capital of the world." Ninety-five percent of the nation's soft-shell crabs come from here, and you'll see them swimming in long tanks at the docks, where they are kept until they have shed their shells and are ready to market.

If you think of this trip as a visit to the quaint past, you will be disappointed. The crab farms on pilings at the harbor, the fishing boats and shanties along the shore, and the narrow, carless lanes of the island are picturesque, but there is nothing quaint or cute about Tangier. The homes are modest and plain, the yards surrounded by plain chain-link fences, and the putt-putt of motorbikes is heard everywhere.

The appeal of the island is the look it affords at a way of life little changed for centuries. Unfortunately, it is a lifestyle hardly seen by the crowds who file off the boat, get in line for the big family-style noonday meal at Hilda Crockett's, and see nothing beyond the tour conducted by island ladies via golf cart, dodging teenagers careening about on bikes as they go.

To get the feel of the place you have to walk away from the crowds, maybe forgo the quantity of food at Crockett's for the fresh quality at one of the little hole-in-the-wall cafes or, better yet, picnic by the water after stopping at one of the homes whose signs offer crab cakes and fresh bread for sale.

Then stroll away from the one and only main road to the eerie beauty of the marshes or to the life along the side lanes, narrow, unpaved paths without road signs or house numbers, where groups of youngsters call to each other in accents from another age.

Tangier was discovered and named by Captain John Smith back in 1608, but it remained the hunting and fishing grounds of the Pocomoke Indians until 1666. History has lost the first name of the Mr. West who bought the island from the Indians that year for two overcoats. West, in turn, sold to John Crockett, who in 1686 moved here from Cornwall with his family. Almost all of today's 900 residents are descendants of Crockett, whose four sons and daughters married mainlanders and proceeded to bring them back to populate Tangier, where they lived off the rich oyster and crab grounds surrounding the island. They added the names Parks, Thomas, and Pruitt, which account for most of the families today. Long isolated from the rest of the world, the people on Tangier still retain accents similar to the Cornish that John Crockett spoke all those years ago but that is now punctuated with local slang.

Tangier's present residents are fishermen, crabbers, and oystermen, like all the generations who came before them, and they still work hard wresting a living from the sea, rising at dawn and boarding their wooden boats to defy the elements. Although some things are changing on Tangier, what with the advent of motorbikes and cable TV, some other things have not changed at all. There is still no doctor on the island, and residents continue to bury their dead in their own gardens in raised concrete boxes to keep water from seeping in at high tide. And as yet, there is no crime on Tangier, no need to lock the door by day or night.

The lifeblood of the island, the livelihood that binds everyone together, and the ever-present dependence on the weather and the sea also have not altered with the centuries. Understanding the power of nature has made these islanders churchgoing and God-fearing people who worship as well as work together. Rustic, hardworking, honest Tangier shows us an interdependence among neighbors and a sense of caring and community that our mechanized modern world can rarely match.

Area Code: 804

DRIVING DIRECTIONS   Irvington is on Route 3, near the tip of Virginia's Northern Neck. From D.C., take I-95 south to Route 3 east. The approximate distance from D.C. is 135 miles.

ACCOMMODATIONS   *The Tides Inn,* Irvington 22480, 438-5000 or (800) 552-2461 in Virginia, (800) 843-3746 out of state, E–EE; MAP available • *Windmill Point Resort,* Windmill Point 22578, 435-

1166, M • *The Inn at Levelfields,* P.O. Box 216, Lancaster 22503, 435-6887, M–E, CP • *Hope and Glory Inn,* P.O. Box 425, 634 King Carter Drive, Irvington 22480, 438-6053 or (800) 497-8228, restored 1890s schoolhouse, grand lobby, whimsical decor, folk art, M–E, CP • *Cedar Grove,* Route 1, Box 2535, Reedville 22539, 453-3915, attractive bed-and-breakfast home overlooking the bay, M, CP • *Bailey-Cockrell House,* 793 Main Street, Reedville 22539, 453-5900, pretty Victorian on the waterfront, antiques, M, CP • *The Gables,* 659 Main Street, Reedville 22539, 453-5209, sea captain's mansion on Cockrell Creek, on National Register, M, CP.

DINING   *The Tides Inn* (see above), E–EE • *Windmill Point Resort* (see above), I–M • *Lancaster Tavern,* Route 3, Lancaster, 462-5941, Southern menus in a historic home, an all-you-can-eat, family-style bargain, lunch and dinner, I–M • *de Medici,* 51 School Street, Kilmarnock, 435-4006, fine northern Italian, one of the area's more elegant choices, M • *The Crab Shack at Rappahannock Seafood,* Route 672, Kilmarnock, 435-1605, cheerful decor, water views, the freshest seafood, good for lunch or dinner, I–M.

SIGHT-SEEING   *Historic Christ Church,* off State Road 200, Irvington, 438-6855. Hours: Guided tours from reception center, April to November, Monday to Saturday 10 A.M. to 4 P.M., Sunday 2 P.M. to 5 P.M. Donation • *Mary Ball Washington Museum and Library,* Route 3, Lancaster, 462-7280. Hours: Thursday to Saturday 10 A.M. to 4 P.M. Donation • *Reedville Fishermen's Museum,* Main Street, Reedville, 453-6529. Hours: May through October, daily 10:30 A.M. to 4:30 P.M.; November to late December, Friday through Monday; March, April, Saturday-Sunday. Closed January, February. $ • *Belle Isle State Park,* Route 354, Lancaster County, 462-5030. Hours: Daylight hours, year-round. **Cruises:** Cruises leave from Reedville May to mid-October. Reservations requires. Phone for current schedules and rates. *Tangier Island Cruises,* 453-2628 • *Smith Island Cruises,* 453-3430.

INFORMATION   *Northern Neck Travel Council,* 479 Main Street, P.O. Box 1707, Warsaw, VA 22572, 333-1919 or (800) 393-6180; www.northernneck.com.

Landlubbing on the Eastern Shore

The Bay Bridge spanning Chesapeake Bay to Maryland's Eastern Shore is a four-and-a-half-mile crossing to another world. Ignore the buildup on the main highway. When you get to Talbot County, you've found a landscape of shady villages whose homes date back 200 years, to open fields where corn and potatoes grow—and to 600 miles of bay and river waterfront filled with boats of every size and shape and purpose. Many of the boats belong to fishermen, for this is a seafood lover's paradise, where even gas stations post signs in summer proclaiming "Crabs for Sale."

In Colonial times, a planter aristocracy grew rich here growing tobacco, while those who had no land became hardworking watermen, living off the bay's bounty of oysters, clams, and crabs. The dichotomy between the two lifestyles can still be seen three centuries later, especially in Talbot County, often referred to as the "Colonial capital" of the Eastern Shore.

Talbot, with its working fishing fleet, waterfront estates, picturesque homes and harbors, and posh shops, is a microcosm of the Chesapeake mix, which is possibly why it has attracted so many of the wealthy city folks who enjoy escaping here. They say that 200 bona fide millionaires live along the rivers and inlets of the county, people with names like Houghton, Chrysler, and du Pont, many of them ensconced in some of the 100 or more remaining eighteenth-century manor houses.

Their presence, along with the shops and restaurants serving growing numbers of sailors and tourists, adds a new dimension—including the growing number of nonscenic discount outlets and fast-food stops on the highway. But they haven't spoiled the original flavor that makes a visit to the Eastern Shore unique. So settle into one of Talbot County's choice inns, get out the map, and prepare to sample the varied pleasures of the Chesapeake. Several lodgings let you stay directly on the water, including one of those historic waterfront estates, Combsberry, where you can experience the good life firsthand.

St. Michaels, bordering the broad Miles River, is a good bet for other lodgings, as well as a good starting point for a landlubber's tour. Once a shipbuilding center for bugeyes and Baltimore clippers, the handsome harbor is now a popular port of call for weekenders, as well as home to the Chesapeake Bay Maritime Museum.

This fine museum, where James Michener did much of the research for his book *Chesapeake,* is a place to get a real feel for the role the water has played in Chesapeake history. You'll see the largest floating fleet of historic bay boats in existence—the skipjacks and bugeyes and log canoes of days gone by. One highly visible exhibit is the Hooper Strait Lighthouse, one of the last three remaining Chesapeake cottage-type lighthouses on stilts, where you can climb up for the view, examine the magnifying lenses that sent the light miles out to sea, see the lighthouse keeper's potbellied stove and iron bed, and even read a bit of his diary.

Other exhibits include the Point Lookout Bell Tower, a one-ton fog bell once found at the mouth of the Potomac; a waterfowl building featuring decoys; a boatbuilding shop; a building with exhibits tracing the history of the bay; and maritime displays of all kinds, including ships' bells, ship models, marine paintings, and black-and-white photos.

If you want to venture out to sea, board the 65-foot cruise boat *Patriot,* berthed at the museum, for an hour and a half, 11-mile cruise on the Miles. It's a good way to see watermen working crab-laden trotlines, as well as some of the hidden mansions along the water. You can also rent your own sailboat or pedal boat at the Town Dock Marina and other marinas around the harbor.

Pick up a copy of the St. Michaels walking tour either at the Maritime Museum or at one of the local shops to see some of the landmarks of the town, the oldest in Talbot County. People here still like to tell about how the British were outwitted during the Revolutionary War when the lights in town were blacked out and lanterns were posted in the fields to misdirect the cannon fire. Most of the oldest sites are clustered between Talbot Street and the water. Among them is St. Mary's Square, where you can tour the St. Mary's Museum, a restored and furnished Colonial home, and see other historic homes and churches dating from the late seventeenth to early nineteenth centuries.

You'll need no guide to the shops on Talbot Street or to the seafood restaurants along the mast-filled harbor. Busiest is the Crab Claw, where they serve up 100 bushels of steamed crabs on a busy summer day. Among the shops, Flamingo Flats will interest cooks for its enormous stock of hot sauces, barbecue, Cajun, Caribbean—you name it. Stop in at the Chesapeake Trading Company for a cup of coffee or fresh-squeezed lemonade and look over the excellent stock of books, specializing in cooking, sailing, and travel in the Chesapeake area.

A ten-mile drive straight out Route 33 and across the Knapps Narrows drawbridge to Tilghman's Island makes for a complete change of scene. Off the highway and down winding lanes on the way are some delightful inns.

Tilghman is the no-frills home port to the last working skipjack fleet, as well as to scores of sport fishermen. The skipjacks are broad-beamed sailboats used for dredging oysters. The sails remain because state conservation law forbids oystering in power boats for fear they might take up too many of the shellfish, depleting the next year's crop. If you wander down to Dogwood Harbor in summer, you'll likely see the fishermen there repairing their craft in preparation for the colder months ahead.

Even better, you can sign on for a sail on the *Rebecca T. Ruark,* the oldest working skipjack on the bay, and learn about the island and the oysterman's life from Captain Wade Murphy, who has been at this most of his life. You'll not only learn how a skipjack does its job, but see it in action, as Captain Murphy dredges up, cleans, and serves the freshest oysters you may ever taste.

This is one of several ways to get out on the water from Tilghman. *The Lady Patty,* a beautifully restored 1935 Chesapeake sailing yacht goes out daily, the *H.M. Krentz* is another chance for a skipjack sail, and Island Kayak conducts guided kayak ecotours and "sunset paddles."

Harrison's Chesapeake House on Tilghman is the center for fishing charters and for family-style seafood dinners with a water view. Tilghman also has a trio of very appealing inns on the water.

As you leave Tilghman, you'll see a sign on the highway for decoys, leading to the Mission Road workshop of carver Dan Vaughn. The setting is island funky, but the decoys are works of art.

The next stop on a Talbot tour is Oxford. Take the road back past St. Michaels and watch for the turnoff to the south leading to the scenic countryside through Royal Oak to Bellevue. And keep your eye out for a bit of antiquing along the way.

In Bellevue, you can board the Oxford-Bellevue Ferry, America's oldest operating ferryboat. History has it that it was started up in 1683, the first keeper subsidized by the Talbot County Court to the tune of 2,500 pounds of tobacco annually. Now the little ferry takes just six cars at a time across the water to the serene, shady, brick-paved lanes of Oxford, a town of old homes, white picket fences, and enormous charm.

It is a surprise to learn that this tiny village of 850 people was once Maryland's largest port. Now it is a sailor's and stroller's delight. The harbor is a glorious sight in August, when as many as 300 sailboats, colorful spinnakers unfurled, sail out in the annual Oxford Regatta.

Just opposite the harbor is one of Talbot County's most appealing larger lodgings, the Robert Morris Inn, built about 1710 by the father of Robert Morris Jr., the man who was known as the "financier of the American Revolution." The dining room here is renowned. You'll also find no more delightful spot for a steamed crab feast than the outside deck of the Pier Street restaurant, overlooking the Tred-Avon River in Oxford.

As for seeing Oxford sights, all it takes is a stroll along those herringbone brick lanes. The Custom House on the water is a replica of the original, but the home called Byeberry, facing the town creek, has been standing since 1695; Jena, the white clapboard house off Oxford Road, dates from 1700; and nearby Plimhimmon is flanked by stately Osage orange and ginkgo trees and a willow oak estimated to be 350 years old. Stop at the little local museum if you want some accurate town history.

Oxford and Easton are 12 miles and many light-years apart. Compared with Oxford, this county seat (population 9,400) seems positively citified, its gift shops and shopping centers bearing witness to the influence of the newcomers who have come to Talbot County.

However, Easton has managed to retain some of its history. You'll get a delightful lesson at the historical society complex on South Washington, an 1810 Federal town house and a 1700s Quaker cabinetmaker's cottage flanking a lovely English garden. The society conducts town walking tours, or you can pick up a map at the museum or at local shops and do your own thing in the historic district along Washington, Harrison, and intersecting streets, such as Goldsborough, Dover, and West. Two principal sights are the 1791 Talbot County Court House and the 1682 Third Haven Meeting House, said to be the nation's oldest frame building devoted to religious worship.

At the corner of Dover and Harrison you'll find the Tidewater Inn, the stately pride of the Eastern Shore, and headquarters for the wonderful Waterfowl Festival held in Easton each November (see page 208). There are also many handsome homes in town.

Easton has an active arts community, with changing art exhibits at the Academy Arts Museum, housed in two nineteenth-century structures, and music, drama, and other entertainment at the nicely restored Avalon Theater, an art deco theater dating to 1921. Antiquers will also be happy here, with more than a dozen shops to choose from.

The word *Chesapeake* means "great shellfish bay," and as you'll discover, feasting on seafood, which means mainly crab in summer, is one of the greatest pleasures here in every town, whether you hammer away at Old Bay–spiced steamed crabs served on newspapers or sit down to a Crab Imperial dinner.

One final nonculinary recommendation: On the way to or from a Chesapeake weekend, detour for the bit of history at Wye Oak. The Wye Oak, Maryland's state tree, is 400 years old and, with a circumference of 37 feet, the largest white oak in the country. It is carefully tended by the state on a protected site by the road, where tourists pause to gaze and take snapshots, turning their cameras this way and that, trying to fit the enormous tree into their picture.

Just beyond is the Old Wye Church, a 1721 jewel whose restoration was financed by Arthur Houghton, a Steuben Glass executive who is a member of the vestry and one of those Talbot County millionaires. The actual work was done by the same architects responsible for Williamsburg's Bruton Parish. The arrangement of the window-high pews is authenticated from a drawing in the vestry records dating back to 1723. The patterned green brocade box pews, the arched windows, and the bargello chair seats and petit-point kneeling cushions at the altar rail, the handiwork of local women, are lovely to see and worth the detour.

For a souvenir of your visit, go down to the Old Wye Grist Mill on the river, where they've been grinding grain since 1680, and pick up flour for some baking of your own. They'll gladly supply the recipes.

Area Code: 410

DRIVING DIRECTIONS Easton is on Route 50, about 26 miles south of the Chesapeake Bay Bridge. From D.C., take Route 301/50 across the bridge, then follow Route 50 south to Easton. The approximate distance from D.C. is 73 miles. A bypass off Route 50 leads to Route 33 west to St. Michaels, and Route 333 heads west to Oxford; each is about 12 miles from Easton.

ACCOMMODATIONS St. Michaels: In town: *Bob Pascal's St. Michaels Harbour Inn and Marina,* 101 North Harbor Road, 21663, 745-9001, prime location, 46 newly renovated rooms and suites, many with balconies directly on the harbor, some Jacuzzis, E–EE • *Victoriana Inn,* 205 Cherry Street, 21663, 745-3368, delightful lawn with a harbor view, , E–EE, CP • *Two Swan Inn,* 208 Carpenter Street, 21663, 745-2929, 1720 home on the water, M, CP • *The Parsonage Inn,* 210 North Talbot Street, 21663, 745-5519 or (800) 394-5519, attractive 1883 brick home, outside deck, M–E, CP • *Hambleton Inn,* 202 Cherry Street, 21663, 745-3350, pleasant bed-and-breakfast near the harbor, nice porches, but lacks a central living room, E–EE • *Five Gables Inn and Spa,* 202 North Talbot Street, 21663, 745-0100 or (877) 466-0100, two newly restored 1800s buildings across from each other on the main street, excellent spa services, E–EE, CP • *Rigby Valliant House,* 123 West Chestnut Street, 21663, 745-3977, modest home, quiet street, reasonable rates, M, CP • *Kemp House Inn,* 412 Talbot Street, P.O. Box 638, 21663, 745-2243, small, cozy, M, CP • *Old Brick Inn,* 401 South Talbot Street, 21663, 745-3323, 12 rooms in restored 1816 inn and newly built carriage house, eclectic decor, some fireplaces, patio with small pool, M–EE

Outside town, on the water: *Inn at Perry Cabin,* 308 Watkins Lane, 21663, 745-2200, 40+ lavish rooms in Laura Ashley decor, the most elegant inn in the area, EE, CP • *Bay Cottage,* 24640 Yacht Club Road, 21663, 745-9369 or (888) 558-8008, cozy early 1900s home on the water, many Oriental antiques, pool, E, CP; private cottage, EE, CP • *Inn at Christmas Farm,* 8873 Tilghman Island Road, Wittman 21676, 745-5312 or (800) 987-8436, charming suites in the farmhouse and in an 1893 chapel moved to the property, swimming pond, barnyard with horses, sheep, peacocks, E, CP • *Wades Point Inn,* P.O. Box 7, St. Michaels 21663, 745-2500 or (888) 923-3466, airy bed-and-breakfast home five miles outside town with perfect spot on the water, M–EE, CP.

Tilghman Island: *Lazyjack Inn,* 5907 Tilghman Island Road, 21671, 886-2215 or (800) 690-5080, breezy, pretty, appealing 160-year-old island home overlooking the harbor; beams, quilts, and some Jacuzzis,

E–EE, CP • *Tilghman Island Inn,* Coopertown Road, Knapps Narrows 21671, 886-2141 or (800) 866-2141, modern building with marsh views, recently renovated, water views, some whirlpools, pool, tennis court, M–E.

Oxford: *Robert Morris Inn,* 314 North Morris Street, P.O. Box 70, Oxford 21654, 226-5111, historic charmer, great range in room size and amenities, many rooms in Sandaway building have waterfront porches, M–EE • *Combsberry,* 4837 Evergreen Road, Oxford 21654, 226-3533, restored eighteenth-century country manor on the banks of Island Creek, formal gardens, elegant decor, EE, CP • *1876 House,* 110 North Morris Street, Oxford 21654, 226-5496, nineteenth-century bed-and-breakfast home on Oxford's lovely main street, M, CP.

Easton: *The Inn at Easton,* 28 South Harrison Street, 21601, 822-4910 or (888) 800-8091, M–E, CP; suites, E–EE, CP • *Tidewater Inn,* 101 East Dover at Harrison Street, Easton 21601, 822-1300 or (800) 237-8775, in-town inn, elegant, M–E • Also see pages 211-212.

DINING **St. Michaels:** *Bistro St. Michaels,* 403 South Talbot, St. Michaels, 745-9111, intimate French bistro, highly recommended, E • *208 Talbot,* at that address, St. Michaels, 745-3838, fine dining in an 1800s home, E–EE • *Ashley Room,* Inn at Perry Cabin, St. Michaels (see above), total elegance, prix fixe, EE • *Harbour Lights,* St. Michaels Harbour Inn and Marina (see above), wonderful water views, E • *Town Dock,* 125 Mulberry Street, St. Michaels, 745-5577, known for its talented chef/owner, crab cakes, and friendly service, music on weekends, M–E • **Tilghman Island:** *Harrison's Chesapeake House,* P.O. Box B, Coopertown Road, Tilghman, 886-2121, longtime no-frills standby for seafood, M • *Tilghman Island Inn* (see above), seafood with a New Orleans accent, can be excellent but erratic, M–EE • **Oxford:** *Robert Morris Inn,* Oxford (see above), wonderful ambience, great crab cakes, M–EE • *Latitude 38,* 26342 Oxford Road, Oxford, 226-5303, a local favorite, creative menu in an offbeat location behind a gas station, E • **For crab lovers:** *Crab Claw,* Navy Point, St. Michaels, 745-2900, busiest place in town, I–M • *Pier Street,* Pier Street Marina, Oxford, 226-5171, outdoor deck, water views, I–M • For Easton, see page 212.

SIGHT-SEEING *Chesapeake Bay Maritime Museum,* Navy Point, St. Michaels, 745-2916. Hours: Summer, daily 9 A.M. to 6 P.M., spring and fall, daily 10 A.M. to 5 P.M.; January, February, Friday to Sunday and holidays only. $$$ • *St. Mary's Square Museum,* St. Mary's Square, St. Michaels, 745-9561. Hours: May through October, Saturday and Sunday 10 A.M. to 4 P.M. Donation • *Historical Society of Talbot County,* 25 South Washington Street, Easton, 822-0773. Hours:

Tuesday to Saturday 10 A.M. to 4 P.M., Sunday 1 P.M. to 4 P.M., closed Sunday January, February, $; house tours, $; guided walking tours, $ • *Academy Art Museum,* 106 South Street, Easton, 833-2787. Hours: Monday to Saturday, 10 A.M. to 4 P.M., Wednesday to 9 P.M., $, free on Wednesday • *Oxford Customs House,* foot of Morris Street, 226-5734. Hours: April to late autumn, weekends 3 P.M. to 5 P.M. Free • *Oxford Museum,* 101 South Morris Street, 226-5331. Hours: April 15 to October 15, Friday to Sunday 2 P.M. to 5 P.M. Free • *Oxford-Bellevue Ferry,* 745-9023. Hours: June 1 to Labor Day, Monday to Friday 7 A.M. to 9 P.M., Saturday and Sunday 9 A.M. to 9 P.M.; rest of year, weekdays 7 A.M. to sunset, weekends 9 A.M. to sunset. Closed December through February. Boats run every 25 minutes. $$ per car, $ per passenger • *Wye Mill,* Route 662 (off Route 50) Wye Mills, 827-6909. Hours: Mid-April to early November, Monday to Friday 10 A.M. to 1 P.M., Saturday and Sunday 10 A.M. to 4 P.M. Mill operates first and third Saturday each month. Free • **Boat and bike rentals:** *St. Michaels Town Dock Marina,* 305 Mulberry Street, 745-2400 • *Wheel Doctor,* 1013 South Talbot Street, St. Michaels, 745-6676.

Chesapeake Bay Cruises: *Patriot,* Chesapeake Bay Maritime Museum, St. Michaels, 745-3100. Hours: May to October, daily 11 A.M., 12:30 P.M., 2:30 P.M., 4 P.M. $$$$ • *Rebecca T. Ruark,* 21308 Phillips Road, Tilghman Island, 886-2176, delightful cruises on the oldest working skipjack on the bay • *Skipjack H.M. Krentz,* Tilghman, 745-6080, midday and sunset cruises on another authentic working skipjack • *The Lady Patty,* Knapps Narrows Marina, Tilghman, 886-2215 or (800) 690-5080, restored sailing yacht, day and sunset cruises; check current schedules • *Dockside Express,* P.O. Box 803, St. Michaels, 886-2643, environmental tours, lighthouse cruises, sunset cruises • *Island Kayak, Inc.,* Tilghman Island, 886-2083, guided ecotours, kayak rentals; phone for information • *Tidewater Kayak,* 10022 Chapel Road, Easton, 819-3284, rentals and guided tours • **Fishing charters:** Harrison's Sportfishing Center, Chesapeake House, Tilghman Island, 886-2121; also sunset cruises, check current offerings.

INFORMATION *Talbot County Office of Tourism,* Courthouse, 11 North Washington Street, Easton, MD 21601, 770-8000; www.talbot county.md • *St. Michaels Business Association,* P.O. Box 1221, St. Michaels, MD 21663, (800) 660-9471; www.stmichaelsmd.org.

Away from It All in the Highlands

Virginia's Western Highlands is for escapists, people who want to leave the crowds for a cool rural countryside hugged by rugged mountains. The mountains in question are the Alleghenies, which begin to the west where the Blue Ridge Mountains leave off. Within them are lakes, mineral springs, and some of the least populated, most beautiful areas in the mid-Atlantic.

But though the setting may be wild, you don't have to rough it in the Highlands. In Bath County, the west-central portion of the highlands, there are several fine lodgings, including the famous Homestead resort in Hot Springs (see page 289), whose golf courses and restaurants are available even to those staying in more modest bed-and-breakfast inns nearby.

Bath County was founded more than 250 years ago by pioneers of mostly Scotch-Irish descent. The first settler was John Lewis, who came with his wife to Fort Lewis, northwest of Staunton, in 1732. That property is now the site of the Fort Lewis Lodge, a farm resort.

Visitors were attracted to the mineral springs in the area as early as 1750. John Lewis's son, Andrew, obtained a patent for the Hot Springs area and with a partner built the first Homestead in 1766, a building that stood until a fire in 1901. M. E. Ingalls, president of the Chesapeake and Ohio Railroad, headed a group of investors who bought the hotel in 1891 and were responsible for rebuilding it after the fire.

The Homestead is the grandest, but it is just one of several unique lodgings in the area. Several attractive bed-and-breakfast inns welcome guests. About four miles north of Hot Springs in the hamlet of Warm Springs, The Inn at Gristmill Square is a minivillage made up of five nineteenth-century buildings, former homes and shops that now house guest rooms and an excellent restaurant in the former mill house. Three tennis courts and an outdoor pool are on the property.

Meadow Lane Lodge is notable for its wonderful surroundings, a 1,600-acre estate with a tennis court, miles of walking trails, and frontage on the Jackson River for swimming, fishing, or canoeing. Rooms are in the main lodge or two cottages on the property.

The Hidden Valley Bed and Breakfast west of Warm Springs is quite remarkable. This award-winning restoration of an 1851 columned Greek Revival brick mansion is the only inn in America in the midst of a national forest. It was the setting for the movie *Sommersby* with Jodie Foster and Richard Gere. Guests here stay in Victorian splendor and have 180 acres of the Hidden Valley Recreation Area at their disposal for hiking and fishing.

Farther east, and north of Millboro Springs, is the historic Fort Lewis Lodge, a 3,200-acre mountain farm. Rooms in the rustic main farmhouse, which is decorated with wildlife art and local handcrafted furniture, include three special bedrooms in the round silo. Also on the grounds are hand-hewn log cabins that are perfect hideaways.

Having chosen a place to stay, you can devote yourself to the abundance of outdoor recreation amid exceptional scenery. The southern region of the George Washington National Forest comprises some 176,809 acres that include Lake Moomaw, a 2,630-acre lake with beaches and excellent fishing. Hidden Valley Recreation Area on the Jackson River is also part of the forest.

Douthat State Park, 3,000 feet high in the Alleghenies, includes some of Virginia's most outstanding mountain scenery, as well as a 30-acre lake stocked with trout, a boat rental, and a sandy swimming beach. Forty miles of wooded hiking trails are prime. The top of a mountain trail yields wonderful vistas of rolling mountains as far as the eye can see. Ranger programs include guided hikes, canoe tours, talks, and family activities. The restaurant has a glass-enclosed porch overlooking the lake. Rustic cabins are available by the week if you want to stay here.

You can find all kinds of guided excursions in the region. The Allegheny Outdoor Center, headquartered in neighboring West Virginia, offers mountain bike rentals and tours in Virginia, and guided canoe and kayak touring on Lake Moomaw and Sherwood Lake. Highland Adventures in Monterey sponsors caving, rock climbing, and mountain bike excursions. The Homestead Stables offer horseback riding and carriage rides. In this county, where 89 percent of the land is forest, almost every road is a scenic woodland drive, including the main highway, Route 39 from Warm Springs to Millboro Springs.

If clouds should gather, you can relax and sample the thermal springs that made this area famous. The Jefferson Pools in Warm Springs are natural rock pools sheltered in their original nineteenth-century bathhouses. In their prime, they were considered the gateway to a tour of the area's hot springs, a pastime popular with society of the day both for health reasons and for socializing. Now kept up by the Homestead, they have been preserved close to their original state. There are separate pools for men and women, so no need for modesty. The 98.6-degree water circulates gently to soak away your aches and cares.

The many shops at the Homestead also will help to pass the time, along with some of the local galleries. A unique stop awaits in the quaint village of Bacova, about seven miles west of Warm Springs on Route 687. The Bacova Chapel was built by hand in 1920 and served the community for more than 50 years. When age began to take its toll, the chapel was saved in 1998 by new owners who restored it as a gallery filled with period oil paintings and antique prints and watercolors, plus antiques and a line of custom furniture created in the Warm Springs Valley.

The Warm Springs Gallery features original art and fine crafts by regional artists and artisans, as does the Allegheny Highlands Arts & Crafts Center to the south in Clifton Forge, which includes only juried work. Michel Cafe in Clifton Forge is a fine stop for dinner. If you stay, check the country music programs at the Historic Stonewall Theatre.

Or you can spend an evening listening to classical music at the Garth Newel Music Center, where concerts are held in a hilltop auditorium every Saturday and Sunday. The strains of Vivaldi and Bach are sure to soothe the savage hiker and biker.

Area Code: 540

DRIVING DIRECTIONS   From D.C. take I-81 south to exit 225, Route 275 west, to Route 250 west. Turn left at Churchville on Route 42, continue south to Millboro Springs, take Route 39 west to Warm Springs, then go south on Route 220 to Hot Springs. The approximate distance from D.C. is 200 miles.

ACCOMMODATIONS   *Inn at Gristmill Square,* P.O. Box 359, Warm Springs 24484, 839-2231, M–E, MAP • *Fort Lewis Lodge,* HCR 3, Box 21-A, Millboro 24460, 925-2314, E, MAP • *Meadow Lane Lodge,* HCR 01, Box 110, Warm Springs 24484, 839-5959, M, CP • **Bed-and-breakfast inns:** *Vine Cottage Inn,* U.S. 220, Hot Springs, 24445, 839-2422 or (800) 410-9755, M, CP; shared baths, I, CP • *Kings Victorian Inn,* U.S. 220, Route 1, Box 622, Hot Springs, 24445, 839-3134, M, CP • *Anderson Cottage,* Old Germantown Road, Warm Springs, 24484, 839-2975, I–M, CP • *Hidden Valley Bed & Breakfast,* off Route 621 in Hidden Valley Recreation Area, P.O. Box 53, Warm Springs 24484, 839-3178, M, CP • *Three Hills Inn,* Route 220, Box 9, Warm Springs, 24484, I–M, CP; suites, M–E, CP.

DINING   *The Homestead,* Route 220, Hot Springs, 839-1776: *The Dining Room* (coat and tie required for dinner), prix fixe, EE, and *The 1776 Grill,* elegant but less formal, M–E. Lunch choices include *Cafe Albert* on Cottage Row. and the *Casino Club, Cascades Club,* and *Lower Cascades Club,* on the golf courses, I–M • *Sam Snead's Tavern,* Main Street, Route 220, Hot Springs, 839-7666, named for the legendary native son, in historic building, varied menu, I–E • *Country Cafe,* Route 220, Hot Springs, 839-2111, country cooking, I–M • *Waterwheel Restaurant,* Inn at Gristmill Square (see above), continental menu, M–E • *Michel Cafe,* 424 East Ridgeway Street, Clifton Forge, 862-4119, everything from steak au poivre to Allegheny mountain trout, I–M. • *Douthat Lakeview Restaurant,* Douthat State Park,

862-8100, Wednesday to Sunday Memorial Day to Labor Day, weekends Easter to Memorial Day, September, October, seving lunch, Saturday and Sunday brunch, I, dinner, I–M.

SIGHT-SEEING   *Garth Newel Music Center,* off Route 220, Warm Springs, 839-5018. Year-round concerts. Summer series, Saturday evenings 5 P.M., Sunday afternoons 3 P.M. Phone for current schedule $$$$$ • *Jefferson Pools,* off Route 39, Warm Springs, 839-5346 or (800) 838-1766. Hours: Daily mid-April through October, 10 A.M. to 6 P.M. • *Allegheny Highlands Arts and Crafts Center,* 439 East Ridgeway Street, Clifton Forge, 862-4447. Hours: May to December, Monday to Saturday 10 A.M. to 4:30 P.M.; rest of year, closed Monday. Free • Phone the following for recreation information: *George Washington National Forest,* Warm Springs Ranger District, Hot Springs, 839-2521; *The Forest Place Visitor Center,* U.S. 220, one mile north of Hot Springs, 839-5281. Hours: Tuesday to Saturday 10 A.M. to 5 P.M., Sunday noon to 5 P.M. • *Douthat State Park,* from I-64, take exit 27 in Clifton Forge, turn north on State Route 629 for three miles to park entrance sign, 862-8100 • *Allegheny Outdoor Center,* White Sulphur Springs, WV, (888) 752-9982 • *Highland Adventures,* Monterey, 468-2722 • *Homestead Stables,* 839-1766.

INFORMATION   *Bath County Chamber of Commerce,* P.O. Box 718, Hot Springs, VA 24445, 839-5409 or (800) 628-8092; www.bathcountyva.org • *Alleghany Highlands Chamber of Commerce,* 214 West Main Street, Covington, VA 24426, 962-2178; www.alleghenyhighlands.com.

Appalachian Arts at Augusta

Augusta was the name given to West Virginia in the early days, when it was still part of the state of Virginia and the first homesteaders were making their way west into the Appalachian Mountains to carve a new life out of the wilderness.

Today Augusta means a series of workshops where people of all walks of life come with the common goal of learning and preserving the Appalachian arts of those early settlers—and a gala weekend festival where these arts are celebrated.

It is the perfect opportunity to appreciate anew the skills and talents nurtured long ago in West Virginia's hill country and to find renewal in the unchanged beauty of the mountains themselves.

Ingenuity was a necessity in this rugged highland region. The crafts of the mountain people were born of practical need, for they had no choice but to make everything for themselves. You might say their music was a necessity as well, because it brought them joy, a precious commodity where life is hard. Music also was a means of worship and a way to pass on treasured stories and traditions from one generation to the next.

Three Elkins-area women, fearful that these time-honored folkways would be forgotten in the fast-paced modern world, began the first Augusta workshops back in 1972 and have seen them grow beyond their fondest dreams. Now sponsored by Davis & Elkins College, which is set among the hilltops overlooking town, the Augusta Heritage Center attracts more than 2,000 participants to this town of 7,400 each year. Even more arrive to share the grand finale weekend.

The Augusta Heritage Workshops are held at the college for five weeks, beginning in July. The summer program has proven so popular that weeks are now scheduled in April and October as well. Participants come from every state in the union to study with an 80-year-old musician or a young fifth-generation basket maker; to master blacksmithing, bluegrass, or stained glass; to get the hang of white oak basketry, wood carving, storytelling, clogging, or making a quilt.

Some come hoping to pick up old-time musical savvy, the fine points of playing the banjo or the dulcimer or the fiddle. They want to share the dances and tunes and storytelling that are long-treasured traditions of the mountains.

All of these crafts and arts, music and dance, and more are on display for the final Augusta Festival weekend in mid-August, a showcase of the talents of Augusta's instructors. The weekend features many crafts demonstrations and entertainment of every kind—clogging and folk dancing; singing and storytelling; dances celebrating the heritage brought to the hills by Scottish, Irish, English, French, and African-American settlers; and lively musical jams. Workshops for the kids and homemade food fill out a full round of festivities.

The scenery adds greatly to the pleasures of a visit. Nestled in a valley on the northwestern slope of the Appalachians, Elkins is surrounded by the ridges of the Cheat and Rich Mountains and some of the greatest wilderness country on the East Coast. It is headquarters for the Monongahela National Forest, nearly a million acres of West Virginia woodlands. Its region, the Potomac Highlands, boasts 603 miles of native brook trout streams, 24 prime white-water rafting rivers, and 110 mountain peaks over 4,000 feet high, keeping things nice and cool even in midsummer.

The best of the easily accessible outdoors is 35 miles east of Elkins in the Canaan Valley, which according to legend got its name in 1753 from settlers who were so moved by its beauty they cried out, "Behold, the land of Canaan." Now known as "kuh-nayn" (accent on the last syllable), the Canaan Valley State Park sits 3,200 feet above sea level and is surrounded by peaks rising to well over 4,100 feet. Canaan is one of the state's superbly developed, moderately priced resort parks, with a pleasant lodge, an 18-hole golf course and a driving range, tennis, swimming, miniature golf, and chair lift rides up the slopes that serve skiers in the winter. An indoor complex provides a swimming pool, whirlpool, sauna, and exercise room. The park also offers some 6,000 acres of lush, verdant forests and clear mountain streams for hiking, horseback riding, fishing, and canoeing. In the summer, arts and crafts and nature programs are offered.

On the way from Elkins to Canaan, watch for the Old Mill on Route 32 in Harman. The 1877 water-powered gristmill still turns. Upstairs is a shop with a large selection of crafts by West Virginia artisans. Among the special events you may encounter here are demonstrations of the grinding of grain, spinning and weaving on an 1830s loom, and a state artist, craftsperson, or musician in residence showing off his or her talents.

From Canaan Valley continue ten miles north on Route 32 to Davis for spectacular scenery at Blackwater Falls State Park, where the Blackwater River takes a dramatic plunge to boulders 60 feet below, then continues winding its turbulent way down to Blackwater Canyon in a series of falls and cascades that descend another 1,350 feet in ten miles. Blackwater Falls Park offers its own lodge with scenic views, horseback riding, swimming, and unlimited nature walks in the cool of the Monongahela Forest. For hikers, the Allegheny Trail begins here, continuing 150 miles south to Greenbrier County.

Most unusual of all the natural wonders in the vicinity is the Dolly Sods Wilderness Area in Red Creek. Situated in a high wild section of the Allegheny Plateau, which rises 4,000 feet above sea level, this spot has been described as a bit of Canada gone astray, with a starkly beautiful terrain reminiscent of Arctic tundra. Winds are so fierce in winter that limbs do not grow on the windward side of trees, leaving stately spruces standing like tall masts with their sails blasted to one side. The diversity of unusual plants attracts many naturalists.

Dolly Sods is also rich in wildlife—deer, beavers, black bears, foxes, raccoons, bobcats, and snowshoe hares are a few of its denizens. With 25 miles of trails, it is a mecca for hikers, berry pickers, and photographers and provides magnificent vistas of the eastern ridges. The tower near Red Creek Campground gives a full 360-degree mountain panorama.

Also within easy reach of Elkins is the Spruce Knob–Seneca Rocks National Recreation Area. It serves majestic Spruce Knob, West Virginia's highest point at 4,860 feet, and Seneca Rocks, an outcropping of 900-foot-high cliffs of Tuscarora sandstone that is a challenge to even the most venturesome rock climbers. The Seneca Rocks Climbing School teaches climbing techniques and offers guided hikes. Many are happier watching the action from the base and picnicking along the bank of the North Fork River. The Seneca Rocks Visitor Center, operated by the U.S. Forest Service, offers films, nature talks, guided hikes, and other programs.

A visit to Augusta and its surroundings will leave you with fresh appreciation for the simple mountain people whose highly personal arts and crafts have special appeal in our mass-produced age and for the mountains that inspired them.

Area Code: 304

DRIVING DIRECTIONS   Elkins is at the intersection of Routes 33 and 219. From D.C., take I-66 west to Route 81 south. At Harrisonburg, Virginia, turn west on Route 33 to Elkins. The approximate distance from D.C. is 200 miles.

ACCOMMODATIONS   Most lodgings offer special rates for Augusta participants. *Cheat River Lodge,* Route 1, P.O. Box 115, Elkins 26241, 636-2301, lodge and log homes along the river; lodge, I; two-and three-bedroom houses, E • *Cheat Mountain Club,* P.O. Box 28, Durbin 26264, 456-4627, private hunting lodge gone public, on trout stream in the forest, excellent food, E–EE, AP • *Graceland Inn and Conference Center,* Davis & Elkins College, Elkins 26241, 637-1600 or (800) 624-3157, restored Victorian mansion plus adjacent conference center building, tennis, fitness center, indoor pool, M–E; conference center rooms, I • **Bed-and-breakfast homes in and around Elkins:** *Warfield House,* 318 Buffalo Street, Elkins 26241, 636-4555 or (888) 636-4555, convenient to the college, M, CP • *The Retreat at Buffalo Run,* 214 Harpertown Road, Elkins 26241, 636-2960, I, CP • *Tunnel Mountain Inn,* Route 1, P.O. Box 59-1, Elkins 26241, 636-1684 or (888) 211-9123, mountainside fieldstone home four miles from town, I–M, CP • *Hutton House B & B,* Routes 219/250, Huttonsville 26273, 335-6701 or (800) 234-6701, Victorian inn on National Register, about 20 miles south of Elkins, I–M, CP • Too remote for taking part in the Augusta activities, but well worth knowing about as back-to-nature getaways, are *North Fork Mountain Inn,* P.O. Box 114, Cabins 26452, 257-1108, recently built, secluded mountainside log lodge in Smoke Hole Canyon, attractive rooms, great views from the porch, M, CP • *Smoke Hole Lodge,* c/o P.O. Box 953, Petersburg, 28647, 257-1539, remote rustic lodge reached via four-wheel drive (yours or theirs), no electricity or phone, hearty meals, escapists love it, E, MAP • **Motels in Elkins:** *Best Western Motel of Elkins,* Route 33, 26241, 636-7711, indoor pool, I • *Elkins Days Inn,* 1200 Harrison Avenue, 26241, 637-4667, I • *Elkins Motor Lodge,* Harrison Avenue, 26241, 636-1400, I. See also Canaan Valley, pages 256–257.

DINING   *Cheat River Inn,* Route 33, Elkins, 636-6265, best in the area, excellent trout, I–M • *CJ Maggies,* 309 Davis Avenue, Elkins, 636-1730, I–M • *1863 Tavern,* Elkins Motor Lodge (see above), M • *Graceland* (see above), American and continental dishes, M–E • *Brooks Landing,* 203 Virginia Avenue, Petersburg 26847, 257-1049, Victorian ambiance, I–M • *The Front Porch Restaurant,* above Harper's Old Country Store, junction of Routes 28, 55 and 33, Seneca Rocks, 567-2555, pizza, subs, panoramic view, open till 9 P.M., I. See also Canaan Valley, page 257.

SIGHT-SEEING   *Augusta Heritage Workshops and Augusta Festival,* Augusta Heritage Center, Davis & Elkins College, Elkins, WV 26241, 636-1903; www.augustaheritage.com. Five weeks of workshops, July and early August; weekend Augusta Festival, early August. Contact for current schedules and rates. Ask also about April Dulcimer Week and October Old-Time Week • *The Old Mill,* Route 32, north of Harman, 227-4466. Hours: Memorial Day to Labor Day, Monday through Saturday 10 A.M. to 5 P.M. Donation • *Dolly Sods Wilderness and Scenic Area,* Route 19 off Route 32, four miles north of Harman. Information from Forest Supervisor, Monongahela National Forest, 200 Sycamore Street, Elkins, WV 26241, 636-1800 • *Spruce Knob–Seneca Rocks National Recreation Area,* Seneca Rocks, 567-2827. Visitor Center hours: April through October, daily 9 A.M. to 5:30 P.M.; rest of year Saturday, Sunday 9 A.M. to 4:30 P.M. Hours can change, so best to call and check. Free • *Canaan Valley Resort State Park, Blackwater Falls State Park,* and all West Virginia state park and forest information available toll-free, (800) CALL-WVA, or on the Internet, www.wvparks.com.

INFORMATION   *Randolph County Convention & Visitors Bureau,* 200 Executive Plaza, Elkins, WV 26241, 636-2717 or (800) 422-3304; www.randolphcounty.com • *Potomac Highlands Travel Council,* 1200 Harrison Street, Elkins, WV 26241, 636-8400 or (800) 999-7292; www.wvonline.com; www.potomachighlands.org.

Feasting and Festing in Annapolis

With a superb setting on a river opening to Chesapeake Bay and a heaping helping of history and charm, Annapolis is a fascinating port of call. Time your visit right, and a festive visit to the Middle Ages and a seafood feast can be added to the agenda.

Well over a century before anyone dreamed of establishing a national naval academy, Annapolis was already the state capital and a thriving port. More than 300 eighteenth-century buildings remain in the town to attest to its prosperous past, some of them open for fascinating touring.

But most of all the history of Annapolis is tied to the sea, a connection you can't miss, since the city dock and its narrow waterway extend the harbor almost into the heart of the city. Part of the fun of an Annapolis visit is boarding one of the boats for a cruise on the bay. In summer, these waters are a sea of sails, a longtime favorite for mid-Atlantic sailors.

The dock is also a fine starting point for getting a sense of bygone days with a walking tour past the picturesque homes and enticing shops. The historic area of the town is compact, and it is easy to navigate on foot. On-site tours are available when you visit the two major attractions of the city, the Maryland State House and the U.S. Naval Academy. Maps and self-guiding tours are available at the Visitor Center and at the City Dock information booth.

If you are a first-time visitor, you may prefer to start with one of the excellent walking tours available. Three Centuries Tours are led by a guide in Colonial garb who will fill you in on local lore. You can also rent a taped 45-minute tour, narrated by Walter Cronkite, at the Historic Annapolis Foundation Museum Store.

The store, which is located at the foot of Main Street, is a logical starting point for touring. It is located in a restored victualing warehouse that once stored food for Revolutionary War troops. A scale model here shows the waterfront as it was from 1751 to 1791, when Annapolis was the principal seaport of Upper Chesapeake Bay. Other exhibits tell more about the early trade and commerce of the area.

The next stop is Market Space, the picturesque square at the end of the dock, where seafood to go is a local institution.

Cornhill is one of the many narrow streets radiating from Market Space that are lined with historic homes, some of them tippy with age. Different-colored plaques are used to tell you which of the town's three centuries each home represents. Dark green marks seventeenth-century structures; bronze is for Georgian homes from 1735 to 1790; brick red is for eighteenth-century vernacular homes; blue identifies the Federal period from 1784 to 1840; light green means Greek Revival style from 1820 to 1860; and purple classifies Victorians from 1837 to 1901. Other styles from 1837 to 1930 have a gray plaque, and yellow is used for especially distinctive twentieth-century structures.

Among the smaller houses are the local showplaces, fine mansions belonging to signers of the Declaration of Independence. They carry special bronze plaques signifying an eighteenth-century building of national importance. One of these open to the public is the home of Charles Carroll, said to have been the wealthiest man in the colonies, and the only Catholic to sign the Declaration of Independence.

Follow Cornhill Street to its end, and you'll find yourself gazing at the State House, which is the country's oldest capitol in continuous legislative use. It served as the nation's capitol in 1783 and 1784. Inside you'll see the Old Senate Chamber, where Congress received George Washington's resignation as commander in chief and where the Treaty of Paris was ratified, officially ending the Revolutionary War.

From here, follow State Circle around to Maryland Avenue to discover some of the shops and art galleries that make Annapolis a browsing and antiquing mecca. The Annapolis Country Store at number 53 is a good spot for small souvenirs such as pottery, potpourri, wicker, and old-fashioned painted porcelain soap dishes.

Main Street is another block recommended for shoppers. It is more attractive than ever, thanks to a renovation that included burying the utility wires. The League of Maryland Craftsmen store at number 216 represents over 150 state artists and artisans.

Two notable homes open for touring on Maryland Avenue are the Chase-Lloyd House, known for its grand columned main hall, and the Hammond-Harwood House, considered one of the finest Georgian homes in the country.

Follow Maryland to Prince George Street and make a right turn for the William Paca House, built in 1763 by one of the Declaration signers, who was also an early governor of the state. The dignified brick home and its exquisite gardens are the city's finest. If you can only tour one home, this is the best choice.

Veer left past the Paca House onto East Street and then right on King George to reach the magnificent waterfront campus of the U.S. Naval Academy. Stop at the handsome visitors center on the water to see a video and exhibits and inquire about guided tours. The museum and chapel are high points on the campus tour, but a stroll amid the quadrangles to see the midshipmen in their spiffy uniforms is enough to give you a feeling of the proud tradition that has been carried on here since 1845. Take a walk along the seawall for an incomparable view of the sailboats tacking to and fro across the Severn River and into Chesa-peake Bay.

By now you'll no doubt be ready to get out to sea yourself. You can choose anything from a 40-minute cruise of the harbor or a 2-hour sail to a full day's outing. Several cruises concentrate on the ecology of the bay, with naturalists on board.

Upon your return, sample one of the excellent restaurants in town, specializing, of course, in seafood. Feast on crabs, oysters, mussels, gumbo, chowder, and all the other special dishes that make a visit to Chesapeake Bay so delicious. Water taxi service is a delightful way to get to the many restaurants in the Eastport area. If you want a giant sampling, wait for the second week in September, when the Maryland Seafood Festival takes place at Sandy Point State Park outside Annapo-lis, near the Bay Bridge.

You can add an even more unusual diversion to your agenda by joining the jugglers, jesters, jousters, knights, and ladies at the Mary-land Renaissance Festival, which goes full tilt on weekends from August through late October. Drive west on Route 50 to exit 23B, Route 450, turn left, then left at the first light and right at the next light onto Crownsville Road and follow the signs back to the sixteenth century.

This is one of only a dozen locations in the nation where you can see this kind of revelry, a combination Renaissance-style street fair and daylong nonstop entertainment by some 200 performers in Tudor cos-tumes. There's something for every taste, from good-natured mock adventures in King Henry VIII's court to full combat jousting. Over the course of the day, dancers cavort, falcons soar over a trainer's watchful eye, archers practice their sport, and knights of old match wits and swordsmanship in the Living Chess Game.

In the center of it all is a mock village of thatched booths where more than 100 artisans and merchants offer anything from flower gar-lands bedecked with flowing ribbons to tarot card readings of your future. All the booths have a Renaissance theme. You can buy a spear or a shield, have your face painted, pick up a pair of Robin Hood boots or a tankard of ale, or buy a candle or a piece of blown glass in the shape of a dragon, a castle, or a unicorn.

Strolling troubadours, jesters, and storytellers keep everyone amused, and if you should tire of just watching, you can try your mettle at archery or darts. To add to the atmosphere, dozens of costumed actors stroll about impersonating typical townspeople, right down to the bawdy balladeers, masters of the off-color tune.

All of it is a lot of fun, but nothing compares with the grand finale, when trumpet blares and timpani introduce a jousting duel between two knights in full armor. It's a rousing send-off that makes a return to the twentieth century seem very tame indeed.

Area Code: 410

DRIVING DIRECTIONS   Annapolis is on Chesapeake Bay, off Route 50/301. From D.C., take Route 50 east to exit 24, Route 70/ Rowe Boulevard. The approximate distance from D.C. is 33 miles.

PUBLIC TRANSPORTATION   Frequent inexpensive light-rail and bus transportation via Dillon's Bus Service to Annapolis from Washington and Baltimore, (800) 827-3490. Limousine service is available from nearby Baltimore-Washington International Airport; there is a free shuttle from the Baltimore Amtrak station to the airport for those arriving by train. If you stay in the historic district, no car is necessary.

ACCOMMODATIONS   All are zip code 21401. Expect minimum stays on weekends. *Loews Annapolis,* 126 West Street, 263-7777 or (800) 23-LOEWS, best in town, E • *Historic Inns of Annapolis,* 58 State Circle, 263-2641, three historic preservations include the Maryland Inn, Governor Calvert House, and Robert Johnson House, all E–EE, CP • *Annapolis Marriott Waterfront Hotel,* Compromise and St. Mary's Streets, 268-7555, prize location on the water, EE • **Bed and breakfast inns:** *Gibson's Lodgings,* 110 Prince George Street, 263-2523, charming small guest houses in historic district, M–E, CP • *Jonas Green House,* 124 Charles Street, 263-5892, historic bed-and-breakfast, one of city's two oldest homes, still in original family, M–E, CP • *Chez Amis,* 85 East Street, 263-6631, former corner store, now quaint bed-and-breakfast, E, CP • *College House Suites,* 1 College Avenue, 263-6124, two elegant suites in a brick town house, E–EE, CP • *Prince George Inn,* 232 Prince George Street, 263-6418, 1884 town house, M, CP • *William Page Inn,* 8 Martin Street, 626-1506 or (800) 364-4160, pleasant wooden Victorian home, quiet, convenient location, M–E, CP • *Maryrob Bed and Breakfast,* 243 Prince George Street, 268-5438, elegant 1864 Victorian, just two guest rooms, M, CP • *Harborview Boat & Breakfast,* P.O. Box 3057, 268-9330 or (800) 877-9330, overnight stay on privately owned, moored yacht; can accommodate two or four, rate includes a one-hour scenic cruise, EE, CP • *Annapolis Bed and Breakfast Association,* P.O. Box 744, Annapolis 21404, 263-6124, www.annapolisbandb.com.

DINING   *Treaty of Paris,* Maryland Inn (see above), charming, reserve well ahead, M–E; weekend jazz entertainment in King of France Tavern • *Corinthian,* Loews Annapolis Hotel (see above), fine American cuisine, E • *Cafe Normandie,* 185 Main Street, 263-3382, excellent French cafe, I–E • *Piccola Roma Ristorante,* 200 Main Street, 268-7898, popular Italian, reliably good food, M–E • *Phlilips Annapolis Harbor,* 12 Dock Street, 990-9888, outpost of Baltimore's famous seafood emporium, same sensational crab cakes and a water-front view, I–E • *Middleton Tavern,* 2 Market Place, 263-3323, historic 1750 tavern with the town's favorite outdoor terrace, I–E • *Chick & Ruth's Delly,* 165 Main Street, 269-6737, local institution for breakfast and lunch I • **Outside the town center:** *Carrol's Creek Cafe,* 410 Severn Avenue, Eastport, 263-8102 (a short water taxi ride away or a few minutes' drive across the Spy Creek bridge), waterfront setting, fish specialties, good brunch, M–E • *O'Leary's,* 310 Third Street, Eastport, 263-0884, the freshest seafood cooked any way you like it, I–EE • *Fred's Tiffany Room Restaurant,* 2348 Solomons Island Road, 224-2386, Italian and seafood, tops for crab cakes, M–EE • *Cantler's River-side Inn,* 458 Forest Beach Road, 757-1311, eat outside on the river, great crabs and seafood, I–M • *Northwoods,* 609 Melvin Avenue, 269-6775, small and excellent, continental and Italian, M–E.

SIGHT-SEEING *Maryland State House,* State Circle, 974-3400. Hours: Daily 9 A.M. to 5 P.M.; tours at 11 A.M. and 3 P.M. Free • *U.S. Naval Academy,* King George & Randall Streets, 263-6933; www. navyonline.com. Grounds open daily 9 A.M. to 5 P.M. *Armel-Leftwich Visitor Center,* Gate 1, information, audiovisual presentation. Hours: March to December 9 A.M. to 5 P.M., January, February to 4 P.M. Guided tours, $$$; check current schedule • *U.S. Naval Academy Museum,* 293-2108. Hours: Monday to Saturday 9 A.M. to 5 P.M.; Sunday 11 A.M. to 5 P.M. Free • *William Paca House and Garden,* 186 Prince George Street, 263-5553. Hours: March to December, Monday to Saturday 10 A.M. to 5 P.M., Sunday noon to 5 P.M. January, February. Friday, Saturday, 10 A.M. to 4 P.M., Sunday noon to 4 P.M., $$$$ • *Hammond-Harwood House,* 19 Maryland Avenue, 269-1714. Hours: Monday to Saturday 10 A.M. to 4 P.M., Sunday noon to 4 P.M. $$ • *Charles Carroll House,* 107 Duke of Gloucester Street, 269-1737. Hours: Friday, Sunday, noon to 4 P.M., Saturday 10 A.M. to 2 P.M. $$ • *Historic Annapolis Foundation Museum Store and Welcome Center, Victualing Warehouse,* 77 Main Street, City Dock, 268-5576. Hours: Daily 10 A.M. to 5 P.M. Free.

Walking tours: Call for current schedules and rates; reservations may be necessary. *Three Centuries Tours,* 48 Maryland Avenue, 263-5401 • *Annapolis Walkabout,* 223 South Cherry Grove Avenue, 263-8253.

Boat tours: Check all for current schedules and fees. **Watermark Cruises,** Slip 20, City Dock, 268-7600, many choices: 40- and 90-minute cruises, day excursions to St. Michaels • *Schooner Woodwind,* Pusser's Landing, Marriott Hotel, 263-7837, two-hour sails on a 74-foot wooden yacht • *Beginagain,* City Dock, 626-1422, daily sails on the bay • *Liberté, the Schooner,* Chart House Restaurant pier, 263-8234, charters for 1 to 25.

Festivals: ***Maryland Renaissance Festival,*** between Routes 450 and 178, c/o P.O. Box 315, Crownsville, MD 21032, 266-7304. Weekends, late August through mid-October, 10:30 A.M. to 7 P.M. $$$$$ • ***Maryland Seafood Festival,*** 151 West Street, Annapolis, 268-7676; www.mdseafoodfestival.com. Held second weekend in September, Friday to Sunday noon to 8:30 P.M. at Sandy Point State Park, Route 50/301, just before the Chesapeake Bay Bridge.

INFORMATION ***Annapolis and Anne Arundel County Conference and Visitors Bureau,*** 26 West Street, Annapolis, MD 21401, 280-0445; www.visit-annapolis.org

Fall

Overleaf: Autumn apple seller in the Shenandoah Valley. *Photo courtesy of Eleanor Berman.*

Who's Who in Colonial Fredericksburg

Everyone who was anyone in early America seems to have played a role in the history of Fredericksburg, Virginia.

For starters, there were the Washingtons. George Washington, who once said, "All that I am I owe to my mother," showed his filial gratitude by buying a home for his widowed mother in Fredericksburg, near the mansion where his sister, Betty Washington Lewis, lived in style in one of the loveliest homes in Colonial America. George, a local boy who made good, said his last farewell to Mary Ball Washington in her Fredericksburg home and rode off with his mother's blessing to be inaugurated as the first president of the United States.

The Washington family homes are among more than 350 original buildings remaining in the 40-block historic district to tell of the illustrious past of this settlement along the Rappahannock River.

Come and follow the footsteps of the Founding Fathers, who plotted the American Revolution here in a tavern built by Washington's brother, Charles, and visit the office where James Monroe practiced law before he became president of the United States. Stand on the spot where Thomas Jefferson declared religious freedom a legal right in Virginia, then walk the silent battlegrounds where blue and gray troops decided the fate of the Civil War a century later, keeping the young states of America united.

The spirit of the past even seems to have rubbed off on present-day Fredericksburg, inspiring a new generation of artisans who re-create handicrafts of the Colonial era. Dropping in on the local pewter-, gold-, and coppersmiths adds to the fun of a visit, as do dining and living in historic quarters and visiting the many antique shops that have burgeoned in the historic district.

Begin at the Visitor Center on Caroline Street for a free film that will fill you in on local lore. Then you'll be ready to see the sights for yourself. You can do that on your own or on guided tours via Old Town Trolley or horse-drawn carriage. Guided walking tours are also available, including Living History Experiences with costumed guides.

Whichever method you choose, you'll soon learn that George Washington grew up on Ferry Farm, right across the Rappahannock River, where Mrs. Washington was still living when her concerned son moved her into town. It was here that the famous legends of chopping down the cherry tree and tossing a coin over the Rappahannock were born. The farm has been saved from development by the Kenmore Association and has been declared a National Historic Landmark. Currently you can visit and walk the grounds with a self-guiding brochure and take part in family programs.

The law offices of James Monroe were located just a few blocks from Mrs. Washington's home. Another monument marks the spot where Thomas Jefferson met with a committee in 1777 to draft the Virginia Statute for Religious Freedom, which later was incorporated into the U.S. Constitution as the First Amendment to the Bill of Rights. Jefferson considered this statute one of his most important achievements.

All of these are among the 29 historic stops marked on the free walking and driving tours available at the center.

You might begin with a visit to the house of the mother of the father of our country. Mary Ball Washington spent her last 17 years in this cozy home, which is still filled with her favorite possessions. When General Lafayette stopped by to pay his respects to his commander's mother, he found her at work in her beloved garden, which is restored much as she left it, planted with boxwoods along a brick walkway to separate the vegetables from a lush English-style flower garden.

Mrs. Washington is buried on the estate of her daughter, at a favorite spot where she often came to meditate and pray. A marker has been installed in her honor.

Betty Washington's showplace home, Kenmore, stands on Washington Avenue, just a couple of blocks from her mother's house. The impressive brick residence built in 1752 by Betty and her husband, wealthy planter Fielding Lewis, originally was the main house of an 863-acre plantation. The house is known for the exquisite decorative plasterwork carving on the ceilings and cornices that made it one of the most elaborate homes of Colonial times. Two of its rooms are included in the book *100 Most Beautiful Rooms in America.*

Betty married well, but not because she was a beauty. Her portrait shows a striking resemblance, nose and all, to brother George, 16 months her senior.

If you take a walk along Washington Avenue, you'll see the fine Victorian homes that went up later in Fredericksburg, after the Kenmore land was subdivided.

Over at the Rising Sun Tavern, built around 1760 by Washington's youngest brother, Charles, the period furnishings remain, and you can almost hear the echoes of the history makers who dined and plotted in this "hot-bed of sedition"— men like Washington, Jefferson, Patrick Henry, and the Lees of Virginia. Have a spot of spiced tea, take a look at the stand-up desk said to have belonged to Thomas Jefferson, and listen to the tavern's story, told by a costumed hostess.

Another fascinating stop on the tour is the Hugh Mercer Apothecary Shop. Once again you are stepping back 200 years, this time to learn about the medicines and surgical treatments—such things as leeches, lancets, and crab claws—that Dr. Mercer might have prescribed for your ailments. Mercer, a personal friend of George Washington, practiced medicine here for 15 years, with Mary Washington as one of his many noted patients. He left to join the revolutionary cause and gave his life at the Battle of Princeton.

The tavern, shop, and Mary Washington House are all maintained by the Association for the Preservation of Virginia Antiquities (APVA). Their fourth property, Saint James's House, was owned by another Mercer named James, the Washingtons' attorney, and sits on land that George Washington had bought from his brother-in-law, Fielding Lewis. The beautifully furnished eighteenth-century gentleman's home is open only by appointment and for special events, including the annual mid-September Living Legacies show held at the APVA properties. The show, featuring exhibits and demonstrations of eighteenth- and nineteenth-century skills, is a special treat for quilt lovers.

The annual Christmas candlelight tour on the first weekend in December is another lovely time for a visit to Fredericksburg.

One more interesting bit of history is the James Monroe Law Office–Museum and Memorial Library. A onetime governor of Virginia, Monroe held many high offices, including that of minister to France, and his office contains some of the furniture in rich mahogany with inlaid brass that he brought back with him from Europe. The Louis XVI desk is where he signed his annual message to Congress in 1823, including the section that became known as the Monroe Doctrine, declaring the United States all the Americas' protector from foreign aggression. Besides the unusually fine furnishings, there are displays of some of the costumes worn by the Monroes at the court of Napoleon and the exquisite gems owned by Mrs. Monroe.

The Fredericksburg Area Museum and Cultural Center interprets Fredericksburg history from prehistoric times to the twentieth century in six permanent galleries, and offers changing exhibits on history as well. It is housed in the 1814 Town Hall/Market House.

The walking-driving tour will point out other places of interest, including historic churches, the campus of Mary Washington College, and, on the other side of the river, the charming eighteenth-century home called Belmont, where painter Gari Melchers lived and worked. His studio and gardens remain on a lovely site overlooking the Rappahannock.

It is something of a miracle that so many of these early buildings survive, because Fredericksburg, located exactly midway between Union headquarters in Washington and the Confederate capital in Richmond, was a highly sought prize that changed hands seven times during the Civil War and was the scene of four bloody battles. The first, in 1862, was the most one-sided battle of the war, resulting in a smashing victory for Lee's forces, ensconced on Marye's Heights, high above the Rappahannock. Another victory came the following year at nearby Chancellorsville, but at a terrible cost. It was here that Stonewall Jackson, the brilliant Confederate general who was Lee's most trusted subordinate, was mortally wounded by an unwitting shot from his own troops. A shrine to Jackson stands about 15 miles south of Fredericksburg.

The Wilderness Campaigns outside town were followed by the Battle at Spotsylvania Court House in 1864, the most intense hand-to-hand combat of the war. It was one of Lee's last successful stands, but one whose heavy Confederate losses led to the eventual end of the war.

The Fredericksburg National Cemetery contains the graves of more than 15,000 Union soldiers, and the Confederate Cemetery holds many more, including those of five rebel generals, evidence of the terrible toll taken here on both sides.

The Fredericksburg/Spotsylvania National Military Park offers films describing the battle action and maps of a self-guided tour of the battle sites in the park. A second visitors center, with its own audiovisual program, is open at the Chancellorsville Battlefield, about ten miles west of Fredericksburg.

Sophia Street is where some of Fredericksburg's 20-plus antique shops begin. Many more are one block away on Caroline Street. The largest selection under one roof can be found at the Willow Hill Antique Court of Shoppes, 1001 Caroline. Other Caroline Street cooperatives, with wares from a dozen or so dealers, are Upstairs/Downstairs, number 922, and Antique Gallery of Fredericksburg, number 1023. More multiple-dealer shops can be found on William Street.

Art is part of the Fredericksburg scene as well, at the Montrose and Premier Galleries, both on Caroline Street.

The most delightful shopping, however, is at the workshops of the Fredericksburg craftspeople. The Copper Shop at 1707-B Princess Anne Street is headquarters for a father-son team of artisans, Alan Green II and Alan the third. Their graceful hand-forged Fredericksburg lamps, contemporary versions of traditional Colonial designs, hang in all 50 states and in 44 foreign lands, and their made-to-order weather vanes, in shapes from cigar-store Indian to rock guitar, are true collector's items.

Handsome handcrafted bowls, plates, and candlesticks can be found at Cardinal Pewter, 526 Wolfe Street, and at the workshop and small salesroom of pewtersmith Ralph Gooch are burnished goblets, plates, mugs, and bowls that are shaped at the wheel into designs that are a beautiful blending of function and art. Many people collect the Christmas ornaments he makes in a different historic design each year. Michael Bender is a goldsmith practicing traditional methods to create jewelry and other items in gold, silver, platinum, copper, and bronze. His studio is at 110 Hanover Street.

The craftspeople are a living continuation of the Colonial spirit, bringing the Fredericksburg of the past gracefully into the present.

Area Code: 540

DRIVING DIRECTIONS Fredericksburg is at the intersection of Routes 1 and 3, just off I-95. From D.C., follow I-95 south to the Fredericksburg exits. The approximate distance from D.C. is 50 miles.

PUBLIC TRANSPORTATION The Amtrak station is in the heart of town, and there are commuter trains to D.C. morning and evening. No car is necessary in the town center.

ACCOMMODATIONS *Kenmore Inn,* 1200 Princess Anne Street, 22401, 371-9229, 1700s home-turned-inn, convenient, M, CP • *Fredericksburg Colonial Inn,* 1707 Princess Anne Street, 22401, 371-5666, small motel-style rooms, but with nice old-fashioned furnishings, I–M, CP • *Sheraton Inn,* 2801 Plank Road, I-95 and Route 3, 22404, 786-8321, M • **Bed-and-breakfast inns:** *The Richard Johnston Inn,* 711 Caroline Street, 22401, 899-7606, charming and convenient, fireplaces, outdoor patio; the "summer kitchen" room with brick floors and enormous fireplace is special, M, CP • *Littlepage Inn,* 15701 Monrovia, Spotsylvania, 22408, 854-9861 or (800) 248-1803, rooms and suites in restored historic plantation and outbuildings, on National Register, M–E, CP.

DINING *Le Lafayette,* 623 Caroline Street, 373-6895, charming 1729 home, French cuisine, M–E • *Andrew's Mediterranean Bounty,* 600 William Street, 370-0909, Mediterranean fare, recommended locally, I–M • *Merriman's,* 715 Caroline Street, 371-7723, arty atmosphere and innovative menus, I–M • *La Petite Auberge,* 311 William Street, 371-2727, French café, I–M • *Ristorante Renato,* 422 William Street, 371-8228, good Italian, I–E • *Moonlighting on the Rappahannock,* 503 Sophia Street, 371-1175, overlooking the Rappahannock River, sandwiches to full meals, I–M • *The Riverview,* 1101 Sophia Street, 373-6500, steaks and seafood, riverfront patio, M • *Olde Mudd Tavern,* 5144 Mudd Tavern Road, off I-95, Thornburg exit (south of Fredericksburg), 582-5250, early American and Civil War era decor, M–E • *Smythe's Cottage and Tavern,* 303 Fauquier Street, 373-1645, contemporary and Colonial dishes in a cozy early-1800s setting, M • *Sammy T's,* 801 Caroline Street, 371-2088, informal, good spot for lunch, I–M.

SIGHT-SEEING Passport to History discount block tickets for eight major sites available at Visitor Center and participating properties. *Mary Washington House,* 1200 Charles Street, 373-1569. Hours: March 1 to November 30, daily 9 A.M. to 5 P.M., December to February 10 A.M. to 4 P.M. $$ • *Kenmore Plantation,* 1201 Washington Avenue, 373-3381. Hours: March through December, Monday to Saturday

10 A.M. to 5 P.M., Sunday noon to 5 P.M.; January and February, Saturday 10 A.M. to 4 P.M., Sunday noon to 4 P.M. $$$ • *Rising Sun Tavern,* 1304 Caroline Street, 371-1494. Hours: March 1 to November 30, daily 9 A.M. to 5 P.M.; December to February, 10 A.M. to 4 P.M. $$ • *Hugh Mercer Apothecary Shop,* 1020 Caroline Street, 373-3362. Hours: March through November, 9 A.M. to 5 P.M.; December through February 10 A.M. to 4 P.M. $$ • *James Monroe Museum,* 908 Charles Street, 654-1043. Hours: March through November, daily 9 A.M. to 5 P.M.; December to February, 10 A.M. to 4 P.M. $$ • *Fredericksburg Area Museum & Cultural Center,* 907 Princess Anne Street, 371-3037. Hours: March through November, Monday to Saturday 10 A.M. to 5 P.M., Sunday 1 P.M. to 5 P.M.; rest of year to 4 P.M. $$ • *Belmont,* 224 Washington Street, Falmouth, off Route 17 east headed toward Falmouth, 654-1015. Hours: May 1 to November 30, Monday to Saturday 10 A.M. to 5 P.M., Sunday 1 P.M. to 5 P.M.; rest of year to 4 P.M. $$ • *Ferry Farm,* State Route 3, east of Fredericksburg (phone for exact directions), 370-0732. Hours: March through December, Monday to Saturday 10 A.M. to 5 P.M., Sunday noon to 5 P.M. January, Feburary, Saturday 10 A.M. to 4 P.M., Sunday noon to 4 P.M. $ • *Fredericksburg/Spotsylvania National Military Park,* Visitor Center, 1013 Lafayette Boulevard (U.S. 1) and Sunken Road, 373-6122. Hours: Daily 9 A.M. to 5 P.M. $$; under 16, free • *Chancellorsville Battlefield Visitor Center,* off Route 3, west of I-95, 786-2880. Hours: 9 A.M. to 5 P.M. $$; under 16, free • **Guided tours:** Most tours leave from Visitor Center (see below); ask at center or phone for current schedules. *Jane B. Beale and Friends, the Living History Company, Inc,* walking/driving tours re-creating history, 899-1776 • *Trolley tours:* 60-minute tours, 898-0737 • *Carriage tours:* 45-minute tours, 654-5511.

INFORMATION *Fredericksburg Visitor Center,* 706 Caroline Street, Fredericksburg, VA 22401, 373-1776 or (800) 678-4748; www.fburg.com. Daily 9 A.M. to 5 P.M. Free orientation film.

Sweet Season in Hershey

Kids are sweet on Hershey, Pennsylvania. But then so are their parents and grandparents and uncles and aunts.

It's hard not to love a chocolate-covered town where even the streetlights are shaped like chocolate kisses, where the main downtown intersection is at Chocolate and Cocoa, and all the street signs have Hershey Bar lettering.

But you will please more than your sweet tooth in the place known as Chocolate Town, U.S.A. In Hershey there are magnificent gardens with 8,000 rosebushes featuring 250 varieties of blooms, a fine zoo, a museum of Pennsylvania life, a super amusement park with six scream-guaranteed roller coasters, tennis courts, five golf courses, and a lavish spa facility, all waiting after your chocolate tour is over.

There are few destinations with so many ways to please the whole family, and there is no better time for a weekend visit than early autumn. The days are a bit cooler then, and crowds of vacationing families have gone home, but Hersheypark remains open on weekends, and the roses are still in bloom.

Milton Hershey, who made a fortune on candy bars, would no doubt be surprised if he could see what has happened in his town. Hershey never planned all these attractions with tourists in mind. Having made his first million on caramel candies in Lancaster, in 1904 the former farm boy came back to his hometown, known then as Derry Church, to build a chocolate factory in a cornfield. Hershey never had children of his own, so he adopted his workers, dedicating himself to making their town a pleasant place to live. The first parks, gardens, museum, and zoo were strictly for their benefit.

But from the start people wanted to see how this new confection called milk chocolate was made, and the factory began offering tours to meet the demand. Savoring the sweet smells, the free samples, and the atmosphere of this unusually pleasant little town, visitors sent their friends. In 1928 the count was 10,000; by 1970 it was pushing a million, and the factory could no longer accommodate the crowds.

Chocolate World was built in 1973 to take the place of the old tour and was updated for its 25th birthday in 1998. It is almost everyone's first stop in Hershey. The free trip in a Disney-like automated car whisks you off on a make-believe journey to watch the story of chocolate unfold from bean to candy bar. There's no longer the chocolate smell that was so luscious in the real factory, but well over a million and a half tourists took the ride last year anyway, and, as in the old days, enjoyed free samples at the end of the tour. The complex includes a cafeteria and a shop filled with chocolate treats.

Opposite Chocolate World is Hersheypark, once the place where factory employees came to picnic, play ball, go boating, and be entertained at the pavilion. Hershey kept improving the facilities, adding a swimming pool and convention hall that doubled in season as an ice-skating rink.

Some of the major structures in town, including the lavish Hotel Hershey, went up during the Depression as part of Hershey's campaign to provide jobs. The elegant Mediterranean-style 235-room hotel was recently refurbished, including the addition of a three-story, $7 million spa and fitness center with an indoor pool. The spa offers traditional European-style services plus some sweet, unique Hershey touches such as a whipped cocoa bath or a chocolate fondue wrap.

Looking out for the children of the town, Hershey bought a carousel and, as a 20th birthday present to the town, a roller coaster. Once again the crowds grew, and the evolution into an amusement park seemed only natural. Planning for Hersheypark began in 1971, and it has grown to 110 landscaped acres. The 1919 carousel now has a lot of company, including six roller coasters. One of the newest is the Lightning Racer, billed as America's first double track, racing/dueling wooden roller coaster.

There are 60 rides in all, from the "scream machines" to gentle go-rounds for the tots. Midway America, a celebration of nostalgic American amusement parks, offers a 100-foot-tall Ferris wheel and the Wildcat, a 1920s-style wooden roller coaster. Though the look is vintage, this roller coaster is far from tame. Advances in technology allow it to maintain speeds up to 45 miles per hour.

A growing number of water rides includes Canyon River Rapids, simulating a raging white-water rafting trip; Frontier Chute-Out, a quadruple-flume water-slide ride; and the Coal Cracker, featuring a 35-mile-per-hour splashdown.

There is continuous live entertainment at theaters scattered through the park. One of the most popular shows is the dolphin and sea lion presentation at the Aquatheatre.

Almost everyone's favorite souvenir of Hersheypark is a photo taken with the life-size candy-bar characters who greet visitors. Don't forget your camera.

Mr. Hershey's zoo has come a long way, too. It began as Hershey's own private animal collection, one of the country's largest, housed at the park for all to see. ZooAmerica now represents the major natural regions of North America—waters, deserts, woodlands, plains, and forests—and is stocked with plants and animals indigenous to each zone in replicas of their native habitats. You'll see alligators in the swamps; pumas, bison, and eagles in Big Sky Country; bears and timber wolves in the forest; wild turkeys, bobcats, otters, and raccoons at home in the woodlands.

There's more than enough to fill a Saturday here, and more still to come for Sunday. All ages can appreciate the beauty of the Hershey Gardens. From its start in 1936 when Hershey ordered that "a nice rose garden" be planted near his new hotel, the garden has grown to 23 acres. In addition to the many varieties of roses, there are themed gardens, including a Japanese garden, herb and perennial gardens, ornamental grasses, and a seasonal display garden. September marks the beginning of a spectacular array of chrysanthemums.

The garden includes a Butterfly House housing more than 25 varieties of beautiful North American butterflies. The iron trusses supporting the butterfly mesh enclosure were part of the framework for the original greenhouse built for Mr. Hershey in 1930.

Even the Hershey Museum proves to be more than you might expect.

It's less overwhelming than a lot of museums and, for that very reason, makes its points unusually well. One exhibit tells the story of the town's unusual founder, Milton Hershey. In addition, you get a compact tour through the changing lifestyles of America as it happened in south-central Pennsylvania, and a Pennsylvania German collection of furniture, ceramics, textiles, and folk art that is one of the largest in existence. Try to time your visit to coincide with the noon performance of the Apostolic Clock, with moving carved figurines depicting the Last Supper.

One other Hershey institution has nothing to do with tourists. The Milton Hershey School was founded in 1909 by Milton and Catherine Hershey to provide a free home as well as an educational center for orphan boys. Now coed, the school tries to create an atmosphere of family life for its residents, with 92 homes spread across 10,000 acres of campus. Each house provides room for 12 to 16 children and house parents. The educational program, which extends through high school, includes time for work on community projects and the opportunity to learn a trade or prepare for college, according to each student's abilities and inclinations.

Founders Hall, a striking domed limestone building constructed as a tribute to the Hersheys, serves as church, theater, and concert hall for the school. A film about the school is shown here regularly, and you can take a self-guided tour. Some of the profits from the Hershey enterprises are used to supplement the endowment Milton Hershey left to the school.

Where to stay in Hershey? The natural choices are the excellent Hershey-run establishments, either the grand Hotel Hershey or the attractive, recently expanded motel-style Hershey Lodge. Both properties offer pools, tennis, golf, spa services, and many other activities, and with package plans, including all of the admissions, they may well fit into your budget.

If not, there are less-expensive motel choices in town and nearby, and the Union Canal House is a reasonable bed-and-breakfast inn in the area.

The only problem with Hershey is fitting it all into one weekend. You may just decide to take it in installments. That way you can come back to see the tulips bloom in the spring.

Area Code: 717

DRIVING DIRECTIONS Hershey is on Route 422, about ten miles east of Harrisburg, close to routes I-81, I-78, and I-76. From D.C., take I-95 north, exit at I-695, the Baltimore Beltway, then take I-83 north to Harrisburg and Route 322 east to Route 422 into Hershey. The approximate distance from D.C. is 110 miles.

PUBLIC TRANSPORTATION   Amtrak and buses to Harrisburg and air service to Harrisburg Airport, 15 minutes away. Hershey accommodations provide service from Harrisburg.

ACCOMMODATIONS   *Hershey Resorts,* Hershey 17033, toll-free (800) 533-3131: *Hotel Hershey,* indoor and outdoor pools, tennis, lawn bowling, bicycle rentals, EE, CP or MAP; *Hershey Lodge,* indoor and outdoor pools, minigolf, game room, spa, E (children under 18 free in same room). Both hotels offer many package plans including meals, lodging, and admissions and much lower off-season rates; call for information and brochure. For less expensive lodgings, try *Best Western Inn,* U.S. 422 and Sipe Avenue, Hershey 17033, 533-5665, M–E, CP • *Comfort Inn,* 1200 Mae Street, Hershey 17036, 566-2050, indoor pool, M–EE, CP • *Days Inn,* 350 West Chocolate Avenue, Hershey 17033, 534-2162, I–E, CP • *Milton Motel,* 1733 East Chocolate Avenue, Hershey 17033, 533-0369, I–E • *Spinner's Motor Inn,* 845 East Chocolate Avenue, Hershey 17033, 533-9157 or (800) 533-5842, I–E, CP • *White Rose Motel,* 1060 East Chocolate Avenue, Hershey 17033, 533-9876, M • **Bed-and-breakfast:** *Pinehurst,* 50 Northeast Drive, Hershey 17033, 533-2603, in a brick mansion built by Hershey for orphan boys, M, CP • *Union Canal House,* 107 South Hanover Street, Union Deposit, 17033, 566-0054, bed-and-breakfast in a historic building, M, CP.

DINING   First choices, once again, are the Hershey properties: *Hershey Lodge,* 533-3311, includes *Hershey Grill,* steaks, seafood, pasta, M–E; *Lebbie Lebkicher's,* nostalgic decor, varied menu, pasta, pizza, main courses, open for three meals, I–M • *Fireside Steak House,* prime cuts, fresh seafood, E • *Hotel Hershey,* 533-2171: *Circular Dining Room,* elegant dining room, jackets requested, E–EE; *Fountain Cafe,* informal setting, M–E. • Other recommendations: *Catherine's at Spinner's,* Spinner's Motor Inn (see above), handsome decor, wide menu, I–E • *Dimitri's,* 1311 East Chocolate Avenue, 533-3403, seafood, steak, Greek dishes, I–E • *Union Canal House* (see above), continental, M–EE.

SIGHT-SEEING   *Chocolate World,* 534-4900. Hours: April to December, daily 9 A.M. to 5 P.M., may be later on weekends and in summer; rest of year, Monday to Saturday, 9 A.M. to 5 P.M., Sunday 11 A.M. to 5 P.M. Free • *Hersheypark,* Hours: Mid-May to Labor Day, selected September weekends. Opening time 10 A.M., closing varies with season, phone for current operating hours. $33.95 • *Hershey Museum,* 534-3439. Hours: Daily 10 A.M. to 5 P.M. $$$ • *ZooAmerica,* 534-3860. Hours: Daily 10 A.M. to 5 P.M.; mid-June to August, to 8 P.M. $$$ • *Hershey Gardens,* 534-3492. Hours: April 1 to September 30, daily 9 A.M. to 6 P.M., Memorial Day through Labor Day to 8 P.M. on weekends,

October, open weekends only, to 5 P.M. $$$ • *Founders Hall,* 520-2000. Hours: Mid-march to December, daily 10 A.M. to 4 P.M.; rest of year to 3 P.M. Free. See Hershey Christmas activities, pages 241–242.

INFORMATION *Hershey,* information and reservations, 300 Park Boulevard, Hershey, PA 17033, (800) HERSHEY; www.800Hershey. com.

Currents of History at Harpers Ferry

In Harpers Ferry, West Virginia, the date is 1860, not long after the day when John Brown and his band marched into town to free the slaves and inscribe the town indelibly in American history.

Then as now, Harpers Ferry was a beautiful spot, set at a bend where two mighty rivers, the Potomac and Shenandoah, meet after carving steep gorges in the surrounding wild, wooded Appalachian Mountains. It is a picture still worthy of Thomas Jefferson's 1780s description as "one of the most stupendous scenes in nature."

The town was all but destroyed by bloody Civil War battles and a series of floods afterward, but since the National Park Service took over in 1960, Harpers Ferry has come back to life as a historical park. It has been reconstructed to look the way it was at its most important moment in history and populated with costumed guides who spin fascinating tales of the momentous events that took place here long ago.

Here's a living history lesson in a setting that is at its most spectacular bathed in autumn color, and a chance to get out and walk amid the mountain scenery as well. You can continue tracing history at Antietam, the fabled battlefield just across the river in Maryland, where part of the Harpers Ferry saga continued to a tragic conclusion.

Everything at Harpers Ferry seems to have stood still for the last century—the dresses in the window of the general store have bustles, the smithy is hard at work at his open hearth, and you must visit the combination telegraph, ticket, and post office when you want to communicate with the outside world. All the tradespeople are in period dress.

If you come for Election Day, held here in mid-October, you'll find yourself in the thick of the 1860 election, with the chance to cast your presidential ballot for Stephen Douglas, John C. Breckenridge, or John Bell, all of whom will be trying to sway your vote. There will be debates, speeches, a temperance rally, and a parade typical of nineteenth-century American elections. If you favor a certain Republican candidate, one Abraham Lincoln, you're out of luck. He had no elector in what was then Jefferson County, Virginia, and thus was not an option.

Start your visit with a stop at the Visitors Bureau to get the lay of the land and a schedule of talks, then join the group sitting in the shade of an ancient tree, where a guide in period dress is explaining the events that once shook this peaceful scene.

The rivers were Harpers Ferry's beginning and ending. The town's story really started in 1748, when the powerful waters of the Potomac and the Shenandoah tempted Robert Harper to stake out a claim here. A millwright and architect, Harper gained a patent on 125 acres of land from Lord Fairfax; bought a cabin, a canoe, and a corn patch; and built himself a mill powered by the rushing water. The town was named for the ferry service Harper took over from an earlier settler.

The rivers' strong currents were also the attraction that inspired George Washington in 1790 to choose Harpers Ferry as the site for the National Armory and Arsenal, which grew into one of the largest factories in early America. It occupied 20 brick workshops and offices along the river and employed 400 people. The town prospered also as a center of commerce with cotton and flour mills, sawmills, an iron foundry, inns, and a number of shops. It was an important stop for the Baltimore and Ohio Railroad and the Chesapeake and Ohio Canal.

All of that began to change when abolitionist John Brown fixed on Harpers Ferry and its armory as the starting point on his crusade to free the slaves. Brown and his 22-man "army of liberation" came across the B&O Railroad bridge over the river in the dark of night on October 16, 1859, and occupied the armory before the startled townspeople realized what had happened. His wild dream was that thousands of slaves would join him and follow him north into Pennsylvania. Instead, the alarm went out, and the raiders were forced to barricade themselves in the army fire engine and guard house. They were captured when reinforcement troops commanded by Colonel Robert E. Lee and Lieutenant Jeb Stuart stormed the building on October 18, breaking down the door with a ladder. Two of the ten men killed were Brown's sons.

John Brown was tried and hanged at nearby Charles Town in December, but on the day of his execution he wrote a last message that proved prophetic. It read, "I, John Brown, am now quite certain that the crimes of this guilty land will not be purged away but with blood." Sixteen months later his words came true when the Civil War began.

In April 1861, when Virginia seceded from the Union (West Virginia remained part of Virginia until 1863), federal troops set fire to the arsenal, but townspeople extinguished the flames, and the cache of machinery and weapons was sent to Richmond to outfit the Confederate army.

Even without the arms, Harpers Ferry's railroad and river supply lines made it the central point of access to the Shenandoah Valley, and both sides wanted it badly. It changed hands eight times, the biggest battle occurring in September 1862, when Confederate troops under General Stonewall Jackson seized the town and captured the 12,700-man Union garrison, the largest Union surrender in the Civil War.

By the end of the war the town was devastated, and many residents had fled. Those who did come back hoping to start anew had their hopes dashed by a series of disastrous floods in the late 1800s. For years after, the ruined town stood almost desolate.

There's much to see today in the historic park—the shops, the small brick engine house where John Brown hid, the John Brown Museum, the Civil War Museum, and the Master Armorer's House, with exhibits on the history of gunmaking, including the first handmade flintlock rifles made for the U.S. Army in Harpers Ferry in 1803.

When you've retraced the fateful history of the town, climb the old stone steps to the oldest surviving building, the house Robert Harper built the year he died. It has been refurbished to represent a tenant's dwelling of the 1850s, complete with quilts, cooking pots, and wash-stand.

Thomas Jefferson was a guest here while Harper House served as an inn from 1782 to 1803. Up the hill at Jefferson Rock you can share the view that inspired him to write, "The passage of the Patowmac [sic] through the Blue Ridge is . . . worth a voyage across the Atlantic." Behind the rock is the graveyard where Robert Harper and his wife are buried.

On High Street, leading up the hill from the park, a dozen or so shops hope to tempt visitors with gifts or souvenirs or snacks of ice cream or fudge. The best of the lot is the bookstore run by the Harpers Ferry Historic Association, stocked with more than 500 titles on the Civil War, regional history, and Americana. A couple of attractive little restaurants also offer refreshments with a view. Farther up the hill in Bolivar, another cluster of antique shops and crafts stores awaits.

If you want to enjoy more views and a hike in the autumn woods, there are several hiking trails within the park, the Appalachian Trail is nearby, and the C&O Canal towpath is just across the river, a spectacular route for hiking or biking near the Potomac. Rafting on the river is another popular pastime. Ask for further information at the park visitor center.

There are a few small, convenient bed-and-breakfast homes in town, some with no more than two bedrooms, but Harpers Ferry's best-known lodging, the Hilltop House, is showing its 100-plus years. A wider choice is found in neighboring towns. In Charles Town, the site of a popular thoroughbred racetrack and gaming complex, the Carriage House, a grand early 1800s home on Main Street, gets the nod for convenience, but even nicer are two choices out in the countryside. The Cottonwood Inn is a warm, comfortable farmhouse with a book-lined living room and a hammock out back, while Hillbrook is country elegant, a showplace done with taste and charm and widely known for elegant multicourse gourmet lunches and dinners.

Two more top choices are in Shepherdstown, a quaint village that boasts of being the oldest in West Virginia. The six-room Thomas Shepherd Inn is cozy, and the Bavarian Inn, a resort perched on a cliff, offers perfect views of the Potomac. Shepherdstown's tippy buildings are filled with interesting shops, the Opera House built in 1909 is one of the oldest movie theaters in the country, and Ye Olde Sweet Shoppe Bakery gets mail orders nationwide for its fat- and cholesterol-free whole-grain European breads.

This town also offers some of the area's best dining. Try the excellent German specialties at the Bavarian Inn, the trendy menu at the Yellow Brick Bank, or lunch or sandwiches and lighter fare with delightful ambience at the Old Pharmacy Cafe, where you can enjoy dessert at an old-fashioned 1911 marble soda fountain.

In Shepherdstown, you'll be just across the bridge from Sharpsburg and the Antietam battlefield. Following his victory at Harpers Ferry in 1862, Stonewall Jackson moved on to join General Lee's forces at Antietam Creek near Sharpsburg, where the Confederate force making its first attempt to carry the war into the north was brutally mowed down by Union fire in the bloodiest battle of the war. Twenty-three thousand men were killed or wounded here. It is a moving story told vividly by the film in the National Park Service headquarters and equally well in Union General Joseph Hooker's written report of the encounter: "In the time I am writing, every stalk of corn in the northern and greater part of the field was cut as closely as could have been done with a knife and the slain lay in rows precisely as they had stood in their ranks a few moments before." The battle was critical because British aid to the Confederacy depended on the outcome.

Follow the markers of the battle, and you will find that corn waves peacefully again in the silent fields once soaked in blood, and country inns stand on ground where part of the battle was fought, happy contrasts to the sad events that took place here more than a century ago.

Area Codes: 304 for West Virginia; 301 for Maryland

DRIVING DIRECTIONS   Harpers Ferry is off Route 340, between Frederick, MD, and Winchester, VA. From D.C., take I-270 north to Frederick, then 340 west. The approximate distance from D.C. is 50 miles.

PUBLIC TRANSPORTATION   Amtrak provides regular service from Washington.

ACCOMMODATIONS   Harpers Ferry: *Jackson Rose Bed and Breakfast,* 1141 Washington Street, P.O. Box 641, Harpers Ferry

25425, 535-1528, nicely furnished historic 1795 home, M, CP • *Briscoe House,* 828 Washington Street, Box 1024, Harpers Ferry 25425, 535-2416, two suites in an 1880s home, M, CP • *Between the Rivers,* 500 East Ridge Street, Harpers Ferry 25425, 535-2768, one room with whirlpool tub, another with mountain views, M, CP • *Harpers Ferry Guest House,* 800 Washington Street, P.O. Box 1079, Harpers Ferry 25425, 535-6955, a newly built Victorian, three rooms with quilts and four-poster beds, M, CP • **Charles Town:** *Hillbrook Inn,* Summit Point Road, Route 2, P.O. Box 152, Charles Town 25414, 725-4223 or (800) 304-4223, best in the area, EE, MAP • *Cottonwood Inn,* RR 2, P.O. Box 61-S, Charles Town 25414, 725-3371 or (800) 868-1188, M, CP • *The Carriage Inn,* 417 East Washington Street, Charles Town 25414, 728-8003 or (800) 867-9830, M, CP • *Washington House Inn,* 216 South George Street, Charles Town 25414, 725-7923 or (800) 297-6957, Victorian charm, M, CP • **Shepherdstown:** *Bavarian Inn and Lodge,* Route 480 at the Potomac River Bridge, Postal Route 1, Box 30, Shepherdstown 25443, 876-2551, M–E • *Thomas Shepherd Inn,* German and Duke Streets, P.O. Box 3634, Shepherdstown 25443, 876-3715 or (888) 889-8952, M–E, CP • **Inns located on the Antietam battlefield:** *Antietam Overlook Farm,* Porterstown Road, Keedysville, MD 21756, (301) 432-4200 or (800) 878-4241, suites and fireplaces, private porches, M–E, CP • *Inn at Antietam,* 220 East Main Street, P.O. Box 119, Sharpsburg, MD 21782, handsomely furnished, (301) 432-6601, M–E, CP • *Piper House,* Route 65, Sharpsburg, MD 21782, (301) 797-1862, M, CP.

DINING *The Anvil,* 1270 Washington Street, Harpers Ferry, 535-2582, American, pub and restaurant, outdoor patio, most popular in town, M–E • *Hillbrook Inn* (see above), seven-course delicious extravaganza, including wine, by reservation only, dinner Thursday to Sunday, EE; lunch daily, E. • *Bavarian Inn* (see above), Bavarian and American dishes, M–E • *Yellow Brick Bank,* 201 West German Street at Princess Street, Shepherdstown, 876-2208, M–E • *Old Pharmacy Cafe & Soda Fountain,* 131 West German Street, Shepherdstown, 876-2085, good stop for lunch, I • *Charles Washington Inn,* 210 West Liberty Street, Charles Town, 725-4020, 1788 home, best in town, M.

SIGHT-SEEING *Harpers Ferry National Historic Park,* 535-6223; www.nps.gov/hafe. Information Center, High Street. Hours: Daily 8 A.M. to 5 P.M. Living-history interpretations and special events held Memorial Day to Labor Day. Election Day annual celebration in mid-October. Cars, $$; persons on foot or bike, $$, good for seven days • *Antietam National Battlefield,* Route 65, Sharpsburg, MD, (301) 432-5124; www.nps.gov/anti/. Hours: Visitor center, Memorial Day to Labor Day, daily 8:30 A.M. to 6 P.M.; rest of year to 5 P.M. $; under age 17, free. *Chesapeake & Ohio Canal National Park Headquarters,*

Ferry Hill Place, off Route 34, Sharpsburg, MD, (301) 739-4200. Hours: daily 8 A.M. to 4:30 P.M.

INFORMATION *Jefferson County Convention & Visitors Bureau,* off U.S. 340, P.O. Box A, Harpers Ferry, WV 25425, 535-2627 or (800) 848-TOUR; www.jeffersoncounty.com/cvb.

Victorian Week in Cape May

You might call it "Gingerbread by the Sea."

A national landmark and America's oldest seaside resort, Cape May, New Jersey, is a national treasure of Victoriana. With 600 prize Victorian houses within 2.2 square miles, it boasts an irresistible collage of pastel paint, curlicues and cupolas, ornate railings, columned porches, and towers and turrets looking out to sea.

After the summer crowds recede, Cape May takes time out to celebrate its extraordinary heritage with an annual ten-day early October extravaganza known as Victorian Week, a chance to really appreciate this town's charms. On the docket are tours, tours, and more tours. There are trolley tours and guided walking tours through the quaint streets to fill you in on the town's event-packed 179-year history. House tours let you see what lies behind those ornate facades by romantic gaslight, and INNteriors tours let you visit the town's famous inns and guest houses. By night, you can take a guided stroll to admire the lamplit stained-glass windows that fill the town with a radiant glow.

You can also watch a fashion show of Victorian dress, attend elegant Victorian dinners, and enjoy band concerts, lectures, and demontrations of Victorian arts. Want more? Browse for Victorian antiques and jewelry, or attend a Victorian Mystery Dinner where guests try to figure out whodunit. Special antique and crafts shows are scheduled as well.

Victorian Week is a one-of-a-kind event that puts you right in the spirit of a one-of-a-kind town filled with wonderful inns and dining as well as old-fashioned charm.

Whatever season you arrive in Cape May, it's a good idea to hop aboard the sightseeing trolley or join the walking tours to find out how this exceptional town came to be. You'll learn that America's largest collection of homes of the 1880s resulted from a fire that all but destroyed the city in 1878. Before that, Cape May was the prime vacation spot on the East Coast, attracting many luminaries, including seven U.S. presidents, who came to stay in its elaborate wooden hotels. The blaze of 1878 was so devastating that 30 acres of the town were laid bare.

Ironically, it was that disaster that prompted so many wealthy people, most from the Philadelphia area, to come in and build on the suddenly available tracts of land. They were further encouraged by the railroad, which offered a year's free transportation to anyone who would help recoup its suddenly vanished tourist trade.

The homes that went up were smaller than the originals, but they were even showier, products of an era when having money meant flaunting it in the form of elaborate exterior decoration. "The fancier, the better" seems to have been the Victorians' motto.

The dozens of Victorian homes now transformed into inns add to the pleasure of a Cape May visit. Many serve afternoon tea to guests and in colder weather have cozy and welcoming fireplaces in the parlor. The acknowledged showplace is the Mainstay Inn, once an elegant gambling club, still with its original 14-foot ceilings, tall mirrors, ornate plaster moldings, elaborate chandeliers, and cupola with an ocean view. The current owners have kept much of the original furnishings, and on most Saturdays and Sundays at 4 P.M. they offer tours and tea in the parlor to show off their place. Check for their Victorian Week schedules. Those who want more creature comforts may opt for the recently renovated Captain's Quarters across the street, which has gas fireplaces, whirlpools, and kitchenettes.

The Abbey, just across the way, is another inn with striking architecture. Queen Victoria and Captain Mey's are other attractive choices among the many pleasant inns on Columbia, Hughes, Ocean, and Jackson Streets. All are an easy stroll to the center of town or to the beach.

For ocean lovers, there are two choices farther from town. Columns by the Sea, a 20-room mansion, located directly across from the quietest end of the beach, has fine ocean views, as does Rhythm of the Sea, a change of pace in Victorian Cape May with airy rooms and Craftsman-style furnishings.

One of the most lavish lodgings in town is the Southern Mansion, a restored villa turned into a boutique hotel, filled with antiques, and with a 48-foot ballroom and 25 enormous guest rooms. The Angel of the Sea and its sibling, the Peter Shields Inn, call themselves bed-and-breakfast inns, but their size also puts them into the small-hotel category.

The title of grandest hotel belongs to the historic 110-room Congress Hall, which reopened in spring 2002, fresh from a $20 million restoration. With its green lawns, majestic columns, and verandas, the hotel has been a landmark for over 150 years, and actually served as the summer White House for President Benjamin Harrison. John Philip Sousa, who led concerts here, composed "The Congress Hall March" in August 1882. The hotel's verandas face the ocean.

The restoration was done by the owners of the handsome Virginia Hotel, another rebirth of a lodging well past its hundredth birthday. The Virginia offers inn ambience with hotel comforts and conveniences such as TV and telephones, and one of the town's best dining rooms.

One must on any Cape May sightseeing tour is the Physick Estate, an authentically restored 1879 Victorian mansion with 18 rooms, a sunken marble bathtub, a tiled fireplace, and elaborate chandeliers. The shop has some unique Victorian gifts, and the Carriage House, in addition to changing exhibits, has a tearoom offering a lovely afternoon tea.

It should be noted that not all of Cape May's attractions are of the Victorian variety. The long strand of beach offers plenty of room for in-season sunning. The promenade beside the beach is perfect for walking or jogging anytime the weather cooperates. Recently, the Victorian Week tour roster has widened to include an Ocean Walk along the beach, telling about the local marine life, plus a boat tour that fills you in on wetlands ecology and marine life along with Cape May architecture and traditions.

A short drive will bring you to Cape May Point, where the Atlantic meets Delaware Bay, one of the few places where you can see both the sunrise and the sunset over water. Sunset Beach on the bay is ideal for watching the sun go down and also is the place to sift through the sand for the plentiful pieces of polished quartz known as Cape May diamonds. The restored 1859 Cape May Lighthouse rewards the 199-step climb to the top with breathtaking views of the Jersey Cape. The Lighthouse is now operated by the Mid-Atlantic Center for the Arts and on selected days in season offers a unique living-history experience, with an actor portraying the last keeper, regaling visitors at the top with tales of life and work in the 1920s.

Besides being a treat for Victoriana buffs and beach walkers, Cape May in autumn is happy hunting grounds for bird-watchers. You'll be following in the footsteps of John James Audubon and Roger Tory Peterson if you head for Cape May Point State Park or the 180-acre Cape May Migratory Bird Refuge, owned by the Nature Conservancy. Both are sanctuaries for spotting birds of prey, such as hawks and falcons, as well as exotic and endangered species, like the least tern, black skinner, and piping plover, which stop for food and shelter before crossing the mouth of Delaware Bay. The New Jersey Audubon Society operates the Cape May Bird Observatory with two centers; stop by for a schedule of field trips and programs.

Back in town, Washington Mall beckons with three blocks of shops, as well as sidewalk cafes, ice cream parlors, and a bookstore where you can pick up the Sunday papers.

All over town are restaurants with a growing reputation among gourmets, many ranked among the best in the state. Among the long-time top offerings are the Ebbitt Room at the Virginia Hotel, Frescos, 410 Bank Street, Water's Edge, and the Washington Inn. Newer entries winning praise include Daniel's on Broadway, Union Park, and the Peter Shields Inn. By the time you read this, there will no doubt be even more choices.

If children are along, you may want to take a drive to Historic Cold

Spring Village, a complex of 20 restored buildings representing a nineteenth-century farm, with working craftsmen offering demonstrations and farm animals to be admired. A bit farther north is Leaming's Run Gardens and Colonial Farm, 25 themed gardens and a reconstructed farm.

On the way home, there is a worthwhile detour off Route 47 to Wheaton Village in Millville. This little-touted attraction is a re-created working craft village on the site of a former glass factory, one of several that prospered in this part of New Jersey a century ago. The 1888 factory has been restored and offers demonstrations of early glassblowing techniques. A crafts arcade is filled with artisans demonstrating such nineteenth-century arts as weaving, wood carving, tinsmithing, pottery making, and the creation of stained glass. Youngsters also love the three-quarter-mile trip around the lake in an old-fashioned train.

The main attraction, however, is the Museum of Glass, one of the best of its kind. Exhibits follow glassmaking history from the first handblown bottles, used for drink, strong and otherwise, to Tiffany, art deco, and art nouveau designs. Early lamps, pressed glass, cut glass, lead crystal—name your favorite and you will find it here, among the displays of almost every kind of glassware ever made by hand or machine. It's all the more attractive because the museum is built around a court and has tall windows that make good use of natural light to show off its displays. If you want a souvenir or an early start on your Christmas shopping, you can buy glassware in the village store and paperweights in a special shop that has a most comprehensive collection, ranging in price from $5 to $5,000.

Glassmaking is another side of the 1880s in southern New Jersey—a bonus on a visit to Victorian Cape May.

Area Code: 609

DRIVING DIRECTIONS Cape May is at the tip of southern New Jersey, the last exit on the Garden State Parkway. From D.C., the shortest way is to take the Cape May–Lewes Ferry, a 70-minute ride across Delaware Bay. Take Route 50/301 across the Chesapeake Bay Bridge, then follow Route 301 to Route 404 east, which merges with Route 18 and Route 9 east to Lewes. For ferry schedules and current rates, call (302) 645-6313. To travel by car, take I-95 north across the Delaware Memorial Bridge into New Jersey, then follow Route 49 south to Route 47 south, which merges with Route 9 into Cape May. The approximate distance from D.C. is 195 miles.

PUBLIC TRANSPORTATION Bus service from Philadelphia via New Jersey Transit (215) 569-3752. A car is not necessary in Cape May.

ACCOMMODATIONS All zip codes are 08204. Prices vary by season and are usually at the lower end in fall, winter, and early spring, highest in summer. **Inns:** *Mainstay Inn,* 635 Columbia Avenue, 884-8690, E–EE, CP; also *Officer's Quarters* of the Mainstay, a separate building, all suites with fireplaces, whirlpools, and kitchenettes, EE, CP • *The Abbey,* 34 Gurney Street, 884-4506, M–EE • *The Queen Victoria,* 102 Ocean Street, 884-8702, M–EE, CP • *Captain Mey's Inn,* 202 Ocean Avenue, 884-7793 or (800) 981-3702, M–EE, CP • *The Inn on Ocean,* 25 Ocean Street, 884-7070 or (800) 304-4477, E, CP • *Columns by the Sea,* 1513 Beach Drive, 884-2228, E–EE, CP • *Rhythm of the Sea,* 1123 Beach Avenue, 884-7788 or (800) 498-6888, E–EE, CP • *Inn at 22 Jackson,* 22 Jackson Street, 884-2226 or (800) 452-8177, all suites, E–EE, CP • *Beauclaire's Bed & Breakfast,* 23 Ocean Street, 898-1222, small and charming, M–E, CP • *Cliveden Inn,* 709 Columbia Avenue, 884-4516 or (800) 884-2420, M–E, CP • *Twin Gables,* 731 Columbia Avenue, 884-7332 or (800) 966-7332, modest but moderately priced for Cape May, M–E, CP. Contact the Chamber of Commerce for a long list of additional inns and motels.

Hotels: *Virginia Hotel,* 25 Jackson Street, 884-5700 or 800-732-4236, M–EE, CP • *Congress Hall,* 251 Beach Drive, 884-8421 or (800) 842-6922, I–E • *The Southern Mansion,* 720 Washington Street, 884-7171 or (800) 381-3888, EE, CP • *Angel of the Sea,* 5–7 Trenton Avenue, 884-3369 or (800) 848-3369, 27 rooms, inn ambience, many ocean views, M–EE, CP • *Peter Shields Inn,* 1301 Beach Drive, 884-9090, Georgian Revival mansion, E–EE, CP.

DINING Critics' picks: *Daniel's on Broadway,* 416 South Broadway, West Cape May, 898-8770, new American in a Victorian home, E–EE • *Ebbitt Room,* Virginia Hotel (see above), elegant and long among the tops in town, E–EE • *410 Bank Street,* at that address, 884-2127, Cajun, mesquite grill, E–EE • *Frescos,* 412 Bank Street, 884-0366, well-prepared northern Italian, E–EE • *Union Park Restaurant,* Macomber Hotel, 727 Beach Drive, 884-8811, former Ebbitt Room chef wins raves in new quarters, EE • *Washington Inn,* 801 Washington Street, 884-5697, gracious 1856 home, consistently excellent, M–EE.

Water views: *The Pelican Club,* 501 Beach Avenue, 884-3500, new penthouse outpost of the Washington Inn, M–EE • *Peter Shields Inn Restaurant,* 1301 Beach Drive, 884-9090, elegant dining, E–EE • *Water's Edge,* Beach Drive and Pittsburgh Avenue, 884-1717, creative menus, highly regarded, M–EE • *Tisha's,* 714 Beach Drive, 884-9119, eclectic menu, pretty and unpretentious, M–E • *Cabanas Beach Bar and Grill,* 429 Beach Avenue, 884-4800, downstairs for light fare, I; upstairs for the view and full meals, E • *Henry's on the Beach,* 702

Beach Drive, 884-8826, serving all three meals at reasonable prices, I–M.

Strictly seafood: *Axelsson's Blue Claw,* Ocean Drive, 884-5878, E • **The Lobster House,** Fisherman's Wharf, 884-8296, very popular, expect long lines, M–EE • *The Raw Bar,* Fisherman's Wharf, no frills take-out to eat at tables on the dock, I–M.

More good choices: *Louisa's,* 104 Jackson Street, 884-5882, tiny cafe that is a find, no reservations so expect a line in season, M • *Cucina Rosa,* 301 Washington Street Mall, 898-9800, casual Italian, pastas, I; other dishes, M • *Peaches at Sunset,* 1 Sunset Boulevard, West Cape May, 898-0100, interesting menu, Thai and Indian influences, M–E. • *Mad Batter,* 19 Jackson Street, 884-5970, eclectic menu in a gingerbread house, top choice for breakfast or brunch, M–E • *The Twinings Tea Room,* Carriage House, Emlen Physick Estate, 1048 Washington Avenue, 884-5404, elegant tea luncheons and afternoon teas, M.

SIGHT-SEEING *Mid-Atlantic Center for the Arts (MAC), Physick Estate,* 1048 Washington Street, P.O. Box 340, Cape May 08204, 884-5404, www.capemaymac.org. MAC sponsors *Victorian Week,* ten days of special events and tours in mid-October. Hours for tours of the Physick House ($$) and Cape May Lighthouse ($$) and various walking, trolley and inn tours change with the seasons; pick up the pamphlet *This Week in Cape May* at information centers or contact MAC for current information. MAC also sponsors year-round events including antique, craft, music, food and flower festivals, and Christmas festivities • *Cold Spring Village,* 720 Route U.S. 9 (exit 4A from the Garden State Parkway), Cape May, 898-2300. Hours: June to Labor Day daily 10 A.M. to 4:30 P.M.; Memorial Day to mid-June and Labor Day through September, weekends only. $$ • *Leaming's Run Gardens and Colonial Farm,* U.S. 9, Garden State Parkway exit 13, Cape May Court House, 465-5871. Hours: Mid-May to mid-October daily 9:30 A.M. to 5 P.M. $$ • *Wheaton Village,* 1501 Glasstown Road, off Wade Boulevard, Millville (from Cape May take Route 47 north and west and watch for signs), 825-6800 or (800) 998-4552. Hours: April to early January, daily 10 A.M. to 5 P.M.; mid-January to March, Wednesday to Sunday 10 A.M. to 5 P.M. $$$, family rates • *Cape May Bird Observatory/New Jersey Audubon Society,* Birding hotline: 861-0466. Two locations, both open daily 10 A.M. to 5 P.M.; Northwood Center, 701 East Lake Drive, Cape May Point; Center for Research and Education, 600 Route 47 North, Cape May Court House, 861-0700.

INFORMATION *Greater Cape May Chamber of Commerce,* P.O. Box 556, Cape May, NJ 08204, 884-5508; www.capemaychamber.com.

The Fairest of Fairs in Waterford

Waterford, Virginia, population 200, still bears a remarkable resemblance to the nineteenth-century village that grew up around a mill on the banks of Catoctin Creek—and that's just the way the residents like it.

When talk of development of the farmlands outside town threatened change years ago, some townspeople had an inspired idea. The Waterford Foundation was formed in 1943 to preserve the open spaces. To raise money toward this goal, they held a crafts fair with their picturesque town as a living backdrop.

Today the annual Waterford Homes Tour and Crafts Exhibit has grown to a giant three-day early-October celebration covering every inch of the town, an event that has been accurately dubbed "the fairest of fairs." What's more, the timing couldn't be better, for Waterford is near the heart of Loudoun County, the pastoral hunt country just an hour from Washington, and the fair coincides with the fall steeplechase season, providing a double reason for the trip.

Put on your walking shoes—the terrain is hilly—and get ready to meet more than 140 top-notch craftspeople showing traditional skills, from silversmithing to leather work. Bookbinders, furniture makers, and artisans creating traditional folk art are among the demonstrators. Visitors are sometimes allowed to get into the act, too, and try their hands at stitching on a quilt, throwing a pot on a kickwheel, or working the wooden toys children played with 200 years ago.

Be forewarned: You will need a blindfold not to succumb to the urge to buy some of the handsome wares that tempt at every turn. But then, why pass up the chance? Besides the crafts demonstrators filling buildings and spilling out onto every sidewalk, field, and empty space, thousands of finished crafts are up for sale in the Mill. One of the quaint buildings of the town may be full of dried flowers, another hung with photos and fine art. The Country Store is stocked with freshly baked goods and homemade jellies.

The arts and crafts are the big attractions, but only the start of the fun. To make it all the merrier, music fills the streets—a string band here, a chamber music group there, a folksinger around the corner. The militia camps in Waterford during the fair, reenacting the skirmish that took place during the Civil War, and you never know when you'll spy a soldier slipping through the trees or a fife and drum corps marching through the town.

There are houses to tour, from tiny Quaker dwellings dating from the town's 1733 founding to the imposing eighteenth-century miller's house to Victorian classics built at the turn of the century. Class is in session in the one-room schoolhouse, run about the way it might have been on a typical day in 1880.

Come early if you want to find a convenient place in the parking fields in Waterford, and allow plenty of time to browse and buy. When you need a refreshment break, you'll find choices all around town—at the old school, the Bond Street Barn and Mill area, the Schooley Mill Barn, and the Hardware Store, to name a few main locations. You can have sausage or pita sandwiches or Brunswick stew, or head for the barbecue pit outside. There's an apple butter pot simmering nearby, offering yet another fine souvenir to take home.

Waterford has limited lodgings, the best being the eighteenth-century log-and-stone Milltown Inn on 15 acres in the countryside. That leaves the happy choice of headquartering either around Leesburg, 5 miles away, or about 15 miles farther in Middleburg. Whichever of these charming towns you choose, it's worth taking time to see the other.

Quaint, "old town" Leesburg, the county seat, was named for Francis "Lightfoot" Lee. Modern development is mushrooming just beyond Leesburg's historic core, but the old town remains as it was, another place with the look of the past. The layout of the main streets, some of the stone structures, and one log house date back to 1758, when the town was founded.

Start at the Loudoun Museum for a slide-show orientation, a printed walking tour, and a look at 200 years of town artifacts. Then take a walk on Market, Loudoun, and King Streets, where there are fine old homes, and past Courthouse Square, where Loudoun freeholders penned the Loudoun Resolves, a protest of the Stamp Act and a plea for American rights and liberties written two years before the Declaration of Independence. You'll find many antiques shops along the way, including 50 dealers under one roof at the Leesburg Antique Gallery of Shoppes at 7 Wirt Street, parallel to King.

The most appealing inn in Leesburg is the Norris House, an 1806 bed-and-breakfast home nicely furnished with antiques.

It will take only an hour or so to do the old part of Leesburg, leaving time for the town's most impressive sights, the mansions in the nearby countryside. Oatlands, a pillared white Classical Revival beauty, was built at the beginning of the nineteenth century by George Carter, a great-grandson of the famous planter Robert "King" Carter. The spacious rooms are decorated with spectacular ornamental plaster cornices and moldings and furnished with choice French, English, and American antiques. The formal terraced gardens are among Virginia's finest. Once the center of a thriving 3,400-acre plantation, Oatlands is now set on 261 acres that serve as the site for point-to-point races, fairs, and an annual monthlong 1880s-style celebration of Christmas.

Morven Park is another storybook estate, built in the 1780s by Maryland governor Thomas Swann and enlarged in the early twentieth century by Virginia governor Westmoreland Davis. Besides the superbly furnished mansion with treasures from around the world, formal gardens, and nature trails, Morven Park offers a carriage museum displaying more than 100 horse-drawn vehicles. The grounds here are also the scene of equestrian events, including important steeplechase races in spring and fall.

Head out into the country to see some of the beautiful farmland and visit one of Loudoun County's scenic wineries. Fields of Flowers is a unique stop, a farm where you can pick your own colorful blooms by the bouquet or by the bucketful. Annual spring and fall organized farm tours are a good chance to see some of the most picturesque farms. Check the Loudoun Convention and Visitors Association for tour dates, and for names of other farms that welcome visitors anytime.

Tarara Winery is the largest of the wineries, with a scenic hilltop location and pleasant outdoor deck. They've recently added guest rooms for those who want to stay for a while. Loudoun Valley Vineyards also has pleasant views from a glass-walled tasting room and deck.

While you're out in the country, make a stop at Old Lucketts Store, seven miles north of Leesburg on Route 15. The funky exterior of the former general store belies the treasures inside, wares from 20 antique dealers from country primitive to art deco. Purcellville is another recommended stop for antiquers, with several stores on one street just off Route 7 in the middle of the village.

Residents are fighting off development to the south in Middleburg, the posh village considered the heart of hunt country. Some of Loudoun County's wealthiest residents, America's landed gentry, live on the manicured estates behind split-rail fences in the hill country outside Middleburg. It is land that has been aptly compared with the lush rolling English countryside. The people here cherish their narrow unpaved roads, the better to discourage tourists and developers.

Middleburg itself is a mixed breed of colonial charm and horsey chic. It was a way station for horsemen traveling to and from the Shenandoah Valley as early as 1728, when it was known as Chinn's Crossing and the present Red Fox Tavern was called Chinn's Ordinary. One frequent visitor was young George Washington, stopping off on his way to the valley as a surveyor for Thomas, Lord Fairfax. Many of the stone buildings from the early days still stand.

But instead of stagecoaches, the roads into town these days bring Mercedes-Benzes and horse vans. You never know what horse-loving D.C. celebrity you may see out shopping on Middleburg's Washington Street, where antique stores and boutiques alternate with shops selling shiny boots and saddles. Almost every shop sign features a fox or horse or dog, and many of the clothes and gifts for sale follow the same hunting motifs.

The horse people settle here to breed and train their mounts and take part in the fox hunts, races, and shows that are the social fabric of the county. The hunts are strictly private affairs, but everyone is invited to the colorful steeplechase events that take place throughout the Loudoun countryside in spring and fall. All you need to enjoy the day, Loudoun-style, is a blanket for sitting on the grass and a sumptuous tailgate lunch. Glenwood Park, home to some of the main events, has spectacular mountain views to add to the pleasure of the events.

You'll see that some steeplechase spectators like to picnic in style, bringing out portable tables with linen cloths, candles, and the family silver for the occasion. Checking out the culinary spreads is part of the day's entertainment.

Steeplechasing is a natural sport for fox hunters, who learn to jump fences and walls in pursuit of their prey. The name *steeplechase* originated in Ireland, where the first recorded horseback chase actually was to a church steeple. On a typical day here there are races over flat ground, over brush jumps, and over timber (split-rail fences). A point-to-point race means exactly that: contestants race from one specified point on the course to another. Some of the horses are bred and ridden by professionals; others are trained and mounted by their amateur owners, more often for glory and trophies than for monetary prizes.

The races are informal affairs, and viewers are free to sit in the shade, mill about, or go up to the fence for a closer view. The racers in their stable colors and the officials in elegant red coats and black riding hats make a pretty picture against the green fields, English racing prints come to life in modern Virginia.

Lodgings in and around Middleburg are choice. You can sleep in a canopy bed at the historic Red Fox Inn or have Colonial decor and modern comfort at additions to the inn such as the Stray Fox. Or stop over at the Middleburg Country Inn or the Middleburg Guest Suites, attractive suites right above the shops on Washington Street. The Long-barn, tucked into the woods, is a renovated barn with country elegance.

Out in the countryside, many special inns await. The 1763 Inn, set on 50 acres of rolling countryside, offers a pool, tennis courts, and a variety of rooms, including rustic charmers in a converted stable. Many rooms have fireplaces, whirlpools, canopy beds, and patios or decks. It is located nine miles to the west in Upperville, the home of a lovely church donated by the late Paul Mellon and the center for the spectacular Loudoun County stable tour held each Memorial Day weekend. Many of us would be happy to be bedded in quarters equivalent to those of Loudoun's favorite steeds!

For an authentic sample of the charm of this region, you can't beat Oakland Green, a beautifully preserved Quaker farmhouse on a narrow dirt road in the countryside in Lincoln, about midway between Leesburg and Middletown. The house was built in four attached sections, including a log house circa 1730 and a stone wing built in the 1740s. It has been occupied by the Brown family for nine generations and is filled with wonderful family antiques. The reasonably priced suite in the log house is a find, offering a comfortable beamed living room with a fireplace, two baths, and a big bedroom. A second bedroom is available if needed. Two more bedrooms are in the main house. Guests here enjoy magnificent grounds shaded by old trees, and a secluded swimming pool.

The Ashby Inn in Paris and the Little River Inn in Aldie are cozy restored 1800s houses in picture-book small towns; Ashby has a highly regarded dining room. Poor House Farm is a plantation circa 1814, on 12 serene acres with lodgings in the main house as well as cottages on the grounds. Buckskin Manor dates to the 1750s and still has some of the original log walls and beams, though the house has been nicely renovated with spacious guest rooms. The 65-acre lawn offers a fishing pond and swimming pool.

Settling on one inn is almost as difficult as fitting in the many attractions of Loudoun County in one weekend. Hunt country is an area that sounds the call for a return trip.

Area Codes: Leesburg, 703; Middleburg and Waterford, 540

DRIVING DIRECTIONS Waterford is near Leesburg in Loudoun County, the horse country west of Washington. From D.C., take Route 7 or the Toll Road, Route 267, west to Leesburg, then Route 9 west, and turn right on Route 662 north to Waterford. For Middleburg, take Route 50 west, follow Route 15 north to Leesburg and proceed as above. The approximate distance from D.C. to Leesburg is 35 miles; to Waterford, 40 miles; and to Middleburg, 50 miles.

ACCOMMODATIONS Lodgings in towns: *The Norris House Inn,* 108 Loudoun Street, Leesburg 20175, 777-1806 or (800) 644-1806, M–E, CP • *Red Fox Inn,* 2 East Washington Street, Middleburg 20118, 687-6301 or (800) 223-1728, E • *Middleburg Inn and Guest Suites,* 105 West Washington Street, Middleburg 20118, 687-3115 or (800) 432-6125, E–EE • *Middleburg Country Inn,* 209 East Washington Street, Middleburg 20118, 687-6082 or (800) 262-6082, weekdays, M–E, CP; Friday, Saturday, E–EE, MAP • **Lodgings in the countryside:** *Oakland Green,* Route 2, P.O. Box 147, Leesburg 20160, 338-7628, historic charm, pool, I, CP • *Milltown Farms Inn,* 14163 Milltown Road, P.O. Box 34, Waterford 20197, 882-4470 or (888) 747-3942, M–E, CP • *Poor House Farm,* 35304 Poor House Lane, Round Hill 20141, (540) 554-2511, M–E, CP • *The Longbarn,* 37129 Adams Green Lane, P.O. Box 208, Middleburg 20118, (540) 687-4137, M, CP • *Buckskin Manor,* 13452 Harpers Ferry Road, Purcellville 20132, 668-6864 or (888) 668-7056, M–E, CP • *Little River Inn,* Route 50, Aldie 20105, (703) 327-6742, M, CP • *1763 Inn,* Route 50, Upperville 20184, (540) 592-3848, M–EE, CP • *The Ashby Inn,* Route 1, P.O. Box 21-A, Paris 20130, (540) 592-3900, main house, E–EE, CP • *Good-*

stone Inn, 36205 Snake Hill Road, Middlebury 20117, 687-4645, lavishly restored historic estate on 265 acres, EE, CP.

DINING *Tuscarora Mill Restaurant,* 203 Harrison Street SE, Leesburg, 771-9300, contemporary setting, M–E • *Lightfoot Cafe,* 11 North King Street, Leesburg, 771-2233, American-style bistro, M–EE • *Laurel Brigade Inn,* 20 West Market Street, Leesburg 22075, 777-1010, traditional menu, M • *Green Tree,* 15 South King Street, Leesburg, 777-7246, authentic Colonial recipes, M–E • *Eiffel Tower Cafe,* 107 Loudoun Street SW, Leesburg, 777-5142, charming French cafe, M–E • *Red Fox Inn* (see above), M–EE • *Black Coffee Bistro,* 101 South Madison Street, Middleburg, 687-6456, bistro fare in a 1790s home, M–E • *Back Street Cafe,* 4 East Federal Street, Middleburg, 687-3122, informal setting for Italian, big salad bar, live jazz on weekends, I–M • *Hidden Horse Tavern,* 7 West Washington Street, Middleburg, 687-3828, cozy, seafood and pasta specials, M–E • *Coach Stop,* 28½ Washington Street, Middleburg, 687-5515, unpretentious local favorite, I–M; try the Horseman's Special Breakfast • *Ashby Inn* (see above), M–E • *1763 Inn* (see above), German/American, I–E • *The Upper Crust,* 4 Pendleton Street, Middleburg, 687-5666, bakery and cafe, good lunch choice, I.

SIGHT-SEEING *Waterford Homes Tour and Crafts Exhibit,* sponsored by Waterford Foundation, Inc., P.O. Box 142, Waterford 20197, 882-3018, www.waterfordva.org. Three days beginning the first Friday in October, 10 A.M. to 5 P.M. $$$$$ • *Loudoun Museum,* 14–16 West Loudoun Street, Leesburg, 777-7427. Hours: February through December, Monday to Saturday 10 A.M. to 5 P.M., Sunday 1 P.M. to 5 P.M. $ • *Oatlands,* Route 15, south of Leesburg, 777-3174. Hours: Late March to late December, Monday to Saturday 10 A.M. to 4:30 P.M., Sunday 1 P.M. to 4:30 P.M. $$$$ • *Morven Park,* Old Waterford Road off Business Route 7, Leesburg, 777-2414. Hours: April to October, Tuesday to Friday noon to 5 P.M., Saturday 10 A.M. to 5 P.M., Sunday 1 P.M. to 5 P.M.; November, Saturday, Sunday noon to 5 P.M. $$$ • **Steeplechase racing:** For current schedules, check with the Convention and Visitors Association or write to Virginia Steeplechase Association, P.O. Box 1158, Middleburg 20118, 687-3455. Among major races usually held in early October are the Virginia Fall Race Meet at Glenwood Park, Middleburg, and the Morven Park Race meet near Leesburg • **Vineyards:** Phone each for hours and driving directions. *Tarara Winery,* 13648 Tarara Lane, Leesburg, 771-7100 • *Willowcroft Farm Vineyards,* 38906 Mt. Gilead Road, Leesburg, 777-8161 • *Loudoun Valley Vineyards,* 38516 Charlestown Pike, Waterford, 882-3375 • *Meredyth Vineyards,* off Route 628, P.O. Box 347, Middleburg, 687-6277 • *Piedmont Vineyards,* 2546-D Halfway Road, P.O. Box 286, Middleburg, 687-5528. This is just a sampling; countact the Convention and Visitors Association for a full wine trail listing.

INFORMATION *Loudoun Convention and Visitors Association,* 108-D South Street SE, Leesburg, VA 20175, 771-2170 or (800) 752-6118; www.visitloudoun.org; www.middleburg.com.

Dropping in on the du Ponts of Delaware

Louis XVI would feel right at home if he were to drop into Nemours, the palatial pink French chateau built by Alfred I. du Pont, great-grandson of Louis's minister of finance.

When Louis and his court ran into trouble and Pierre Samuel du Pont de Nemours fled to the New World in 1800, he founded an American dynasty that would by the 1920s be the nation's wealthiest family, one whose estates would have done credit to royalty. The du Pont properties now open to the public make for some of the most spectacular sight-seeing in the East.

Headquarters for a du Pont weekend really should be the Hotel du Pont in Wilmington, which reflects the resources of the family behind the name. It was for a time, in fact, the residence of Pierre S. du Pont, who didn't marry until he was 40 and divided his time between an apartment on the top floor of the hotel and his nearby Pennsylvania estate, now known as Longwood Gardens.

Built by the company in 1911 as part of its corporate complex in downtown Wilmington at twice the usual cost of a first-class hotel of its size, the block-square white stone Italian Renaissance building offers comfortably modern guest rooms in gracious surroundings. Even if you don't stay here, don't miss the Green Room with its arching two-and-a-half-story windows and gold chandeliers, and the Brandywine Room, with Italian walnut paneling and a million dollars' worth of Wyeths and other paintings on the walls.

To learn how the du Pont dynasty began, start at the Hagley Museum, which tells the tale of the first black-powder mills along the Brandywine, as well as the story of early American industry from the first water-powered mills to the steam-powered engines of the late nineteenth century. The 240-acre grounds of Hagley include the Georgian-style home of original Pierre's son, Éleuthère Irénée, who founded the company that eventually grew into the world's most powerful gunpowder manufacturer.

The founder lived with his domain in full view right out the window of his mansion, known as Eleutherian Mills. Five generations of du Ponts lived in this home built in 1803, and the furnishings of the 12-

room home are all the more interesting for revealing their changing tastes. Empire, Federal, and Victorian periods are highlighted in various room settings.

On Blacksmith Hill, part of the workers' community has been restored to show the lifestyle of the early families who lived on the property. Nearby is the school where workers' children were educated before there was a public school in the area. At the base of the hill, a restored machine shop of the 1880s offers a picture of change in the workplace, the din of old power tools replacing the quiet, painstaking hand-tooling of earlier artisans. In fall, the grounds are home to an annual craft fair with some 40 artisans demonstrating and selling their wares.

To see what had become of the du Ponts a century later, take an afternoon tour at Nemours, built from 1909 to 1910 by Alfred I du Pont. It is named for the original family estate in France, and worthy of the European royalty that inspired it. The opulent 102-room mansion is remarkable. Its ornate paneling, carved and gold-leaf-adorned ceilings, crystal chandeliers, priceless antique furnishings, paintings, silver, Oriental rugs, Aubusson carpets, and ornate screens are dazzling in their magnificence. Many of the furnishings have royal origins. One of the chandeliers once hung in Schoenbrun Palace in Austria, where Marie Antoinette grew up. Outdoors, the 1488 English Gates came from Wimbledon Manor, the estate given by Henry VIII as a gift to his wife Catherine Parr in 1543, and the Russian Gates were made for the palace of Catherine the Great outside St. Petersburg.

There are portraits of the family founder, as well as of Louis XVI and his wife, Marie Antoinette, but also many family photos and paintings of children and much-loved adopted stray pets, evidence that this was, in fact, a warm, family home. Throughout there are reminders of some of the unusual interests of Alfred du Pont, who, aside from his wealth, was quite an accomplished man—an inventor who held 200 patents, a horseman, and a champion sailor with many trophies. He liked modern devices, and the house included the very latest in bathrooms, as well as its own generator and a room for bottling spring water. There were also gadgets such as an exerciser with a saddle seat that simulates the gait of a horse, a steam cabinet, a bowling alley, a pull-down screen for films, and a billiards room with lights made to swivel so they cast no shadows on the tables.

As if the home were not enough, there are acres of gardens inspired by Versailles, resplendent with reflecting pools and fountains; a 200-foot carillon; and the Temple of Love, with a life-size statue of Diana. Amid the pomp, there is another reminder that this was a family's home—the little gray house called the Wren's Nest, a combination schoolhouse and playhouse for the children on the estate. Visitors are also taken to the Chauffeur's Garage to view the antique cars and a motor launch owned by the family, and a pony cart used by the children on the estate.

Nemours will fill your afternoon and your senses. Come Sunday, you can start fresh among the legendary formal gardens of Pierre Samuel du Pont (known to all as P.S.) at Longwood in Kennett Square, Pennsylvania, about a 20-minute drive from Wilmington. Local legend has it that Alfred I. built his fabulous Nemours estate because he was jealous of rival cousin P.S.'s showplace, and Longwood is still considered by many to be the most fabulous of all the du Pont estates. In fall, the chrysanthemum display is outstanding.

Du Pont was inspired when he visited the Villa d'Este outside Rome early in this century and reportedly said, "It would be nice to have something like this at home." His first efforts became the scene of a garden party in 1914 that was such a smash, it inspired the creation of fountains to make the next year's event even more spectacular.

The gardens continued to grow. A huge conservatory was added when Pierre decided things were "rather dreary in winter," and the countryside in front was transformed into Longwood's main Fountain Garden. When a ballroom was added in 1928, a 10,010-pipe Aeolian organ was installed behind fabric walls at one end of the room. It is still used regularly for public concerts.

When the Open Air Theater was enlarged in 1926, an elaborate new fountain system was built and illuminated by 600 multicolored lights. It debuted to wild acclaim in 1927. Still not satisfied, du Pont worked for another four years to create the spectacular fountains that still thrill visitors today.

The gardens, among the finest in America, are kept up to their creator's standards, offering more than 1,100 varieties of plants. The conservatory, nearly four acres with 20 indoor gardens, ensures dazzling blooms whatever the weather, and a yearlong calendar of special events, including gardening and cooking demonstrations, plant walks, art exhibits and concerts, and special children's activities, ensures that there is something to see and do anytime you visit. The children's garden is guaranteed to charm all ages.

The Longwood Heritage Exhibit, located in the former Pierce–du Pont residence on the grounds, offers a video and some fascinating exhibits tracing the development of the gardens.

Longwood is the greatest of the du Pont gardens, but the most remarkable of all the family homes awaits at Winterthur, the estate of Henry Francis du Pont, about ten minutes from Longwood on Route 52, heading back toward Wilmington. It holds one of the nation's finest assemblages of early American antiques.

Henry du Pont was one of the first to recognize the importance of American craftsmanship. In 1923 he began to amass the finest from the period between 1640 and 1860, not only furniture but curtains, bed hangings, rugs, lighting fixtures, silver pieces, and ceramics. Not content with isolated objects, he went on to comb the eastern seaboard for paneling, fireplaces, mantels, doors, and carved ceilings from the finest homes of the period, dismantling and reinstalling them at Winterthur as proper background for his collections. Eventually there were almost 175 room settings. After living pleasurably with his antiques for close to 30 years, du Pont in 1951 turned his home into a museum and educational facility, moving into the Regency-style villa that now serves as the Museum Store.

The 45-minute general tour is a sampler of American interiors that span two centuries. Decorative Arts tours are more in-depth guided itineraries exploring a variety of period settings. The house changes seasonally and features Yuletide decorations in November and December and fresh flowers from the garden in warmer months.

The Galleries at Winterthur add an important dimension to a visit. They offer self-guided exhibits to further understanding and appreciation of fine craftsmanship. The Galleries can be seen on their own as a museum of American design, or in conjunction with a house tour.

A permanent exhibit on the ground floor, "Perspectives on the Decorative Arts in Early America," focuses on the meaning of objects in everyday life. The separate Dorrance Gallery holds the quite extraordinary Campbell Collection of some 125 soup tureens. The Touch-It Room features hands-on areas, including a child-sized period room setting, a small general store, and kitchen and lighting exhibit tables.

The Henry S. McNeil Gallery on the second floor offers three illuminating exhibits. A replica of the Dominy Shops, a woodworking and clockmaking shop on Long Island, displays the changing tools used by one family of craftsmen over four generations, spanning the seventeenth through twentieth centuries. Pieces from Winterthur's fine collections are used to demonstrate "Clues for Collectors," 14 points of connoisseurship used by experts to help identify and evaluate furniture. "Survivals and Revivals" shows how seven nineteenth- and twentieth-century furniture makers copied the designs and workmanship of earlier craftsmen. Also on the second floor is the Graves Gallery for changing exhibitions.

Not the least of the pleasures of Winterthur are the gardens, a 983-acre woodland carefully planted to maintain a natural look. Henry du Pont was as avid a gardener as a collector, and his plantings include a vast collection of exotic and native plants. The gardens have been restored to their original glory, and a three-acre Enchanted Woods section has been added, complete with Troll Bridge, Faerie Cottage, Tulip Tree House, Bird's Nest, and Fairy Flower Labyrinth.

Tanbark and turf paths wind through shaded woodland and over rolling hillsides, bringing lovely vistas into view at every turn. Though most famous for spring displays, the garden's foliage and flowers are lovely in fall as well. Lavender cups of colchicums cover the hillsides in September, joined by fall daffodils and white autumn crocuses in

October, all set against a backdrop of scarlet and gold leaves and bright berried shrubs. It's a heavenly stroll on a fine fall day, but there is a tram tour from mid-April through October for the less energetic.

The grounds of Winterthur host several special events, including point-to-point steeplechase races in early May, a tradition for more than two decades, and a fine craft show over Labor Day weekend, featuring the work of nearly 200 artisans as well as music, fireworks, and food from popular area restarants.

Both Winterthur and Longwood have excellent restaurants on the grounds. Reservations are usually necessary for the very popular Longwood facility, though there is a cafeteria for those who have not planned ahead.

If you have already visited Longwood or Winterthur, you can still spend a rewarding Sunday getting to know the city of Wilmington (see pages 43–48) or taking in some of the lesser-known du Pont landmarks around town. A drive out Route 100 shows you the best of the beautiful Brandywine countryside, the prime estate country that includes many more du Pont residences not open to the public. You'll get a view of one of the grandest—the imposing chateau of Irénée du Pont, known as Granogue—if you turn off to Smith's Bridge Road.

Just north of town is the 328-acre Bellevue State Park, the former estate of William du Pont and a fine place for a break. His mansion, Bellevue Hall, has been renovated and can now be hired for private entertaining functions. Du Pont surrounded his home with lavish facilities: tennis courts, equestrian stables, gardens, and a picturesque pond amid woodlands and fields overlooking the Delaware River. Walking and jogging are popular activities in the park A fitness track a mile and one-eighth long circles a catch-and-release fishing pond stocked with bass, catfish, and sunfish, while the nearby exercise trail offers a refreshing workout. Hiking trails allow you to explore other parts of the estate. If you prefer cycling, paved paths lead you on a leisurely tour.

What else have the du Ponts left to their state of Delaware? Everything from Route 52, built privately by P.S. to provide a smooth ride to Longwood, to Route 13, the major road leading south to Dover and the beaches. The latter route was made possible by Coleman du Pont, a state and U.S. senator who made a $4 million contribution when he decided his state really ought to have a better north-south artery to conduct him to his business in the capital. Alfred I. du Pont contributed toward the road to Philadelphia so that he could drive more easily to concerts and operas in his homemade automobile. This preoccupation with roads and motor cars eventually culminated with the du Pont Company becoming a major stockholder in General Motors, adding substantially to the family's fortune.

Dropping in on the du Ponts is a fascinating experience, one that may convince you that we did have royalty in America after all.

<u>Area Code: 302</u>

DRIVING DIRECTIONS   Wilmington is off I-95. From D.C., take I-95 north, stay left approaching the Delaware Memorial Bridge, and follow the signs for Wilmington. The Delaware Avenue exit leads to the center of town. The approximate distance from D.C. is 110 miles.

PUBLIC TRANSPORTATION   Wilmington has frequent Amtrak and bus service. The city can be reached by air via Philadelphia International Airport, about 25 miles away. Shuttle service connects the airport to major city hotels.

ACCOMMODATIONS   See Wilmington listings, page 46, and Brandywine listings, pages 231–232.

DINING   See Wilmington listings, page 47.

SIGHT-SEEING   *Hagley Museum,* off Route 141, Greenville, 658-2400. Hours: Daily March 15 through December, 9:30 A.M. to 4:30 P.M.; rest of year, guided tours available on weekdays at 1:30 P.M., full hours on weekends. $$$$ • *Nemours,* Rockland Road, off Route 141, 651-6912. Hours: May through November, Tuesday to Saturday, guided tours at 9 A.M., 11 A.M., 1 P.M., and 3 P.M., Sunday 11 A.M., 1 P.M., and 3 P.M.; reservations required, under 16 not admitted. $$$$ • *Winterthur,* Route 52, outside Wilmington, 888-4600 or (800) 448-3883. Hours: Monday to Saturday 9 A.M. to 5 P.M., Sunday noon to 5 P.M. General admission to the Galleries and gardens, $$$$; special tours, $$$$$, include 45-minute Introduction to Winterthur and in-depth Decorative Arts tours, one or two hours. Reservations recommended for house tours. All tours include garden tram rides and self-guided garden tours • *Longwood Gardens,* Route 1, Kennett Square, PA, (215) 388-1000, recorded information (800) 737-5500. Hours: April to October, daily 9 A.M. to 6 P.M.; rest of year, 9 A.M. to 5 P.M. Send a self-addressed, stamped business-size envelope for schedule of year-round activities. $$$$$ • *Bellevue State Park,* 800 Carr Road, two miles north of Wilmington, off I-95 Marsh Road exit, 577-3390. Daylight hours. Park admission, free; fees for riding and other special activities. For other Wilmington attractions, see pages 41–48.

INFORMATION   *Greater Wilmington Convention and Visitors Bureau,* 100 West 10th Street, Suite 20, Wilmington, DE 19801, 652-4088 or (800) 422-1181; www.visitwilmingtonde.com.

Riding High on the Cass Railroad

"Wild and Wonderful," read the license plates in West Virginia. They're right.

The Mountain State has the most wide open spaces and most spectacular scenery to be found in the eastern United States. Two-thirds of the state is covered with wild mountain ranges, ravines, and gorges, once poetically described by Henry David Thoreau as places where "the morning wind forever blows, the poem of creation is uninterrupted."

A visit is a rejuvenation and a joy for urban dwellers any time of year, but in autumn when the hills turn into Technicolor, it is nothing less than fantastic—especially when viewed from the windows of the Cass Scenic Railroad.

The Cass was a logging railroad built in 1901. The present tracks, now incorporated into a unique state park, are the last 11 miles of 3,000 miles of logging lines that once covered the state. Unlike standard steam locomotives, the Shay logging locomotives used here are driven by direct gearing to the wheels, enabling them to climb the steepest grades and swing around hairpin curves while hauling heavy loads.

Today those engines provide a thrilling excursion that is especially fine in autumn. Whistling off from the depot in the onetime lumbering town of Cass, the engines pull passenger cars converted from old lumber flatcars on an uphill run to the 4,842-foot summit of Cheat Mountain, the spot known as Bald Knob, the state's second-highest peak.

The first part of the ride takes in two zigzag switchbacks, then moves into the open fields and Whittaker Station. Here you can leave the train for a breathtaking view of the autumn-brilliant wilderness, enjoy a picnic lunch, and visit a reconstructed logging camp known as Whittaker Camp #1. In summer, special dinner runs end with barbecues here.

Afterward, you can opt to return to the starting point, making for a 90-minute round trip, or continue on the 22-mile climb to the top, a four-and-a-half-hour round trip winding up, down, around, and through woodlands that are a fingertip-close kaleidoscope of autumn color—yellow hickories and poplars, bright orange sumacs and sassafras, crimson maples and dogwoods, and a mix of scarlet and gold on sugar maples that positively dazzles the eye.

By the top, the climate has changed so dramatically, you might as well have driven 800 miles north to Canada. Be sure to bring a jacket.

Along with the ride comes a running commentary. You'll learn about the days at the turn of the century when these tracks were laid to reach a valuable stand of red spruce atop Cheat Mountain, turning tiny Cass into a boomtown. The lumberjacks brought from Canada and the northern states descended periodically to spend their pay and, when it was all gone, climbed back up the mountain to start all over again.

All that's left of Cass today is a handful of houses and the Cass Country Store, once the company store of the West Virginia Pulp and Paper Company and the largest wood structure east of the Mississippi. Now the store makes the most of the railroad traffic with gifts, food, and a couple of little museums. It's a good place to pick up a picnic for your trip.

When your ride is over and while you are in the neighborhood, you may want to visit the futuristic home of the National Radio Astronomy Observatory in Green Bank. This national research center and its huge telescopes seem out of place here in the countryside, but it's definitely the right place if you want to learn about radio astronomy. A 15-minute movie and a 40-minute narrated bus tour are offered.

Hikers and bikers can hook up with the Greenbrier River Trail below Cass, an 80-mile-long former railbed of the C&O Railway now maintained by the state for recreation. The location along the river is a fine one.

Nor is a train ride the only way to view the remarkable scenery in this part of wild, wonderful West Virginia. North of Marlinton off Route 219, Route 150 is a 25-mile semicircular drive known as the Highland Scenic Highway, which takes you through cranberry backcountry and over the Williams River for more unforgettable mountain views. Over half the road is above 4,000 feet, with several outstanding overlooks to take in the vistas below.

At the southern end of the highway is the Cranberry Mountain Visitor Center, where you can learn about the additional sights and activities waiting in this section of the Monongahela National Forest. Don't miss the Cranberry Glades, where a boardwalk gives easy access to the bogs and a look at such exotic flora as bog rosemary, buckbean, a carnivorous plant called horned bladderwort, and many species of orchids, beard flowers, and beaked rush. Just to the west of the glades off Route 39, a three-quarter-mile trail takes you 250 feet down a steep ravine past the three falls of Hills Creek. The final waterfall, almost five stories high, is the second highest in the state.

Surrounding the Cranberry Glades are 53,000 acres of backcountry wilderness, a favorite haunt for hikers, campers, and fishermen going after the trout in the Cranberry and Williams rivers.

For Civil War buffs, continue south on 219 to Droop Mountain Battlefield State Park, a few miles below Hillsboro. It was the site of one of the most fiercely contested battles of the war. Eight thousand men took part in the bloody battle to drive the Confederates out of the fertile lands of the Greenbrier Valley. Today the lookout tower offers a peaceful view of the valley, lovely in autumn or when the rhododendrons bloom in July. Nearby Beartown State Park offers a boardwalk meander through a maze of house-high boulders.

Pulitzer and Nobel prize–winning author Pearl Buck's home, a National Register Historic Site, is also nearby, in the valley of Hillsboro. The white clapboard home where Buck was born in 1892 still has some of its original Victorian furnishings. The home is supposed to be open from May to the end of October, but posted hours aren't always observed, so it's best to phone and check before you make the trip.

The closest lodgings to the train are the modest cottages at Cass. Inn and condominium accommodations atop the mountain at Snowshoe Ski Resort, only about 15 miles away, have the advantage of resort facilties, including golf. Snowshoe also offers a growing Mountain Biking Center. Elk River Inn in Slatyfork, a pleasant low-key place to stay and dine, is also a center for mountain biking expeditions.

Those who want to be close to some of the spectacular scenery of this region might opt for the Cranberry Mountain Lodge, in an isolated mountaintop location adjacent to the Cranberry Back Country and Wilderness Area, with hundreds of miles of trails. To the southeast is 10,000-acre Watoga State Park, the largest in West Virginia, filled with verdant woodland and all kinds of recreational facilities, including many hiking trails, horseback riding, and an 11-acre lake. Through October, the park offers comfortable rustic cottages and a restaurant.

Two detours will add more variety to the weekend. Tiny Helvetia still has the look of its Swiss origins and excellent bratwurst, sauerbraten, and other old-country fare at the Hutte Restaurant. If you want to stay around, one of the old houses in town is now the Beekeeper Inn.

To add a touch of civilization and charm to your trip to the mountains, you might choose to drive farther south to Lewisburg. The white-columned General Lewis Inn is a winning old place, dating back to 1830, when stagecoaches like the one now sitting out front used to travel along the James River and Kanawha Turnpike (now Route 60), bringing visitors to the mountains.

This simple inn is full of beams and fireplaces, country antiques, and old-fashioned warmth. There are curios everywhere and a "memory hall" hung with tools and memorabilia of the early mountain settlers. On a chilly day, the fire will be going in the sitting room, and they'll be serving tea and scones, the latter heaped with thick rich cream and strawberries. At dinner, the fare turns Southern: fried chicken, pork chops, Virginia ham, and homemade corn sticks and biscuits.

Lewisburg is one of the oldest towns in West Virginia, and the whole center of town is a National Historic District. Originally called either Camp Union or Fort Savannah, it was renamed in 1774 to honor General Andrew Lewis, a local Indian-fighter, and became an important way station on the turnpike. The Civil War battle of Lewisburg in 1862 was won by the North, but the town remained a Southern outpost for most of the war.

Today's Lewisburg is a spiffy cluster of fine old homes with wide porches and churches dating back to Colonial times. The Old Stone Church, circa 1796, is surrounded by pioneers' graves, many bearing names still associated with the area. The local walking tour, available at the Visitors Center, takes you past many early homes on Washington Street and its surrounding avenues, to the 1837 Greenbrier County Courthouse and the North House Museum, an 1820 mansion containing collections of early local memorabilia.

There are also a number of interesting small shops and galleries for browsing on Washington Street and neighboring blocks in the Historic District, featuring contemporary crafts, folk art, and lots of antiques.

The Visitors Center also offers a brochure providing a self-guided tour of the Battle of Lewisburg; you'll see bronze markers of the battle around town.

If you are looking for more sights around Lewisburg, Lost World Caverns has several large chambers with intriguing stalactite and stalagmite formations, one more than 40 feet high and 25 feet around.

For a totally different kind of attraction just outside town, you can visit the famous Greenbrier, one of America's landmark resorts (see page 289). The hotel is grand, and the mountain views are lovely, but even the Greenbrier can't touch the majesty of the climb up Cheat Mountain aboard the old Cass Railroad.

Area Code: 304

DRIVING DIRECTIONS Cass is off Route 28/92 between Routes 250 and 219. From D.C., take Route 66 west, then I-81 south. At Staunton, Virginia, take Route 250 west to Bartow and turn left onto 28 south, watching for the turnoff to Cass between Greenbank and Dunmore. The approximate distance from D.C. is 230 miles. From Route 219, turn north on Route 28/92 at Marlinton.

ACCOMMODATIONS *Cass Cottages,* Cass Scenic Railroad State Park, P.O. Box 75, Cass 24927, (800) CALL-WVA, 12 restored turn-of-the-century rustic log cabins accommodating six to ten, M • *Elk River Inn,* U.S. 219, Slatyfork 26291, 15 miles from Cass, 572-3771, home cooking, inn with private baths, I–M, CP; farmhouse with shared baths, I, CP; two-bedroom cabins, E • *Morning Glory Inn,* U.S. 219 North, Slatyfork, 26291, 572-3771, pleasant new lodge, M–E • *Pleasant Valley Farm,* Route 219, HC 69, P.O. Box 225, Slatyfork 26291, 572-2319, farmhouse on 900 acres, views, I–M, CP • *Sweet Thyme Inn,* Route 28/92, Greenbank, 456-5535, 1890 homestead, M • *The Current,* HC 64, P.O. Box 135, Hillsboro 24946, 40 miles from Cass, 653-4722, simple homey bed-and-breakfast, shared bath, I; suite with private bath, M, CP • *Jerico B & B,* Jerico Road, Marlinton 24954, 799-6241, I–M, CP; cabins, I–E • *Old Clark Inn,* 702 Third Avenue, Marlinton 24954, 799-6377 or (800) 849-4184, I–M, CP • *Nakiska Chalet,* HC 73, Box 24, Valley Head, 26294, 339-6309, hot tub, sauna, I–M, CP • *Beekeeper Inn,* P.O. Box 42, Helvetia 26224, 924-6435, M, CP • *General Lewis Inn,* 301 East Washington Street, Lewisburg 24901, 645-2600, M • *Snowshoe Mountain Resort:* P.O. Box 10, Snowshoe 26290, 15 miles from Cass, 572-5252. (All are highest during ski season.) Choices include: *Whistlepunk Inn,* P.O. Box 70, alpine decor, pool, sauna, hot tub, best on the mountain, M–E • Mountaintop ski lodges: *Inn at Snowshoe,* I–E • *Spruce Lodge,* least expensive lodging, I • *Highland House,* I–M; *Rimfire Lodge,* I–M • Silver Creek Lodge, pool, sauna, fitness center, M • Many condominiums available, M–E. Two state lodges are usually rented by the week but available nightly when not filled: *Cranberry Mountain Lodge,* Lobelia Road, six miles off U.S. 219, Hillsboro, reservations c/o 125 Elm Street, Wheeling, 26003, 242-6070 or (800) CALL-WVA, one lodge cabin accommodating up to 16 people, I–M • *Watoga State Park,* three miles off Route 219, north of Hillsboro, HC 82, P.O. Box 252, Marlinton 29454 (35 miles southwest of Cass), 799-4087 or (800) CALL WVA, cabins, I.

DINING   *Elk River Inn* (see above), I–M • *Country Roads Cafe,* Route 219, Hillsboro, 653-4335, I • *Red Fox Restaurant,* Whistlepunk Village, Snowshoe Mountain, 572-1111, top choice in the area, M–EE • *Brandi's,* Inn at Showshoe (see above), casual, I–M • *Hutte Restaurant,* Helvetia, 924-6435, I–M • *General Lewis Inn* (see above), I–M.

SIGHT-SEEING   *Cass Scenic Railroad State Park,* Route 28, Cass (between Dunmore and Greenbank), 456-4300 or (800) CALL-WVA. Hours: Memorial Day to Labor Day, daily (except no Bald Knob runs on Monday); Labor Day to late October, weekends only except daily during Fall Color Schedule, October 1 to mid-October. Two-hour rides to Whittaker Station, 10:50 A.M., 1 P.M., 3 P.M. Trains to Bald Knob, four and a half hours, noon. $$$$$ • *National Radio Astronomy Observatory,* Route 92, Greenbank, 456-2011. Hours: Mid-June to Labor Day, daily 9 A.M. to 4 P.M.; early June, September, and October, weekends only. Free • *Cranberry Mountain Nature Center,* Junction of Route 150 and Routes 39/55, 653-4826. Hours: April through November, daily 9 A.M. to 5 P.M. Free. • *Droop Mountain Battlefield State Park,* U.S. 219, Droop, 653-4254. Park open daylight hours; museum open 8 A.M. to 5 P.M. Free. Also adjoins Beartown State Park • *Pearl S. Buck Birthplace Museum,* off U.S. 219, Hillsboro, 653-4430. Hours: May to October, Monday to Saturday 9 A.M. to 5 P.M., Sunday 1 P.M. to 5 P.M.; rest of year, by appointment. $$ • *North House Museum,* 301 West Washington Street, Lewisburg, 645-3398. Hours: Monday to Sat-

urday 10 A.M. to 4 P.M. $$ • *Lost World Caverns,* Fairview Road, Lewis-
burg, 645-6677. Hours: Daily 9 A.M. to 5 P.M.; mid-May to Labor Day
to 7 P.M. $$$$ • *Elk River Touring Center,* U.S. 219, Slatyfork, 572-
3771, mountain bike rentals, touring.

INFORMATION *Pocahontas County Convention and Visitors
Bureau,* P.O. Box 275, Marlinton, WV 25954, 799-4636 or (800)
336-7009; www.pocahontascountywv.com; see also www.potomac
highlands.org • *Lewisburg Visitors Center,* 105 Church Street, Lewis-
burg, WV 24901, 645-1000 or (800) 833-2068.

Mr. Jefferson's Legacy in Charlottesville

Here in gentle, magnolia-studded Charlottesville, Virginia, the lines get
long outside Monticello, the home of Thomas Jefferson, but the crowds
stand patiently. They've heard it's worth the wait.

Few homes anywhere so radiate the personality of their builders, and
in this case the builder was one of America's most remarkable men.

Author of the Declaration of Independence, governor of Virginia,
president of the United States, founder of the University of Virginia—
none of these titles do full justice to the tall, redheaded man the
townsfolk still refer to as Mr. Jefferson. Albemarle County was his
birthplace, Monticello his passion, and here is where you must come
to get to know something about Mr. Jefferson the man—not just the
brilliant writer, diplomat, and champion of freedom, but the loyal
friend, gracious host, avid gardener, and architect who was far ahead of
his time.

Although Monticello draws the crowds, almost everywhere you go
in and around this scenic city at the foot of the Blue Ridge Mountains
still bears the Jefferson imprint. The Jefferson-designed rotunda, lawns,
and colonnades at the University of Virginia earned a citation from the
American Institute of Architects almost two centuries after their cre-
ation as an outstanding achievement in American architecture. Court
Square downtown is where Jefferson strolled with his fellow patriots
James Monroe and James Madison, discussing law and liberty. Later,
Monroe came to live at Ash Lawn–Highland Plantation to be near his
friend, settling on a site personally selected by Jefferson, who sent his
own gardeners to plant the orchards.

And all the vineyards now thriving in surrounding Albemarle
County are carrying on the growing of grapes for wine that the fore-

sighted Jefferson began in the 1700s. They even call themselves the Monticello Viticultural Area.

You can see Jefferson's legacy any time of year, but a good reason for braving the crowds in fall is the bonus backdrop of color provided by the autumnal mountains that Jefferson called the Eden of the United States. October has an added lure, since it is usually the month when the Monticello Wine and Jazz Festival is held at the Boar's Head Inn. Later in the month, the Virginia Film Festival takes place at the University of Virginia, a treat for film buffs that is growing in stature every year.

An excellent place to begin a visit is at the Monticello Visitors Center, where a fascinating exhibit, "Thomas Jefferson at Monticello," explores the many facets of his life and shows some 400 objects and artifacts, including personal family memorabilia and artifacts discovered during recent archaeological excavations on the Monticello grounds. The exhibit gives you background that makes a visit to Monticello far more meaningful.

The best plan to beat the crowds at the home is to get up early enough to reach Monticello soon after the gates open at 8 A.M. A bus will take you from the ticket booth to the 867-foot hilltop where Jefferson enjoyed a commanding view of the countryside he loved best.

For 40 years, from the day he inherited the land and gave it the name Monticello ("little mountain") at the age of 24, Jefferson continually dreamed about and planned for perfecting his home. He was responsible for every detail of its design, construction, furnishing, and several remodelings.

Jefferson chose a classical design rather than the Georgian architecture popular in his day. Except for the dome, familiar from countless photographs, the architectural plan gives a 33-room house the appearance of a one-story home.

The house was a wonder in its time, causing one visiting French nobleman to write, "Mr. Jefferson is the first American who has consulted the Fine Arts to know how he should shelter himself from the weather." Enter and you are in the unmistakable presence of genius, in a home of unmatched grace and elegance, flooded with natural light, yet with a sense of intimacy within each room.

Jefferson's keen mind, interest in the scientific, and delight with gadgets can be seen everywhere: in the dumbwaiter used to transport wine from the cellar and the revolving serving door that allowed the servants to set out food without entering the dining room; in a set of glass doors connected to open simultaneously when the first is set ajar; and in the seven-day clock in the entrance hall that recorded the day as well as the hour. Like the 14 skylights that bathe the house with light, they were innovations in their time.

His practical bent is evidenced by Monticello's stairs, which are narrow and tucked away out of sight. Jefferson thought the then common practice of installing elaborate stairways a waste of floor space.

His own sanctum—bedroom, sitting room, library, and study— is a high point of the tour. Above the bed is a long, narrow closet with port-hole windows for light and ventilation, reached by a stepladder kept in a closet at the head of the bed. He used the revolving chair, Windsor bench, and revolving-top table for reading and writing, sitting in a half-recumbent position to ease his rheumatism. A telescope is installed in the south window.

Jefferson's library once held 6,700 volumes. They went to the fed-eral government in 1815, forming the nucleus of the present Library of Congress. The volumes now at Monticello are a selection of duplicates.

His attention to his garden design was as inventive as his interest in architecture. Both ornamental and vegetable gardens and two orchards were part of his plan for a self-supporting estate, and the gardens have been restored to his meticulously laid-out design, with 250 varieties of vegetables and 122 kinds of fruit. The stables and slave quarters, smokehouse, kitchen, and other outbuildings of the plantation commu-nity are the latest part of the estate to be restored. Tours of this area and the gardens are available.

From Monticello, it is a short drive to Ash Lawn–Highland, the home of Jefferson's friend James Monroe. The modest yellow frame Colonial is cozy and filled with family memorabilia. The grounds, with their peacocks and boxwood gardens, are exceptional. Special events, concerts, plays, and crafts displays are often held here.

You may have to face another line if you want the traditional South-ern buffet of fried chicken, black-eyed peas, biscuits, and apple cobbler served up daily for lunch at the Ordinary, a converted log house adjoin-ing Michie (pronounced "mickey") Tavern. Tours are offered in the tav-ern itself, one of the oldest in Virginia, moved to its present site from a well-traveled coach road northwest of town. Many of the original fur-nishings and utensils remain, along with the ballroom where dancers twirled two centuries ago. The tour continues through several outbuild-ings, which include the small Virginia Wine Museum and the Meadow Run Grist Mill.

To see more of Mr. Jefferson's town, proceed downtown to Court Square, where the original Albemarle Court House was built in 1762 and it was not unusual to see three future American presidents, Jeffer-son, Madison, and Monroe, chatting on the green. Many of the historic buildings here have been renovated into business and legal offices and shops.

Two blocks south of Court Square, a stretch of Main Street has been turned into a pedestrian mall. The shops include a number of used-book stores. The array of wares in the Hardware Store is fun, and there is also a funky little cafe that is a good bet for lunch.

Antiquers will find a pleasant lunch at the 1817 Tea Room Cafe on West Main Street, and a large selection of wares at DeLoach Antiques next door. Among the town's many stops for antiques, the most attractive setting and largest selection is at the 1740 House outside town at 3449 Ivy Road (Route 250 west), where top-quality pieces are displayed in a historic tavern.

Almost 100 artists work in Charlottesville. You can see and talk to more than 40 of them in their studios at the McGuffey Art Center at 201 Second Street, NW, just one block off Main Street.

In the lush horse country outside of town, fall is a busy season. The oldest steeplechase race in America, the American Grand National, is held at Foxfield Race Course west of Charlottesville each year, and the Farmington Hunt Club annual fall horse show takes place in October.

You can also stay in the countryside in a variety of lovely lodgings. Clifton is one of the choicest, a columned eighteenth-century manor house that manages to be both elegant and comfortable. It belonged to William Randolph, whose son Thomas Mann Randolph, an early governor of Virginia, was married to neighbor Thomas Jefferson's daughter, Martha. You can stay in the historic main house or equally engaging quarters in the Carriage House, the Livery, and the Randolph law office.

Guesthouses, the local bed-and-breakfast registry, offers many listings on country estates, as well as in fine antebellum homes in town. Among the local bed-and-breakfast inns, the Inn at Monticello stands out. Located just outside town and convenient for sightseeing, the mellow mid-1800s manor house is well furnished and has lovely mountain views.

Farther into the country, Prospect Hill is a romantic 1732 plantation house with rooms in the former slave quarters, and High Meadows Vineyard Inn is a landmark home with two sections, 1832 and 1882, and furnishings appropriate to each. More luxurious lodgings are in a contemporary carriage house. Dinner each night is preceded by a wine tasting.

Then we have Keswick Hall, a 48-room country hotel on 600 acres, including formal gardens and an Arnold Palmer golf course. The showplace estate has been renovated by Sir Bernard Ashley of the Laura Ashley family to the tune of $40 million and includes million-dollar homes on some of the property. The hotel is, of course, decorated with the famous Ashley fabrics, no two rooms alike, but all with a selection of choice antiques.

The countryside is also the place to visit the vineyards that are helping to fulfill Jefferson's vision of native Virginia wines. Of the vineyards in the region, Barboursville claims the distinction of being the picturesque ruins of a home designed by Thomas Jefferson, and Oakencroft boasts proudly of being the only winery with a female owner and winemaker. The Jefferson Vineyards are on 650 acres adjoining Monticello, including the land where Jefferson had his first grapes planted. White Hall Vineyards, a modern winery, has outstanding mountain views.

You will have the chance to sample and buy all of the local products at the annual Monticello Wine and Jazz Festival, held usually at the Boar's Head Inn in early October. The wine is still young, so don't judge it by California standards. The most appealing thing about these winemakers is their enthusiasm for their work.

For a final appreciation of Jefferson's genius, visit the magnificent grounds of the University of Virginia. Guided tours go out frequently from the Rotunda, the famous landmark he designed with dome and columns inspired by the Pantheon in Rome. Today it is a monument to Jefferson, displaying his statue and copies of the drawings and writings of the "academical village" he envisioned and brought to life.

The Rotunda steps lead out to the Lawn, tiers of greenery flanked by facing columned arcades. The most coveted student lodgings are those in these historic arcades, awarded each year to honor students.

Beyond the arcades are gardens enclosed by serpentine walls and more arcaded rows of rooms, known as East and West Range, for graduate students. A poor student named Edgar Allan Poe lived in West Range arcade until his gambling debts forced him to withdraw. His room is open to visitors.

The Rotunda was begun in 1821, and Thomas Jefferson saw the first students enroll in the school in 1825, just one year before his death. Among his many accomplishments, he considered his role as founder of the university one of the greatest. For his own gravestone epitaph he wrote, "Here was buried Thomas Jefferson, Author of the Declaration of American Independence, of the Statute of Virginia for Religious Freedom and Father of the University of Virginia." These mattered more to Jefferson than titles like governor or president.

Jefferson also wrote, "All my wishes end where I hope my days will end . . . at Monticello." He got his wish. Thomas Jefferson is buried just down the path from the home he loved, and where he died at age 83 on July 4, 1826, the 50th anniversary of the Declaration of Independence.

Area Code: 434

DRIVING DIRECTIONS   Charlottesville is at the intersection of I-64 and Route 29. From D.C., take I-66 west to Route 29 south. The approximate distance from D.C. is 125 miles.

ACCOMMODATIONS   *Boar's Head Inn* at the University of Virginia, Route 250, 22905, 296-2181, elegant, longtime local landmark, tennis, golf, spa, E–EE; inquire about sports packages • *Clifton,* 1296 Clifton Inn Drive, 22911, (888) 971-1800, 1799 mansion, charming and elegant, fireplaces, pool, tennis, lake, fine dining, E–EE, CP • *Silver Thatch Inn,* 3001 Hollymead Road, off Route 29 north, 22911, 978-4686 or (800) 261-0720, charming inn and restaurant, E, CP • **Bed-and-breakfast inns:** *The Inn at Monticello,* 1188 Scottsville

Road (Highway 20 South), Charlottesville 22902, 979-3593, country house two miles from Monticello, M–E, CP • *200 South Street,* at that address, Charlottesville 22901, 979-0200 or (800) 964-7008, nicely furnished restored home in town, walking distance to dining, M–E, CP; suites, EE, CP • *1817 Historic Bed and Breakfast,* 1211 West Main Street, Charlottesville 22903, 979-7353 or (800) 730-7443, in-town Federal home turned inn, small rooms filled with antique furnishings that are for sale, M–E, CP • *Inn at Court Square,* 410 East Jefferson Street, Charlottesville 22901, 295-2800, oldest house in town transformed into an antique-filled small inn, E–EE, CP.

Outside town: *Prospect Hill,* 2887 Poindexter Road, Trevilians 23093, (800) 277-0844, wonderful restored plantation, fine food, pool, EE, MAP • *High Meadows Vineyard Inn,* 55 High Meadows Lane, off Route 20, Scottsville 24590, 286-2218 or (800) 232-1832, restored historic home, contemporary carriage houses with fireplaces, skylights, hot tubs, noted for wine-tasting programs, E–EE, MAP • *Keswick Hall,* 701 Country Club Drive, Keswick 22947, 979-3440 or (800) 274-5391, ultimate luxury, indoor and outdoor pools, golf, tennis, spa, EE.

DINING **Bizou,** 119 West Main Street, 977-1818, affordable nouvelle comfort food, outdoor dining on the mall, I–M • *C & O Restaurant,* 515 East Water Street, 971-7044, French specialties, a longtime favorite, M–E • *Continental Divide,* 811 West Main Street, 984-0143, tasty Southwestern, great margaritas, worth the wait, I–M • *Hamilton's,* 1st and Main Streets, Downtown Mall, 295-6649, on the mall, fairly priced American menu, M • *Historic Michie Tavern,* 683 Thomas Jefferson Parkway (Route 53), 977-1234, tourist standard for Colonial lunch buffet, I • *Ivy Inn,* 2244 Old Ivy Road, 977-1222, Victorian home, regional cuisine, M–E • *L'Avventura,* 220 Market Street West, 977-1912, regional Italian with wines to match, M • *Metropolitain,* 214 West Water Street, 977-1043, excellent nouvelle cuisine, one of the best in town, M–EE • *OXO,* 215 West Water Street, 977-8111, a standout, former Keswick Hall chef, creative dishes, fine dining, E • *Mono Loco,* 200 West Water Street, 979-0688, fun, Cuban-inspired menu, M • *Old Mill Room,* Boar's Head Inn (see above), fine dining in a former grist mill, popular Sunday brunch, E • *Petra,* 210 West Water Street, 295-6787, American bistro fare, M • *Silver Thatch Inn* (see above), country French, E • *Southern Culture,* 633 West Main Street, 979-1990, Gulf coast cuisine, best for gospel Sunday brunch, M • *Starr Hill Restaurant and Brewery,* 709 West Main Street, 977-0017, lively ambience, homemade beer, live music upstairs many nights • The following are by advance reservation only: *Clifton* (see above), prix fixe, EE • *Ashley Room,* Keswick Hall (see above), prix fixe, EE • *High Meadows* (see above), prix fixe, includes pre-dinner wine tasting, EE • *Prospect Hill* (see above), prix fixe, EE.

SIGHT-SEEING *Monticello,* Route 53, 984-9822. Hours: March to October, daily 8 A.M. to 5 P.M.; rest of year 9 A.M. to 4:30 P.M. $$$$$ • *Ash Lawn–Highland,* 1100 James Monroe Parkway (Route 795), 293-9539. Hours: March to October 9 A.M. to 6 P.M.; rest of year 10 A.M. to 5 P.M. $$$$ • *Historic Michie Tavern,* Route 53, 977-1234. Hours: Daily 9 A.M. to 5 P.M. $$$. Money-saving President's Pass available for all three above attractions. • *Monticello Visitors Center,* Route 20 south, 977-1783. Hours: Exhibit, "Thomas Jefferson at Monticello," March through October daily 9 A.M. to 5:30 P.M., rest of year to 5 P.M. Free • *University of Virginia Rotunda and Central Grounds,* U.S. 29 and 250 Business, in the center of town, 924-7969. Guided tours daily from the rotunda, 10 and 11 A.M.; 2, 3, and 4 P.M. Free • *Virginia Film Festival* c/o Department of Drama, University of Virginia, Charlottesville 22903, 982-5277, (800) UVA-FEST, usually late October. Check current dates • *Monticello Wine and Jazz Festival,* annual day-long event at Boar's Head Inn, usually in early October; phone 296-4188 for dates and information.

INFORMATION *Charlottesville/Albemarle Convention & Visitors Bureau,* Route 20 south, P.O. Box 178, Charlottesville, VA 22902, 977-1783 or (877) 386-1102; www.charlottesvilletourism.org. Visitor Center hours: Daily 9 A.M. to 5 P.M.

Autumn Adventures in the Poconos

Once upon a time, the unusual little town of Jim Thorpe, Pennsylvania, was a tourist mecca. During its glory years in the mid-1800s it was known as "the Switzerland of America" for its extraordinary location in a steep gorge between high mountains along the Lehigh River. At that time the town was called Mauch Chunk, named for the high hill on the opposite side of the Lehigh, which the Indians dubbed "Macht Tschunk," or "Mountain of the Bears," because the shape resembled a crouching bear.

The town's fortunes waned, but the scenery did not. Renamed and rapidly being restored to its nineteenth-century look and feel, Jim Thorpe is enjoying a renaissance that merits a visit. There's no better time than in autumn, when 18,000 square miles of surrounding wilderness in the western Poconos light up in a million shades of crimson, gold, and russet.

The town is particularly festive during its annual foliage festival the second weekend in October. And while you are learning about a curious little chapter of American history, you can sample a bit of outdoor adventure, taking in the flaming foliage via diesel train, bicycle, or river raft, or from a mountaintop.

Strolling the streets of town, lit up by the glowing hills that enfold it, is a treat in itself in autumn. Because it was hemmed in by mountains, Mauch Chunk grew vertically instead of horizontally. Many of the buildings, such as the 1869 St. Mark's Episcopal Church, are built directly against the side of the mountain. Stop at the tourist welcoming center in the 1888 New Jersey Central Railroad Station for a walking tour that will tell you the story of Mauch Chunk's rise and fall.

The town's original prosperity derived from its status as a river port, the shipping center for the rich deposits of anthracite coal being mined in the surrounding mountains. You can still see the towpath of the old Lehigh Canal, which was dug to connect to the Delaware Canal in Easton so that the coal could be shipped out. English, Welsh, and Irish immigrants were attracted to the area, and building boomed in the town that soon became the county seat of Carbon County.

The early reliance on canals ended in the 1850s as Mauch Chunk became a prominent rail transfer point for coal, largely through the formation of the Lehigh Valley Railroad by Asa Packer, a local self-made millionaire and philanthropist.

The first railroad in America, an 18-mile gravity track known as the Switchback, was actually built between Mauch Chunk and Summit Hill. At first it was used to transport coal into town, then to bring tourists up for the view. Gravity brought the cars downhill; mules towed them back to the top. In the early 1900s, a trolley car was added to carry tourists to the fabulous views of Flagstaff Park, which sat atop the mountain just outside town. During the Big Band era, the famous Dorsey Brothers, natives of nearby Lansford, played here in the "Ballroom in the Clouds."

You can learn about all this history and see working models of the switchback railroad and canal locks at the Mauch Chunk Museum and Cultural Center.

Mauch Chunk at its prime boasted 13 millionaires, but the decline of the coal industry brought a halt to its prominence, and hard times followed. In the 1950s, a small effort to revitalize began, and local citizens were asked to contribute a nickel a week to a redevelopment fund. About that time the famous American Indian athlete, Jim Thorpe, died in poverty, and his wife, having heard about the town's spirit, offered his name in exchange for a proper burial and memorial. In 1954 three adjacent areas, Mauch Chunk, Upper Mauch Chunk, and East Mauch Chunk, combined to form one borough renamed Jim Thorpe. Thorpe's Memorial, a 20-ton granite mausoleum, can be seen a half mile east of town on Route 903.

The new town hoped that the recognition that followed its name change would encourage an economic recovery, and finally that has indeed begun to happen.

Among the prominent downtown buildings to be seen on a walking tour are the handsome Lehigh Coal and Navigation Building, dating back to 1884, and St. Mark's Episcopal Church, which boasts Tiffany windows, gold, marble, and brass furnishings, and a three-story wrought-iron elevator. The stone Carbon County Courthouse is also worth a visit for its elaborate oak-paneled skylighted courtroom, but it is open only on weekdays. The handsome 1881 Opera House has undergone restoration and is now home to musical comedies and other performances. It is listed on the National Register of Historic Buildings.

The imposing local jail, now a museum, was infamous for its association with the "Molly McGuires," the violent forerunners of the labor union movement. Five of its members were hanged here. The last, Tom Fisher, left a handprint on the wall of cell 17, which he declared would remain forever as proof of his innocence. The outline is still visible today despite efforts to remove it.

Race Street took its name from the race, or track, that ran water down the street's center to the mill at the foot of the hill. It contains a row of 16 houses known as Stone Row, almost unchanged in appearance since they were built in the 1840s. Stone Row had become run-down, but much of it, too, is undergoing renovation, and delightful new shops are occupying many of the old homes.

Millionaire's Row is the lineup of fine homes on both sides of Broadway built by the wealthy of Mauch Chunk between 1860 and 1890. Wealthiest of all was Asa Packer, president of the Lehigh Valley Railroad and founder of Lehigh University, whose treasure-filled 1860 Victorian mansion on a hill overlooking town is open for guided tours. Next door, the restored home of Harry Packer, Asa's youngest son, is now an elegant bed-and-breakfast lodging, though weekends are devoted to murder-mystery shenanigans and carry a high price tag for a town that otherwise boasts happily moderate rates.

The handsome old Mauch Chunk Opera House on West Broadway has been nicely renovated and once again offers live entertainment. Check the current schedule.

The main lodging in town is the Inn at Jim Thorpe, a restored 1840s building done up nicely with Victoriana. Also appealing is the tiny Hotel Switzerland, whose bar is the social center of Jim Thorpe. The simple rooms upstairs are country-fresh. Owners of several of the Victorian homes in town also take in bed-and-breakfast guests.

Shops are multiplying in Jim Thorpe, and you'll find some pleasant browsing in shops and galleries on Race Street and Broadway. The restored Hooven Mercantile Company, a former spice and coffee warehouse on Susquehanna Street, offers shops and displays of local memorabilia. Upstairs is the delightful H.O. Scale Model Railroad, a two-level display featuring 13 separate model trains and more than 200 miniature buildings. Among the variety of crafts for sale is one unique to the region—coal sculpture and jewelry, which you can see at the Coal Bin.

A short stroll away in Asa Packer Park, a 15,000-pound hunk of black diamond carbon coal is on display, a sample of why the town once prospered.

Plan the rest of your stay according to your inclinations. The railroad station is the departure point for nostalgic train rides into the fall countryside. The "Flaming Foliage Rambles" are 33-mile round trip excursions that last two and three-quarters hours.

The old switchback trail is a prime lure for hikers, along with several other trails in Mauch Chunk Lake State Park, four miles west of town. The park offers 2,100 acres, including the 345-acre lake for fishing, picnicking, and boating, with boat rentals available.

More scenic trails await at Lehigh Gorge State Park, which meanders for 25 miles from Jim Thorpe to White Haven along the Lehigh River. The closest access is along Coalport Road on the east side of Jim Thorpe.

Many raft trips are offered through the gorge. Once the spring high water recedes, the trips are labeled "floats" and described as "great for beginners." Special "Color Cruises" are scheduled in the fall. You can also sign on for bicycle tours or rent mountain bikes in town.

And then we have Skirmish, billed as a "friendly war game," actually an adult version of Capture the Flag, with two teams competing to capture each other's flags from bases in a wooded area. Combatants use specially designed air pistols to splat their opponents with colored liquid. It's not everyone's idea of fun, but some people love it and come back again and again. There's no question that it's unique.

And so is Jim Thorpe, a small town being brought back to its former charm in a mountain setting that needed no improvement. Mark it down as a fascinating autumn destination.

Area Code: 505

DRIVING DIRECTIONS   Jim Thorpe is on Route 209, reached off Route 476, the Pennsylvania Turnpike Extension. The scenic route from D.C. is to take I-95 north to I-695 outside Baltimore and connect with I-83 north. At Harrisburg, turn east on I-81 and continue east as it merges with I-78. (Do not follow I-81 north to Hazleton.) Just before Allentown, take Route 476, the Turnpike Extension, to Route 209 west into town. Alternate route: Follow I-95 to Philadelphia, connect with I-76 north, then I-276 west to Route 476 north and proceed as above. From the northeast, take Route 80 to Route 476 south and proceed as above. The approximate distance from D.C. is 223 miles.

ACCOMMODATIONS   *The Inn at Jim Thorpe,* 24 Broadway, 18229, 325-2599 or (800) 329-2599, M, CP, suites, E–EE, CP • *Hotel Switzerland,* 5 Hazard Square, 18229, 325-4563, I, CP • *The Victorian Bed & Breakfast,* 68 Broadway, 18229, 325-8107 or (888) 241-4460, 1860 townhouse filled with Victoriana, rooms, I–M, CP, suites M–E, CP • **Broadway House,** 44-46 West Broadway, 325-9100 or (877) 412-3247, period home with modern conveniences, views from decks, operated by Mauch Chunk Museum, M. CP • *The Minnie Victoria,* 723 North Street, Jim Thorpe, 18220, 325-9992 or (866) 288-3229, nicely funished Victorian, M, CP • *Riverdance,* 504 North Street, Jim Thorpe 18229, 325-2961, in-town bed and breakfast home, I–M, CP • *Tiffany's Grand Victoria Bed & Breakfast,* 218 Center Street, 18229, 325-8260 or (888) 541-2206, an 1846 home in a quiet neighborhood, outdoor pool, I–M, CP • *Harry Packer Mansion,* Packer Road, 18229, 325-8566, M–E, CP, $$ CP; monthly "Mystery Weekends," EE, MAP • *Arbor Glen,* Jim Thorpe 18229, 325-8566, deluxe suites in a wooded setting outside town, managed by Harry Packer Mansion, E–EE, CP.

DINING   *J.T.'s All American Steak & Ale House,* Hotel Switzerland (see above), 325-4563, cozy atmosphere, I–M • *The Emerald Restaurant & Molly McGuire's Pub,* Inn at Jim Thorpe (see above), a top pick in town, I–M • *Black Bread Cafe,* 45-47 Race Street, Jim Thorpe, 325-8957, fine dining in casual atmosphere, M–E •*Macaluso's at The Lantern Lodge,* Routes 209 and 93, Nesquehoning (just outside Jim Thorpe), 669-9433, Italian, ignore the decor, the food is fine, I–M. • *Sunrise Diner,* 3 Hazard Square, 325-4093, 50s-style diner, jukebox, etc, open 24 hours weekends, I–M.

SIGHT-SEEING   *Asa Packer Mansion,* Packer Road, 325-3229. Hours: Memorial Day through October, daily 11 A.M. to 4:15 P.M.; November, December, April to late May, weekends only, $$ • *Harry Packer Mansion,* Packer Road, 325-8566. Hours: Sunday 1 P.M. to 3 P.M. $ • *Rail Tours, Inc.,* Central Railroad Station, PO Box 285, 325-4606. Hours: Mid-May through Labor Day, 40-minute train rides Saturday, Sunday, and holidays, $$; Lake Hauto Specials, June 30 to Labor Day, 19 miles, 1¾ hours, $$$$; Flaming Foliage Rambles, October weekends, 2¾ hours, $$$$$; reservations advised • *Mauch Chunk Museum and Cultural Center,* 41 West Broadway, 325-9190. Hours: Tuesday to Sunday, 10 A.M. to 4 P.M., $$ • *Old Mauch Chunk Model Train Display,* Hooven Mercantile Co., 41 Susquehanna Street, 325-4371. Hours: mid-June to Labor Day, Sunday to Friday, noon to 5 P.M., Saturday 10 A.M. to 5 P.M.; early June, Labor Day to October 31, closed Monday, Tuesday; January to May, November, December, Saturday, Sunday noon to 5 P.M., $$ • *The Old Jail Museum and Heritage Center,* 128 West Broadway, 325-5259. Hours: Memorial Day to Labor

Day, daily except Wednesday, noon to 5 P.M.; September, October weekends only. $$ • *St. Mark's Episcopal Church,* Race Street, 325-2241. Hours: Memorial Day through October, tours daily; phone for current hours. $$ • *Pocono Whitewater Adventures,* Route 903, 325-3655 or (800) WHITEWATER, rafting trips, bicycle tours, Skirmish adventures; special weekends in foliage season. Phone or write for current offerings and rates • *Jim Thorpe River Adventures, Inc.,* 1 Adventure Lane, 325-2570 or (800) 424-RAFT, rafting trips, inquire about current offerings • *Blue Mountain Sports,* Route 209, 325-4421 or (800) 599-4421, mountain bike rentals, shuttle service to trailheads.

INFORMATION *Jim Thorpe Chamber of Commerce,* P.O. Box 164, Jim Thorpe, PA 18229, (888) JIM-THORP; www.visitjim thorpe.com. Pocono Mountains Vacation Bureau Visitor Center is in the Railroad Station.

On Top of the World in Shenandoah

Virginia's Skyline Drive is a wonder. It wiggles its way heaven-high astride the Blue Ridge Mountains for 105 miles, smack through the exquisite wilderness of Shenandoah National Park, with tiers of dusky mountain ridges honing into breath-catching views at every bend.

Down below, the lush rolling Piedmont horse country stretches away to the east. To the west lies the Shenandoah Valley of fable and song, and the Shenandoah River, dividing in order to fork its way around the 40-mile stretch of Massanutten Mountain.

There's plenty of time to enjoy the views. The pace on the drive is a leisurely 35 miles per hour, there are only four entrances in over 100 miles, and there are 71 overlooks along the way, allowing you to pull off to contemplate the scenery or take a walk in the woods whenever the spirit moves you.

A beautiful spot year-round, the park takes on an extra glow in autumn, and even the crowds can't spoil the glory as the golds and crimsons of the season begin working their way down from the mountaintop, bathing the hills in radiant color.

If you are able to stay in one of the two park lodges, Skyland or Big Meadows, you'll have a ringside seat at your window. Both areas offer lodge rooms or suites plus cabins. If you want to rough it just a bit, the Lewis Mountain area is cabins only, and they use outdoor grills for cooking.

But not to worry if the park lodging is full. All of the Shenandoah Valley is aflame in October, and the views are fabulous even outside the park, especially on the roads cutting across the mountains, like Route 211, where the apple sellers are out in force, adding still more color with festoons of Confederate flags behind their baskets of ripe, red fruit.

You could spend a happy weekend just contemplating the serene countryside at Jordan Hollow Farm, a restored Colonial horse-farm-turned-country-inn in Stanley, about 12 miles from the Skyline Drive. The original farmhouse serves as a cozy dining room, where the food is top-notch. The 21 guest rooms in newly constructed lodges have rustic charm and admirable views from their porches. This is still a working horse farm, with both lessons and trail rides available.

Shenandoah Valley Farm and Inn in McGaheysville offers six moderately priced and very private guest cottages on the grounds of a 150-acre working cattle farm with magnificent grounds and views. Other inns with mountain views include Killahevlin on a hilltop in Front Royal, and the Iris Inn in Waynesboro.

Two excellent resorts are also nearby, Bryce Mountain and Massanutten, each offering handsome condominium lodgings, golf and tennis, and striking mountain vistas. Massanutten also has hotel accommodations.

Those who want the dining choices and additional activities of a small city can find them near the southern end of the Skyline Drive in Harrisonburg, off Route 33, or Staunton, off Route 250.

Harrisonburg, a small city centered around a classic Southern courthouse square, boasts one of the most elegant inns in the valley, the 1888 Joshua Wilton House, which includes a much-lauded restaurant. Just down the street is the small but excellent Virginia Quilt Museum, where you can be sure of seeing a high-quality display. Walk a little farther on South Main and you will find a couple of interesting crafts galleries, and interesting photos and other exhibits at the Center of American Places, an organization dedicated to preserving the classic places and landscapes of America. Antiquers will find over 50 dealers at the Rolling Hills Antique Mall on East Market Street.

Staunton offers an attractive, hilly Victorian downtown with plenty of dining choices. A unique stop here is the Museum of American Frontier Culture, a living museum outside town that re-creates the farms of England, Ireland, and Germany, the cultures that settled this part of Virginia. There is also an American farmstead from the valley, reflecting the blend of European influences. It is well worth a detour.

Another Staunton attraction is the Woodrow Wilson Birthplace and Museum, quite an interesting portrayal of Wilson and the nation during the years of his presidency. Right across the street, and within walking distance of town, is the Sampson Eagon Inn, a beautifully restored and furnished antebellum mansion, circa 1840.

The modest old-fashioned Buckhorn, 12 miles west of Staunton, is known for its bountiful Southern cooking and peanut butter pie. At the Buckhorn, you can ask for the room where Stonewall Jackson and his wife once slept.

Strasburg, an easy drive to the start of the drive in Front Royal, is another choice for antiquing and sightseeing as well as lodging, and Washington, Virginia, off Route 211, is one of the most appealing towns in the Shenandoah Valley. See pages 38–41 for more details.

Having settled in, you'll find plenty of activity to keep you busy both in and out of the park.

Shenandoah was authorized as a national park in 1926, and the state then purchased and donated to the federal government nearly 300 square miles cradling over 196,000 acres of the Blue Ridge Mountains. In the early 1800s, settlers spread from the fertile valley into the uplands. Here, scattered in ridges and hollows, they used the mountain for grazing, lumbering, and growing crops. By the time the park was established, more than half of the population had left the mountain area, and the remaining residents sold their land or were relocated with government assistance.

The recreational facilities and the Skyline Drive were both "Depression babies," monuments built by Franklin Roosevelt's Civilian Conservation Corps. Over the years, more than 95 percent of the land has returned to forest filled with more than 100 species of trees. The deer, bears, bobcats, turkeys, and other animals that were becoming rare or absent have also returned. The largest remaining open area, Big Meadows, has an abundance of wildflowers and berries that attract both wildlife and humans.

Besides gazing at the views in the park, you may take one of the many ranger-guided programs or pick up a guide for self-guided walks. Almost 500 miles of footpaths give you a close-up view of nature at its best. There are walks for everyone, from short strolls to more than 101 miles of the Appalachian Trail. Nine of the hikes lead to waterfalls.

One of the most popular trails is Old Rag Mountain, one of the most spectacular in the northern Virginia Blue Ridge. It features a rock "obstacle course," a 7.2-mile circuit over, under, and around large boulders and through a narrow natural rock tunnel. Be forewarned; it gets crowded.

Another favorite is the 6.25-mile section of the Appalachian Trail from Fishers Gap to Skyland, which edges Franklin Cliffs for an astonishing valley view, then crosses a ridge between Hawksbill and Naked Top Mountain. A side trail leads to the summit of Hawksbill, at 4,050 feet the highest point in the park.

Wherever you wander, you'll find natural beauty, mountain creeks, waterfalls, and a rich variety of plants and wildlife. Some 200 species of birds have been spotted within the park.

Horseback riders can rent mounts at Skyland Lodge and enjoy scenic guided walks along 150 miles of horse trails, and canoeists can go down into the valley to enjoy the mountain views from the waters of the Shenandoah River. Shenandoah River Outfitters of Luray will provide the canoes.

Some of the great sights in the Shenandoah Valley are underground in the eight huge limestone caverns beneath the valley's floor. The best known and most spectacular is Luray Caverns, where the soaring formations and crystal pools are a true natural wonder. Some of the shapes are eerie; others are nature's whimsy, bearing an uncanny resemblance to giant slabs of bacon and fried eggs. Most amazing of all is the Great Stalacpipe Organ, the world's largest musical instrument, a series of huge stalactites that produce melodious concert music when they are struck with rubber-tipped hammers. You can bring your camera with you into the caves, by the way. One section is lit with 25,000 watts, allowing for photos without a flash.

Part of the Luray Caverns complex, which includes a motel, tennis courts, and golf course, is a museum of 75 historic cars and carriages, with displays dating all the way from a 1755 Conestoga wagon to a 1946 Daimler.

Luray is the king of caverns, but when you've seen one cave, you haven't quite seen them all. Shenandoah Caverns is smaller, but it holds its own wonders, especially the sparkling Diamond Cascade and the vaulted-ceilinged Grotto of the Gods. An added attraction here is the American Celebration on Parade, an eye-popping parade of animated floats depicting American entertainment and political history.

Civil War buffs will want to see the Hall of Valor Civil War Museum at New Market Battlefield, one of the clearest displays of the course of the war, especially the battles in Virginia.

An alternate way back east to D.C. past the apple stands on Route 211 brings you to the village of Sperryville. On the third weekend in October, the annual Apple Harvest Celebration fills the town with booths and crafts, entertainment, and food. It's the perfect place to watch apple butter being made and to stock up on cider and apples from the nearby orchards. The Sperryville Antique Market holds all manner of treasures in a building that was once an apple warehouse. A few miles farther is Washington, Virginia, and its fine dining choices.

Gourmet dining adds to the pleasure, but the memories that will linger longest are those of heavenly autumn vistas of the Blue Ridge Mountains. Driving among the peaks on the Skyline Drive leaves you feeling on top of the world!

Area Code: 540

DRIVING DIRECTIONS   From D.C., take I-66 west to the northern end of the Skyline Drive at Front Royal. The approximate distance from D.C. is 76 miles. For other destinations in the valley, continue west on I-66 to Route 81 south. Other entrances to the drive are at Routes 211, 33, and 250/I-64.

ACCOMMODATIONS *Shenandoah National Park,* all lodging reservations are through Aramark National Park Lodging, P.O. Box 727, Luray, VA 22835, (800) 778-2851, www.visitshenandoah.com. Lodgings include: *Skyland Resort,* lodge open early April to late November, lodge rooms, M; suites, M–E; cabin rooms, I–M • *Big Meadows Lodge,* late April through October, lodge rooms, I–M; suites, M–E; cabin rooms, I–M • *Lewis Mountain Cabins,* late May through early November, cabin rooms, I; two rooms with connecting bath, M. All park rates are higher in October • *Jordan Hollow Farm Inn,* 326 Hawksbill Park Road, Stanley 22851, 778-2285 or (888) 418-7000, M–E, CP • *Shenandoah Valley Farm and Inn,* 882 Bloomer Springs Road, McGaheysville 22840, 289-5402, cottage units, I • *Killahevlin,* 1401 North Royal Avenue, Front Royal 22630, 636-7335 or (800) 847-6132, M–E, CP • *Iris Inn,* 191 Cinquapin Drive, Waynesboro 22980, 943-1991, recently built cedar and brick building on 20 acres, with decks or balconies for most rooms, M, CP; suites, E, CP • *Joshua Wilton House,* 412 South Main Street, Harrisonburg 22801, 434-4464, elegant Victorian in town, M, CP • *Stonewall Jackson Inn,* 547 East Market Street, Harrisonburg 22801, 433-8233 or (800) 445-5330, restored 1885 home on two acres, I–M, CP • *Sampson Eagon Inn,* 238 East Beverley Street, Staunton 24401, 886-8200 or (800) 597-9722, beautifully decorated, M, CP • *Belle Grae Inn,* 515 West Frederick Street, Staunton 24401, 886-5151 or (888) 541-5151, best rooms are in Victorian homes adjoining the main inn, E, CP • *Buckhorn Inn,* 2487 Hankey Mountain Highway, Churchville 24421, 337-6900, I, CP • **Resorts:** *Bryce Resort,* P.O. Box 3, Basye 22810, 856-2121 or (800) 821-1444, condo units from studios to villas, M–EE • *Massanutten Village,* P.O. Box 1227, Harrisonburg 22801, 289-4984 or (800) 207-MASS, hotel rooms, I; condos vary with size, M–EE. See also Strasburg, pages 7–8, and Washington/Sperryville, page 41.

DINING *Big Meadows Lodge* and *Skyland Resort* (see above), both serve all three meals, I–M • *Panorama Restaurant,* U.S. 211 and Skyline Drive, (800) 999-4714, additional park facility open mid-May to early November and early spring weekends, pizza, subs, Southern dishes, fine views, I–M • *Jordan Hollow Farm Inn* (see above), M • *Bryce Resort* (see above), restaurant with pleasant views, M • Joshua *Wilton House* (see above), dining room, formal menu, widely praised, prix fixe, EE; cafe menu, eclectic selections, M • *Belle Grae Inn* (see above), main dining room, M–E; bistro, I–M • *Staunton Station,* 42 Middlebrook Avenue, Staunton, restored railroad station complex includes *The Pullman,* 36 Middlebrook Avenue, Staunton, 885-5663,

American menu, soup and salad bar, I–M; *Depot Grille,* 885-7332, old freight depot, seafood and steaks, M; and the *Whistlestop Soda Shop,* a delightful 1880s ice cream parlor, I • *L'Italia,* 23 East Beverley Street, Staunton, 885-0102, Italian, I–M • *The Pampered Palate Cafe,* 26–28 East Beverley Street, Staunton, 886-9463, excellent lunch choice, I • *Buckhorn Inn* (see above), bountiful old-fashioned buffets, I, except Friday seafood buffet, M.

SIGHT-SEEING *Shenandoah National Park,* 999-3500; www.nps. gov/shen. Dickey Ridge Visitor Center, milepost 4.6, Byrd Visitor Center, milepost 51, Loft Mountain Visitor Center, Milepost 79.5. Hours for all: late spring to late fall, daily 9 A.M. to 5 P.M. Admission, $10 per car, good for seven days • *Virginia Quilt Museum,* 301 South Main Street, Harrisonburg, 433-3818. Hours: Monday, Thursday to Saturday, 10 A.M. to 4 P.M., Sunday 1 P.M. to 4 P.M. $$ • *Museum of American Frontier Culture,* U.S. 250, Staunton, 332-7850. Hours: Mid-March through November, daily 9 A.M. to 5 P.M.; rest of year 10 A.M. to 4 P.M. $$$$ • *Woodrow Wilson Birthplace & Museum,* 18–24 North Coalter Street, Staunton, 885-0897. Hours: March through October, daily 9 A.M. to 5 P.M.; rest of year 10 A.M. to 5 P.M. $$$ • *Luray Caverns,* U.S. 211 and 340 Bypass, Luray, 743-6551. Hours: Spring and fall, daily 9 A.M. to 6 P.M.; June 15 to Labor Day, daily to 7 P.M.; rest of year, Monday to Friday 9 A.M. to 4 P.M., Saturday, Sunday 9 A.M. to 5 P.M. $$$$$ • *Shenandoah Caverns,* Route 730, New Market, 477-3115. Hours: Spring and fall, daily 9 A.M. to 5:15 P.M.; summer to 6:15 P.M.; winter to 4:15 P.M. $$$$$ • *New Market Battlefield Park,* 8895 Collins Drive, New Market, 740-3102. Hours: Daily 9 A.M. to 5 P.M. Park, free; Hall of Valor, $$ • *Shenandoah River Outfitters,* 6502 South Page Valley Road, Luray, 743-4159 or (800) 6-CANOE-2, tube, canoe, and kayak rentals; phone for current rates.

INFORMATION *Shenandoah National Park,* c/o Superintendent, 3655 U.S. Highway 211 East, Luray, 22835, 999-3500; www.nps.gov/ shen • *Shenandoah Valley Travel Association,* 277 West Old Cross Road, P.O. Box 1040, New Market, VA 22844, 740-3132 or (877) VIS-ITSV; www.svta.org.

Carving a Niche in Easton

The ducks and geese are everywhere—in carvings, paintings, photographs, and displays in every shop window. There's no mistaking who's king in Easton, Maryland, come early November, when the annual Waterfowl Festival gets under way.

Some 20,000 people flock to the Eastern Shore each autumn for this weekend celebration of wildlife art that fills the town to overflowing. More than 400 artists display their work. A visit leaves little doubt as to the special niche this very American folk art has carved for itself among collectors and admirers, and you needn't be a bird lover to enjoy the show.

Whether you go home with a $1,500 prize decoy or a $15 carved tern, you'll have a festive day. As a bonus, there are those luscious Chesapeake Bay oysters in their November glory, not to mention the prime views of live V-shaped formations of the real ducks and geese overhead this time of year, honking in for their annual winter stay.

Some of the world's best carvers come to show and sell their work in Easton, and some of the finest antique decoys go up for display and sale at an annual auction. Paintings by the nation's most renowned waterfowl artists can be found in several locations, and a special building is set up for sculptors. The Talbot County Historical Society auditorium shows off work by photographers. A "collector's gallery" of exceptional nineteenth- and twentieth-century art and sculpture is housed at the Avalon Theater. At the high school, the big Buy, Sell, and Swap display brings scores of dealers and collectors ready to make a deal on antique decoys, rare books, and all manner of memorabilia. The Easton Middle School becomes a gift shop for the weekend, devoted to waterfowl-related arts and crafts, which means anything from stained glass and ceramics to needlework, leather, and clothing, all with bird and hunting-dog motifs. Many items are not available in commercial shops.

Those who become inspired can register in advance for master classes in painting and photography or attend seminars by prominent artists and conservationists at the Historical Society Museum, intended to educate visitors about wildlife, both in nature and in art.

Adding to the fun is the chance to listen in on the goose- and duck-calling contests and to watch the shooting, retriever, and fly-fishing demonstrations.

An annual event since 1970, the show—now run by some 1,500 volunteers—has raised more than $4 million for wildlife conservation causes. They have managed to organize a potential mob scene into relative order. Efficient shuttle buses are in constant motion ferrying visitors from one site to another, so you can leave your car in the public parking lots and forget about the traffic hassles in town. Ducky signs clearly mark the bus stops.

It's worth a wait in line to see the stars of the show, the carvers and painters. Originally, wildfowl carvings meant working decoys, lifelike models of ducks and geese and shorebirds that were used by hunters to lure the birds. The ducks and geese actually floated in the water; the shorebirds were mounted on rods and stuck in the sand as if scanning the surf for food.

The best of these decoys are recognized today as whimsical, nostalgic works of folk art, and their prices have risen dramatically. Prizes that used to be found at flea markets for small change may now sell for $1,000 and way up. Among the most sought-after pieces are those made prior to World War II, before the advent of mass-produced decoys. Collectors also treasure signed decoys by acknowledged masters like Lem and Steve Ward, brothers from Crisfield, Maryland, who worked in the 1960s. Knowledgeable aficionados say that you can still buy a pretty good old decoy for a few hundred dollars, but extremely rare pieces have gone for more than $30,000 at auction.

As interest in the bird carver's art has grown, the craft has evolved to become closer to realistic sculpture, amazing in its intricacy and detail. The work of many top contemporary carvers is beautiful and can be appreciated by anyone who enjoys artistic workmanship, regardless of the subject matter. The Ward Museum of Wildfowl Art, a permanent showcase in Salisbury, to the northeast on U.S. 50, is well worth a detour to see the best of the art, including winners of an annual competition.

If the lines for exhibits get to you and you want a break, stop for some of the cold oysters al fresco served at stands set up by local service organizations, then have a stroll through town. All of Easton is decked out for the occasion, but with a sense of humor about it all. There are displays everywhere poking gentle fun at the hunters, like a rubber boat with a giant goose dressed in camouflage at the helm. In the boat is his prey, a trussed pair of hunters. Hunters, incidentally, are often the most ardent conservationists, abiding strictly by legal limits and working hard to preserve the wetlands, so as to encourage the abundant flocks that give them so much sporting pleasure.

Shop windows in Easton are filled with carved ducks and geese and shorebirds of every size and species. Inside the shops you can find almost anything imaginable with bird motifs—goosey sweatshirts, pillows, skirts, and pocketbooks; gold jewelry in the shape of ducks on the wing; dhurrie rugs with ducky designs; ties and even toilet seats adorned with birds in flight.

Although this is not the ideal time for a peaceful stroll through Easton, a walk still can give you a good idea of the flavor of the town that is the hub of the lower Eastern Shore. Easton grew inland from the water, centered on a church and a court of justice. The Third Haven

Meeting House on South Washington dates back to 1682 and is said to be the nation's oldest frame building devoted to religious worship. It was built at the head of the Tred-Avon River so that congregants could come to services by boat.

The Talbot County Court House on North Washington is a 1794 successor to the building put up in 1712 to serve Talbot County. It became the focus of the settlement that was actually known as Talbot Court House until 1786, when residents petitioned for incorporation. Easton became the "Colonial capital" of the Eastern Shore. Many fine early homes remain, like Foxley Hall, a 1775 home at Goldsborough and North Aurora Streets, and the 1803 Thomas Perrin Smith House at 119 North Washington.

The Historical Society of Talbot County, housed in a nineteenth-century building, features a museum with changing exhibitions and guided tours of two restored houses, the Joseph Neall House, built in 1795, and the James Neall House, circa 1810. The society offers guided walking tours of Easton, or if you want to see more on your own, you can pick up a walking tour pamphlet and follow Washington and its parallel neighbors West and Harrison, as well as the intersecting streets of Dover and Goldsborough.

At the corner of Dover and Harrison you'll find the Tidewater Inn, the stately pride of the Eastern Shore, and one of the headquarters for the Wildfowl Festival. Down the block on Harrison is the chic small Inn at Easton, with a notable dining room, and Mason's, a popular local restaurant.

Named one of America's "100 best art towns" in a recent book, Easton has an active arts community, with changing art exhibits at the Academy Art Museum, housed in two nineteenth-century structures, and music, drama, and other entertainment at the nicely restored Avalon Theater, an art deco theater dating to 1921. Each will have programs devoted to wildlife during the festival weekend.

Festival tickets include a visit to the Chesapeake Bay Maritime Museum in St. Michaels, a fine place to get a sense of the role water has played in Chesapeake history, and to see the largest floating fleet of historic bay boats in existence. The museum's landmark is the Hooper Strait Lighthouse, one of the last three remaining cottage-type lighthouses on the bay. A stroll around St. Michaels, a village that retains much of its nineteenth-century character, is also rewarding. Read more about St. Michaels on page 130.

Two other popular attractions during the weekend are retriever demonstrations at area ponds, showing the uncanny skills of the hunting dog, and the world championship goose-calling contest, held at the high school auditorium. A fly-fishing demonstration is another favorite event.

However fascinating the wildfowl exhibits may be, save part of a day for a look at the real thing, the waterfowl that flock so abundantly here in late fall and winter. The Chesapeake Bay region is one of the main intersections of the migratory paths of more than 37 species of water-fowl, including the biggest of the migrating birds, whistling swans, which may weigh as much as 25 pounds. Although spotting and identifying birds on the wing is a skill that takes years to develop, you don't need a first-name acquaintance with them to appreciate the bevies of beauties to be seen overhead, on the ponds, and in the marshes.

The best place for close-up views is the Blackwater National Wildlife Refuge, to the south of Easton, 12 miles below Cambridge. This stretch of more than 24,000 acres, mostly rich tidal marsh, was set aside in 1933 as a protected haven for migratory wildfowl. It soon became a favorite wintering area for Canada geese using the Atlantic flyway. In autumn, at the peak of the annual migration, thousands of geese and ducks can be found here. Among the residents that have been spotted spending the winter are tundra swans, snow geese, and some 20 duck species, including colorful mallards, black ducks, blue-winged and green-winged teals, wigeons, and pintails.

Other feathered residents include the great blue heron and the bald eagle; the endangered national bird is found here in its greatest numbers in the East, north of Florida. Another endangered species sometimes seen here is the peregrine falcon. Ospreys arrive in spring and stay through early fall, using the nesting platforms that have been placed throughout the marsh.

The refuge is also a year-round home for towhees, woodpeckers, brown-headed nuthatches, bobwhites, and woodcocks, and such mammals as white-tailed deer, raccoons, opossums, skunks, red foxes, gray squirrels, and the Delmarva fox squirrel.

You can spot all kinds of residents along a three-and-a-half-mile or six-and-a-half-mile wildlife drive among the ponds, woods, fields, and marshes, or on walking trails.

Blackwater is an appropriate end to a wildfowl weekend, a chance for a live appreciation of the grace that inspires the Easton bird carvers.

Area code: 410

DRIVING DIRECTIONS Easton is on Route 50, south of the Chesapeake Bay Bridge. Take Route 50/301 across the bridge and turn south on Route 50. The approximate distance from D.C. is 73 miles.

ACCOMMODATIONS See pages 134–135 for best accommodations in Easton and neighboring Oxford and St. Michaels. Rooms here are booked months ahead for the Waterfowl Festival weekend, so here are a few more options: ***Harbourtowne Resort,*** off Route 33, St. Michaels 21663, 745-9066 or (800) 446-9066, 111-room resort with golf, driving range, putting green and a great waterside location, motel-style rooms, E–EE • ***Bishop's House,*** 214 Goldsborough Street, Easton 21601, 820-7290 or (800) 223-7290, very Victorian bed-and-breakfast home circa 1880, M, CP • *Chaffinch House,* 132 South Harrison Street, Easton 21601, 822-5074 or (800) 861-5074, 1893 Queen Anne Victorian, M, CP • *John S. McDaniel House,* 14 North Aurora Street, Easton, 21601, 822-3781, in-town bed-and-breakfast, M, CP • **Area motels** (may be higher for Waterfowl Weekend): *Comfort Inn,* Route 50, Easton 21601, 820-8333, M • *Holiday Inn Express,* 8561 Ocean Gateway, Easton 21601, 819-6500, M, CP • *Days Inn,* Route 50, Easton 21601, 822-4600 or (800) 638-9146, I–M, CP • *Atlantic Budget Inn,* 8058 Ocean Gateway (Route 50), Easton, 21601, 822-2200, M • *Econo Lodge,* 8175 Ocean Gateway (Route 50), Easton 21601, 820-5555, M • *Best Western St. Michaels Motor Inn,* Route 33, St. Michaels 21663, 745-3333, M.

DINING *The Inn at Easton,* 28 South Harrison Street, 21601, 822-4910 or (888) 800-8091, excellent creative chef, prix fixe, EE • *Hunter's Tavern,* Tidewater Inn, Dover and Harrison Streets, 822-1300, elegant, Eastern Shore decor, decoys, M–E • *Mason's,* 22 South Harrison Street, 822-3204, attractive setting, interesting and varied menu, highly recommended locally, M–E • *Out of the Fire,* 11 Goldsborough Street, 770-4777, arty setting, stone hearth oven, good Mediterranean fare, wine bar, M–E • *Washington Street Pub,* 20 North Washington Street, 822-9011, informal, I–M • *Rustic Inn,* Talbotown Shopping Center, Harrison Street, 820-8212, rustic decor, family-friendly, M–E • *Legal Spirits Tavern,* 42 East Dover Street, 820-0765, casual, I–M • *Eagle Spirits,* The Easton Club, 28449 Clubhouse Drive, 820-4100, pleasant dining room overlooking golf course, I–M. See page 135 for St. Michaels and Oxford.

SIGHT-SEEING *Waterfowl Festival,* usually the second weekend in November. Information and current rates, 40 South Harrison Street, P.O. Box 929, Easton 21601, 822-4567; www.waterfowlfestival.org • *Historical Society of Talbot County,* 25 South Washington Street, Easton, 822-0773. Hours: Tuesday to Saturday 10 A.M. to 4 P.M. $; house tours and walking tours, each $ additional • *Chesapeake Bay Maritime Museum,* Navy Point, St. Michaels, 745-2916. Hours: Daily 9 A.M. to 5 P.M. Admission included with Waterfowl Festival ticket during festival weekend; otherwise $$$ • *Academy Art Museum,* 106 South Street, Easton, 833-2787. Hours: Monday to Saturday, 10 A.M. to 4 P.M., Wednesday to 9 P.M., $, free on Wednesday • *Blackwater National Wildlife Refuge,* 2145 Key Wallace Drive, Cambridge, 228-2677. Visitor center open Monday to Friday 8 A.M. to 4 P.M., Saturday, Sunday 9 A.M. to 5 P.M. Wildlife Drive and outdoor facilities open dawn to dusk. $$ per car.

INFORMATION *Talbot County Office of Tourism,* Courthouse, 11 North Washington Street, Easton, MD 21601, 770-8000; www.talbot county.md.

The Inn Crowd in Bucks County

William Penn, who had his pick of Pennsylvania, chose to build his country home along the Delaware River in Bucks County, reportedly telling some friends that it was even lovelier than the English countryside he had left behind.

This bucolic enclave of hills, streams, covered bridges, and mellowed stone farmhouses has been drawing people ever since. At the turn of the twentieth century, the pastoral views inspired one of the nation's first art colonies. Later they lured some of America's top creative talents, people like Oscar Hammerstein II, Moss Hart, George S. Kaufman, James Michener, and Pearl Buck, who chose Bucks County for their country homes.

Nowadays it is inn lovers who flock to Bucks County, where choosing among the historic homes now serving as lodgings is one of life's pleasanter dilemmas. Should it be the Inn at Ford Hook Farm, the gracious estate of seed king David Burpee, or Oscar Hammerstein's Highland Farms, where Stephen Sondheim was a frequent guest and the late Henry Fonda was married under the grape arbor? High Victorian style and a six-course dinner at Evermay, country charm at Ash Mill Farm, or the elegant ambience, pool, and tennis court at Pine Tree Farm?

The list goes on and on, and so do the pleasures of a Bucks County visit: walking along the canal, riding a mule barge, leisurely gliding in a canoe down the Delaware, riding an old-fashioned steam train, roaming through galleries and antique shops, visiting historical sites, or just gazing at some of the most enchanting back-roads scenery in the East.

You might start your visit Saturday morning in New Hope, the picturesque artists' colony that is the heart of Bucks County. Here, a labyrinth of paths and alleyways offers almost 100 shops and galleries for browsing. New Hope, however, is far from undiscovered, and you'll understand why an early start is advisable when you see the number of tourists converging here as the day goes on.

Still, there is good reason for the crowds. Here's where you can take that nostalgic ride on one of the last operating mule-drawn canal barges in the country or climb aboard the New Hope & Ivyland Rail Road for a 50-minute round trip to Lahaska, through some of Bucks County's prettiest countryside.

Tucked among the gift and gewgaw shops are some finds. A few special shops and galleries to note are Golden Door (a historic stone building) for Bucks County traditional landscape paintings, A Mano for handcrafts, and Three Cranes for Oriental pieces and interesting clothing, all found on Main Street. Antiquers will find a host of shops on Bridge Street.

The sightseeing spot here is the Parry Mansion, with ten rooms displaying the furnishings and decor that might have been used by the family whose successive generations lived here for 182 years. Come evening, the Bucks County Playhouse, the famous old theater in a restored gristmill, will likely have something interesting on tap. It has been named the official state theater of Pennsylvania.

When the New Hope sidewalks begin to overflow with shoppers, it's time to visit the tourist office at the corner of Main and Mechanic to stock up on maps and guides and then head out for the shops that run almost nonstop along Route 202 to Doylestown. Peddler's Village, a nicely landscaped Colonial-style complex, has more than 70 shops crammed with wares of every kind, along with quite an elegant inn, the Golden Plough, several dining places, and Carousel World, where you can ride on the whimsical steeds of a restored 1922 carousel.

You can't miss the newest shopping attraction in the area, Penn's Purchase, a village of factory outlets from Anne Klein fashions to OshKosh overalls.

Nor will you need a guide to find the many other antique shops along Route 202. Three big antique shows are held each year; ask the dealers or contact the Bucks County Conference & Visitors Bureau for this year's dates and locations.

Continue on to Doylestown for a unique sightseeing complex known as the Mercer Mile, the legacy of a genuine American genius and eccentric, Henry Chapman Mercer. One of the nation's leading archaeologists, he had a passion for collecting early American tools, and that led to a midlife career change. Mercer became so intrigued with the tools used by the old Pennsylvania German potters and tile makers that he determined single-handedly to perpetuate the dying craft. He apprenticed himself to one of the potters, rented a decrepit kiln, and soon exhibited a talent that brought him a new kind of fame. Mercer tiles can be seen from the casino at Monte Carlo to the Gardner Museum in Boston to the tile floor in the Pennsylvania state capitol at Harrisburg.

Mercer called his enterprise the Moravian Pottery and Tile Works. The factory is now a living history museum, but it is the least of Mercer's monuments. The most incredible display of tiles is in his own home, Fonthill, a castlelike concrete fantasy of columns, balconies, beams, towers, arches, and winding stairs. Tiles are everywhere: on columns and beams; serving as headboards, tabletops, and ceilings; and even lining the stair steps.

And then there is the Mercer Museum, housing Mercer's huge collection of 50,000 hand tools for some 130 crafts. There are tools once used by butchers, dairymen, cooks, and coopers; carpenters, weavers, leather workers, and printers; doctors, clock makers, surveyors, and seamstresses. Each trade's tools are set up in separate cubbies surrounding spiral stairs. The stairs encircle a six-story-high vaulted core where handcrafted objects of every conceivable kind are suspended: chairs, cradles, barrels, whaleboats, baskets, bellows, cigar-store Indians, even a Conestoga wagon.

Across from the Mercer Museum is Doylestown's equally important attraction, the James A. Michener Art Museum, endowed by and named for the author who is the town's most famous native son. It is handsomely housed in the ornate 1884 building that was once the Bucks County jail. The prison yard is now a courtyard enhanced by a sculpture garden. Since opening in 1988, the museum has been expanded twice, most recently in 1996.

The galleries concentrate on nineteenth- and twentieth-century regional American art, with changing exhibits as well as a permanent collection of work by Pennsylvania Impressionists, including the noted early 1900s New Hope School of painters. The Abstract Expressionist paintings collected by James Michener and his wife, Mari, are also on display.

A special exhibition honors the life and work of James A. Michener, with original furnishings from his early Doylestown office, where he wrote *Tales of the South Pacific*. The Mari Sabusawa Michener Wing features a multimedia interactive exhibition, "Creative Bucks County," with displays on the many notable people who have lived in the area.

The Reading Room, dedicated to a renowned Bucks County woodworker, the late George Nakashima, overlooks the courtyard and sculpture garden. The Japanese-style library includes an installation of classic furniture from Nakashima's studio. The museum's Espresso Cafe offers drinks and light fare.

With these important sights, plus some of the best lodging and dining in the county, Doylestown is an excellent home base for a weekend.

Sunday is the time for the back roads and countryside. Despite the growing number of contemporary homes that are changing the landscape, the stone houses and barns that are the special trademark of Bucks County remain, and they make for a beautiful drive. Some of those farmhouses are now among the county's list of special lodgings.

Part of the fascination is that no two stone houses are alike. Even their colors and textures vary according to the native stones used for construction. You'll see mostly limestone and shale in central Bucks, and craggier granite in the upper regions. Notice the double houses with twin doors, the big trilevel barns, and the "bride and groom" trees that flank many of the doorways. The trees were planted long ago for good luck by newlyweds who hoped their love would flourish along with the saplings.

The main roads are River Road (Route 32) and Routes 611 and 413, and you can't go wrong making your way back and forth. One possible route is to follow winding River Road north. The thin strip of land paralleling the road between the canal and the river is officially called Delaware Canal State Park, but generally it is just referred to as the towpath, because it was once used by the mules that pulled barges down the canal. Now hikers and bikers ply the path.

The drive will take you through the sleepy town of Lumberville, where the Cuttalossa Inn is a perfect spot for brunch or lunch beside a waterfall. Then it's on to Point Pleasant, where you may be tempted to pause for an hour to see the river from one of its nicest perspectives, by canoe. Point Pleasant Canoe and Tube can provide all the necessary gear, and even novices need not worry about this placid stretch of water.

Twelve covered bridges remain on the back roads of Bucks County. With a free map from the Conference & Visitors Bureau to guide you, you'll find four of these along scenic detours as you proceed up the river between Point Pleasant and Erwinna. Stover-Myers Mill in Erwinna, circa 1800, still has its old machinery intact and is a local historic site. A two-and-a-half-mile detour west of River Road in Upper Black Eddy will bring you to a curiosity, three and a half acres of huge boulders known as Ringing Rocks because many of the rocks, when struck, actually do ring.

From here, continue west on Route 32 to the connection with Route 611 and proceed south through more charming towns such as Pipersville, near the Cabin Run and Loux covered bridges. Not far away, near Dublin, is Green Hills Farm, where Pulitzer and Nobel prize–winning author Pearl Buck lived and worked for 40 years. Her 1835 stone house is filled with Oriental antiques.

If you take a drive to lower Bucks County, you can see Pennsbury Manor in Morrisville, William Penn's reconstructed seventeenth-century country plantation estate overlooking the Delaware. Along the way you'll pass Washington Crossing Historic Park, with many interesting sights for touring and the 100-acre Bowman's Hill Wildflower Preserve for roaming.

And then there is still that matter of choosing a Bucks County lodging of your own. Do you want river views from your room at the 1740 House? Or would you rather visit Barley Sheaf Farm, 1740 stone farmhouse where George S. Kaufman once entertained the Marx Brothers and Lillian Hellman? At the Golden Pheasant, you can have a private suite with a deck overlooking the canal, and stroll over for a gourmet dinner in one of the most romantic dining rooms in Bucks County.

If you find it hard to decide on a favorite, you'll be in good company. You can join the legions who keep returning happily to Bucks County to make up their minds.

Area Code: New Hope and Doylestown, 215; 610 where noted

DRIVING DIRECTIONS   New Hope is on Route 32, River Road. From D.C., take I-95 north into Pennsylvania, then north on Route 32.

The approximate distance from D.C. is 175 miles. From the north or west, follow Route 202 to Route 32.

ACCOMMODATIONS *Ash Mill Farm,* 5358 York Road (Route 202), Holicong 18928, 794-5373, charmingly furnished 1790 stone farmhouse, M–E, CP • *Barley Sheaf Farm,* 5281 York Road, Route 202, Holicong 18928, 794-5104, 30-acre farm estate, pool, M–EE, CP • *Evermay on the Delaware,* 899 River Road (Route 32), Erwinna 18920, (610) 294-9100, handsome Victorian, E–EE, CP • *Golden Pheasant Inn,* 763 River Road (Route 32), Erwinna 18920, (610) 294-9595, rooms above the restaurant in country French decor, canal views, one very private suite, M, CP • *The Inn at Fordhook Farm,* 105 New Britain Road, Doylestown 18901, 345-1766, M–EE, CP • *Highland Farms,* 70 East Road, Doylestown 18901, 340-1354, E, CP • *Mill Creek Farm,* 2348 Quarry Road, P.O. Box 816, Buckingham 18912, 794-0776, eighteenth-century home, horse farm on 100 acres, attractive rooms, E, CP • *Pine Tree Farm,* 2155 Lower State Road, Doylestown 18901, 348-0632, E, CP • *1740 House,* River Road (Route 32), Lumberville 18933, 297-5661, attractive smallish rooms, most facing the canal, M, CP • *Tattersall Inn,* Cafferty and River Roads (Route 32), Point Pleasant 18950, 297-8233 or (800) 297-4988, gracious manor house, M–E CP • *Stone Ridge Farm Bed & Breakfast,* 956 Bypass Road, Dublin, 18917, 249-9186 or (877) 855-BARN, restored 1810 barn on a ten-acre horse farm, special, M–C, CP.

Inns are small and fill quickly. If all of the above are booked, here are some very pleasant alternatives: *The Bucksville House,* 4501 Durham Road, Kintnersville 18930, (610) 847-8948, cozy country decor, off the tourist track about 20 minutes north of New Hope, M, CP • *Fox & Hound Bed & Breakfast of New Hope,* 246 West Bridge Street, New Hope 18938, 862-5082 or (800) 862-5082, 1850s stone manor on two acres, half a mile from town center, some Jacuzzis, fireplaces, M–E, CP • *Inn at Phillips Mill,* River Road (Route 32), New Hope 18938, 862-9919, country French decor, small pool, M, CP • *Mansion Inn,* 9 South Main Street, New Hope 18938, 862-5082, luxurious in-town inn, E–EE, CP • *Maplewood Farm Bed & Breakfast,* 5090 Durham Road, Route 413, Gardenvlle, PA, informal farmhouse amid sheep-filled meadows, pool, M–E, CP • *Wedgewood Inn,* 111 West Bridge Street, New Hope 18938, 862-2570, antique-filled Victorian for those who want to be in the center of New Hope, E–EE, CP • *Whitehall Inn,* Pineville Road, New Hope 18938, 598-7945, pool, tennis, afternoon tea, chamber music, E, CP • Most inns have two-night minimums; these do not: *Golden Plough,* Route 202 and Street Road, Peddler's Village, Lahaska 18931, 794-4004, nicely furnished small hotel, M–EE, CP • *Plumsteadville Inn,* Route 611 and Stump Road, Plumsteadville

18949, 766-7500, well-furnished rooms above a popular restaurant, M–E, CP; suites, EE, CP.

DINING *Black Bass Hotel,* River Road (Route 32), Lumberville, 297-5770, perfect riverside setting, 1740 building, good choice for Sunday brunch, dinners, E • *Bucks Bounty,* 20 River Road, Erwinna, (610) 294-8106, soaring ceiling, interesting decor and menu, reasonble, I–M • *Carversville Inn,* Carversville and Aquetong Roads, Carversville, 297-8100, Southern menu, quaint old inn, M • *Centre Bridge Inn,* 2998 North River Road, New Hope, 862-9139, lovely spot on the river, M–EE • *Chef Tell's Manor House,* 1800 River Road, Upper Black Eddy, (610) 982-0212, 1803 manor on the river, eclectic, including some German specialties, well-known chef, M • *Cuttalossa Inn,* River Road (Route 32), Lumberville, 297-5082, great location but only fair food, M–EE; best for lunch or brunch, I–M • *Evermay* (see above), six-course dinner, prix fixe, EE • *Golden Pheasant Inn* (see above), romantic choice, charming country French decor, solarium dining in season, M–EE • *Hotel du Village,* 2535 North River Road, New Hope, 862-9911, rustic atmosphere, country French menu, M–E • *Inn at Phillips Mill* (see above), 862-9919, romantic setting, French menu, E–EE • *La Bonne Auberge,* Village II, Mechanic Street, New Hope, 862-2462, classic French, expensive but highly regarded, EE • *The Landing,* 22 North Main Street, New Hope, 862-5711, town's best river view, dependable American cuisine, M–E • *Plumsteadville Inn* (see above), excellent American fare in a 1751 inn, M-E • *Waterlilies,* 5738 Route 202 at Route 263 intersection, Lahaska, 794-8588, informal setting, good food, reasonable prices, M–E • Also see Lambertville, NJ, page 13.

Doylestown: *Black Walnut,* 30 West State Street, Doylestown, 348-0708, elegant French-American, EE • *Cafe Arielle,* 100 South Main Street, Doylestown, 345-5930, well-reviewed French fare in a restored mill, M–E • *Roosevelt's Blue Star,* 52 East State Street, Doylestown, 348-9000, American cuisine, fresh ingredients of the season, M–E • *Sign of the Sorrel Horse,* 4424 Old Easton Road, Doylestown, 230-9999, elegant continental in a onetime gristmill, prix fixe, EE • *State Street Cafe,* 57 West State Street, Doylestown, 340-0373, American fare, airy setting, recommended for lunch, M.

SIGHT-SEEING *Parry Mansion,* South Main Street, New Hope, 862-5652. Hours: May to mid-December, Friday to Sunday 1 P.M. to 5 P.M. $$ • *New Hope Canal Boat Co.,* 149 South Main Street, New Hope, 862-0758. Hours: Mule-drawn barge rides, May to October, daily noon to 4:30 P.M., April, Friday to Sunday. Best to check current schedule. $$$ • *New Hope & Ivyland Rail Road,* Bridge & Stockton Streets, New Hope, 862-2332. Hours: late May through early November, Monday to Friday 11 A.M. to 4 P.M., Saturday and Sunday 11 A.M. to 5 P.M.; rest of year, usually Friday, Saturday, Sunday, except January through early April, Saturday and Sunday only. Special "Santa Express" schedules late November and December. Times vary with seasons, so best to call. $$$$ • *Mercer Museum,* 84 South Pine Street, Doylestown, 345-0210. Hours: Monday to Saturday 10 A.M. to 5 P.M., Sunday noon to 5 P.M. $$ • *Fonthill,* East Court Street at Route 313, Doylestown, 348-9461. Hours: Tours offered Monday to Saturday 10 A.M. to 5 P.M., Sunday noon to 5 P.M. Reservations suggested. $$ • *Moravian Pottery and Tile Works,* 130 Swamp Road at East Court Street, Doylestown, 345-6722. Hours: Daily 10 A.M. to 4:45 P.M. $$ • *James A. Michener Art Museum,* 138 South Pine Street, Doylestown, 340-9800. Hours: Tuesday to Friday 10 A.M. to 4:30 P.M., Saturday and Sunday 10 A.M. to 5 P.M. $$; under age 12, free • *Grand Carousel,* Peddler's Village, Routes 202 and 263, Lahaska, 794-8960, includes a ride on a restored antique carousel. Hours: March to December, Monday to Thursday 10 A.M. to 5 P.M., Friday and Saturday 10 A.M. to 9 P.M., Sunday 11 A.M. to 5:30 P.M.; rest of year, Monday to Friday 10 A.M. to 5:30 P.M., Saturday 10 A.M. to 6 P.M. $$ • *Pearl S. Buck Home,* 520 Dublin Road, Perkasie, 249-0100. Hours: March through December, tours Tuesday to Saturday 11 A.M., 1 P.M., and 2 P.M.; Sunday 1 P.M. and 2 P.M. $$ • *Washington Crossing Historic Park,* Route 32 south of New Hope, P.O. Box 103, Washington Crossing, 493-4076. Hours: Tuesday to Saturday 9 A.M. to 5 P.M., Sunday noon to 5 P.M. park admission, $ per car; Park and Memorial Building, free. Inclusive admission to Thomson-Neeley House, McConkey Ferry Inn, Taylor House, and Bowman's Hill Tower, $$ • *Pennsbury Manor,* 400 Pennsbury Memorial Road, Morrisville (near Tullytown), 946-0400. Hours: Guided tours Tuesday to Saturday 9 A.M. to 5 P.M., Sunday noon to 5 P.M.; last tour begins at 3:30 P.M. $$ • *Bucks County Playhouse,* 70 South Main Street, New Hope, 862-2041. Hours: April through December; phone for current offerings.

INFORMATION *Bucks County Conference & Visitors Center,* 3207 Street Road, Bensalem, 19020, (888) 359-9110; www.bccvb.org • *New Hope Chamber of Commerce,* 1 West Mechanic Street, 18938, 862-5880; www.newhopepa.com.

An Early Thanksgiving on the James River

Forget all those stories about the Pilgrims. Down in Virginia, they'll tell you that the first official Thanksgiving was celebrated not in Massachusetts at all, thank you, but at Berkeley Plantation on the James River in 1619, two years before the Pilgrims celebrated the first Thanksgiving in Massachusetts. Virginians even persuaded a Massachusetts native, the late President John F. Kennedy, to issue a Thanksgiving Proclamation in 1963 recognizing their state's claim.

But being the gracious folks they are, the Virginians didn't try to change the familiar national observance. They simply added a ceremony of their own at Berkeley on the first Sunday in November. It isn't a large celebration, but it is a perfect opportunity to remember the importance of the Virginia Colony by visiting the great plantations along the James, as well as the settlements at Jamestown, where the first permanent English colony in America began in 1607.

Some 104 passengers sailed up the James River aboard three tiny ships to found that first settlement. A mixed crew of well-heeled gentlemen, skilled artisans, and indentured servants, they faced hunger, sickness, Indians, and the rigors of the wilderness in their new home. More settlers arrived, but during "the starving time" of 1609–1610, 440 of the 500 inhabitants perished. Yet survivors learned to conquer frontier living and survived. Jamestown was the capital of the sprawling Virginia Colony and an active community for almost 100 years. It was during that time that the idea of representative government was developed. The capital was moved to Williamsburg in 1699.

All that remains of the original town is the seventeenth-century Church Tower. At Jamestown, where the Virginia settlers landed, foundations and artifacts have been excavated; a 1608 glass factory has been re-created, complete with demonstrations of the old craft; and paintings and markers have been created as clues to the world of newly established "James Cittie."

Knowledgeable National Park Service rangers lead walks and give talks that help put the pieces into perspective. Many of Jamestown's residents have been forgotten, but statues remain to honor Pocahontas, the Indian princess whose marriage to Englishman John Rolfe helped improve relations between their two peoples, and to commemorate Captain John Smith, the explorer who was president of the Jamestown Council from 1608 to 1609. The remains of the settlement called New Towne, established after 1620, help show the further development of the community.

Just next door on the mainland, at Jamestown Settlement, you can board reconstructions of the three ships—the *Susan Constant,* the *God-speed,* and the *Discovery*—that made the long ocean voyage to America and marvel that these tiny vessels ever survived. Under the auspices of the Jamestown-Yorktown Foundation, this is part museum, part living history program. A visit begins in the indoor complex, where a 20-minute film tells about the beginnings of the settlement, and exhibits in the English, Powhatan Indian, and Jamestown galleries fill out the story.

Outside are reconstructions bringing to life the area before and after the English arrived. The Indian Village is based on archaeological findings, with houses made of sapling frames covered with reed mats. Interpreters demonstrate the Powhatan way of life.

The reconstruction of the first fort carved out of the forest has high wooden palisades protecting the tiny wattle-and-daub structures that were used for everything from homes to churches and armories. Once again, costumed interpreters are on hand, showing the crafts and trades of the era, such as blacksmithing, carpentry, and open-hearth cooking.

You could spend an instructive weekend just following the Colonial Parkway north from Jamestown into Williamsburg, the second Virginia capital, now a restored Colonial town that has preserved better than any other single spot the lifestyle of eighteenth-century America. The seeds of the American Revolution were sown here, and the fate of the new nation was sealed with the final victory ending the Revolutionary War at Yorktown, the destination at the far end of the Colonial Parkway.

The National Park Service facility at Yorktown includes a visitor center, where a film is shown describing the siege, the battlefield itself, the site of George Washington's headquarters, and some of the homes used for meetings.

Tiny Yorktown is still an active town, and well worth a stroll since it retains the look of long ago.

The Yorktown Victory Center nearby is a separately run facility, also under the auspices of the Jamestown-Yorktown Foundation. A major museum exhibit, "Road to Revolution," traces the events that led to America's declaring its independence and paints a picture of the daily life of the people who lived during the Revolution. In a novel approach, the "Witnesses to Revolution" gallery shows the impact of the Revolution on ten individuals, told through their personal writings and observations. Re-creations outside include a Continental army camp and an eighteenth-century farm.

One way to fit all of this in might be to save the wealth of Williamsburg sight-seeing for another visit, but to get the flavor of the town now by staying here. The James River plantations lie about midway between Williamsburg and the present capital of Richmond, 50 miles and an hour's drive away, and either town serves as a good home base for the weekend.

Even better are some of the interesting countryside bed-and-breakfast possibilities in the heart of the plantation area near Charles City. North Bend Plantation, circa 1819, is a Virginia Historic Landmark on 250 acres that was used as headquarters by General Sheridan in 1864. The owners, George and Ridgely Copland, have family roots deep in Virginia history, and their home is filled with fascinating memorabilia. Piney Grove at Southall's Plantation is an intriguing mix of 1800 log cabin and fine residence, recently restored into a welcoming small inn. A few other properties, still amid working farms, also have accommodations for bed-and-breakfast guests.

Three fine restaurants, Coach House Tavern at Berkeley Plantation, Indian Fields Tavern, and David's White House Restaurant, have added appealing dining choices to the area.

Route 5, the plantation route between the two towns, is one of the oldest roads in the country. It follows an old Indian trail paralleling the river. As plantations and villages grew up beside the river, an overland route was built connecting them, known as the "new market road" because it literally connected the old markets of Williamsburg with the newer ones in Richmond. The road played a prominent part in both the Revolutionary and Civil Wars.

Heading west from Williamsburg, you are entering the lush agricultural region where the new English colonists began to make fortunes growing tobacco and other crops. Some of Virginia's most magnificent plantations were built here, and some are now open to the public, offering dramatic proof of how much things had progressed in the new colony in just one century.

The undisputed queen of the plantations is Shirley, the oldest plantation in Virginia and a rare continuity of one family spanning nearly four centuries. It was founded six years after the settlers arrived at Jamestown in 1607 to establish the first permanent English colony in the New World. Edward Hill in 1638 acquired a portion of the original grant. The present mansion was begun in 1723 by Edward Hill III, a member of the House of Burgesses in the Virginia Colony, when Elizabeth Hill, great-granddaughter of the first Hill, married John Carter, eldest son of Robert "King" Carter, uniting two great early Virginia families. It was completed in 1738 and is largely in its original state. The superb red Flemish bond brick buildings in the Queen Anne forecourt are recognized as architectural gems unique in America.

The Hills and Carters entertained the Byrds, the Harrisons, Washington, and many other prominent early Virginians here. Ann Hill Carter, mother of Robert E. Lee, was married in one of these rooms to Governor Harry "Lighthorse" Lee. The famous general spent several years in his mother's home, where he received part of his schooling. The tenth generation of the family to live in the home resides upstairs and allows the public in to see the stunning great rooms downstairs. The original family portraits, silver, and furniture remain, along with a tall carved cantilevered walnut staircase remarkable for its lack of visible support.

Shirley's 800-acre estate continues to be a working farm, producing corn, barley, wheat, and soybeans. Besides the main house, many outbuildings have been preserved, among them a large two-story kitchen, laundry, smokehouse, dovecote, stable, and two sturdy brick barns.

Sherwood Forest Plantation was the home of America's tenth president, John Tyler, from 1842 to 1862. The gracious white-columned and porticoed Colonial home was built in 1730 and redone by John Tyler when he retired from the White House in 1845 with his second wife, Julia Gardiner Tyler. Columns and other architectural details added by the Tylers reflect the Greek Revival influence of their day. The 68-foot ballroom designed for dancing the Virginia reel made this the longest frame house in America, some 300 feet.

The house has remained in the Tyler family for more than 150 years. In the mid-1970s, it was restored by President Tyler's grandson, Harrison Ruffin Tyler, and his family, who remain in residence. The home is elegantly furnished and filled with family memorabilia and portraits. Scars left on the doors and woodwork during the Civil War remain. Also unique to this home is the legend of the Gray Lady, who has been heard rocking in the parlor for more than 200 years. The fine gardens are also open for self-guided strolls. Box lunches are available at Sherwood Forest by advance reservation.

Two other homes of note are Westover, built about 1730 by William Byrd II, the founder of Richmond, and Evelynton, named for Byrd's daughter and once part of the Westover estate. Westover is best known for its gardens and their elaborate entrance gates.

Evelynton has the look of an old Georgian plantation house but is actually a 1937 structure on the site where the home of family patriarch Edmund Ruffin was burned during the Civil War. Ruffin has a unique spot in history—he fired the first shot of the Civil War at Fort Sumter. Portraits of the Ruffin family hang on the walls. The 60-acre site with formal English boxwood gardens and lush lawns is part of a 2,500-acre working farm, still owned and operated by the Ruffin family.

The culmination of a plantation tour is Thanksgiving at Berkeley. The early Georgian mansion built by Benjamin Harrison IV in 1726 is said to be the oldest three-story brick house in Virginia and is matched only by the Adams House in Massachusetts for producing two presidents: Benjamin's son, William Henry Harrison, and his great-grandson (also Benjamin). The younger Benjamin Harrison came home to Berkeley to write his inaugural address in the room where he was born. Every president from Washington to Buchanan enjoyed Berkeley's famous hospitality. Ten acres of formal terraced boxwood gardens and lawn extend a full quarter mile from the front door to the James River.

Berkeley claims several firsts in America. The first bourbon was supposedly made here in 1622, and that same year, the first organized American war, an Indian massacre, took place on the grounds. The first commercial shipyard opened here in 1695, the first pediment roof went up in 1726, and while General Butterfield was quartered here with General McClellan's Union troops in 1862, Butterfield composed the music for taps.

But the first that is celebrated with ceremony each year is the one entered in the seventeenth-century records of the Berkeley Company. These papers commission Captain John Woodlief and 38 Englishmen to settle 100 acres in Virginia and to designate the date of their landing as an annual day of thanksgiving, the first official American Thanksgiving.

On the first Sunday of November, that landing is remembered at Berkeley. Some years have seen reenactments and festivities, others simply a prayer service. House tours are always part of the events. Though you can follow the service today with a proper turkey dinner at the Coach House Tavern, there were no turkey feasts, cranberry sauce, or pumpkin pie at that first Thanksgiving, which is possibly why the Massachusetts observance is more popular.

What Berkeley's ceremonies do offer is another reminder of the importance of Virginia's settlers in building the nation we call America. And that alone is reason enough for thanksgiving.

Area Code: 804

DRIVING DIRECTIONS   Virginia's plantation road is Route 5, between Richmond and Williamsburg. From D.C., take I-95 south to I-295 south to exit 22A, Route 5, Charles City Plantations and Jamestown. From Richmond, drive east on Route 5 to the plantations and Jamestown. The approximate distance from D.C. to Berkeley Plantation is 135 miles.

PUBLIC TRANSPORTATION   Closest airports are Richmond and Norfolk.

ACCOMMODATIONS   *North Bend Plantation,* 12200 Weyanoke Road, Charles City 23030, 829-5176, M–E, CP • *Piney Grove Bed and Breakfast at Southall's Plantation,* 16920 Southall Plantation Lane, Charles City 23030, 829-2480, M–E, CP • *Orange Hill B&B,* 180401 The Glebe Lane, Charles City 23032, 829-5936 or (888) 889-7781, renovated farmhouse on 50 acres of working farmland, M–E, CP • *Colesville Plantation,* 9600 John Tyler Memorial Highway, Charles City 23030, 829-6433, eighteenth-century farmhouse on a working 355-acre plantation, M, CP • *Jasmine Plantation,* 4500 North Court House Road, Providence Forge 23140, 966-9836 or (800) NEW KENT, eighteenth-century farmhouse on 47 acres, M–E, CP. See also Williamsburg, pages 236–237, and Richmond, page 29.

DINING   *Indian Fields Tavern,* Route 5, Charles City, 829-5004, restored home, excellent food, M–E • *Coach House Tavern,* Route 5 at

Berkeley Plantation, Charles City, 829-6003, dinner by reservation only, E • *David's White House Restaurant,* 3560 Courthouse Road, Providence Forge, 966-9700, regional favorites, highly regarded chef, M. See also Williamsburg, page 237, and Richmond, pages 29–30.

SIGHT-SEEING *Virginia Thanksgiving Festival, Inc.,* P.O. Box 5182, Richmond, 23220. Held the first Sunday in November at Berkeley Plantation, Route 5, Charles City, 829-6018. Best to check current hours, events, and admission fees for the festival • *Colonial National Historical Park,* information from superintendent, P.O. Box 210, Yorktown 23690, 898-3400; www.nps.gov/colo. Hours: Visitor centers open 9 A.M. to 5 P.M. at Jamestown and Yorktown sites, each $$, under 17, free • *Jamestown-Yorktown Foundation,* P.O. Box 1607, Williamsburg, 253-4838 or (888) 593-4682. The foundation operates two properties: *Jamestown Settlement,* Route 31 and the Colonial Parkway. Hours: Daily 9 A.M. to 5 P.M. $$$$; *Yorktown Victory Center,* hours: Daily 9 A.M. to 5 P.M. $$$; a combination ticket for two sites above is available • **James River Plantations:** *Berkeley Plantation,* Route 5, Charles City County, 829-6018. Hours: Daily 8 A.M. to 5 P.M. $$$$ • *Shirley Plantation,* Route 5, Charles City, 829-5121. Hours: Daily 9 A.M. to 5 P.M. $$$$ • *Sherwood Forest Plantation,* 4501 John Tyler Highway (Route 5), Charles City, 829-5377. Hours: Daily 9 A.M. to 5 P.M. House and garden tours, $$$$; gardens alone, $$ • *Evelynton Plantation,* 6701 John Tyler Highway (Route 5), Charles City, 829-5075. Hours: Daily 9 A.M. to 5 P.M. $$$$ • *Westover,* 7000 Westover Road, off Route 5, Charles City, 829-2882. Hours: Daylight hours, gardens and grounds only. A money-saving combination ticket for Berkeley, Evelynton, Sherwood Forest, and Shirley plantations is available for $30 at any of the properties.

INFORMATION *James River Plantations,* P.O. Box 218, Charles City, VA 23030, (800) 704-5423; www.jamesriverplantations.org • *Charles City County,* P.O. Box 66, 10900 Courthouse Road, Charles City, VA 23030, 829-0217; co.charles-city.va.us.

Winter

Overleaf: Winter at Valley Forge, Pennsylvania. *Photo courtesy of Mont-gomery County Convention & Visitors Bureau.*

Christmas Cheer in West Chester

West Chester, Pennsylvania, is a town that wears its history well.

The brick-paved streets lined with Federal town houses are reminiscent of the charm of Society Hill or Georgetown, but there are many more architectural styles as well. Over a period of more than 300 years, the seat of Chester County has acquired a wealth of fine architecture, from stone farmhouses to massive-columned Greek Revival structures designed by the architect of the nation's capitol. Because of these elaborate columned buildings, this little town was once dubbed the Athens of Pennsylvania.

Come Christmas, all of the town is decked out with Victorian decorations and filled with cheer guaranteed to gladden the heart of even the Scroogiest. The annual West Chester Old-Fashioned Christmas celebration in early December offers live music, walking tours, art and crafts, homemade goodies, holiday greens, special shop window displays, and seasonal entertainment from puppets to Christmas choirs. Naturally, Santa wants to be part of the fun. He presides over the Friday night parade that follows the lighting of the community Christmas tree on the courthouse lawn.

Most special of all is the annual Holiday House Tour, scheduled on the first Saturday of each December to benefit the local YWCA, a tradition now well into its third decade. There are at least a dozen stops on the tour, offering the chance to visit some of the most beautiful of the area's homes. The historic houses are all the more interesting because so many contain family heirlooms handed down from generation to generation.

To make things even nicer, you can stay in a historic bed-and-breakfast inn in town or at a variety of accommodations in the surrounding Brandywine Valley. Especially lovely are some of the farms in the rolling countryside. My favorite is Whitewing Farm, a gracious 1700s Pennsylvania farmhouse on 43 beautiful acres, a short drive away and adjacent to Longwood Gardens. Accommodations include one suite in the main house and other well-decorated rooms in the carriage house, stables, and gatehouse on the grounds, each with a small library for guests. In summer, amenities include a pond, swimming pool, and ten-hole chip-and-putt golf course. In winter, the farm is a Christmas-card setting.

To get your bearings in West Chester, first take a walk along High Street to see the parade of architectural variety. You'll discover the green serpentine stone that is characteristic of the area; gingerbread Victorian porches; porticoed doorways; iron-lace fences; and those famous Greek columns near the corner of High and Market Streets, adorning the courthouse, a local bank, and a church. Both the firehouse and the public library are Gothic buildings boasting Tiffany windows. Fine examples of the residential life of the 1800s can be seen in the Greek Revival houses on "Portico Row" on Miner Street, and almost any of the side streets provide delightful vistas of red-brick Federal row houses.

Having admired the homes from the outside, you'll be able to appreciate them even more on the house tour. The homes are different every year, but always a treat. Tanglewood, the handsome home of the president of West Chester University, is sometimes included.

Many of the look-alike row houses in town hold surprises added by their modern owners. Skylights and eclectic furnishings and color schemes blend surprisingly well with the original exposed brick and giant hearths of the antique homes. All of the houses are decorated with old-fashioned greenery, bows, and lavish trees, making them all the more welcoming for visitors.

The YWCA building turns into a crafts bazaar the night before the event, featuring handmade gifts, decorations, and baked goods. Several community organizations take part in setting up Victorian soup-and-sandwich parlors offering homemade foods and baked delights. On Saturday, the Y keeps children busy and happy making holiday gifts, cards, wraps, and foods while their parents are touring houses.

The Chester County Historical Society Museum, a pleasure to visit in any season, often adds a special exhibit for the holidays. This exquisite small museum offers nine galleries with permanent and changing exhibits, and a History Center and research library that draw genealogists from near and far. The collections include tall case clocks, regional furniture, embroidery, porcelain, and silver. The pieces are particularly fine, the kinds of antiques that are often featured on the covers of magazines for collectors.

West Chester offers two change-of-pace attractions. QVC, a home shopping network seen on cable TV, offers studio tours for a behind-the-scenes look at electronic retailing. If the timing is right, you can watch broadcasts in progress from an observation deck. The attractive workshop of Simon Pearce on the Brandywine River provides a catwalk where you can watch glassblowers creating fine pieces of clear glass, which are for sale in the adjacent shop. Seconds in the shop are a good value. The excellent food served in the restaurant is served on Pearce glass and pottery.

When the pleasures of West Chester are completed, you have more Christmas treats in store at three other traditional Brandywine Valley observances within a few minutes' drive. The Brandywine River Museum, noted for its Wyeth collections, will be offering its annual display of toy trains, children's illustrations, and giant trees decorated with whimsical ornaments known as "critters," made from natural materials—the same lovely ornaments that have been selected to adorn the White House Christmas tree in past years. There's a popular annual critter sale the first weekend in December. In alternate years, a special Christmas display shows off the wonderful antique doll collection of Ann Wyeth McCoy.

At Longwood Gardens, the grounds turn into a wonderland of twinkling lights at Christmas, with lighted topiary, reindeer, and a sleigh on the way to the conservatory, abloom with four acres of red and white poinsettias and exquisitely decorated trees. To make things even nicer, some 100 musical events are held here throughout the holidays. The Terrace Restaurant here serves delicious food, so reserve in advance to ensure a table for lunch or dinner. There's a cafeteria for those who did not plan ahead.

A few minutes across the Delaware border, Winterthur, the famous house-museum of American furniture and furnishings from 1640 to 1860, has its exquisite period rooms specially decorated for Christmas, with a new theme each year.

It's a pre-Christmas outing all but guaranteed to send you home filled with the old-fashioned spirit of the season.

Area Code: 610

DRIVING DIRECTIONS   West Chester is off Route 202, west of Philadelphia and north of Wilmington. From D.C., take I-95 north to Wilmington, then Route 202 north. Alternate route: Exit from I-95 at Route 272, just after the Susquehanna River Bridge, and follow Route 272 to Route 1 at Nottingham. Continue north on Route 1 to Chadds Ford, then north on Route 202 to West Chester. The approximate distance from D.C. is 126 miles.

ACCOMMODATIONS   *Broadlawns,* 629 North Church Street, West Chester 19380, 692-5477, spacious, attractive in-town Victorian, M–E, CP • *Faunbrook,* 699 West Rosedale Avenue, West Chester 19382, 436-5788, Victorian showplace tucked away on the edge of town, I–M, CP • **Inns in the nearby countryside:** *Whitewing Farm,* 370 Valley Road, West Chester 19382, 388-2664, exceptional, best choice in the area, E–EE, CP • *Meadow Spring Farm,* 201 East Street Road (Route 926), Kennett Square, 19348, 444-3903, folksy, warm, M, CP • *Sweetwater Farm,* Sweetwater Road, P.O. Box 86, Glen Mills 19342, 459-4711, elegant, E–EE, CP • *Hamanassett,* 725 Darlington Road, P.O. Box 129, Lima 19037, 459-3000, 28-room stone 1870 mansion in secluded wooded setting, room, M–E, CP • *Harlan Log House,* 205 Fairville Road, Chadds Ford 19317, 388-1114, authentically furnished eighteenth-century Quaker farmhouse, E, CP • *Hedgerow,* 268 Kennett Pike (Route 52), Chadds Ford 10317, 388-6080, two well-furnished carriage house suites with space and privacy, E, CP • *Penns-*

bury Inn, 883 Baltimore Pike (Route 1), Chadds Ford 19317, 388-1435, exceptional furnishings in a 1714 farmhouse, pool, but very close to busy Route 1, E–EE, CP • *Fairville Inn,* Route 52, Fairville 19357, 388-5900, restored 1820s home, lovely decor, new carriage house with private decks, E–EE, CP • *Brandywine River Hotel,* Routes 1 and 100, Chadds Ford 19317, 388-1200, intimate 40-room hotel, E, CP • *Duling-Kurtz House,* South Whitford Road, Exton 19341, 524-1830, nicely furnished rooms, good restaurant, M, CP.

DINING *Simon Pearce on the Brandywine,* 1333 Lenape Road at Routes 52 and 100, West Chester, 793-0948, creative American with an Irish touch, on the Brandywine River, lunch, I, dinner, E • *Iron Horse Restaurant and Brewery,* 3 West Gay Street, West Chester, 738-9600, attractive and lively, pub and full menus, I–M • *The Terrace,* Longwood Gardens (see below), 388-6771, lovely setting for excellent food, popular, so reserve ahead, lunch, I–M, dinner, M • *Maxwell Creed's,* 503 Orchard Avenue at Route 1, Kennett Square, 388-9450, creative continental fare, local mushrooms are a house specialty, M–E • *Chadds Ford Inn,* Route 1, Chadds Ford, 388-7361, atmospheric eighteenth-century tavern, M–E • *The Gables at Chadds Ford,* 162 Baltimore Pike, Chadds Ford, 388-7700, California cuisine in a handsome restored barn, M–E • *Half Moon Restaurant & Saloon,* 108 West State Street, Kennett Square, 444-7232, casual favorite for interesting American fare, I–M • *Mendenhall Inn,* Route 52, Mendenhall, 388-2100, attractive large dining room, convenient lunching for Longwood and Winterthur, lunch, I–M; dinner, E–EE • *Duling-Kurtz House* (see above), attractive setting and good food, M–E • *Pace One,* Thornton-Concord Road, Thornton, 459-9784, restored barn, good bet for Sunday brunch, M–E • *Crier in the Country,* Route 1, Glen Mills, 358-2411, varied menu, M–E • **Historic country inns near West Chester:** *Dilworthtown Inn,* Old Wilmington Pike and Brinton Bridge Road, Dilworthtown, 399-1390, M–EE • *Marshallton Inn,* 1300 West Strasburg Road (Route 162), Marshallton, 692-4367, M–E • See also Wilmington, page 47.

SIGHT-SEEING *YWCA West Chester Holiday House Tour,* 123 North Church Street, 692-3737, first Saturday in December 10 A.M. to 4 P.M. Tickets by mail or at YWCA Saturday morning at 9 A.M. Call to check current date and rates. • *Chester County Historical Society Museum,* 225 North High Street, West Chester, 692-4800. Hours: Monday to Saturday 9:30 A.M. to 4:30 P.M. $$ • *QVC Studios,* 1200 Wilson Drive, West Chester, (800) 600-9900. Hours: Daily 1¼-hour tours on the hour 10 A.M. to 4 P.M.; extended hours in summer. $$$$. Phone for information on being in the studio audience • *Simon Pearce on the Brandywine,* 1333 Lenape Road at Routes 52 and 100, West

Chester, 793-0949, glassblowing workshop and retail shop. Hours: Daily 9 A.M. to 9 P.M. Free • *Brandywine River Museum,* U.S. 1, Chadds Ford, 388-2700. Hours: Daily 9:30 A.M. to 4:30 P.M. $$$ • *Longwood Gardens,* U.S. 1, Kennett Square, 388-1000. Hours: Daily 10 A.M. to 5 P.M., to 6 P.M. April through October, to 9 P.M. during the Christmas season. $$$$$ • *Winterthur,* Route 52, outside Wilmington, DE, (302) 888-4600 or (800) 448-3883. Hours: Monday to Saturday 9 A.M. to 5 P.M., Sunday noon to 5 P.M. General admission to the Galleries and gardens, $$$$; special house tours, $$$$$; Yuletide tours are included with all admission tickets.

INFORMATION   *Chester County Conference and Visitors Bureau,* 601 Westtown Road, Suite 170, West Chester, PA 19380, 344-6365 or (800) 228-9933; www.brandywinevalley.com.

Away from It All in Williamsburg

Yes, that's Patrick Henry over there, expounding on why we need to get rid of those oppressive British. And the woman in the wig? That's Martha Washington. She'll answer your questions about life with George.

Sights like these aren't unusual in historic Williamsburg, a sure cure for the winter doldrums. Virginia's Colonial capital, a town that had a tremendous impact on the early development of our country, is America's favorite historical attraction, and it's easy to see why. You not only come back with new knowledge and feel for the nation's heritage; you have a lot of fun.

Williamsburg is well known for its holiday festivities, when lantern light, caroling, music and dance, festive meals, and holiday trim turn the whole town into a Christmas card come to life.

By all means come for Christmas if you can—but to experience a real escape to another time, come back when the throngs have left. The spell of Williamsburg, sometimes hard to feel amid summer crowds, seems at its best in the calm of winter. Free bus service connecting all the major sights makes sure you stay snug no matter what the weather. If there's a dusting of snow to add a bit of magic, it's the frosting on the cake.

Special Winter in Williamsburg packages offer great seasonal bargains, even at the posh, newly renovated Williamsburg Inn. Special weekends add interest with features such as an annual antiques forum, a look at eighteenth-century cooking or decoration, or a celebration of George Washington's birthday. The Days in History program re-creates activities of special days in Colonial times such as Court Days or Musket Days. And you'll be able to explore the historic district without crowds.

Historic Williamsburg consists of 173 acres of the original town, which was the center of America's wealthiest colony from 1699 to 1780. In practical terms, that means an area roughly ten blocks long and three blocks wide, looking much as it did more than 200 years ago and packed with sights that can easily fill two days or more. Not the least of the pleasure of strolling Williamsburg's main thoroughfare, Duke of Gloucester Street, is the absence of twentieth-century traffic to spoil the illusion of another time.

More than 90 acres of eighteenth-century greens and gardens surround the buildings, lovely when in bloom and adding to the appeal even in winter.

This was a planned city, and within the street plan devised in 1699 are 88 original preserved and restored shops, houses, taverns, and public buildings. Hundreds of public buildings, including the Governor's Palace, the Capitol, homes, shops, and other structures, have been rebuilt according to extensive archaeological research.

Within the historic homes of Colonial Williamsburg are period rooms furnished with choice pieces of the past, from four-poster beds to pottery and pewter and family portraits, chosen from a collection of more than 50,000 items.

All of this is even more memorable if you are lucky enough to stay in one of the lodgings available in the Colonial houses right in the heart of history. The dining places in historic Williamsburg are also a step back in time, housed in real Colonial taverns and serving up atmosphere along with traditional dishes.

The streets and homes of the restoration take on unusual vitality because of the costumed "residents," who provide the community with life beyond that of a Colonial museum piece. Gaolers, militiamen, blacksmiths, coopers, bookbinders, milliners, and silversmiths can all be seen going about their daily routines. In the historic trades shops in town, the artisans will gladly explain their techniques.

While you admire the finery of the much-photographed red brick Governor's Palace you may encounter a resident waiting to air a grievance before the governor and be asked to serve on the jury, one of many ways Colonial Williamsburg helps visitors feel like part of history rather than passive observers.

Your weekend should begin at the Colonial Williamsburg Visitor Center, where an excellent film puts all of the history into perspective. There's a large parking lot here. When you buy your ticket, you'll receive a brochure listing hours, special programs, and events, and including a map showing locations of exhibits, buildings, shopping, and places to dine. The map outlines the route of the free bus and the numbered stops. You can get on and off as often as you like.

Hop on the bus back to the historic area and stroll, savoring the feel of the town and dropping into the various shops and buildings as the spirit moves you.

There are a few "don't miss" stops. A famous Williamsburg highlight is the Governor's Palace, its fine furnishings and gardens betokening the power and prestige of the Crown in Colonial Virginia. Later it became the executive mansion for the first two governors of the independent colony, Patrick Henry and Thomas Jefferson.

Equally impressive is the Capitol, where Henry and Jefferson served in the Virginia Legislature and where the Resolution for American Independence passed without a dissenting vote in 1776, even though this wealthiest of the colonies had the most to lose if its bid for freedom failed.

Raleigh Tavern, where patriots, including George Washington, gathered, is another significant site. A couple of standout homes are the Peyton Randolph House on Nicholson Street and the George Wythe House on Palace Green.

But you needn't feel bound by any special itinerary. The only "right" way to see Williamsburg is at your own pace and according to your own tastes. It's the ambience of the town that matters far more than any single attraction.

This mammoth restoration began in 1926 through the chance meeting of a minister and a millionaire. Dr. William A. R. Goodwin, rector of the Bruton Parish Church, where the people of Williamsburg have worshiped since 1674, sat next to John D. Rockefeller Jr. at a Phi Beta Kappa dinner and gained his interest in saving the neglected former capital.

The restoration efforts and the galleries at Williamsburg continue to expand. The DeWitt Wallace Gallery, funded largely by a $14 million grant from DeWitt and Lila Wallace, cofounders of *Reader's Digest,* enables historic Williamsburg to display some 10,000 of the best items from its astonishing collection of seventeenth-, eighteenth-, and early-nineteenth-century English and American antiques. The gallery is built partially underground and behind the reconstructed 1773 Public Hospital, which was the nation's first hospital for mental patients.

The Abby Aldrich Rockefeller Folk Art Center is filled with superior examples of American folk art dating from the 1730s to the present. The collection of 3,000 objects dates from the 1920s, when Abby Rockefeller began her collection of paintings by unschooled artists, along with weather vanes, quilts, tobacconist figures, canes, and whirligigs, items that had not previously been considered art. When the museum opened in 1957 with her collection of 424 items as a nucleus, it was the first in the nation devoted solely to folk art. It is now one of the nation's leading showcases and a major research center.

Bassett Hall, the Rockefellers' Williamsburg home, is also open for tours. It is a warm family home, surprisingly modest—until you note the 14 sets of fine china, a sign of the Rockefellers' dislike for dining with the same plates on the table every night.

Eight miles east of Williamsburg is Carter's Grove, an 800-acre plantation tract with exhibits spanning four centuries of Virginia history. The 1754 mansion and slave quarters of the period can be toured, along with the Winthrop Rockefeller Archaeology Museum, which tells the story of a lost town's discovery through archaeology and traces the 1619–1622 history of the community, Martin's Hundred, and its principal settlement, Wolstenholme Towne. Visitors can also see the partially reconstructed 1619 village, the ultimate artifact.

There's so much more to see and do in this area, you could easily spend a week. Jamestown, Yorktown, the grand plantations along the James River: all are minutes away. If you come back in spring or summer, there's also the big amusement park at Busch Gardens nearby. Williamsburg is rapidly developing into a major golf center. And just outside town on Route 60 west is a whole maze of outlet malls, including the Williamsburg Pottery Factory, 32 buildings stuffed with just about any merchandise you can imagine. Berkeley Commons Outlet Center has a number of top brands such as Liz Claiborne, Anne Klein, Seiko, Eddie Bauer, and Brooks Brothers.

But Colonial Williamsburg alone is more than enough reason for a trip. It's a welcome escape to yesteryear.

Area Code: 757

DRIVING DIRECTIONS   Williamsburg is on Route 60, off I-64 between Richmond and Norfolk. From D.C., take Route I-95 south, then I-64 east. The approximate distance from D.C. is 162 miles.

PUBLIC TRANSPORTATION   Williamsburg is served by Amtrak and is only 45 minutes from either the Norfolk or the Richmond airport, even closer to Newport News. Limousine shuttle service is available at airports.

ACCOMMODATIONS   *Colonial Williamsburg reservations,* P.O. Box 1776, Williamsburg, VA 23187, 229-1000 or (800) HISTORY. Packages including lodging, some meals, and admission to Colonial Williamsburg are considerably less than these rates individually; ask for current offerings. Golf, tennis, and fitness plans also available in season. Accommodations include *Williamsburg Inn,* EE • *Colonial Houses,* lodgings within the Historic District, EE • *Williamsburg*

Lodge, M–EE • *Woodlands,* M–E • *Governor's Inn,* I–M • *Kingsmill,* 1010 Kingsmill Road, 253-1703, is an alternative within a 15-minute drive, an attractive luxury resort with tennis, golf, racquetball, and health club, E–EE, lower rates in winter. • **Convenient motels**: *Holiday Inn,* 814 Capitol Landing Road at Parkway Drive, 23185, 229-0200 or (800) 465-4329, indoor pool and putting green, I–E • *Four Points by Sheraton,* 351 York Street, 23185, 229-4100, I–M • *Best Western Patrick Henry Inn,* 249 East York Street, 23187, 229-9540, I–M • There are many more motels; write for complete listing.

Bed-and-breakfast inns: Many to choose from. Among the best are *Indian Springs Bed and Breakfast,* 330 Indian Springs Road, 23185, 220-0726 or (800) 262-9165, suites overlooking wooded ravine, quiet location within walking distance of sights, M–E, CP • *Liberty Rose Inn,* 1022 Jamestown Road, 23185, 253-1260 or (800) 545-1825, change of pace, lavish Victorian on a hilltop, E–EE, CP • *Williamsburg Manor,* 600 Richmond Road, 23185, 220-8011 or (800) 422-8011, gracious Georgian brick Colonial, convenient location, M–E, CP • *Colonial Capital Bed and Breakfast,* 501 Richmond Road, 23185, 229-0233 or (800) 776-0570, nicely furnished, convenient, M–E, CP • *The Cedars,* 616 Jamestown Road, 23185, 229-3591 or (800) 296-3591, Colonial charm, M–E, CP • *Williamsburg Sampler,* 922 Jamestown Road, 23185, 253-0398 or (800) 722-1169, cozy eighteenth-century Colonial, M–E, CP.

DINING   In the historic district: Dinner reservations required for all, (800) HISTORY. *Christiana Campbell's Tavern,* Waller Street, seafood, spoon bread, sweet potato muffins, E • *King's Arms Tavern,* Duke of Gloucester Street, quiet and refined, roast beef, game dishes, E • *Josiah Chowning's Tavern,* Duke of Gloucester Street, Brunswick stew, Colonial gambols and bawdy songs in the tavern after dinner, M • *Shield's Tavern,* Duke of Gloucester Street, eighteenth-century tavern decor, working fireplaces, entertainment, spit-roasted meats and eighteenth-century menus, M–E • *Regency Room,* Williamsburg Inn (see above), elegant, excellent, E–EE • All open for lunch, as are inexpensive options such as *A Good Place to Eat,* fast food in Merchants' Square; *Cascades* (cafeteria style) near the visitor center; the *Wallace Gallery Cafe* and two *Clubhouse Grills,* overlooking the inn golf course.

Just outside the Historic District: *The Trellis,* 403 Duke of Gloucester Street, Merchants' Square, 229-8610, notable nouvelle cuisine, M–E • *Berret's,* 199 Boundary Street, Merchants' Square, 253-1847, seafood, I–E. Also recommended: *Le Yaca,* Kingsmill Village shops, 1915 Pocahontas Trail, U.S. 60, 220-3616, fine French menu, E–EE • *Dining Room at Ford's Colony,* 240 Ford's Colony Drive, 565-4100, country club dining, formal Colonial decor, excellent traditional dining, M–E • *Kitchen at Powhatan Plantation,* 3601 Ironbound Road, 220-1200, Colonial ambience, excellent contemporary menu, game and regional dishes, E • *Chez Trihn,* Williamsburg Shopping Plaza, 157 Monticello Avenue, 253-1888, Vietnamese, I–M • *Peking Restaurant,* U.S. 60 Bypass, Kingsgate Center, 229-2288, Chinese, I • *Pierce's Pitt Bar-B-Que,* 443 Rochambeau Drive, 565-2955, far from town but near outlets, very casual, I.

SIGHT-SEEING *Colonial Williamsburg Foundation,* P.O. Box 1776, Williamsburg 23187, 229-1000 or (800) HISTORY; www.colonial williamsburg.org. Hours: Most sites daily 10 A.M. to 5 P.M. unless noted. Ticket prices and hours can change; best to check current information. Admission: Day Pass including transportation and all sites, $32; Freedom Pass, good for one year, $38.

INFORMATION For accommodations and attractions outside the Historic District, *Williamsburg Area Convention & Visitors Bureau,* 201 Penniman Road, P.O. Box 3620, Williamsburg, VA 23185, 253-0192 or (800) 368-6511; www.visitwilliamsburg.com.

Christmas Lights in Pennsylvania

It's appropriate that Christmas should be a special occasion in Bethlehem, Pennsylvania. The city's destiny was fixed on a Christmas Eve in 1741, when a group of pious Moravians gathered in a little log house in an unnamed settlement to light candles and sing. They called the town Bethlehem that night, and ever since, Christmas has been celebrated here in the same simple Moravian tradition, with candlelight, illuminated Moravian stars, and song.

The Moravian Church is unique in many of its customs. The oldest Protestant denomination, it was established in 1457, 60 years before the Reformation in Europe, based on the teachings of an earlier Bohemian religious reformer, Jan Hus; its members numbered about 200,000 during Martin Luther's time. By the end of the Thirty Years' War the membership had dwindled, but in 1722 the church was revived on the estate of Count Ludwig von Zinzendorf in Saxony, and followers built the town of Herrnhut nearby. From here they came as missionaries seeking converts in the New World.

The Christmas rites they brought with them from their German

homeland are still observed in Bethlehem and in another early settlement, the tiny Pennsylvania Dutch town of Lititz. Each Moravian
church and home traditionally hangs a many-pointed giant star in the
doorway, similar to the finest ones used in German churches. They also
display another German tradition, the putz, an elaborate creation of
detailed scenes from the Nativity using many natural materials in the
settings. In the churches on Christmas Day, as the story is read, the
appropriate scenes are lit. Afterward carols are sung.

A Christmas trip to share these lovely traditions adds a delightful
dimension to the holiday and also provides the opportunity for a family
celebration that can include some of the more familiar observances held
each year in Hershey, Pennsylvania. Since the Moravian displays are on
view from early December until the end of the month, they are an
excellent way to extend the joy of the season.

Bethlehem's glowing celebration has brought it the name "America's
Christmas City." All of the town is aglimmer with thousands of tiny
white lights in the windows of homes and public buildings alike. Atop
South Mountain, above the Lehigh University campus, the huge lighted
Star of Bethlehem is visible for miles, a beacon drawing thousands for
the famed Candlelight bus tours, which give visitors a chance to see the
town transformed by twinkling candlelight. Reservations are highly
recommended for these popular tours.

The Candlelight Tours are led by guides in traditional Moravian
attire who tell the story of the town's unique history as the bus traces
the same paths used by early settlers more than two centuries ago. The
tour sets out from the Christmas-tour information center at Broad and
Guetter Streets and moves through the historic area. On Church Street
it passes the Bell House, the Brethren's House, Central Church, and
other Moravian structures remaining from Colonial times, all with a
single lighted candle in each window. Past the eighteenth-century Colonial Industrial Quarter, two more historic buildings, the John Sebastian
Goundie House and the 1758 Sun Inn, come into view on Main Street.

Then the route crosses the Hill-to-Hill Bridge, with scores of Christmas trees lighting the way, toward the star shining atop South Mountain. The Lehigh Valley below, a fairyland of glimmering lights, is pure
magic.

Later, take a stroll in town to see the Moravian stars hanging in doorways and inside the vaulted Central Church, where a giant star six feet
in diameter is a much-treasured local tradition. Elaborate stars were
first made in Herrnhut in 1850. They usually have 26 spikes—18 four-
sided points and 8 triangular points—though some showpieces, such as
the ones here and in Lititz, may contain as many as 110 points.

The delicate and difficult crafting of these intricate displays is an art
that is often passed down from generation to generation. Originally
constructed with a rigid metal core, the stars are now made of paper,
softly lighted to give off a white or yellow glow. Stars in various shapes

and sizes can be purchased in the Moravian Room of the Moravian Book Shop in town, along with beeswax candles, another Moravian holiday tradition.

The largest Bethlehem putz (from a sixteenth-century Saxon word meaning "to decorate") also is set up in the Central Church. Originally created in the mountains of medieval Germany, the putz differs from other Nativity representations in its emphasis on landscape settings of natural materials such as moss, plants, rocks, evergreen sprigs, and tree stumps. Planning must start months before Christmas, when moss is collected from the woods and kept cool and moist to furnish a green foundation for the scenery. Canopies of stars are often used to represent the nighttime skies, and there may be simulated lakes made of mirrors.

The putz seeks to tell the whole Christmas story from the angel's message, or Annunciation, to the flight into Egypt, with each scene a separate entity. Each is constructed anew every year by members of Moravian congregations. No two are exactly alike from church to church, since they are an expression of each builder's conception of the Nativity story. The only given is the scene of the Christ Child in the manger with Mary and Joseph in attendance.

Other scenes often used show the angel appearing to Mary, the Magi following the star, shepherds on a hillside with their sheep, and an angel bearing glad tidings. Two other putz scenes may be viewed at the East Hills Moravian Church on Butztown Road, and the Edgeboro Moravian Church on Hamilton Avenue. In addition to the elaborate community putzes in local churches, Moravian families usually make their own putzes in miniature, also with natural materials for the landscapes. Families share their creations by visiting each other's homes on Christmas Day.

Though the nighttime scene is the most memorable one, there is much to see in Bethlehem by day in the Historic District, the site of the original Moravian settlement, and in the restored buildings of one of early America's most prosperous industrial areas. Gemein House, the oldest of the original buildings, is now the Moravian Museum, filled with mementos of the early settlers. While you are in town, have a meal at the historic Sun Inn on Main Street. You'll be joining a guest roster that includes George Washington, John Adams, and General Lafayette.

Many other special events are held during this period. Costumed guides lead one-hour walking tours through the Historic District, sharing stories of the people who made this colonial village a center of culture in early America. Carriage rides take in Victorian neighborhoods as well as the Colonial Moravian buildings. All of the town's museums have holiday decor and special exhibits for Christmas.

Music in an integral part of things. The noted Bach Choir of Bethlehem (see page 20) holds an annual concert of Bach music in praise of the Nativity, concluding with the audience joining the choir in traditional carols. The faculty of Moravian College presents candlelight concerts on weekends in lovely Christ Church, and organ concerts with guest artists take place during the week in the 1751 Old Chapel of Central Moravian Church.

The Christkindlmarkt, a family holiday market, is held each year under heated tents, showcasing handmade crafts, holiday crafts, and decorations. Moravian stars and hand-painted Christmas ornaments are among the special items for sale, and strolling entertainers, specialty foods, and a children's shopping area are among the attractions. The event takes place across from Bethlehem's Colonial Industrial Quarter, where tours usually take place on December weekends. There is usually an appearance by Belsnickel, the Pennsylvania German version of Santa Claus, and other special activities for children.

If you prefer a small-town setting for an introduction to a Moravian Christmas, the candlelit homes of Lititz have much village charm to offer. A walk down Main Street takes you past more than a dozen houses dating to the mid-1700s. Toward the end of the block are the brick and stucco buildings of the Moravian Church Square, which includes the church itself, as well as the original Brethren's and Sisters' Houses and the 1767 Linden Hall, one of the oldest girls' schools in the country. During the week after Christmas, the Lititz church offers half-hour light shows featuring the scenes of its putz.

Among the homes is the stately Victorian mansion built at 19 East Main Street by General John Sutter, who retired here after striking it rich in the California Gold Rush. The general was the first in Lititz to have indoor plumbing, not to mention a large wine cellar stocked with California wines. His home has been authentically restored and is used as an office by the Lititz Farmers First Bank. Sutter is buried in the Moravian Cemetery at the rear of the church. The pleasant local inn, which dates back to 1754, bears his name.

Two other nonreligious attractions in Lititz are favorites at any time of year. In 1861 a local resident, Julius Sturgis, opened the first commercial pretzel bakery in America in one of the town's historic homes. The house, built in 1784, has been restored and contains a museum where visitors can see pretzels being baked in the original 200-year-old ovens. There are tours of the modern pretzel plant also. Guests from 8 to 80 have fun here trying their hand at some fancy pretzel twisting. They are rewarded with diplomas proclaiming their mastery of the art.

Wilbur's Chocolate Company, with displays of historical candy-making equipment, tempts with demonstrations of how hand-dipped chocolates are made today. Sample boxes are for sale at outlet prices.

Christmas is not the only time when candles mark a holiday in Lititz. If you should ever happen to come back to this town on the Fourth of July, you'll find Lititz Springs Park lit with one of the country's most unusual Independence Day displays, a mammoth show of candlelight.

If you are looking for more Christmas lights, you'll find them in ample supply just a short drive away in Hershey, Pennsylvania. Hersheypark's Christmas Candylane glows from mid-November with lavish decorations and more than a million lights. As many as 40,000 visitors have come on a holiday Saturday night to enjoy the spectacle. Brass bands and Yuletide carolers stroll the lanes, and the Music Box Christmas Show takes place in a heated theater. It's too cold for roller coasters, but you can take a horse-drawn carriage ride, or catch the Candylane Twilight Express for a steam-powered trip through Santa's Magical Forest. You can visit a miniature train display and have breakfast with Santa, ensconced in his workshop with real live reindeer.

The Chocolate World visitor center is decked out for the holidays, and continues to offer its free animated tour to see how chocolate is made. The shops, of course, are crammed with chocolate gift ideas, as well as old-time ornaments. Hershey lodgings get into the holiday spirit with special events, and to add to the fun, if there's snow, cross-country skiing, sledding, and tobogganing are available at the Hotel Hershey.

For a final dazzle of lights, make a detour on the way to or from Hershey, from Route 78 to Route 183 south to Bernville and down the clearly marked dark country road that takes you to the stupendous display known as Koziar's Christmas Village. It all began in 1948 when William M. Koziar began putting on a show of lights for his neighbors. Soon there were crowds, and the home became known as the Christmas House. The displays grew, and so did the crowds, until the present village was born. There are now more than half a million Christmas lights, along with two huge barns filled with handmade items, souvenirs, and a super-duper toy train display. Yes, this one is decidedly commercial, but the kids oohing and aahing haven't been known to complain.

Area Codes: 610 for Bethlehem; 717 for Lititz and Hershey

DRIVING DIRECTIONS   For Bethlehem driving directions, see page 23. From Bethlehem to Lititz or Hershey, follow Route 22 west; it will merge with Route 78. Turn off on Route 501 south to Lititz; turn off on Route 743 south to Hershey. To go directly to Lititz, follow directions to Lancaster, page 123, then take Route 501 north for 7 miles. The approximate distance from D.C. is 113 miles. For direct Hershey routes, see page 161. The approximate distance from D.C. is 110 miles.

ACCOMMODATIONS   *General Sutter Inn,* 14 East Main Street, Lititz 17543, 626-2115, rooms, M; suites, M–E • *The Alden House,* 62 East Main Street, Lititz 17543, 627-3363 or (800) 584-0753, charming bed-and-breakfast in 1850s style, M, CP • *Swiss Woods Bed and Breakfast,* 500 Blantz Road, Lititz 17543, (800) 594-8018, delightful secluded chalet-style inn overlooking a lake, M–E, CP. See also Bethlehem, page 23; Hershey, page 162.

DINING *1764 Restaurant,* General Sutter Inn, Lititz (see above), M–E • See also Bethlehem, page 23; Hershey, page 162; Lancaster area, page 124.

SIGHT-SEEING Bethlehem: *Candlelight Tours:* Evening bus tours offered hourly daily (weather permitting) from the Visitor Center starting at 5 P.M., late November through December. Reservations are suggested. $$$. Phone 868-1513 to reserve and recheck current hours and rates • *Central Church Moravian Putz,* 866-5661. Phone for current dates and hours • *Christmas Walking Tours,* late November through December, daily 3 P.M. and 5 P.M. from the 1810 Goundie House on Main Street, $$$ • *Horse-drawn Carriage Rides,* late November through December, daily 2 P.M. to 9 P.M., leaving every 20 minute from the Visitor Center. $$$ • *Bethlehem Bach Choir of Bethlehem Christmas Concerts,* 423 Heckewelder Place, Bethlehem 18018, 866-4382 or (888) 743-3100, www.bach.org. Contact for this year's dates and locations • *Candlelight Concerts,* Christ Church, late November through December, Saturday, Sunday 6 P.M. $$$ • **Music in the Old Chapel,** Old Chapel, Central Moravian Church, Monday to Friday, 4:30 P.M. Free • *Christkindlmarkt,* c/o Musikfest, Banana Factory, 211 Plymouth Street, Bethlehem, 861-0678. Market is held at Main and Spring Streets. Hours: Late November to mid-December, Thursday (except Thanksgiving) to Saturday, 11 A.M. to 8 P.M., Sunday 11 A.M. to 6 P.M. $$$ • *Colonial Industrial Quarter,* 459 Old York Road, access via Union Boulevard, 691-0603. Hours: Usually Saturday and Sunday in December, but subject to change—best to check. $$ • See additional Bethlehem sightseeing, pages 23–24.

Lititz Moravian Church Christmas Putz Scene, 8 Church Square, Lititz, 626-8515. Hours: Usually December 26–31, 7 P.M. to 9 P.M., half-hour presentations. Free; donations welcome. Best to check church for current dates and hours • *Sturgis Pretzel House,* 219 East Main Street, Lititz, 626-4354. Hours: Monday to Saturday, 9 A.M. to 4:30 P.M. $ • *Christmas in Hershey,* Candylane hotline, (800) HERSHEY. Candylane hours: Mid-November through mid-December, Wednesday to Sunday; daily rest of December, except closed Christmas day. Hours vary; phone for times. Candylane and Chocolate World admission, free; fees for rides, museum, and theaters • *Koziar's Christmas Village,* off Route 183, Bernville, (610) 488-1110, early November to January 1, Monday to Friday 6 P.M. to 9 P.M. Saturday and Sunday from 5:30 P.M. to 9:30 P.M. $$$.

INFORMATION *Bethlehem Tourism Authority and Visitors Center,* 52 West Broad Street, Bethlehem, PA 18018, 868-1513 or (800) 360-8687; www.bethtour.org • *Pennsylvania Dutch Visitors Bureau,*

501 Greenfield Road, Lancaster, PA 17601, 299-8901, free or (800) 723-8824; www.800padutch.com • *Hershey,* information and reservations, 300 Park Boulevard, Hershey, PA 17033, (800) HERSHEY; www.800hershey.com.

Strutting in the New Year in Philadelphia

It won't be "Auld Lang Syne" but "Oh, Dem Golden Slippers." On January 1, to the tune of hundreds of strumming banjos, that lively song traditionally leads off the annual Mummers Parade, strutting 20,000 strong through Philadelphia in the world's happiest salute to the New Year.

The much-loved parade has been a tradition since 1901. Fancy brigades in dazzling costume accompanied by brass bands, banjo-strumming string bands, and playful clowns join in the festivities. The parade kicks off at 8:45 A.M. at Fifth and Market Streets and marches nine blocks west to City Hall. Since the string bands heralding the splashiest part of the action don't make their appearance until later, you don't have to get up for the start to join the fun.

The New Year's Day parade attracts nearly a million spectators, and no one goes home disappointed. The feathers and finery, the dazzle of colors, and the imaginative motifs, from comic-strip characters to cheerleaders to Chinese dragons, add up to an unforgettable show. An indoor performance, in the warm Pennsylvania Convention Center, the Fancy Brigade Finale and judging, takes at 6 P.M., after the parade has ended, with the extravagantly costumed participants performing intricate dance routines. Many other special events take place in Philadelphia around New Year's to add to the fun.

The parade, the only one like it in the world, is worth a trip to Philadelphia on its own, but this many-faceted city merits a journey anytime. If you haven't visited recently, you'll discover many exciting changes in the City of Brotherly Love.

The city's most famous attraction, Independence National Historical Park, is in the midst of major improvements, including a sparkling new Independence Visitors Center opened in late 2001, with informative interactive orientations both to the park and to the city. In spring 2002, the Liberty Bell was ensconced in a spacious new pavilion, where understanding of what the bell stands for is enhanced by a new adjoining exhibit hall. Coming to the historic area in 2003 is the $105 million National Constitution Center, a museum that will use interactive exhibits to increase understanding of the meaning and relevance of one of the document on which our nation is based, the U.S. Constitution.

Another new museum, the National Liberty Museum, opened nearby in 2000 to honor Americans and others who have fought injustice and prejudice, from Jackie Robinson to Nelson Mandela, Mother Teresa to Winston Churchill. A Hall of Fame honors America's Nobel prize winners. The museum is marked by a 20-foot Flame of Liberty created by the noted glass artist Dale Chihuly.

On Broad Street, where banners proclaim "Avenue of the Arts," the Kimmel Center for the Performing Arts is a stunning new showplace with a soaring domed top sure to become a city landmark. It is a new home for the Phildelphia Orchestra and several other groups, with the beautiful and historic 1857 Academy of Music one block away continuing as a venue for groups such as the opera and and the Pennsylvania Ballet. The two venues together form an arts center for the entire region.

Philadelphia's riverfront is being transformed by the lavish Penn's Landing Project, a mix of entertainment, shopping, and culture that will include a 20-screen movie theater, a large-screen 3-D auditorium, a new home for the children's Please Touch Museum, and an outdoor amphitheater. Target date is 2003.

In Center City, half a dozen sleek new hotels and shopping complexes have joined the new office towers that are rapidly transforming the skyline, and the city's new restaurants should please even the choosiest diners.

With so many intriguing new features to explore, 150 museums, the fine Philadelphia Orchestra, the bustling Italian Market, the mansions of historic Germantown, the famous cheesesteak shops, the pretzel vendors, the world's largest city park, and the nation's oldest zoo, there is enough here to keep you busy for a month of weekends. Kids absolutely love this city, which is made to order for pint-size fun.

Those who come to see the furs and feathers and fancy capes of the mummers will actually be seeing a festive amalgam of many of the New Year's customs that were brought to this country from other lands. The Swedes and Finns, for example, shot off guns, rang bells, and pounded pots to ward off evil in the New Year. The English and Welsh visited their neighbors to recite poems, and the Germans added the tradition of Belsnickel, the forerunner of Santa Claus, which in turn inspired additional comic masqueraders who rode through the streets shouting and firing guns.

The word *mummer* is found in several of these cultures. In England, it referred to groups of youths who dressed up during Christmas week to perform silent plays about St. George and the Dragon, Father Christmas, and other characters. In German, the word *Mummerkleid* means "disguise."

In Philadelphia, the idea of a holiday open house was adopted by masked callers who were given candies, cakes, fruits, and drinks by their neighbors. The natives also initiated the Carnival of Horns, which drew thousands of costumed characters who celebrated the New Year with a cacophony of noisemakers.

In 1876, groups calling themselves mummers added an annual march to Independence Hall, doing a strut version of a cakewalk that has become a trademark of the parade. The city's official organization of the event may have been more in an effort to control the rowdy revelers than in a spirit of holiday cheer, but the result nevertheless is one of the most exuberant celebrations in the country.

Each of the mummers' clubs has its own name—Golden Crown, Merry Makers, and Shooting Stars, to cite a few— and each has its own requirements for admittance. Some people become involved because of a club in their neighborhood; others begin learning the contagious strut as children and can't wait to become part of a group.

Wearing the trappings of a mummer takes dedication, however. Some mummers have their outfits professionally made, but others create and design their own costumes; some of the fancier outfits cost several thousand dollars. A frame costume carried on wheels with a man inside can weigh as much as 300 pounds and measure 13 or 14 feet high. Other costumes with elaborate headpieces and backpieces strapped on by harnesses weigh as much as 125 pounds. The big parade climaxes a year of work for each participant. Many a last stitch is still being sewn early on New Year's Day.

City hotels make a trip to see the parade even more appealing with weekend and New Year's packages at bargain rates. However, if you want to make this the ultimate romantic New Year's Eve, that's easily arranged. Check into one of the city's luxury lodgings such as the Four Seasons, the Park Hyatt at the Bellevue, the Rittenhouse, Loews, or the Ritz-Carlton Philadelphia; splurge on dinner amid the intimate charm and elegance of Le Bec-Fin, one of the mid-Atlantic's most famous restaurants; and go dancing at any one of the posh new hotels. You can sleep late on New Year's Day and enjoy a memorable brunch in the Four Seasons Fountain restaurant before you head to the parade.

If you prefer more intimate lodgings, two appealing choices await in the Historic District. The Best Western Independence Park Inn, a small hotel, is a stylishly renovated nineteenth-century building, and the Thomas Bond House is a charming Federal-period guest house that once belonged to one of Benjamin Franklin's best friends. Franklin and Bond were two of the trio that founded Pennsylvania Hospital, the nation's oldest public hospital. Located within the boundaries of Independence National Park, the house has been beautifully restored under the auspices of the National Park Service and combines the warmth of a country inn with modern conveniences.

Those who want to take advantage of the funky shops, nightlife, and ethnic eateries on South Street may opt for the Shippen Way Inn just one block away, a 1750 home done in delightful Colonial decor.

Wherever you stay, a good place to begin your sight-seeing is with a stroll through the square mile designated as Independence National Historical Park. You can stand right in the room where Benjamin Franklin and John Hancock framed the Declaration of Independence in Independence Hall; see Carpenter's Hall, where the first American Congress met; gaze at the Liberty Bell; visit Old City Hall, which housed the first U.S. Supreme Court; and see the many other historic monuments tracing our country's birth.

Don't overlook the intriguing underground museum dedicated to Ben Franklin at Franklin Court, where you can see his many ingenious inventions, such as bifocals and library steps, dial up a Franklin witticism on almost any topic, or use a telephone to hear George Washington or John Adams talk about Mr. Franklin's contributions to his country. The telephone number to dial for each past patriot is posted on a giant directory complete with appropriate area codes.

While you are in the neighborhood look into the Curtis Center building, which houses the Norman Rockwell Museum, for an unexpected art treasure. One entire wall of the lobby shows off a Tiffany glass tile mosaic mural, the only one of its kind.

Also near Independence Park are the restored Colonial town houses and cobbled streets of Society Hill, a delightful neighborhood for strolling.

Another unique attraction is the National Museum of American Jewish History, the only museum devoted to Jewish life in this country. The new building includes a modern Sephardic synagogue for the historic Congregation of Mikveh Israel, which has origins in the city dating to 1740.

When you want a break from history, head for the funky shops on South Street, where you won't want to miss a visit to Jim's on the corner of South and Fourth Streets, a favorite among cheesesteak lovers, as you'll see from the long lines.

Philadelphia has shopping diversions for every taste and pocketbook. The Gallery, at Ninth and Market, claims to be the largest urban mall in the nation, with 110 shops and restaurants. The chic designer shops are clustered on Walnut Street, at Liberty Place, and in the Bellevue, and antiquers won't want to miss the lineup of stores on Pine Street, east of Broad Street. If bargains are more your beat, take a short drive to Franklin Mills just north of the city, where there are outlets by the score, including clearance centers for Saks Fifth Avenue, Macy's, Ann Taylor, J.C. Penney, and Sears. Take I-95 north to the Woodhaven Road exit to Franklin Mills Boulevard. Many hotels offer transportation to the mall.

The sight-seeing possibilities in this city are all but endless. Walk narrow Elfreth's Alley, the oldest residential street in the country, or visit the tiny Colonial home where Betsy Ross sewed the first American flag. This neighborhood, known as Old City, is blooming anew with galleries and restaurants.

If the weather is mild, walk down to Penn's Landing on the waterfront, visit the Independence Seaport Museum, and board some of the museum vessels at anchor. Take the ferry here to visit the New Jersey Aquarium, just ten minutes away across the Delaware River in Camden.

If you want to do some museum hopping, head for broad, flag-lined Benjamin Franklin Parkway, Philadelphia's answer to the Champs-Élysées. Climb the stairs that the film *Rocky* made famous for a tour of the Philadelphia Museum of Art, the nation's third-largest art museum. An entire wing, the Annenberg Galleries, is devoted to the museum's great collection of nineteenth-century European art, including masterpieces by Renoir, Matisse, and van Gogh. Other highlights include a notable section of American art, and stunning Oriental-art galleries known for architectural installations such as a seventeenth-century Chinese palace hall, a fourteenth-century Japanese Buddhist temple, and a sixteenth-century carved granite Indian Hindu temple.

Nearby is the Rodin Museum, with the largest collection of the sculptor's works to be found outside of France. Slated to go up across the Parkway is a museum devoted to the Philadelphia-born sculptor, Alexander Calder. Until the museum is a reality, Calder's bold sculptures and stabiles will be seen on the two-acre site of the museum at 22nd Street, in the garden of the Rodin Museum, and on the East Terrace of the Philadelphia Museum of Art, which oversees both the Rodin Museum and the future Calder museum. Some 10 to 15 sculptures will be installed on a rotating basis, some of them monumental in size.

The Pennsylvania Academy of Fine Arts, a spectacularly gaudy, High Victorian showplace, is a work of art in itself. It gives fresh importance to a period often overlooked, America's own Impressionist movement, and painters like Mary Cassatt, who trained at the academy.

At the innovative Franklin Institute Science Museum, on the other side of the parkway, you can pilot a plane, steer a ship, or even walk through a giant human heart in the Science Center building. The museum continues to innovate with exhibits such as "The Sports Challenge," complete with a blimp, JumboTron screen, and Astroturf, where trying your hand at various sports challenges helps to understand the physics, physiology, and material science involved in favorite sports. The new KidScience area takes children five to eight years old on a journey to explore the foundations of science pertaining to light, water, earth, and air. The museum's Mandell Center is a do-it-yourself trip to tomorrow. Here you can leap to the frontiers of medicine, standing inside a human cell a million times larger than life, or manipulate a robot on the surface of the moon. Even the youngest visitors can enjoy touring a space station and imagining themselves as astronauts.

Other popular attractions here are the Fels Planetarium and the Omniverse Theater, where a giant screen puts the audience in the midst of the action.

In other parts of the city you can visit the world-famous Mummy Room and the new Canaan and Ancient Israel Gallery at the University of Pennsylvania Museum, watch coins being made at the U.S. Mint, or discover the world of the dinosaur at the Academy of Natural Sciences.

Children will also have a ball at the Philadelphia Zoo, where they can climb into a gigantic make-believe beehive or up into a tree house with the birds and butterflies. America's oldest zoo recently celebrated its 125th birthday with a host of additions. New features include rare blue-eyed lemurs—the only ones on exhibit in North America; the Lorikeet Exhibit, an interactive adventure where guests can hand-feed nectar to colorful flocks of Australian lorikeets; the new Amphibian and Reptile House; and the show-stopping, state-of-the-art Primate Reserve.

The New Year's Day parade may also make you want to learn more about the mummers, who have their own museum in town with a tile façade as colorful as their costumes. Later in the afternoon when your energy flags, you can be revived by a proper English tea amid luxurious surroundings at the Four Seasons, the Ritz-Carlton, or the Park Hyatt at the Bellevue.

Philadelphia offers pleasures of many kinds, enough to merit many happy returns. But for color, there's nothing to compare with that inimitable march of the mummers. It will send you home to a banjo beat auguring the happiest of New Years.

Area Code: 215

DRIVING DIRECTIONS Philadelphia is reached via I-95 or I-276/76. From D.C., take I-95 north. The approximate distance from D.C. is 135 miles.

PUBLIC TRANSPORTATION Frequent Amtrak trains, plus buses and planes. No car is needed in Center City. Buy a SEPTA DayPass for economical unlimited rides on all buses, streetcars, and subways; it even includes a one-way ride to the airport. The Phlash minibus offers loop transportation around the main city sights, September to late May, 10 A.M. to 6 P.M., rest of year to midnight, by the ride or on a one-day pass, $$; family rates, two adults and three children under 18, are a bargain, $$$$.

ACCOMMODATIONS Ask at all hotels for special New Year's or weekend packages and children's rates, often far below standard rates. **Top of the line:** *Four Seasons,* 1 Logan Square, 19103, 963-1500 or (800) 268-6282, indoor pool, EE • *Park Hyatt Philadelphia at The Bellevue,* 1415 Chancellor Court (Broad and Walnut Streets), 19102,

893-1776, or (800) 233-1234, EE • *The Rittenhouse,* 210 West Rittenhouse Square, 19103, 546-9000 or (800) 635-1042, EE • *Ritz-Carlton Philadelphia,* 10 Avenue of the Arts (Broad Street), 19102, 735-7700 or (800) 241-3333, EE.

Next luxury level: *Embassy Suites Center City,* 1776 Benjamin Franklin Parkway, 19103, 561-1776 or (800) EMBASSY, EE, CP • *Latham Hotel,* 135 South 17th Street, 19103, 563-7474 or (800) LATHAM, EE • *Loews Philadelphia,* 1200 Market Street, 19107, 627-1200, E–EE • *Philadelphia Marriott,* 1201 Market Street, 19107, 625-2900 or (800) 320-5744, adjoining the convention center, indoor lap pool, E–EE • *Omni at Independence Park,* 401 Chestnut Street, 19106, 925-0000 or (800) THE-OMNI, indoor pool, E • *Sheraton Society Hill,* 2nd and Walnut Streets, 19106, 238-6000 or (800) 325-3535, M–EE.

More moderate prices: *Best Western Center City,* 501 North 22nd Street, 19130, 568-8300 or (800) 528-1234, M–E • *Best Western Independence Park,* 235 Chestnut Street, 19106, 922-4442 or (800) 624-2988, small, attractive, E • *Comfort Inn,* 100 North Columbus Boulevard, 19106, 627-7900 or (800) 228-5150, M–E • *Doubletree Philadelphia,* Broad and Locust Streets, 19107, 893-1600 or (800) 222-TREE, indoor pool, E • *Hawthorn Suites,* 1100 Vine Street, 829-8300 or (800) 527-1133, suites with kitchens, E, CP • *Holiday Inn Express Midtown,* 1305 Walnut Street, 19107, 735-9300, M, CP • *Penn's View Hotel,* 14 North Front Street, 19106, 922-7600 or (800) 331-7634, M–E • *Wyndham Franklin Plaza,* 17th and Race Streets, 19103, 448-2000, indoor pool, E.

Bed-and-breakfasts: *Alexander Inn,* 12th and Spruce Streets, 19107, 923-3535 or (877) ALEX-INN, 48-room hotel with bed-and-breakfast ambience, historic building with small but stylish rooms, pleasant sitting/breakfast room, M–E, CP • *Rittenhouse Square Bed and Breakfast,* 1715 Rittenhouse Square, 19103, 546-6500 or (877) 791-6500, luxury B&B, Jacuzzis, some balconies, E–EE, CP • *Shippen Way Inn,* 416–418 Bainbridge Street, 19147, 627-7266 or (800) 245-4873, a charming 1750 town house, beams and antiques, convenient to South Street, M, CP • *Thomas Bond House,* 129 South 2nd Street, 19106, 923-8523, historic Colonial town house, beautifully restored, fine location in the historic district, M–E, CP.

DINING Literally hundreds of possibilities. **Fine dining:** *Le Bec-Fin,* 1523 Walnut Street, 567-1000, splurge at the city's best, EE, or visit the elegant but less pricey downstairs bistro, *Le Bar Lyonnais,* M–E • *Brasserie Perrier,* 1619 Walnut Street, 568-3000, Le Bec-Fin owner does a contemporary American menu, M–EE • *Striped Bass,* 1500 Walnut Street, 732-4444, city's best for seafood, EE • *Avenue B,*

260 South Broad Street, 790-0705, haute Italian from the owner of Striped Bass, across from the Kimmel Center, EE • *Deux Cheminées,* 1221 Locust Street, 790-0200, fine French, prix fixe, EE • *The Fountain,* Four Seasons Hotel (see above), Continental, consistently excellent, EE • *The Founder's,* Park Hyatt at the Bellevue (see above), 790-2814, beautiful room and elegant New American food, EE • *Susanna Foo,* 1512 Walnut Street, 545-2666, gourmet Chinese with a French accent, M–EE • *Ciboulette,* Bellevue Building, 200 South Broad Street, 790-1210, upscale cafe serving appetizers known as "small plates," I–M each, or a tasting menu, EE • *Budakan,* 325 Chestnut Street, 574-9440, fusion Asian cuisine in a striking setting, M–EE • *Monte Carlo Living Room,* 2nd and South Streets, 925-2220, elegant northern Italian, EE • *La Famiglia,* 8 South Front Street, Old City, 922-2803, Italian with high ratings, E–EE • *Opus 251,* 251 South 18th Street, 735-6787, elegant, atmospheric dining in the Philadelphia Art Alliance building off Rittenhouse Square, E–EE.

Other good choices: *Rouge,* 105 South 18th Street, 732-6622, intimate casual cafe from Neil Stein (of Striped Bass), an instant hit, M–EE • *Bleu,* 227 South 18th Street, 545-0342, another casual and popular bistro from master restaurateur Stein, M–E • *Cuba Libre,* 10 South Second Street, 627-0666, Miami celebrity chef comes north, E • *Vetri,* 1312 Spruce Street, 732-3478, cozy quarters for a highly regarded chef, Italian provincial fare, M–E • *Fork,* 306 Market Street, 625-9425, New American bistro fare in the Old City, good value, M • *Prime Rib,* Warwick Hotel, 1701 Locust Street, 772-1701, a favorite for red meat lovers, M–E • *Bistro St. Tropez,* 2400 Market Street, 4th floor, 569-9269, hip, hidden gem in the Marketplace Design Center, M • *City Tavern,* 138 South 2nd Street, 413-1443, 1772 landmark serving creative versions of recipes Washington and Franklin might have enjoyed, M–EE • *Swann Lounge and Cafe,* Four Seasons Hotel (see above), the most elegant light dining in town, M–E • *Rose Tattoo Cafe,* 1847 Callowhill Street, 569-8939, flower-filled decor, excellent New American fare, M–E • *Joseph Poon Restaurant,* 1002 Arch Street, 928-9333, wild decor and unusual Asian dishes; you won't be bored, I–M • *¡Pasion!,* 211 South 15th Street, 875-9895, gourmet nuevo Latino menu in a tropical setting, E–EE • *DiNardo's Famous Seafood,* 312 Race Street, 925-5115, hard-shelled crabs are the house specialty, M • *Philadelphia Fish & Co.,* 207 Chestnut Street, 625-8605, reliable for creative fish dishes, M–E • *Dock Street,* 2 Logan Square, 496-0413, eclectic menu, home-brewed beer, I–E • *White Dog Cafe,* 3420 Sansom Street, 386-9224, a classic, long-time favorite in the university area, informal, interesting menu, M • *Dante's & Luigi's,* 762 10th Street, 922-9501, South Philly Italian old-timer for red sauce, big portions at small prices, I–M • *Saloon,* 750 South 7th Street, 627-1811, trendy, steaks and Italian, E–EE • For a feast of sights, sounds, and food selections at lunchtime, visit the stalls at **Reading Terminal Market,** the nineteenth-century marketplace still thriving at 12th and Arch Streets. For dinner try **Down Home Diner,** 1039 Reading Terminal Market, 12th and Filbert Streets, comfort food, I.

SIGHT-SEEING *Mummers Parade,* January 1, 8:45 A.M.; www. mummers.com. Grandstand seats, 636-1666, $$$$$; order early or you'll have to stand • *Fancy Brigade Finale,* performance and awarding of prizes for parade participants, January 1, Pennsylvania Convention Center, 12 noon and 6 P.M., (800) 462-6811, $$$$$ • For other current New Year's celebrations, check with the Visitors Center • *Independence National Historical Park,* Visitors Center, 6th and Market Streets, 597-8974; www.nps.gov/inde. Hours: daily 9 A.M. to 5 P.M. Free • *Betsy Ross House,* 239 Arch Street, 627-5343. Hours: Tuesday to Sunday 10 A.M. to 5 P.M. Donation • *Philadelphia Museum of Art,* 26th Street and Benjamin Franklin Parkway, 763-8100; www.phila museum.org. Hours: Tuesday to Sunday 10 A.M. to 5 P.M., until 8:45 P.M. on Wednesday. $$$$, under 12, free; pay what you wish all day Sunday • *Franklin Institute Science Museum,* 20th Street and Benjamin Franklin Parkway, 448-1200; www.fi.edu. Hours: Science Center, daily 9:30 A.M. to 5 P.M.; Mandell Center, 9:30 A.M. to 5 P.M. Sunday to Thursday; Friday, Saturday 9:30 A.M. to 9 P.M. Science Center and Mandell Center, $$$$$; separate admission charged for Omniverse Theater Combination tickets available • *Rodin Museum,* 22nd Street and Benjamin Franklin Parkway, 763-8100. Hours: Tuesday to Sunday 10 A.M. to 5 P.M. Donation • *Academy of Natural Sciences,* 19th Street and Benjamin Franklin Parkway, 299-1000. Hours: Monday to Friday 10 A.M. to 4:30 P.M.; weekends and holidays to 5 P.M. $$$$ • *University of Pennsylvania Museum of Archaeology and Anthropology,* 33rd and Spruce Streets, 898-4000, Tuesday to Saturday 10 A.M. to 4:30 P.M., Sunday 1 P.M. to 5 P.M. $$ • *Mummers Museum,* 1000 South 2nd Street, 336-3050. Hours: Tuesday to Saturday 9:30 A.M. to 5 P.M.; Sunday noon to 5 P.M. $$ • *National Museum of American Jewish History,* 55 North 5th Street, 923-3811. Hours: Monday to Thursday 10 A.M. to 5 P.M. Friday to 3 P.M., Sunday noon to 5 P.M. $$ • *Please Touch Museum,* 210 North 21st Street, 963-0667. Hours: Daily 9 A.M. to 4:30 P.M., July 1 to Labor Day to 6 P.M. $$$ (museum will be moving to Penn's Landing around 2003; check location) • *Philadelphia Zoo,* Fairmount Park, 34th Street and Girard Avenue, 243-1100. Hours: March to November, Monday to Friday 9:30 A.M. to 4:45 P.M., weekends and holidays to 5:45 P.M.; rest of year, daily 10 A.M. to 4 P.M. $$$$$ • *U.S. Mint,* 5th and Arch Streets, 408-0114. Hours: Monday to Friday 9 A.M. to 4:30 P.M. May and June also open Saturday 9 A.M. to 4:30 P.M., July and August open daily 9 A.M. to 4:30 P.M. Free • *Independence Seaport Museum,* Columbus Boulevard and Walnut Street, Penn's Landing, 925-5439.

Hours: Daily 10 A.M. to 5 P.M. $$$, includes boarding historic ships •
National Liberty Museum, 321 Chestnut Street, 925-2800. Hours:
Tuesday to Sunday, 10 A.M. to 5 P.M. $$ • *New Jersey State Aquarium,*
1 Riverside Drive, Camden, (609) 365-3300. Hours: March to mid-
September, daily 9:30 A.M. to 5:30 P.M.; rest of year Monday to Friday,
9:30 A.M. to 4:30 P.M., Saturday, Sunday 10 A.M. to 5 P.M. $$$$$ •
Riverlink Ferry leaves frequently from Penn's Landing, Walnut Street
and Columbus Boulevard, $ each way. Phone 925-LINK for current
information.

INFORMATION *Greater Philadelphia Tourism Marketing Corporation,* 123 South Broad Street, Suite 2180, Philadelphia, PA 19109,
599-0776 or (877) GO-PHILA; www.gophila.com. *Philadelphia Visitor Center,* 6th and Market Streets, 965-7676, for information (800)
537-7676; www.phillyvisitorcenter.com. Open daily 9 A.M. to 5 P.M.

Winter Wonder in West Virginia

Winter in the Mountain State is the magic season, the time when brooks
and waterfalls freeze to shimmering crystal, every tall tree and mountain is crowned by whipped-cream white, and sugar-coated panoramas
await around every bend of the road.

In the area called the Potomac Highlands, the snows are bountiful,
an average of 200 inches annually, and so are the mountaintops, 110 of
them with an elevation over 4,000 feet. That means winter pleasures
galore, whether you want to schuss down the slopes, make tracks cross-
country, take a turn on ice skates or a sled, snowshoe through the
woods, or simply stay indoors in front of a cozy fire, enjoying the
snowscape outside the window. With several state parks, and several
downhill mountains and cross-country ski areas to choose from, there is
something here for everyone.

Canaan Valley State Park (pronounced "kuh-nayn," emphasis on the
last syllable) offers the closest drive from the D.C. area and the most
variety. This unique 15-mile-long, 5-mile-wide basin stands 3,200 feet
above sea level, capped with mountains reaching up to 4,280 feet. It is
the highest major valley east of the Mississippi.

The skiers learned about it in the 1940s after pilots began to report
exceptional snow in the valley, often lasting into April. The Washington, D.C., Ski Club used to come for the snowdrifts they called Little
Tuckerman's, in honor of the famous ravine on New Hampshire's Mt.

Washington. In 1954 a rope tow was built, and the first commercial ski area south of the Mason-Dixon Line opened for business. Later the area was chosen as the West Virginia state park system's winter sports center, and the first chairlifts in the state were installed in 1971.

Today, as a four-season resort park, Canaan Valley offers a major ski area, almost 19 miles of cross-country trails, and an outdoor skating rink lit for après-ski fun. A 600-foot snow-tubing hill has its own tow lift, fun for nonskiers as well as a change of pace for skiers. A 250-room lodge provides comfortable motel-type rooms with a view, or you can choose a cabin with a cozy fireplace. A pool, exercise room, sauna, and Jacuzzi await downstairs at the main lodge. The lodge also offers a snack bar for light lunches as well as the big Aspen Dining Room, with moderate prices and a picture window overlooking the night action on the lighted skating rink.

Canaan's ski area boasts a quad chairlift and two triple chairs, with runs as long as 5,000 feet, including a 2,000-foot expert trail ominously named Gravity. Night skiing adds to the fun, and extensive snowmaking augments Mother Nature in her slow seasons. With a vertical drop of 850 feet, the mountain now offers 34 slopes and trails and good professional ski instruction. It's an ideal place to learn the sport, and a particularly welcome destination for families, since shuttle bus service from the lodge transports eager-beaver youngsters who want to hit the slopes before their parents are ready to venture out into the cold. For younger children, a nursery provides care for infants and toddlers, and a special Ski 'n Play program is geared for children ages three to six.

Blackwater Falls State Park is only about ten miles from Canaan Valley in Davis, a village with the look of a western frontier town and some alternative lodgings for those who might not choose to stay in the parks. There's a choice of small inns or several condominium complexes nearby with spacious rentals, and several appealing shops. The Art Company in Davis, a recommended stop to see arts and crafts by regional artisans, includes a nice little cafe for a cup of coffee or lunch.

Blackwater Falls offers its own lodge and dining room, a recently added indoor pool, a hot tub and fitness center, and a dramatic view. The 65-foot waterfall that tumbles down the rocks into the gorge in summer becomes a frozen still life in winter. You can admire the falls from the panoramic overlooks provided around the park or, better yet, put on your long johns and boots and take a walk through the silent snow to enjoy the wonder of winter. There's a great toboggan slide with a rope tow here as well, fun for all ages. A warming hut offers a fireplace and warm drinks when you are ready for a break from the cold.

Blackwater Falls State Park also has a cross-country skiing center and trails with nearly 22 miles of maintained trails and 6 miles of machine-set track. Good skiers can take a challenging 8-mile trail connecting to Canaan Valley. Both state parks offer rentals and lessons, as well as the rare chance to break into fresh powdered snow disturbed only by the early-morning tracks of deer and snowshoe rabbits.

Nearby is the Blackwater Outdoor Center, which offers white-water rafting in summer and ski touring in winter, with special packages including lodging.

For both the unpracticed and the most experienced on cross-country skis, the White Grass Ski Touring Center provides additional options. There are 30 miles of trails over meadows and wooded slopes, half of them machine-groomed, and there are many challenging downhill trails for advanced skiers and those who use Telemark skis, which incorporate some of the features of both downhill and cross-country equipment. The cafe here is a good bet for homemade soups and sandwiches and hot spiced cider and serves dinner on weekends.

Canaan Valley, Blackwater, and White Grass all offer snowshoe rentals, an increasingly popular pastime in this area.

Timberline, a ski area near Canaan with a respectable vertical drop of 1,000 feet, is a lure for both downhill and Nordic skiers. A 250-foot halfpipe is a favorite with snowboarders. Downhillers like the two-mile beginner run, trails providing glade skiing, night skiing on weekends, and the weekend double lift with protective pull-down bubbles to cut the chill, a first in the region. Condominium lodgings are conveniently located near the foot of the triple chairlift, and there's an excellent program for children known as TAK (Timber's Adventure Klub).

Timberline is also a hub for Nordic and Telemark slope skiing. The West Virginia Telemark Series Race held here in February draws participants from throughout the mid-Atlantic region.

True big-league skiing awaits those who are willing to drive farther south to Snowshoe Mountain. The resort actually encompasses two distinct ski complexes. Snowshoe attracts more-experienced skiers, while Silver Creek, halfway down the mountain, provides wide trails and milder terrain perfect for families and novice or intermediate skiers. Silver Creek is almost a ski resort in itself—there's a nine-story hotel at the base of the slopes, with ski-in/ski-out convenience. It also offers night skiing, a terrain park, and a snow-tubing hill with a seven-story drop.

Unlike most areas developed at the base of a mountain, Snowshoe, which bills itself as "Island in the Sky," sits atop a 4,848-foot-high ridge with views that seem to go on forever. You ski down from your lodging, then take the lift back up. The base of the mountain is at an elevation of 3,348 feet, higher than the peaks of many Eastern areas. With a 1,500-foot vertical drop and challenges such as the mile-and-a-half Cupp Run, there is plenty of good skiing. The mountaintop provides ski-village ambience, complete with restaurants, nightlife, and such niceties as Jacuzzis, saunas, and indoor pools.

Accommodations are in lodges, inns, or condominium units, most within walking distance of the lifts and all the activities.

Since Snowshoe Mountain Resort was purchased a few years back by Intrawest, owners of many leading destination resorts, some $100 million has gone into capital improvements, including two new high-speed detachable quads, night skiing, a terrain park and halfpipe, a snow-tubing hill, increased snowmaking, and increased ski terrain, including a double black diamond trail. Many improvements are taking place at the base, with new shops and restaurants and construction of a new mountaintop village planned. For those who want the challenge and the fun of a sophisticated ski area, this is definitely the place.

Skiers in the D.C. area might also remember that the Snowshoe Mountain Resort is part of the Allegheny Front, which catches the winter storm clouds as they move east from the Great Lakes, so that the snows here come early and stay late, long after spring has arrived in the capital. Just in case Mother Nature is not generous with snow, the resort has 100 percent snowmaking coverage.

If you choose this route and also want to get in some cross-country skiing, you will find rentals and trails just down the hill and south a few miles at the Elk River Touring Center in Slatyfork. There's homey lodging here and home-cooked meals, as well.

They work hard in West Virginia to keep the roads clear so you can enjoy the winter snowscapes and outdoor fun, but nonetheless plan on plenty of extra time for the mountain highways. The views here are so spectacular that it's hard to resist the urge to pause and gaze, or to capture it all with a camera.

Area Code: 304

DRIVING DIRECTIONS   From most locations to the east, West Virginia's mountains are best approached from I-81 south in Virginia. From D.C., take I-66 west to Strasburg, Virginia, then Route 81 south. For Canaan, exit at Route 33 and continue west to Route 32 north. The approximate distance from D.C. is 185 miles. For Snowshoe, continue south on I-81 to Staunton, then west on U.S. 250, south on Route 42 to Goshen, then Route 39. At Marlinton, turn north on Route 219 to Snowshoe. The approximate distance from D.C. is 245 miles. A bit longer route to Snowshoe, but one with better roads, is to continue on I-81 to I-60/64 west, then turn north on Route 219 at Lewisburg. From Canaan to Snowshoe, follow Route 33 to Elkins, then Route 219 south.

PUBLIC TRANSPORTATION   Air service to Lewisburg, 65 miles from Snowshoe. Amtrak serves White Sulphur Springs, just outside Lewisburg.

ACCOMMODATIONS   Expect minimum stays at some properties. *Canaan Valley Lodge,* Canaan Valley Resort State Park, Route 1, Box 330, Davis 26260, 866-4121 or (800) CALL-WVA, I–M • *Blackwater*

Falls Lodge, Blackwater Falls State Park, Drawer 490, Davis 26260, 259-5216 or (800) CALL-WVA, I • **Bed-and-breakfast inns: *Brookside Inn,*** Route 1, Box 217-B, Aurora 26705, 735-3563 or (800) 223-4361, mountain lodge with excellent dining room, overlooking Cathedral State Park, M, CP; E, MAP • ***Bright Morning Bed and Breakfast,*** Main Street, Davis 26260, 259-5119, M, CP • ***Meyer House,*** 259-5451, P.O. Box 360, Davis 26260, 259-5451, I, CP, family suite, M, CP • ***Black Bear Resort,*** Route 1, P.O. Box 55, Canaan Valley, Davis 26260, 866-4391 or (800) 553-2327, pool, cross-country skiing; inn, M, chalets, E • ***Deerfield Village Resort,*** Route 1, P.O. Box 152, Canaan Valley, Davis 26260, 866-4698 or (800) 342-3217, condo rentals, M–E • ***Timberline Resort,*** P.O. Box 625, Canaan Valley, Davis 26260, 800-633-6682, slopeside condo rentals, E–EE • ***Elk River Inn,*** U.S. 219, Slatyfork 26291, 15 miles from Cass, 572-3771, modest, homey lodging, home cooking, adjoining Elk River Touring Center, inn with private baths, I–M, CP farmhouse with shared baths, I, CP, two-bedroom cabins, E • ***Snowshoe Mountain Resort,*** P.O. Box 10, Snowshoe 26290, 572-5252. Reservation service for a variety of inns, lodges and condominiums on the mountain; discuss your needs • ***Whistlepunk Inn,*** P.O. Box 70, alpine decor, indoor pool, sauna, outdoor hot tub, inn rooms and condos, best on the mountain, M–E. Also see bed-and-breakfast listings, pages 189–190.

DINING   *Canaan Valley Lodge* (see above), I–M • *Blackwater Falls Lodge* (see above), I–M • *Golden Anchor,* Route 32 south, Canaan Valley, 866-CRAB, seafood with mountain views, M • *Sirianni's Cafe,* Main Street, Davis, 259-5454, pizza and pasta, local favorite, I • *Blackwater Brewing Company,* William Avenue, Davis, 259-4221, hand-crafted beer, German and Italian food, music, I–M • *Bright Morning* (see above), bountiful breakfast buffets, I • *Deerfield Village Restaurant,* Deerfield Village Resort (see above), I–M • *Brookside Inn* (see above), prix fixe, EE • *Elk River Restaurant* (see above), I–M • At Snowshoe Mountain Resort (see above): *The Red Fox Inn,* Whistlepunk Village, best on the mountain, also good for Sunday brunch, M–E • *Goodtime Bobby's Eating and Drinking Emporium,* Mountain Lodge, M • *Auntie Pasta's Ristorante,* the name says it, M–E • *Foxfire Grille,* barbecue, M • *The Junction,* all three meals served in a turn-of-the-century logging mill, I–M • *Brandi's,* Inn at Snowshoe, all three meals, I–M.

SPORTS   Check current prices and conditions at all ski areas. *Canaan Valley Ski Area,* Canaan Valley State Park, Route 1, P.O. Box 39, Davis 26260, 866-4121 or (800) CALL-WVA; www.canaan resort.com • *Blackwater Outdoor Adventures,* cross-country ski center, Blackwater Falls State Park, P.O. Drawer 490, Davis 26260, 259-5216, (800) CALL-WVA; www.blackwaterfalls.com • *Timberline Ski Area,*

Route 1, P.O. Box 625, Davis 26260, 866-4801 or (800) 843-1751 out of state; www.timberlineresort.com • *White Grass Ski Touring Center,* Route 1, P.O. Box 37, Davis 26260, 866-4114; www.whitegrass.com • *Snowshoe Resort,* 10 Snowshoe Drive, Snowshoe 26209, 572-1000; www.snowshoemtn.com.

INFORMATION *Tucker County Convention & Visitors Bureau,* Route 32, P.O. Box 565, Davis, WV 26260, 259-5315 or (800) 782-2775; www.canaanvalley.org; www.wvonline.com.

Celebrating George at Valley Forge

Martha Washington must have baked a mean birthday cake back in the 1700s. No doubt both she and the general would be pleased to know that more than 250 years later, George's birthday remains cause for celebration, and that cake made from Martha's own recipe is one of the main attractions at the annual observance held at Valley Forge, Pennsylvania.

This weekend brings many special events at Valley Forge National Historic Park. Since the Valley Forge area also offers plenty of scenery, shopping, and history beyond the military, it makes a perfect Washington's Birthday weekend outing.

It could not have been a happy birthday for George Washington, quartered with his army at Valley Forge during the freezing winter of 1777–78. During their six-month encampment after triumphant British troops had bested the Americans and occupied Philadelphia, the tired, ill-equipped, and poorly trained Continental army retreated, only to battle new enemies at Valley Forge: hunger, disease, and the fury of a winter that proved fatal to 2,000 of the 12,000-man force.

Nevertheless, the survivors revived their spirit and forged a fighting unit that emerged to defeat the British army at the Battle of Monmouth in nearby New Jersey on June 28, 1778. The park is a monument to their triumph against terrible odds, a victory that buoyed the army for the battles still ahead.

The big National Historical Park at Valley Forge traditionally marks Washington's birthday weekend by re-creating the days of that fateful winter. Costumed in authentic Colonial uniforms, soldiers from the re-created Second Pennsylvania Regiment occupy the Muhlenberg huts where the Continental army lived. Their colorful living-history interpretation of encampment life includes musket-firing demonstrations, drills, and camp crafts, including outdoor cooking.

During the weekend, there are special programs for children, and talks that are historical eye-openers: a closer look at Washington and his officers, their personalities, and their contributions to the war effort.

Women of the Valley Forge Historical Society follow Martha's "Great Cake" recipe and serve up portions to visitors at their museum. Visitors get copies of the recipe for the giant yellow cake studded with fruit and nuts, which calls for 40 eggs, "five pounds of flower [sic]," and a lacing of half a pint of wine plus some fresh brandy.

A film tells more about the role of the area during the War for Independence and the many historic sites in the beautiful park that are open to the public.

Pick up a self-guiding tour map, and drive the marked route through the 3,600-acre complex. If the February fields are blanketed with snow, you might even consider a jaunt on cross-country skis.

Depending on how serious you are about your history, you can spend anywhere from two to four hours touring the sights, which include extensive remains and reconstructions of major forts and lines of earthworks; the Artillery Park, where cannons were massed and gun crews were trained; Washington's Headquarters, in a seventeenth-century home; the quarters of other officers; and the Grand Parade, where General von Steuben rebuilt the army and where the happy news of French support was announced on May 6, 1778. These plus the reconstructed huts, monuments, and markers help to re-create vividly the story of the men at Valley Forge who helped shape our nation's future.

Don't forget a stop at the lovely Washington Memorial Chapel on the grounds, known for its stained-glass windows, and the Museum of the Valley Forge Historical Society, which offers exhibits relating to the Revolution—worth a look even when there is no birthday cake on the menu.

When your park explorations are done, many other pleasures await in the surrounding area. Happily, many are free.

One of the most fascinating is the home of John James Audubon, now part of the Mill Grove Audubon Wildlife Sanctuary just beyond the park entrance. Take the Route 422 expressway west across the Betzwood Bridge, exit at Audubon/Trooper, turn left at the first light, and proceed straight ahead to the scenic estate that was the first American home of the famed naturalist, the first to portray authentically birds and other wildlife from living subjects and their habitats. You'll find samples of his beautiful art here, including the enormous folios of *Birds of America,* rarely seen by the public, and his restored studio and taxidermy room. The colorful murals on the downstairs walls are also extraordinary, done in 1954 as a tribute to Audubon's local adventures. The six miles of scenic marked trails along Perkiomen Creek take you through the settings that inspired young Audubon to begin his illustrious career.

From Mill Grove, turn left at the end of the drive and follow the road (it eventually becomes Route 363) north about ten miles to Route 73. Turn left and you'll find signs directing you to the entrance of the Peter Wentz Farmstead. The eighteenth-century German-style house has been restored in detail to the way it appeared when it was Washington's headquarters before and after the battle of Germantown. One of its surprising features is the bold hand-drawn designs that decorate the walls, an early-American equivalent of wallpaper. In season, the Wentz complex is a working farm, and year-round there are special events and demonstrations of period crafts.

The Valley Forge region abounds with shopping possibilities, beginning with the neighboring King of Prussia Mall, one of the nation's largest, with nine department stores and 450 shops and restaurants. More unusual wares can be found on Route 73 heading toward Skippack Village. The Cedars Country Store on Route 73 has been in continuous operation since 1849, and along with the usual stock of a country store, there are some tempting country collectibles for sale, both here and in adjoining shops.

Temptations also await in quaint quarters about three miles west, at Skippack Village, a community that dates back to 1722. Country antiques and accessories are the specialty, but you'll find almost every kind of antique and craft in the dozens of shops lining the main street of this quaint eighteenth-century village. New development here has brought some upscale dining and an Italian Market that claims to have the best hoagies this side of Philadelphia's South Street.

For a springlike end to a winter weekend, take the half-hour drive to Kennett Square and Longwood Gardens, where the four-acre indoor conservatory is already resplendent with spring bloom. It's a guaranteed spirit lifter in the snowy days of February.

Area Code: 610

DRIVING DIRECTIONS Valley Forge is west of Philadelphia at Route 202 and I-76, the Pennsylvania Turnpike. From D.C., take I-95 north to I-476 to I-76 to Valley Forge. The approximate distance from D.C. is 125 miles.

PUBLIC TRANSPORTATION Valley Forge is served by Philadelphia transportation, just 30 minutes away.

ACCOMMODATIONS All lodgings are less on weekends; ask about packages. *Sheraton Park Ridge Hotel & Conference Center,* 480 North Gulph Road, King of Prussia 19406, 337-1800 or (800) 337-1801, outdoor pool, fitness center, E • *Valley Forge Hilton,* 251 West

DeKalb Pike (U.S. 202), King of Prussia 19406, 337-1200 or (800) 879-8372, M–E • *Radisson Valley Forge Hotel,* 1160 First Avenue at North Gulph Road, King of Prussia 19046, 337-2000 or (800) 325-3535, M • *Comfort Inn Valley Forge,* 550 West DeKalb Pike (U.S. 202 north), King of Prussia 19406, 962-0700, outdoor pool, M • *Wyndham Valley Forge,* 888 Chesterbrook Boulevard, Chesterbrook Corporate Center, Wayne 19087, 647-6700, all suites, indoor pool, sauna, game room, E • *Homewood Suites,* 12 East Swedesford Road, Malvern, 19355, 296-3500, generous breakfasts and evening snacks, indoor pool, M–E, CP • Inns: *Great Valley House,* 1475 Swedeford Road, Malvern, 10355, 644-6759, bed-and-beakfast in 300-year-old stone farmhouse, country decor, on four acres with pool, M, CP • *William Penn Inn,* Route 202 at Sumneytown Pike, Gwynedd 19436, (215) 699-9272, established 1714, oldest continuously operated inn in the state, M–E, CP • *Joseph Ambler Inn,* 1005 Horsham Road, Montgomeryville 19454, (215) 362-7500, 1734 inn on 12 acres, rooms in various historic buildings, furnished with antiques, M–EE, CP • *Historic General Warren Inne,* Old Lancaster Highway, Malvern 19355, 296-3637, 1745 inn, Colonial furnishings, all suites, M–E, CP.

DINING *Kennedy-Supplee Restaurant,* 1100 West Valley Forge Road, King of Prussia, 337-3777, elegantly restored 1852 mansion on the park grounds, excellent food, M–E • *The Baron's Inne,* 499 North Gulph Road, King of Prussia, 265-2550, Old World ambience, convenient to Valley Forge, M–E • *California Cafe Bar & Grill,* 160 North Gulph Road, King of Prussia Mall, King of Prussia, 354-8686, trendy decor, eclectic menu, M–E • *Jefferson House,* 2519 DeKalb Pike, Norristown, 275-3407, attractive country inn with glass-enclosed porch, American and Italian specialties, E • **Colonial-era inns, all with charm:** *William Penn Inn,* Gwynedd (see above), M–E • *The Blue Bell Inn,* 601 Skippack Pike, Blue Bell, (215) 646-2010, George Washington slept here, traditional menus, M–E • *Joseph Ambler Inn* (see above), E • *General Warren Inne* (see above), E • There are several family restaurants, chain and otherwise, in the large King of Prussia shopping mall near Valley Forge. Also see page 232, Chester County, and page 70, for Wayne.

SIGHT-SEEING *Valley Forge National Historical Park,* Route 23, Valley Forge, 783-1077. Hours: Daily 9 A.M. to 5 P.M. Admission free; $ for historic homes; fee for guided bus tours • *Valley Forge Historical Society Museum,* Route 23, Valley Forge National Historical Park, 783-0535. Hours: Tuesday to Saturday 10 A.M. to 5 P.M., Sunday 1 P.M. to 5 P.M. $ • *Mill Grove Audubon Sanctuary,* Audubon and Pawlings Roads, Audubon, 666-5593. Hours: Tuesday to Saturday 10 A.M. to 4 P.M., Sunday 1 P.M. to 4 P.M.; grounds open dawn to dusk. Donation • *Peter Wentz Farmstead,* off Route 363, Worcester, 584-5104. Hours:

Tuesday to Saturday 10 A.M. to 4 P.M., Sunday 1 P.M. to 4 P.M. Free • *Pottsgrove Manor,* West King Street at Route 100, Pottstown, 326-4014. Hours: Tuesday to Saturday 10 A.M. to 4 P.M., Sunday 1 P.M. to 4 P.M. Free • *Longwood Gardens,* Route 1, Kennett Square, 388-1000. Hours: Grounds open daily, 9 A.M. to 5 P.M. in winter, Conservatory open 10 A.M. to 5 P.M. $$$$$.

INFORMATION *Valley Forge Convention and Visitors Bureau,* 600 West Germantown Pike, Plymouth Meeting, PA 19462, 834-1550 or (888) VISIT-VF; www.valleyforge.org.

Getting a Lift at Wintergreen

He loves the wide-open spaces, but she'd rather sightsee or shop. Or she's a hot-dog skier, but he'd rather relax by a pool. Or maybe it's the kids who want to romp in the snow, while Mom and Dad prefer to read or cuddle in front of the fire.

When temperaments don't match, planning a winter weekend can be a problem, but not at Wintergreen, Virginia's spectacular mountaintop resort. There's everything or nothing to do here, all in a matchless setting astride the Blue Ridge Mountains.

Wait until you see the views from this classy complex set on more than 11,000 sky-high acres. With over half of its own land set aside as permanent undisturbed forest and borderlands that include the Blue Ridge Parkway, a 2,400-acre U.S. Park Service reserve, and the George Washington National Forest, Wintergreen's unspoiled vistas go on forever from a ridgeline that reaches an altitude of 3,850 feet. In all, there are more than 6,000 acres of undisturbed wilderness.

They are serious about nature here. The nonprofit Wintergreen Nature Foundation, based at the Trillium House, a former country inn on the property, has exhibits on the region's natural and cultural history and offers more than 100 educational programs each year, including guided hikes, children's nature camps, and slide shows.

It would be worth the trip if you did nothing but gaze out your picture window at the hazy blue ridges spreading out in the distance, especially since the windows are in stylish privately owned condominiums that range from spacious studios to lavish mountain chalets with as many as six bedrooms. Depending on your mood, you can choose a quiet retreat hidden in the trees or be right in the middle of the action on the ski slopes, so the skiers can schuss out the door in the morning, leaving everyone else in peace. Almost all of the accommodations give you a fireplace and deck of your own, and although the tab isn't cheap, it's made a lot more affordable with the option of making your own meals, a special savings where families are concerned. You don't even have to worry about the cooking if you emulate some of the veteran guests who come bearing frozen casseroles made in advance at home.

Because they care a lot about the environment at Wintergreen, all the homes are tasteful, built of natural wood in modernistic architecture that has been carefully regulated to blend into the setting. Not everyone knows that rates here go by the number of bedrooms, not by the views, so by all means request a prime location.

Snowbirds won't have to complain about sissy slopes at Wintergreen if they ski the Highlands, where expert trails offer vertical drops of 1,000 feet and respectable runs more than 4,000 feet long. There's plenty of other terrain for all abilities, a total of 20 trails, and snow-making over 86 acres keeps the hills powdery even in winters when Mother Nature doesn't bless the Virginia slopes. Half the trails are well lighted for night skiing, and five chairlifts, including one quad and three triple-seaters, help hold down the waits in line. A dedicated snow-board park keeps snowboarders happy, and the snow-tubing hill is a family favorite.

The Skyline pavilion building is the home of the ski school. Beginners who rent ski equipment at Wintergreen are offered a free lesson, along with anyone who buys a lift ticket and rents equipment. The GETSkiing instruction program using short skis helps novices advance quickly.

At Stoney Creek, Wintergreen's second golf course, temperatures are 15 degrees above those on the mountain, making this the only resort in the East where you can ski in the morning, bring your lift ticket to the golf pro shop, and play golf in the afternoon. Three indoor courts at the Devils Knob Tennis Pavilion mean you can finish the day with a set in the evening. The Tennis Academy offers instruction here year-round.

If you prefer something more restful, just grab your bathing suit and head for the Wintergarden Spa. Facilities here include a big indoor swimming pool, as well as hot tubs, a Jacuzzi and sauna, and a convenient juice bar. There's also a fitness center if you feel the need for a workout afterward, and you can finish things off with a facial or a massage. Wellness programs, a cosmetology center, and personal trainers also are available here.

The handsome, rustic Mountain Inn is the main center of activity at the resort. Included in the central courtyard design is the Treehouse, near the children's slope, specially designed to accommodate Wintergreen's year-round children's programs.

Inveterate shoppers need go no farther than the redesigned shopping gallery in the Mountain Inn to whip out their credit cards. The offerings include outdoor clothing and equipment, mountain crafts, and lots of tempting gift items. There's a food market on the grounds also, but you'll do a lot better in price if you buy your groceries before you take the two-mile drive to the top of the mountain. When you do eat out, almost all of the Wintergreen restaurants offer children's menus.

For dining variety, you can enjoy fine continental dining at the Copper Mine, less formal fare at the Stony Creek Bar and Grill, or burgers and other light fare with a view at the Edge at Cooper's Vantage, along with live entertainment in the evening. The multimillion-dollar Devils Knob Golf Clubhouse adds the Devils Grill on the 18th hole to the options. The Gristmill Espresso/Cappucino Bar in the lobby is a comfortable place to enjoy an after-dinner coffee.

Or you can head down the hill for a special culinary treat, the down-home country cooking at Rodes Farm Inn. This nineteenth-century brick farmhouse is chockablock with rural charm: red-checked cloths on the tables, handmade quilts on the walls, and a fireplace in every room. The story goes that Rodes Farm came into being when Nelson County native Marguerite Wade welcomed the new developers of Wintergreen back in the 1970s with a nice lunch of fried chicken, homemade biscuits, and all the fixings. Knowing a good thing when they tasted it, they soon made plans to open an inn with Marguerite running the kitchen. Her recipes for chicken, roast beef with gravy, barbecued ribs, and country ham have become all but legendary, and no trip to Wintergreen is complete without a Rodes Farm breakfast with thick homemade apple butter waiting to be spread on the hot biscuits.

An equestrian center at Rodes Farm offers lessons for all abilities and trail rides through the valley.

Wintergreen's final big advantage is location. Many ski areas are so remote that there isn't much to do nearby. But an hour's drive from this plush aerie zips you to Charlottesville, just 43 miles away, and tours of Thomas Jefferson's Monticello, James Monroe's Ash Lawn, and the splendid campus of the University of Virginia. It's only a mile to the Blue Ridge Parkway or another easy drive over to Route 81 and the Woodrow Wilson home in Staunton, the Hall of Valor Civil War Museum at New Market, and the historic campuses of Washington and Lee University and Virginia Military Institute in the charming little town of Lexington.

There is one definite problem with Wintergreen, however, and that is deciding which season here is the best. Winter sports and snowscapes are followed by dogwoods in bloom and such a profusion of wildflowers that seminars and field trips are scheduled in spring. The year-round 18-hole Stoney Creek valley course is highly rated by golfing magazines, and there is a new adjacent nine-hole course. As soon as the weather permits, the par-70 mountaintop Devils Knob course opens, offering 50-mile views and cool mountain breezes. The Wintergreen Golf Academy is the only full-service golf school in Virginia.

There's something here for everyone—24 outdoor tennis courts plus the indoor pavilion; four outdoor pools; the stables; fishing in mountain streams; and 30 miles of hiking trails, including a section of the Appalachian Trail. The new Out of Bounds program adds in-line skating, mountain biking, a 25-foot climbing tower, basketball, volleyball, and a skateboard park with half- and quarterpipes. Children and teens enoy a host of planned programs.

Come autumn, the views rival those of the Blue Ridge Parkway—and without the traffic. The chairlift runs every weekend in October for a lofty view of the color.

Wintergreen lifts the spirits no matter when you come. If you're smart, you will sample all the seasons before you decide on a favorite.

Area Code: 434

DRIVING DIRECTIONS Wintergreen is off I-64 west of Charlottesville. From D.C., take Route 66 west, then Route 29 south to Route 64 west. At exit 107, pick up Route 250 in Crozet and continue west to Route 151 south. Turn left on 151 and continue for $14^2/_{10}$ miles to Route 664. Turn right and Wintergreen is $4^1/_2$ miles ahead. The approximate distance from D.C. is 168 miles.

PUBLIC TRANSPORTATION Air and Amtrak service go to Charlottesville, 43 miles away. Limousine service available from Charlottesville.

ACCOMMODATIONS AND INFORMATION *Wintergreen Resort,* P.O. Box 706, Wintergreen, VA 22958, 325-2200 or (800) 266-2444; www.wintergreenresort.com. Wide range of condominiums, studios to seven-bedroom units. Many package plans available for skiing, golf, and tennis, EE.

DINING *Copper Mine,* continental, M–EE • *Devils Grill,* casual, terrace dining in season, M–E • *Stony Creek Bar and Grill,* casual, overlooking the golf course, I–M • *The Edge,* Cooper's Vantage, casual, live entertainment, I–M • *Rodes Farm Inn,* country cooking, family style, lunch, I; dinner, M.

Beyond the Inner Harbor in Baltimore

Oh, how things have changed in this Cinderella city.

Baltimore used to be overshadowed by its near neighbor, Washington, D.C. But ever since the urban miracle that totally transformed the Inner Harbor in the early 1980s, the tourists have come flocking. The Inner Harbor attractions keep growing, along with the number of visitors, so that an out-of-season visit to Baltimore is a good idea these days to avoid the crowds. Baltimore's cache of fine museums and winter activities such as ice skating at the Inner Harbor make this a perfect cold-weather destination.

While the Inner Harbor is the big draw, it is only the start of Baltimore's pleasures. Those who venture farther afield will discover a big, warm historic mix of neighborhood moods, from ethnic to elegant to Colonial charm, plus a rich heritage and impressive arts that catch many visitors totally by surprise.

No question, the tourists come first for Harborplace and the Gallery, the shiny glass pavilions on the water housing dozens of shops and restaurants that are a constant source of fun, festivity, and good food. They also come to gawk and grin at the 10,000 species of fish, mammals, and birds in the National Aquarium in Baltimore; to board the historic ships in the harbor; and to find out about everything from earth to outer space at the Maryland Science Center, with its planetarium and 3-D IMAX theater, the other star Inner Harbor attractions. The imaginative new Port Discovery Children's Museum will surely please families who come to town, and the baseball and football stadiums at nearby Camden Yard are big draws in their respective seasons.

Sports fans also line up for fun at the ESPN Zone, a restaurant with lots of interactive sports exhibits. It is located in the Power Plant entertainment complex, adjacent to the Inner Harbor, which also houses Baltimore's Hard Rock Cafe, marked by a giant guitar, along with a flagship Barnes and Noble bookstore, one of the most attractive in the chain.

It is hard to believe that this was once an area of rotting wharves so decayed that H. L. Mencken, a native, described it as "smelling like a billion polecats." One and a half billion dollars and a lot of vision turned it into the spark of a revival that is visible for blocks beyond. More new office towers, hotels, and shopping complexes continue to rise, totally changing the face of the city. Some of the newest hotels are in the up-and-coming Inner Harbor East neighborhood, not far from Little Italy.

You can get an eagle's-eye view of all the changes from the Top of the World, atop I. M. Pei's World Trade Center on Pratt Street.

Get an early start to avoid the lines at the National Aquarium in Baltimore. It's worth a wait, however, because it's quite a show, beginning with your walk up a spiraling ramp into a rain forest, then descending a walkway circling the Atlantic Coral Reef and other ocean exhibits. You are eye to eye with the colorful denizens of the deep all the way. Another highlight is the Amazon River Forest exhibit, with exotic inhabitants like a 300-pound anaconda, piranhas, and dwarf caimans, relatives of the American alligator. The Marine Mammal Pavilion stars those perennial favorites, the dolphins. Several shows are presented each day; they are both entertaining and educational.

It takes a full morning to do justice to the aquarium, and if hunger pangs strike when you are done, you could conveniently proceed right across to Harborplace. A host of snack stands, restaurants, and markets await in the Light Street Pavilion and its twin Pratt Street Pavilion, which includes a Planet Hollywood.

If you want more authentic food markets, this is a city long known for its variety of ethnic foods. Seven public markets featuring fresh fruits and vegetables, meats, and seafood from Chesapeake Bay are open here, the newest of them more than 100 years old. The first and still the largest is Lexington Market, a downtown landmark since 1782 and the oldest public market in the country, and a great stop for lunch. Join the locals in line for the delectable chowder and crab cakes at Faidley's, often rated as the city's best. Since the markets are not open on Sunday, you may want to detour here for Saturday lunch.

Shoppers will find plenty of temptations at Harborplace, from well-known stores to specialty boutiques to vendors offering every kind of souvenir imaginable, many emblazoned "Baltimore Is for Crabs." There are more upscale stores across the way at the Gallery.

Antique buffs should note that the city's Antique Row is away from the city center, between the 700 and 800 blocks on North Howard Street and the 200 block of West Read Street. It is easy to reach via the city's aboveground light-rail system.

At some point, you'll probably want to take in the other popular sights around the Inner Harbor: the Maryland Science Center with its planetarium, IMAX theater, computers, and hands-on exhibits, and the harbor ships. A recent addition for winter visitors is the open-air Inner Harbor Ice Rink, a chance to take a few turns in a magical setting or watch a graceful exhibition. Special Harborplace events in winter often include an ice-carving competiton.

For a superb view of the harbor and the busy working port of Baltimore, climb the stairs behind the Science Center to the Colonial streets of Federal Hill. You'll be standing on the spot where 4,000 local citizens celebrated the ratification of the U.S. Constitution. The restored homes in this and many other of Baltimore's older neighborhoods are evidence that the spirit of revival begun at the harbor has been contagious.

Take a long walk or a short drive downhill around Sharp Street for a look at one of the city's prides, the Otterbein Homesteading Project. Residents bought up the blighted eighteenth-century row houses here for a dollar each and carefully restored them, turning the area into a beautiful and vibrant historic district.

The American Visionary Art Museum at the foot of Federal Hill is a wonderful whimsical showcase for work by talented, unschooled artists, the only one of its kind in the country. The 55-foot giant whirligig outside sets the stage. The innovative Joy America cafe on the top floor gets top reviews for dinner as well as lunch.

Fell's Point, the oldest port area in the city, is another neighborhood that should be explored. It still looks remarkably like the salty seafaring community that was laid out in 1763, with its cobbled streets and charmingly restored eighteenth- and nineteenth-century residences and shops. Someone called it a cross between Georgetown and Dublin.

Some of the city's most appealing lodgings are here. The first to open was the Admiral Fell Inn, three Fell's Point town houses put together to make an elegant hostelry on the site of an old seaman's hotel. The Inn at Henderson's Wharf, once a tobacco warehouse, has been beautifully transformed, still preserving the old brick walls. Many of the tastefully furnished rooms look out directly on the water. Celie's Bed and Breakfast offers historic quarters and charm on a more intimate scale.

A walking tour of this compact neighborhood will show you the more interesting sights, including Broadway Market, a miniature version of Lexington Market dating back to 1784; and the Robert Long House, the oldest home in the area, now restored and furnished by the Society for Preservation of Federal Hill and Fell's Point. Much of the new construction along the water is being carried out with architecture that is hard to distinguish from the old, housing even more new shops and cafes. Take a walk to admire the galleries and shops and little theaters, the cafes and clubs that are sprouting like wildflowers, turning Fell's Point into a lively center for young nightlife.

A water taxi service connects the Inner Harbor with Fell's Point, Little Italy, and other tourist attractions.

For a total change of scene, hop the bus that goes from the Inner Harbor up Charles Street, a street of galleries, shops, and popular cafes leading to Mt. Vernon Place. This square of parks and fountains, laid out in 1827 and centered on a 160-foot Washington Monument that predates the one in the nation's capital, is the heart of the elegant, arts-centered part of Baltimore. The 22 buildings around the square and those in some 40 blocks surrounding it are the cream of Baltimore's late-nineteenth- and early-twentieth-century architecture and include the homes of some of the city's most noted earlier residents: Johns Hopkins, Enoch Pratt, and George Peabody, to name a few.

The noted Peabody Conservatory of Music is found on Mt. Vernon Place, and next to it is the Peabody Library, a five-tiered, skylighted Victorian beauty maintained by Johns Hopkins University and containing original manuscripts by Beethoven, Purcell, and Handel. Note that the library is open weekdays only.

Nearby, on West Monument Street, is the Maryland Historical Society, where you can see the original manuscript of "The Star-Spangled Banner," as well as a display of toys, costumes, silver, and furniture, and period rooms of the nineteenth-century Enoch Pratt mansion.

The prize of Mt. Vernon Place is the magnificently restored Walters Art Museum, a miniature palace that has been rightfully called one of America's great museums. On its four floors are the treasures amassed by Henry and William Walters, a father and son whose collections are dazzling in their range and profusion: paintings from every major period of art, plus sculptures, armor, stained glass, Roman sarcophagi, Russian icons, Renaissance bronzes, Sèvres porcelain, jewelry, and silver.

The Hackerman House wing holds one of this country's outstanding exhibits of Oriental art, shown in a dazzling setting, a transformed 1851 Greek Revival mansion attached by a corridor to the original museum. From a collection of more than 3,000 pieces of priceless Chinese porcelains dating as far back as the sixteenth century, 450 jewels have been chosen for display on the first floor. The second floor takes visitors from Chinese Neolithic and Buddhist art to Japanese tea-ceremony objects, scrolls and screens, netsukes, incense games, weapons, and armor. A prime piece is the oldest-known wooden Buddha in existence, dating from A.D. 610.

An equally amazing Baltimore art collection was gathered by two sisters, Claribel and Etta Cone, and you'll find it at the Baltimore Museum of Art. Just continue north on Charles Street past the attractive turn-of-the-century row houses of Charles Village near the Johns Hopkins campus, and you'll come to the museum, where the Cone Collection of Impressionist art is housed in its own wing, fresh from a major two-year renovation. It contains many fine pieces, but the real prize of the collection is the selection of works by Matisse: 42 oils, 18 sculptures, 36 drawings, 155 prints, and 7 illustrated books. You might also want to stop at the museum's American Wing to see the outstanding exhibit of early furniture, and a newer wing devoted to the museum's modern-art collections. The museum cafe, overlooking a sculpture garden, is a fine choice for brunch, lunch, or dinner.

A prime attraction in Baltimore is the birthplace of Babe Ruth, his grandmother's home. It is also a museum for the Baltimore Orioles, full of baseball lore. The Babe would probably feel right at home in Oriole Park at Camden Yards, the home of Baltimore's much-loved baseball team. The stadium was deliberately planned to retain the feel of an old-fashioned ballpark, and it scored a hit right from opening day. It's just a stroll from the Inner Harbor, a good reason to make a return trip in season. The Baltimore Ravens football team is also ensconced in a fine new stadium next to Camden Yards.

Two more only-in-Baltimore sights are the B&O Railroad Museum, where you can explore the nation's first passenger station and climb aboard some magnificent antique trains, and Fort McHenry, where the sight of the high-flying, giant star-spangled banner that inspired Francis Scott Key to write the national anthem still brings a proud swell of patriotism.

Unusual collections that may interest aficionados are on display at the U.S. Lacrosse Hall of Fame, on the Johns Hopkins University campus, and the Jockey Hall of Fame, at Pimlico Racetrack, in spring the site of the Preakness, one of the nation's top races.

Come evening, there is music in the city's striking Joseph Meyerhoff Symphony Hall, as well as opera at the Lyric Opera House, a reproduction of Germany's Leipzig Music Hall. The Morris Mechanic Theatre in the downtown Charles Center is a major stop for national touring companies, and the Center Stage is the respected local regional theater company. Concerts are also presented at the Peabody Conservatory of Music and by the Chamber Music Society of Baltimore at the Museum of Art. In summer, music also fills the air at the tented concert pavilion at Pier 6 on the waterfront.

When it comes to fine dining, the top choices include the elegant and intimate Hampton's at the Harbor Court Hotel, and longtime local favorites such as Tio Pepe and the Prime Rib. There are many choices also along Charles Street, known as Restaurant Row, where the Brass Elephant is highly recommended.

But some of the best of Baltimore eating is found in the city's many modest ethnic neighborhoods. A few recommendations: Aldo's, Boccaccio, and Da Mimmo in Little Italy, and Ikaros in Greektown. Kali's Court, the Black Olive, and John Steven, Ltd., in Fell's Point are among the favorites for seafood.

Scores of luxury hotels have risen to accommodate the growing tourist trade in Baltimore. Once again, Harbor Court gets the nod for elegance. Gracious smaller bed-and-breakfast town houses bring a bit of country-inn ambience to the neighborhoods of the city.

The Inner Harbor has made all of Baltimore come alive, and it is the lure that keeps so many visitors coming. But it is the pleasures beyond the harbor that keep them coming back.

Area Code: 410

DRIVING DIRECTIONS   Baltimore is reached via I-95, I-83, and I-70. From D.C., follow I-95 north or take the Baltimore-Washington Parkway. The approximate distance from D.C. is 37 miles.

PUBLIC TRANSPORTATION Frequent Amtrak and bus service and many air connections via BWI airport.

ACCOMMODATIONS Many hotels offer much better rates on weekend package plans, especially off-season; be sure to ask. **Hotels across from the Inner Harbor:** *Harbor Court Hotel,* 550 Light Street, 21202, 234-0550, small and elegant, EE • *Hyatt Regency,* 300 Light Street, 21202, 528-1234, EE • *Renaissance Harborplace,* 202 East Pratt Street, 21202, 547-1200, EE • *Brookshire Suite Hotel,* 120 East Lombard Street, 21202, 625-1300, all suites, EE, CP • *Baltimore Marriott Inner Harbor,* Pratt and Eutaw Streets, 21201, 962-0202, EE • *Omni Inner Harbor Hotel,* 101 West Fayette Street, 21201, 752-1100, E • *Holiday Inn Inner Harbor,* 301 West Lombard Street, 21201, 685-3500, E • *Days Inn,* 100 Hopkins Place, 21201, 576-1000, M–EE • *Tremont Hotel,* 8 East Pleasant Street, 21202, 576-1200, and • *Tremont Plaza,* 222 St. Paul Place, 21202, 727-2222, both (800) 638-6266, all suites, good value, M–E • **Inner Harbor East:** *Inner Harbor Courtyard by Marriott,* 1000 Aliceanna Street, 21202, 923-4000, E • *Marriott Waterfront,* 700 Aliceanna Street, 21202, 385-3000, EE • **Fell's Point:** *Admiral Fell Inn,* 888 South Broadway, Fell's Point 21231, 522-7377, charming, E–EE, CP • *The Inn at Henderson's Wharf,* 1000 Fell Street, 21231, 522-7777 or (800) 522-2088, on the waterfront, E–EE, CP • **Other locations:** *Clarion Hotel,* 612 Cathedral Street at Mt. Vernon Square, 21201, 727-7101, old-world feel, on the city's nicest square, M–EE • *Doubletree Inn at the Colonnade,* 4 West University Parkway, 21218, 235-5400 or (800) 456-3396, near Johns Hopkins, E.

Inns: *Celie's Waterfront Bed and Breakfast,* 1714 Thames Street, Fell's Point 21231, 522-2323, charming, spacious rooms, M–EE, CP • *Mr. Mole Bed and Breakfast,* 1601 Boston Street, 21217, 728-1179, 1867 home, many antiques, M–E, CP • *Abercrombie Badger Bed and Breakfast,* 59 West Biddle Street, 21201, 244-7227, turn-of-the-century building, antiques, M–E, CP •*Inn at Government House,* 1125 North Calvert Street, 21202, 539-0566, complex of historic town houses, M–E, CP • *Hopkins Inn,* 3404 St. Paul Street, 21218, 235-8600, 1920s building, M–E, CP.

DINING Fine dining: *Hampton's,* Harbor Court Hotel (see above), elegant dining, harbor views, E–EE • *The Prime Rib,* 1101 North Calvert Street, 539-1804, American menu in handsome surroundings, E–EE • *Tio Pepe,* 10 East Franklin, 539-4675, continental/Spanish, M–E • *Charleston,* 1000 Lancaster Street, 332-7373, gourmet American with a Southern accent, M–E • *Polo Grill,* Doubletree Inn at the Colonnade (see above), clublike ambience, excellent reviews, M–EE • *Brass Elephant,* 924 North Charles Street, 547-8480, northern Italian/

Mediterranean in lovely surroundings, E–EE • *Joy America Cafe,* American Visionary Art Museum, 800 Key Highway, 244-6500, contemporary American, harbor view, E.

Fell's Point: *Black Olive,* 814 South Bond Street, 276-7141, attractive and extremely popular Greek restaurant, seafood specialties, M • *Kali's Court,* 1606 Thames Street, 276-4700, another hit Greek seafood choice, M–E • *Pierpoint,* 1822 Aliceanna Street, 675-2080, seafood and Maryland cuisine, M–E • *John Steven Ltd.,* 1800 Thames Street, 327-5561, informal waterfront spot, excellent seafood and sushi, try the oyster-filled "yumbo gumbo," I–M.

Ethnic: *Aldo's Ristornte,* 306 South High Street, Little Italy, 727-0700, M–EE • *Da Mimmo,* 217 High Street, Little Italy, 727-6876, M–E • *Boccaccio,* 925 Eastern Avenue, Little Italy, 234-1322, M–E • *Germano's Trattoria,* 300 South High Street, Little Italy, 752-4515, I–M • *The Helmand,* 896 North Charles Street, 752-0311, intimate setting for delicious Afghan food, I–M • *Ikaros,* 4805 Eastern Avenue, 633-3750, Greek, I–M • *Samos,* 600 South Oldham Street, 675-5292, another Greek favorite, reasonable, I • *Mughal Garden,* 920 North Charles Street, 547-0001, Indian, great lunch buffet, I–M • *Kawasaki,* 413 North Charles Street, 659-7600, Japanese, sushi bar, I–M • *Thai Landing,* 1207 North Charles Street, 727-1234, I–M.

Casual: *Louie's Bookstore Cafe,* 518 North Charles Street, 962-1224, classical music, eclectic menu, I • *Sisson's,* 36 East Cross Street, 539-2093, Cajun in Baltimore's original brewpub, M • *Phillips Harborplace,* 301 Light Street, 685-6600, big and busy for good reason; fresh seafood and great crab cakes, M–E • *Legal Seafoods,* 100 East Pratt Street, 332-7360, a Boston standby moves south with fresh seafood and the clam chowder that made it famous, M–E • *Faidley's Seafood and Raw Bar,* Lexington Market, 200 North Paca Street, 727-4898, many say the crabcakes are Baltimore's best, I–M.

SIGHT-SEEING *Inner Harbor,* Pratt and Light Streets, includes the following: *Harborplace,* two pavilions of food and shops. Admission, free • *National Aquarium in Baltimore,* Pier 3, 501 East Pratt Street, 576-3800. Hours: November to February, daily 10 A.M. to 5 P.M., to 8 P.M. on Friday; March to June and September to October, 9 A.M. to 5 P.M., Friday to 8 P.M.; July/August, daily 9 A.M. to 8 P.M. $$$$$ • *Maryland Science Center & Davis Planetarium,* 601 Light Street, 685-5225. Hours: Early September to mid-June, Monday to Friday 10 A.M. to 5 P.M., Saturday and Sunday 10 A.M. to 6 P.M.; mid-June to early September, Monday to Thursday 10 A.M. to 5 P.M., Friday to Sunday 10 A.M. to 6 P.M., mid-June to Labor Day Monday to Thursday, 9:30 A.M. to 6 P.M., Friday to Sunday 9:30 A.M. to 8 P.M. $$$$$; planetarium is extra • *Baltimore Maritime Museum,* Pier 3, Pratt Street, 396-3454. Hours: Three historic ships to board, Monday to Friday 10 A.M. to 5 P.M., Saturday and Sunday 10 A.M. to 6 P.M. $$$• *Inner Harbor Ice Rink,* Rash Field next to Maryland Science Center, 837-4636. Hours: late November to March, two-hour day and evening skating sessions starting at noon, also special exhibitions. Check for current hours and schedule. Skating, $$; skate rental, $.

Mt. Vernon Place: Charles and Monument Streets; attractions around this square include *George Peabody Library,* 17 East Mt. Vernon Place, 659-8179. Hours: Monday to Friday 9 A.M. to 3 P.M. Free • *Walters Art Museum,* 600 North Charles Street, 547-9000, Tuesday to Friday 10 A.M. to 4 P.M., Saturday and Sunday 11 A.M. to 5 P.M. $$$, free Saturday 11 A.M. to 1 P.M. • *Maryland Historical Society,* 201 West Monument Street, 685-3750. Hours: Tuesday to Friday 10 A.M. to 5 P.M., Saturday 9 A.M. to 5 P.M., Sunday 11 A.M. to 5 P.M. $$.

Other special sights: *Baltimore Museum of Art,* Art Museum Drive, Charles and 31st Streets, 396-7100. Hours: Wednesday to Friday 11 A.M. to 5 P.M., to 9 P.M. first Thursday each month, Saturday and Sunday 11 A.M. to 6 P.M. $$$; under age 19, free; free to all on Thursday • *American Visionary Art Museum,* 800 Key Highway, 244-1900. Hours: Tuesday to Sunday 10 A.M. to 6 P.M. $$$ • *Port Discovery Children's Museum,* 35–43 Market Place, 727-8120. Hours: Labor Day to Memorial Day, Tuesday to Saturday 10 A.M. to 5 P.M., Sunday noon to 5 P.M., June daily, 10 A.M. to 5 P.M., July, August daily 10 A.M. to 6 P.M. $$$$$ • *Babe Ruth Birthplace/Baltimore Orioles Museum,* 216 Emory Street (off 600 block of Pratt Street), 727-1539. Hours: April through October, daily 10 A.M. to 5 P.M.; rest of year to 4 P.M. $$$ • *B&O Railroad Museum,* 901 Pratt Street at Poppleton Street, 752-2490. Hours: Daily 10 A.M. to 5 P.M. $$$ • *Fort McHenry National Monument,* foot of East Fort Avenue, 962-4290. Hours: Daily 8 A.M. to 5 P.M.; early June to Labor Day to 8 P.M. $$; under 17, free • *Lexington Market,* Lexington and Eutaw Streets, 685-6169. Hours: Monday to Saturday 8:30 A.M. to 6 P.M. Free • *Top of the World,* World Trade Center, 401 East Pratt Street, 837-8439. Hours: Observation deck open Monday to Saturday 10 A.M. to 5:30 P.M., Sunday noon to 5:30 P.M., extended hours in summer. $$.

INFORMATION *Baltimore Area Convention and Visitors Association,* 100 Light Street, 12th Floor, Baltimore, MD 21202, 659-7300 or (800) 343-3468; www.baltimore.org. • *Baltimore Visitors Center,* 451 Light Street, Inner Harbor, (888) BALTIMO (225-8466). Open daily.

Tracking the Snow in Western Maryland

When they tell you there is snow awaiting in Garrett County, Maryland, believe it, even if there is nary a snowflake where you live.

I found out for myself driving west on Route 40 from Cumberland, Maryland, one fine February day, when the sun was shining, the sky was blue, and the ground was bare. Then I started to climb—and climb and climb—and a few minutes later, as I crossed the county border, I was looking at a powdery white landscape and was knee-deep in the middle of a snowstorm.

Garrett County is the triangular far end of the state, sandwiched between West Virginia and Pennsylvania. The terrain has more in common with its mountainous neighbors than with the rest of its own state. The second largest and most sparsely populated of Maryland's counties, it lies within the Appalachian Plateau and contains five main mountain ridges with an average elevation of 2,300 feet above sea level. The highest point, Backbone Mountain, stands some 3,360 feet high.

Besides the mountains, trees and lakes are the dominant features of the 662-square-mile Garrett landscape. Three state forests comprising some 75,000 acres of wilderness and six state parks add up to more trees than people and 90,000 acres of parkland—plenty of wide-open space for enjoying nature. Deep Creek Lake, a man-made wonder covering nearly 3,900 acres, is the state's largest freshwater lake.

In spring and summer, the boaters and fishermen and swimmers hold sway in Garrett County; in autumn, the leaf watchers take over; but come winter, this is a snow lover's paradise. The Allegheny Front, which captures moisture moving east from the Great Lakes, accounts for the perennial winter coat of white, even when lowlanders haven't seen a sign of snow. The average is a hefty 97 inches, and some winters the snowfall has topped 200 inches.

Wisp Mountain Resort takes advantage of all that white stuff with 23 downhill trails along the slopes of Marsh Mountain, part of the Allegheny Range. With a respectable elevation of 3,080 feet, a vertical drop of 610 feet, and trails up to two miles long, it is a small mountain, but challenging enough for all but the most expert. New owners are adding snow tubing and more runs on the backside of the mountain. A full schedule of ski races and snowboard competitions add to the fun.

Wisp is ideal for learners, and should the average snowfall fail to accumulate, skiing is still guaranteed by extensive snowmaking that covers 90 percent of the mountain. Most of the trails are also lighted for night skiing to prolong the fun. The Rossignol Adventure Center offers some alternatives to traditional alpine skiing, with rentals and coaching in the use of the parabolic-shaped "Cut Ski," snowboards, and snow-runners. Snowboarders will find their own halfpipe on the mountain.

Cross-country skiers and hikers will also find good going amid gorgeous winter scenery in Garrett County parks. There are cleared and marked trails in New Germany State Park, Deep Creek State Park, and Herrington Manor State Park, the last a scenic five-mile route around Herrington Lake. Trails also can be found at Swallow Falls State Park, where the scenic falls were the site of a 1918 camp used by automotive pioneers Henry Ford, Thomas Edison, and Harvey Firestone. Muddy Creek Falls in Swallow Falls Park is a dramatic 52-foot tumble to the rocks below that turns into a fairy-tale scene frozen in motion in winter.

Herrington Manor State Park is also a mecca for night sledding on Friday evenings, when torches light the run and bonfires and hot chocolate help to keep everyone toasty when they aren't on the slopes. Rentals are available.

Another way to enjoy the superb winter scenery is on horseback. Four stables will be glad to oblige with guided trail rides, from one hour to half-day and whole-day outings.

This is also prime territory for snowmobilers, who have 35 miles of trails to themselves. And hardy fishermen don't give up when the ice covers Deep Creek Lake. They just chop a hole in the ice, drop their lines, and go right on catching yellow perch, pike, and pickerel. The ice fishermen patiently tending their lines add a colorful note to the frozen landscape.

There is a bit of sight-seeing nearby when you want to come in from the cold. The center of things is Oakland, a pleasant little town boasting "Church of Presidents," St. Matthew's Episcopal Church on Liberty Street, where Presidents Grant, Harrison, and Cleveland worshiped while vacationing nearby at Deer Park, once a fashionable resort. President and Mrs. Cleveland spent one week of their honeymoon here in 1886.

The Queen Anne–style Baltimore and Ohio (B&O) Railroad station, fresh from a $1.4 million restoration, was built in 1884 in Oakland and is one of the oldest in the country. John W. Garrett (for whom the county was named) was then president of the B&O Railroad and did much to further its development. During his presidency, the railroad built large summer resorts in Deer Park and Oakland.

The coming of the railroad was also responsible for the growth of Mountain Lake Park, just east of Oakland off Route 135. It became a noted resort attracting thousands each summer for cultural events. Many wealthy families built fine Victorian homes and came for the whole summer to attend dramatic and musical presentations held in a 5,000-seat amphitheater, and to hear speakers like President William Howard Taft, William Jennings Bryan, and the evangelist Billy Sunday. A number of the elegant old homes are being restored, and a portion of the town has been declared a Historic District.

Pennington Cottage, located east of Mountain Lake Park on the south side of Route 135 (the old Oakland and Deer Park Road), is the last reminder of the grand old days of Deer Park. The elaborate 14-room, three-story summer home stands on the grounds of the old resort and now operates as the Deer Park Inn, a restaurant with three upstairs rooms available for bed-and-breakfast guests.

Things are more modest in Garrett County these days, and one of its definite advantages is lodging that seems reasonable compared with rates in some ski areas. The growing number of pleasant bed-and-breakfast inns in the area is a boon for visitors. Savage River Lodge is another choice lodging, with 18 very private luxury cabins nestled amid the 700-acre Savage River State Forest, and gourmet meals.

Garrett County has a number of antique dealers, including three malls. For a full list and map stop at the visitor center and ask for the *Antique Guide* folder.

This is also good place to look for handicrafts. Schoolhouse Earth, two miles north of Deep Creek Lake on Route 42, is one good source. Grand Central Station on Third Street in Oakland has eight shops under one roof, with a wide variety of wares. The Book Market & Antique Mezzanine in Oakland has books old and new and all manner of collectibles. A former Bausch and Lomb plant on Route 135 in Mt. Lake Park has been occupied by Simon Pearce, whose handblown glass is found in fine shops throughout the Northeast. Visitors can watch the craftsmen at work from a balcony above the factory floor and buy their products, including well-priced seconds.

More attractions await to the north of the county in the little town of Grantsville, an Amish-Mennonite community whose Main Street is along the old National Pike. Two local landmarks are the 1797 Stanton's Mill, the county's oldest operating gristmill, and the graceful Casselman Bridge, which was the longest single-span stone-arch bridge in the country when it was built in 1813.

A big draw in Grantsville is Penn Alps, a Mennonite-operated restaurant in a remodeled 1818 log stagecoach stop. Bountiful Pennsylvania Dutch cooking is served up here, and the shop has a big selection of handcrafts from the region.

You can see artisans in action next door at Spruce Forest Artisan Village, where original log cabins and other rustic structures are used as work and display areas for spinners, weavers, potters, stained-glass workers, wood sculptors, bird carvers, and other crafters. A quilt show here in mid-July is a big draw.

More old-fashioned food and ambience can be found down the street at the Casselman Hotel, an 1824 lodging that was also built to serve stagecoach travelers. Antiques are for sale here, as well as an assortment of tempting sweets in the Bake Shop.

Other tasty souvenirs are the hickory-smoked meats, sausages, or bologna; local maple sugar; and homemade jams from Yoder's Country Market in Grantsville.

A worthwhile drive for dinner is south across the West Virginia border to the Brookside Inn, serving some of the most creative food in the area.

Wherever you go in western Maryland in the winter, you'll likely have a snow-covered landscape for company.

Area Code: 301

DRIVING DIRECTIONS Garrett County is west of Cumberland, Maryland, reached via I-68 from the east, Route 219 north and south. From D.C., take I-270 north to Frederick, then follow Route 70 west to I-68 west. At Keysers Ridge, take Route 219 south to Oakland. The approximate distance from D.C. is 188 miles.

ACCOMMODATIONS *Carmel Cove Inn,* Glendale Road, P.O. Box 644, Oakland 21550, 387-0067, charming and elegant inn located in a onetime monastery, hot tub, M–E, CP • *Savage River Lodge,* Mt. Aetna Road, Frostburg 21532, 689-3200, hideaway luxury cabins in the forest, can accommodate four, E • *Lake Pointe Inn,* 174 Lake Pointe Drive, Box 873, McHenry 21541, 387-0111 or (800) 523-5253, comfortable restored rustic 1890 stone farmhouse on the lake, M–E, CP • *Savage River Inn,* Dry Run Road, Box 147, McHenry 21541, 245-4440, contemporary home, peaceful setting in Savage River State Forest, fireplaces, rooms, M, CP; suites, M–E, CP • *Deer Park Inn,* 65 Hotel Road, P.O. Box 58, Deer Park 21550, 334-2308, Victorian landmark, M, CP • *Haley Farm Bed and Breakfast,* 16766 Garrett Highway, Oakland, 21550, 387-9050 or (888) 231-3276, 65-acre working farm, rooms in farmhouse, M, CP; suites in carriage house and barn, E, CP • *The Oak & Apple,* 208 North Second Street, Oakland 21550, 334-9265, Victorian bed-and-breakfast in town, I–M, CP • *Elliott House Victorian Inn,* 146 Casselman Road, Grantsville 21536, 895-4250 or (800) 272-4090, restored 1870 Victorian inn on seven acres along the Casselman River, adjoining Penn Alps and Spruce Forest Artisan Village, hot tub, M–E, CP • *Brookside Inn,* Route 1, P.O. Box 217-B, Aurora, WV 26705, (304) 735-6344, or (800) 588-6344, choice spot across the state line south of Oakland, excellent meals, M, CP; E, MAP • *Wisp Mountain Resort,* 290 Marsh Hill Road, McHenry 21541, 387-5581 or (800) 462-9477 for reservations, slopeside hotel and condos for eager skiers, indoor pool, fitness center; ask about ski packages, M–E • *Will o' the Wisp,* 20160 Garrett Highway, Oakland 21550, 387-5503, lakefront units, studios, and one-bedroom units sleeping four, I–E. Many motels and small resorts are available in the area, and hundreds of cottages can be rented through local realtors; write for full list.

DINING *Deer Park Inn* (see above), top choice, M • *Savage River Lodge* (see above), "gourmet country cuisine," advance reservations required, E • *McClive's,* Deep Creek Drive, McHenry, 387-6172, overlooking McHenry Cove and Wisp ski area, varied menu, I–M • *Cornish Manor,* Memorial Drive, Oakland, 334-6499, elegant manor house, pianist on weekends, continental/American menu, reservations required, M–E • *Point View Inn,* Deep Creek Drive, McHenry, 387-5555, casual, serves all three meals, seafood buffet, salad bar, I–M • *Deep Creek Brewing Company,* 75 Visitors Center Drive, off Route 219, McHenry, informal pub fare, freshly brewed beer, I–M • *Uno's Restaurant,* Route 219, Deep Creek Lake, 387-4866, lakefront setting and wider menu than much of this pizza chain, reliable family choice, I–M. • *Penn Alps,* Route 48, Grantsville, 895-5985, reasonable Pennsylvania Dutch specialties, I–M • *Casselman Restaurant,* Main Street, Grantsville, 895-5266, cozy, baking a specialty, I–M.

SIGHT-SEEING *Wisp Mountain Resort,* P.O. Box 629, McHenry, 387-4911 or (800) 462-9477, phone for current rates, hours. **State Parks:** Phone for information, directions. *Deep Creek Lake State Park,* 898 State Park Road, Swanton, 387-5563 • *Herrington Manor State Park,* County Route 20, five miles northwest of Oakland, 334-9180 • *New Germany State Park,* New Germany Road off U.S. 168, 5 miles south of Gransville, 895-5453 • **Swallow Falls State Park,** Swallow Falls Road, 9 miles northwest of Oakland, 334-9180. **Horseback riding:** Phone for information, directions. *Western Trails,* 387-6155 • *Broken Bar Riding Stables,* 334-3114 • *Small Oaks Riding Stables,* 334-4991 • *Sunny Slope Stables,* 334-4834.

INFORMATION *Garrett County Chamber of Commerce,* 15 Visitors Center Drive, McHenry, MD 21541, 387-4386; www.garrett chamber.com. For snow conditions for downhill and cross country and a list of cross-country ski clinics, see www.skimaryland.com.

Winter Warm-ups in the Poconos

Start with six major ski areas, something for everyone from beginner to mogul master, plus another seven smaller slopes at the resorts. Now add horse-drawn sleigh rides, more than two dozen indoor and outdoor skating rinks, seven year-round riding stables, seven state parks plus a national recreation area with cross-country ski trails, and scores of opportunities for sledding, tobogganing, and snowmobiling.

No wonder so many find Pennsylvania's Poconos the right destination for winter fun.

Poconos downhill skiing and snowboarding are always reliable as long as the nights go below freezing, because all of the major areas have snowmaking covering the entire mountain to ensure good conditions. The major ski areas all have halfpipes for snowboarders.

Lights on the slopes make it possible to keep schussing after the sun goes down at Camelback, the largest of the areas, where most of the 33 trails are lighted. Camelback offers a lighted Half Pipe and Terrain Park for snowboarders and the region's largest snow-tubing slopes. Night skiing is also available at Alpine Mountain, Blue Mountain, Shawnee, and Big Boulder.

Snow tubing has caught on in a big way throughout the region. Sliding down the hill is fun and requires no special skills; it is as easy as sitting in an inner tube. Runs can be found at all the major mountains, as well as some of the resorts.

Jack Frost and Big Boulder offer cross-country ski rentals, as does the touring center at Pocono Manor resort, whose terrain, 40 miles of groomed trails, is one of the area's best. State parks offer more opportunity for gliding through the winter landscape. Among the longer runs are the 13 miles of trails at Hickory Run State Park in White Haven and the 26 miles of trails at Lehigh Gorge State Park in Weatherly.

Though best known for its "couples resorts," you needn't rent a room with a heart-shaped tub to enjoy the Poconos. If a resort is what you have in mind, Skytop Lodge is gracious and grand, standing on a mountaintop overlooking 5,500 unspoiled acres. It is a reminder of another era, a place where gentlemen are still requested to wear coats for dinner. Despite its old-world ways, there's nothing stodgy about Skytop. Young families are as welcome as adult couples, and the facilities are fine. Among the bountiful facilities are a small private ski area, cross-country skiing, ice skating, sledding, a toboggan run, an indoor health club, a pool, and a sauna; the rates include three meals daily. The Inn at Skytop, a recent addition, is a 20-room lodging with lovely views, fireplaces and balconies in every room, and the opportunity to take advantage of all the facilities of the main inn.

If country inns are more your style, the Poconos can deliver. Two winning contenders are in the town of Canadensis. Brookview Manor is a spacious country home refurbished as a fresh and attractive bed-and-breakfast inn in Victorian and country style; some of the rooms have Jacuzzis. Pine Knob is a country Victorian done with warmth and good taste, and with a well-regarded dining room as well. The cottage rooms on the grounds have fireplaces.

The Farmhouse Inn in Mount Pocono, set on six and a half acres surrounded by tall pines, offers four spacious suites located in the main house and an additional house on the property, all with old-fashioned country furnishings and fireplaces. The duplex Caretaker's Cottage, the original icehouse on the farm, is a perfect private romantic hideaway. At the Blueberry Mountain Inn, guests can enjoy a game room and pool table and cross-country ski trails.

Two more possibilities await further north in South Sterling. The Sterling Inn is a mini-resort with the old-fashioned feel of a country inn. Activities include cross-country skiing, ice skating, sledding, and swimming in an indoor pool. French Manor, a turreted fieldstone mansion under the same ownership, was built in the 1930s by famed art collector Albert Hirschorn and has nonstop views from its very private perch atop Hackleberry Mountain. Dinners are served by candlelight in the great room, which has a cathedral ceiling and giant fireplaces at either end. Guests can cross-country ski right on the inn grounds, and also have use of the Sterling Inn facilities.

Families may want to consider cottage colonies such as Naomi Village or Rimrock Country Cottages, where each unit comes with a fireplace, cooking facilities, and a TV and VCR.

For the best of the winter scenery, take in the lofty views from either Pocono Manor or Skytop. Then drive east to the Delaware Water Gap, the deep, tree-covered gorge that is the entrance to the Poconos. This three-quarter-mile-high natural wonder, carved by the Delaware River, is part of a 77,000-acre national recreation area that offers canoeing, hiking, and picnicking in summer and cross-country trails in winter. Even when everything is blanketed with snow, you can pull on your boots and make tracks through the woods for the short walk to Dingman and Silver Thread Falls. The crashing waters are a sight worth the trek.

Snowmobiling is another popular winter sport in the Poconos. Rentals and trails are available at the Jack Frost, Shawnee, and Alpine Mountain ski areas, in many state parks and forests, and at the Mount Pocono Golf Course. Some of the resorts also may open their facilities to the public. Check the current visitors guide.

If shopping is your favorite sport, there is plenty to keep you occupied. Some of the best small shops are in the mountain villages of Canadensis, Cresco, and Mountainhome.

Antiquers should head for the Olde Engine Works Market Place on North Third Street in Stroudsburg, a multi-dealer co-op inside a 100-year-old machine shop. Vitale's Antiques at Storm Street, another multi-dealer mall, specializes in refinished oak furniture, and Ibis at 517 Main Street features decorative arts of the nineteenth and early twentieth centuries, including art deco and art nouveau. Don't overlook the Sunday market at Collector's Cove off Route 33 south of Strouds-burg, where over 100 antique dealers participate.

Stroudsburg also has several worthwhile stops for admirers of fine handcrafts. The Foxglove Gallery, 805 Scott Street, shows a wide variety of work by local artisans, primitive paintings to wrought-iron furniture, and Designer Crafts, 578 Main Street, represents the work of 250 juried artists and craftsmen. The Gallery at Liztech, 95 Crystal Street in East Stroudsburg, features the colorful jewelry of a local artist known as Liztech, plus high-quality crafts of all kinds in a gallery tucked inside a bank building.

Bargain hunters will find over 100 outlet stores at the growing Crossings Factory Outlet just off I-80, exit 45, with brand names such as Tommy Hilfiger, Mikasa, Polo–Ralph Lauren, Reebok, Ann Taylor Loft, and Jones New York. More shopping is available at the smaller Foxmoor Village Outlet Center in Marshalls Creek and at the Pocono Outlet Complex in Stroudsburg.

Several Poconos stops give you a show with your shopping. Callie's Candy Kitchen in Mountainhome has chocolate-covered everything, from strawberries to potato chips, plus a laugh-a-minute candy-making demonstration from the colorful Mr. Callie. Twenty kinds of yummy soft pretzels are the offerings at Callie's Pretzel Factory, where you're invited to taste samples, watch the "pretzel bender" in action, and try bending one of your own. Candle makers can be seen at work at American Candle in Bartonsville and the Pocono Candle Works in East Stroudsburg, and you can tour the winery at Cherry Valley Vineyards just off Route 33 in Saylorsburg, tasting the wines and enjoying the old farm atmosphere.

Come nighttime, you can sample dancing and entertainment at some of the area resorts, or go back to the fireplace in your own cozy inn, a perfect way to warm up to winter in the Poconos.

Area Code: 570

DRIVING DIRECTIONS   Most Pocono locations are reached from I-80. From D.C., take I-95 north to I-695, then I-83 north to Harrisburg. Connect here with I-81 north to I-80 east. The closest of the resorts and ski areas (Big Boulder and Jack Frost) are around Lake Harmony and

White Haven. The approximate distance from D.C. is 225 miles. Camelback Mountain and other resorts are 20 to 25 miles farther to the east off I-80.

PUBLIC TRANSPORTATION   Wilkes-Barre/Scranton Airport, 38 miles away. Bus service from Philadelphia.

ACCOMMODATIONS   *Blueberry Mountain Inn,* Thomas Road, Blakeslee, 18610, 646-7144 or (800) 315-BLUE, farmhouse-style home built in 1994, six rooms, indoor pool, outdoor hot tub, beautiful grounds, M, CP • *Brookview Manor,* Route 447, Canadensis 18325, 595-2451, M–E, CP • *Farmhouse Bed & Breakfast,* Grange Road, Mt. Pocono 18344, 839-0796, M, CP • *The French Manor,* P.O. Box 39, Huckleberry Road, South Sterling 18460, 676-3244, E, CP; suites, EE, CP • *The Pine Knob Inn,* Route 447, Canadensis 18325, 595-2532, M–EE, CP; E–EE, MAP • **Resorts:** *Skytop Lodge,* Skytop 18357, 595-7401 or (800) 345-7SKY (in PA, [800] 422-7SKY), EE, AP (under age 18 free in parents' room except for modest meal charge) • *Sterling Inn,* South Sterling 18460, 676-3311 or toll free (800) 523-8200, E–EE, MAP • **Cottages:** One- to four-bedroom units available, all with cooking facilities. *Naomi Village,* Route 390, P.O. Box 609, Mountainhome, 18342, 595-2432 or (800) 336-2664, E–EE • *Rimrock Country Cottages,* 425 Rimrock Road, Stroudsburg, 18360, 629-2360, E–EE. Free area lodging reservation service: (800) POCONOS.

DINING   *The Cook's Touch,* Route 390, Mountainhome, 595-3599, well-prepared contemporary American menu, reasonable, highly recommended, I–M • *Crescent Lodge,* Routes 940 and 191, Paradise Valley, Cresco, 595-7486, formal ambience, pianist on Saturday, M–E • *Dansbury Depot,* 50 Crystal Street, East Stroudsburg, 476-0500, model-train decor in the 1864 train station, fun stop for lunch or informal dinner, I–M • *Hampton Court Inn Restaurant,* Route 940 East, Mount Pocono, 839-2119, intimate dining, reliable, M–E • *Hazard's Rainetree Restaurant,* Route 191, South Sterling, 676-5090, rustic setting, American menu, good food at good prices, I–M • *Homestead Inn,* Sandspring Drive, Cresco, 595-3171, country ambience and candlelight, M • *Peppe's Ristorante,* Eagle Valley Mall, Routes 209 and 447, East Stroudsburg, 421-4460, Northern Italian, pleasant ambience, I–E • *Pump House Inn,* Skytop Road, Route 390, Canadensis, 595-7501, continental, long established, intimate dining in 1842 former stagecoach inn, M–E • **Advance reservations advised:** *French Manor* (see above), E–EE • *Pine Knob Inn* (see above), M–E • *Skytop Lodge,* Skytop, (see above), prix fixe, EE.

ACTIVITIES   **Skiing:** *Camelback,* Tannersville, 629-1661; snow report, (800) 233-8100 • *Big Boulder,* Blakeslee, 722-0100; snow report, (800) 475-SNOW • *Jack Frost Mountain,* Blakeslee, 443-8425; snow report, (800) 475-SNOW • *Alpine Mountain,* Analomink, 595-2150, snow report, (800) 233-8240 • *Blue Mountain,* Palmerton, (610) 826-7700; snow report, (877) SKI-BLUE • *Shawnee Mountain,* Shawnee-on-Delaware, 421-7231; snow report, (800) 233-4218 • **Cross-country Skiing:** For a free state park guide, phone (888) PA-PARKS • **Snowmobiling:** State forest and state park hotline, 787-5651, for snow conditions • *Alpine Mountain* (see above) • *Jack Frost Mountain* (see above) • *Shawnee Resort,* Shawnee-on-Delaware, (800) SHAWNEE • *Mount Pocono Golf Course,* Mount Pocono, 839-7800 • **Riding stables:** *Carson's,* Cresco, 839-9841 • *Pocono Manor stables,* Summit, 839-0925 • *Mountain Creek,* Cresco, 839-8725, sleigh rides also • *Pocono Adventures,* Mount Pocono, 839-6333.

INFORMATION *Pocono Mountains Vacation Bureau,* 1004 Main Street, Stroudsburg, PA 18360, 421-5791 or (800) POCONOS; www.800poconos.com

A Taste of Spring in Maryland

Some wait for the robin's song, but more eager watchers for spring's first signs keep their eyes on the maples.

Even while nights are still freezing and snow is on the ground, warming sun during the day is enough to trigger the rising of the sap in the maple trees, heralding the start of maple-sugaring season, a welcome assurance that Old Man Winter is on the way out.

Demonstrations of how the sap is turned to tasty maple syrup are an annual event for two mid-March weekends at Cunningham Falls State Park in Thurmont, not far from Frederick, Maryland. It's a chance to watch a longtime American custom, have a welcome break out of doors, and get acquainted with a spirited historic town. Antiquers will find another incentive for the trip, both in Frederick and in New Market, the tiny town six miles to the east.

At the park, rangers are in residence, ready with a video explaining the skills of sugaring that were first taught to early American settlers by the Indians, followed by firsthand outdoor demonstrations of how it's done.

The sap running into the buckets hanging from a "spile," a small hollow spout inserted into the tree, seems as clear and thin as sugar water, but just let it simmer four to six hours in the big iron kettles tended by the rangers, and tempting smells arise as the liquid thickens into the familiar sticky-delicious golden maple syrup. Everyone is fascinated to see how much sap it takes to boil down into a small amount of syrup, which explains why this delicacy comes with such a high price tag.

Watching the process is an educational taste of spring, and you can buy take-home samples of maple candy and maple syrup made in Maryland. You can also enjoy a serving of pancakes and sausage, lavished with you-know-what.

If the weather is cooperatively springlike, Cunningham Falls State Park offers 5,000 wooded acres with 15 miles of trails for walks with opportunities to picnic and to have a look at the 78-foot cascading waterfall for which the park was named. Also within the park is the Catoctin Furnace Historic District, a chance to see the iron furnace that operated from 1774 to 1903 supplying weapons for both Revolutionary and Civil War armies. The stone furnace and the nearby stoneworkers' cottages are listed on the National Register.

This state-run park is on the south of Catoctin Mountain, divided by Route 77 from adjoining Catoctin Mountain National Park north of the highway, a 5,770-acre preserve. Since the National Park Service took over in 1936, the once-depleted forests of black locust, wild cherry, sassafras, and yellow poplar have grown back into their full glory. Camp David, the presidential retreat, is hidden deep among the dense trees, so you won't be able to see it, and it is not open to the public.

What you can see in this park are many panoramic views from the mountain. With more than 25 miles of hiking trails, there is something for everyone. The self-guided Charcoal Trail explains the process of making charcoal, which was used as fuel in the nearby Catoctin Iron Furnace. The Blue Blazes Whiskey Still trail, leading through the forest to the site of the old still, and the Sawmill Exhibit, located near Owens Creek Campground, are more glimpses into a past way of life. Stop at the Visitor Center for information on trails and ranger programs, and visit the exhibits on the natural and cultural resources of the park.

The 300 residents of the Catoctin Mountain Wildlife Preserve and Zoo begin receiving visitors in March.

If woodland rambles don't suit the March weather or your fancy, head for in-town pleasures in Frederick, a town well worth a visit whatever the season.

Frederick's history goes back to 1745, but it was poet John Greenleaf Whittier who immortalized the town's "clustered spires" of church steeples in 1863, when he wrote about a spunky local patriot, 90-year-old Barbara Fritchie. Furious at Confederate troops shooting at Old Glory, Fritchie shamed mighty Stonewall Jackson by imploring, "Shoot if you must this old gray head, but spare your country's flag." A reconstruction of her red-brick house and her shop, where she sold gingersnaps and gloves made by her husband, is open for touring.

Like its legendary heroine, Frederick has not allowed age to dim its spirit. The pleasant mix of historic ambience and modern pleasures has inspired many an urbanite to move here and commute to a job in Baltimore or Washington, each about 45 miles away. The emergence of Frederick as an antiquing center brings lots of visitors to town as well, and some very appealing inns have opened to serve them.

Before you hit the shops, have a look at the charming town. A printed walking tour of the 50-block historic district is available at the Visitor Center on Church Street. Guided tours are offered on Saturday and Sunday at 1:30 P.M. from April through December.

On your own, a good place to start is Court Square, where 12 judges from Frederick County met in November 1765 to issue one of the first official protests against the British Stamp Act, a full eight years before the Boston Tea Party. The nineteenth-century courthouse was converted some years ago to serve as city hall, replacing the original building, which burned in 1861.

The old city hall has its own bit of history to tell. It was here that the city fathers met in urgent session to hear the demands of Confederate general Jubal Early, who demanded ransom in return for sparing the city. Frederick dug down to the tune of $200,000, but Early never got to spend it, because Union troops were waiting for him just outside the city. The Battle of Monocacy delayed him enough to stave off a planned Rebel invasion of Washington, D.C.

On the southern side of the square is one of the famous church spires, belonging to the 1855 All Saints Episcopal Church, which now boasts Tiffany-style and Bavarian stained-glass windows. A local favorite is the cast-iron greyhound put in front of the church rectory by a loving eighteenth-century master. It was rescued from Confederate troops aiming to melt it down for cannonballs and returned to its proper home.

The rest of the city's historic churches can be found within a three-block radius. Stonewall Jackson is said to have fallen asleep during a sermon at the Evangelical Reformed Church, a building whose two towers are modeled after the lanterns of Demosthenes. A free candle-light tour of Frederick's historic houses of worship is held each year during the Christmas season.

Directly across from Court Square is the low, white, double-doored building where two prominent onetime residents—Francis Scott Key, author of the "Star-Spangled Banner," and his brother-in-law, Roger Brooke Taney, chief justice of the United States Supreme Court—had law offices. The Taney/Key Museum is maintained in Taney's home on South Bentz Street, but is open to the public only during special events in town.

Just around the square on Council Street are two fine adjoining early-1800s mansions. The white house on the right is the family home of former Maryland senator Charles Mathias. The red brick Ross House next door was lodging for the Marquis de Lafayette when he visited Frederick after the Revolution. The fine wrought-iron fencing in front of both homes was cast at the old Catoctin Iron Furnace near Thurmont.

The recently renovated National Museum of Civil War Medicine tells an unusual and interesting story, portraying the dramatic role the war played in setting medicine on a path toward the modern era. In meeting the emergency demands of war, doctors of the era made many advances in the use of anesthesia, administration of hospitals, nursing, surgery, and sanitation.

Much additional local lore and memorabilia has been gathered by the Historical Society of Frederick County and can be seen in its museum, located in one of the lovely old homes in the Historic District.

Some outlying sites are also of interest in Frederick. Rose Hill Manor is the Georgian mansion of Maryland's first governor, Thomas Johnson. Inside the mansion, Rose Hill offers the Touch and See children's museum, introducing youngsters to Colonial life. Also on the grounds are a carriage museum, a collection of farm implements, a 150-year-old log cabin, and a blacksmith shop. In season, there are often demonstrations of nineteenth-century crafts such as candle dipping and quilting.

The city's oldest dwelling is Schifferstadt, a 1756 steep-roofed, German-style stone house near the Hood College campus. Check before you make the trip, however, since the house usually does not open until April.

Those who are fascinated by old graveyards should visit the Mt. Olivet Cemetery and the Francis Scott Key Grave and Monument, where the Stars and Stripes fly day and night to honor the man who glorified them. Thomas Johnson and Barbara Fritchie rest here, along with many soldiers who fell in the Civil War and several Revolutionary War militiamen.

Many visitors to the Frederick area never get around to seeing all the historic sights, however, because they have come for a different kind of history—the take-home variety available in a host of antique stores. You can get a full list from the Tourism Council, but you'll find some of the best shops on East Patrick Street, East Street, and North Market Street. Emporium Antiques at 112 East Patrick is of note for wares from 130 dealers.

The most picturesque shopping place is Everedy Square and Shab Row at the corner of East and Church Streets. It was once shabby indeed, but now the old row houses and a former bottle cap factory have been revitalized and hold 35 specialty shops and cafes.

It's easy to find the shops lined up on Main Street in New Market, a charming hamlet about 15 minutes from Frederick that has also been declared a historic district. Drovers on the way to the Baltimore market once led their livestock down the old National Pike, the same street where antiquers now flock to scoop up candlesticks, copper kettles, mahogany dressers, and Victorian high-back beds, not to mention windup trucks, teddy bears, tinware, and tiles. The shops are wall-to-wall, more than 30 of them in a one-mile stretch, housed in the picturesque period homes on Main Street. A printed guide is available at many shops to spell out each shop's specialties. Many of the owners are city dwellers who open for business only on weekends, so be forewarned and don't waste a trip midweek. Everyone who comes to New Market seems to wind up at Mealey's, the popular town restaurant.

Three fine inns are convenient to the shopping and dining variety in Frederick. McCleery's Flat, circa 1876, is a beautifully decorated, grand Empire-style townhouse, a charming oasis right on the town's antique row with prices that are quite reasonable for the quality of the inn. The Tyler Spite House, an 1814 Federal-style home, is also a beauty, offering 14-foot ceilings, marble fireplaces, lots of antiques, and a nice garden and pool out back. Hill House, a three-story Eastlake-style Victorian, is also in the historic district and has four attractive guest rooms.

There are happy choices in the nearby countryside as well. Top choice is the Turning Point Inn, a gracious and spacious home set back from the main road a few miles south of Frederick. Elegant dinners are served here. Spring Bank is a historic brick mansion a couple of miles outside town with caring owners, while the Middle Plantation Inn to the east in Mt. Pleasant is a new building built from old logs and beams, furnished in Victorian style, and set on 26 acres. Fifteen miles away in Middletown, Stone Manor offers sumptuous suite lodging and fine dining in an elegant manor house on 114 acres. Part of the house dates back to the 1760s. And it isn't far to Antietam, where more inns beckon.

Another alternative for nature lovers who want to stay out among the maples is Ole Mink Farm Cabins, located just south of Cunningham Falls Park. It offers you the chance to live in a cozy log cabin, an oak bungalow, or a cathedral-ceilinged chalet, with your own fireplace or woodstove to warm the March evenings. You'll be secluded in the woods high in the Catoctins with all the comforts of home and plenty of firewood to burn. And to add a final sweet taste, you can have maple syrup on your French toast in the morning.

Area Code: 301

DRIVING DIRECTIONS Frederick is at the intersection of I-70, I-270, Route 340, and Route 15. From D.C., follow Route 270 north. The approximate distance from D.C. is 45 miles.

ACCOMMODATIONS *McCleery's Flat,* 121 East Patrick Street, Frederick 21701, 620-2433 or (800) 774-7926, M, CP • *Tyler Spite House,* 112 West Church Street, Frederick 21701, 831-4455, EE, CP • *Hill House,* 12 West Third Street, Frederick 21705, 682-4111, M, CP •

Turning Point Inn, 3406 Urbana Pike (Route 355), Urbana, 21704, 831-8232, M, CP, guest cottages, M–E, CP • *Middle Plantation Inn,* 9549 Liberty Road, Frederick 21701, 898-7128, M, CP • *Spring Bank Inn,* 7945 Worman's Mill Road, Frederick 21701, 694-0440, note that most bedrooms share baths, M, CP • *Stone Manor,* 5820 Carroll Boyer Road, Middletown 21769, 473-5454, EE, CP • *Ole Mink Farm Recreation Resort,* 12806 Mink Farm Road, Thurmont 21788, 271-7012, two-night minimum, M–EE, depending on size of cabin • For Antietam inns, see page 167.

DINING *Brown Pelican,* 5 East Church Street, Frederick, 695-5833, pelicans on the walls, excellent eclectic choices on the menu, M–E • *Tauraso's/Victor's Saloon & Raw Bar,* Everedy Square, 6 East Street, Frederick, 663-6600, soaring space and lots of choices, seafood and Italian dishes, wood-fired pizza oven, I–M • *di Francesco's Italian Restaurant,* 26 North Market Street, Frederick, 695-5499, I–M • *The Province,* 131 North Market Street, Frederick, 663-1441, creative American menu, M • *Brewer's Alley Restaurant & Brewery,* 124 North Market Street, Frederick, 631-0089, lively brewpub, regional cuisine and wood-fired oven pizza, I–M • *Crabapples Delicatessen,* 111 West Patrick Street, 694-7373, good spot for lunch, I • **Outside town:** *Turning Point Inn* (see above), lovely decor and excellent food, E–EE • *Stone Manor* (see above), gourmet fare, prix fixe, EE • *Cozy Restaurant,* 105 Frederick Road, Thurmont, 271-7373, family-style dinners, lots of important visitors to Camp David have dined in this no-frills cafe, I–M • *Mealey's Restaurant,* 8 Main Street, New Market, 865-5488, a local tradition, M–E.

SIGHT-SEEING *Maple Syrup Demonstrations,* William Houck Area, Cunningham Falls State Park, 14309 Catoctin Hollow Road off U.S. 15 north, Thurmont, 271-7574. Usually held on two successive weekends early to mid-March, 10 A.M. to 3:30 P.M. Free. Call to check current dates and times. Park is open daylight hours daily year-round. Visitor Center hours: Monday to Friday 10 A.M. to 4:30 P.M.; Saturday, Sunday 8:30 A.M. to 5 P.M. $ • *Catoctin Mountain National Park,* Route 77 west off U.S. 15, Thurmont, 663-9330. Daylight hours daily. Free admission • *Catoctin Wildlife Preserve and Zoo,* 13019 Catoctin Furnace Road, Thurmont, 271-3180. Hours: March through November, daily 9 A.M. to 5 P.M., later in summer; petting zoo 10 A.M. to 5 P.M. $$$$ • *Barbara Fritchie House and Museum,* 154 West Patrick Street, Frederick, 698-0630. Hours: April through September, Monday and Thursday to Saturday 10 A.M. to 4 P.M.; Sunday 1 P.M. to 4 P.M., October-November, Saturday, Sunday 10 A.M. to 4 P.M. $ • *Schifferstadt,* 1110 Rosemont Avenue, Frederick, 663-3885. Hours: April through mid-December, Tuesday to Saturday 10 A.M. to 4 P.M.; Sunday noon to 4 P.M. $; students, free • *Children's Museum of Rose Hill*

Manor Park, 1611 North Market Street, Frederick, 694-1648. Hours: April through October, Monday to Saturday 10 A.M. to 4 P.M.; Sunday 1 P.M. to 4 P.M., November, Sunday 1 P.M. to 4 P.M. $$ • *National Museum of Civil War Medicine,* 48 East Patrick Street, Frederick, 695-1864. Hours: mid-March to mid-November, Monday to Saturday 10 A.M. to 5 P.M.; Sunday 11 A.M. to 5 P.M., rest of year to 4 P.M. $$$ • *Historical Society of Frederick County Museum,* 24 East Church Street, Frederick, 663-1188. Hours: Monday to Saturday 10 A.M. to 4 P.M.; Sunday 1 P.M. to 4 P.M. $; children free • *Frederick Brewing Company,* 4607 Wedgewood Boulevard, Frederick, 694-7899. Hours: Tours and tastings, Saturday and Sunday 1:30 P.M. Call for reservations. Free • **Guided walking tours:** *Frederick Visitor Center,* 19 East Church Street, 694-7433: Hours: April through December, 90-minute tours weekends and Monday holidays at 1:30 P.M. $$ • For Antietam information, see page 167.

INFORMATION *Tourism Council of Frederick County,* 19 East Church Street, Frederick, MD 21701, 664-4047 or (800) 999-3613; www.visitfrederick.org.

First Resorts of the Mid-Atlantic

Go ahead. You deserve it. In a hectic world filled with fast food and Formica, everyone ought to be entitled to splurge once in a while to experience the good life the way it used to be and still is at the two great tradition-filled, five-star resorts of the mid-Atlantic, the Greenbrier in White Sulphur Springs, West Virginia, and the Homestead, in Hot Springs, Virginia.

Bigger than life and far more serene, each of these splendid dowager queens still offers the kinds of pleasures the privileged enjoyed in a more gracious era. Twenty-two-foot ceilings and crystal chandeliers, high tea in the afternoon, carriage rides, multicourse meals, and a staff that outnumbers the guests remain traditions that have been cherished ever since the long-ago days when Southern aristocracy came to take the waters at the mineral springs that inspired the building of both hotels.

That's not to say that these opulent mountain oases have not kept up with today's taste for more vigorous activity, and on a scale befitting their penchant for lavishness. Among the Greenbrier's 6,500 acres, in addition to 12 acres of magnificent formal gardens, you will find three

18-hole golf courses, 20 tennis courts (5 of them indoors), platform tennis, indoor and outdoor swimming pools, trap and skeet shooting, horseback riding, mountain biking, hiking trails, and fishing streams stocked with trout and bass.

Not to be outdone, The Homestead's 15,000 mountain acres boast their own three golf courses; eight tennis courts; lawn bowling; a children's playground and clubhouse; and more chances to ride, hike, shoot, swim, or fish. In winter, both hotels add ice skating to the list, and the Homestead offers ski slopes as well.

Even at that awkward in-between season, when winter snow has vanished but spring has not yet arrived, you'll find plenty to keep you happy at these indoor-outdoor complexes, from bowling alleys, billiards tables, and indoor pools to spas, fitness centers, and saunas.

Hot mineral baths and marvelous massages are available at both spas, so you can soak away your troubles or have them kneaded away, just as visitors have done for the past two centuries. Both hotels have spent millions recently in spa renovations and improvements.

Off-season is a perfect time to come, in fact, if you want to take advantage of lower rates and weekend packages. Each hotel schedules special weekends and theme activities to pick up business when things get slow, such as wine tastings or big-band weekends. The Greenbrier also has its own highly regarded cooking school, La Varenne at the Greenbrier, and a full roster of gourmet cooking classes given by its own culinary staff.

These two friendly rivals, 45 minutes apart in the Alleghenies, have much in common, yet each has a distinct flavor and personality, and its own share of history to tell.

Step into the Greenbrier and you are overwhelmed with space, color, and lavish decor. People have been coming to White Sulphur Springs to take the cure ever since the 1770s, when the word got out about a Mrs. Amanda Anderson, a lady crippled with rheumatism who immersed herself in the odoriferous waters and, when she emerged, pronounced herself miraculously cured.

The first permanent cottages, Paradise Row and Alabama Row, were built at the springs in the 1800s and are still standing, the former used as lodging, the latter now housing an art colony where handicrafts are for sale. More cottages continued to go up, and before long aristocratic Southern families began making a ritual of coming to drink the waters three times a day.

The Presidents' Cottage Museum serves as a reminder that some 25 U.S. presidents have visited the Greenbrier from its early days right up to the present. Another illustrious guest was Robert E. Lee, who made the hotel his summer home after the Civil War.

The original stately hotel building that went up in 1858 had one of the largest ballrooms in America. Many a Southern belle twirled her skirts here, hoping to bewitch a beau on the dance floor. During the

Civil War, the hotel changed hands several times and served as a hospital for both sides.

That first hotel, fondly known as Old White, was torn down after the Chesapeake and Ohio Railroad took over in 1910 and built the tall-columned Georgian structure that is still the hotel's core, sparing no expense to make it the epitome of lavishness. In those days it was known as the Jewel of the South. For 37 years, guests were met at the train by horse-drawn carriages and driven to the hotel, where a seven-piece orchestra awaited along with long-skirted hostesses offering lemonade. Many others came in their private railroad cars.

After serving as a hospital once again during World War II, the Greenbrier was redecorated on an even grander scale in the late 1940s by interior designer Dorothy Draper, whose imprint remains throughout. With a budget of $10.5 million, a more-than-tidy sum in those days, she filled the walls and halls with the floral prints and vivid colors of her own patented designs. Each of the 650 rooms is different from the next, but all are in the oversize patterns Draper felt were necessary to fill such soaring spaces. The pink rhododendrons that abound here in spring are the most common motif, found in the china and the hotel logos, and all through the hallways.

Though each room is redecorated regularly, most of the fabrics are reproductions of Draper's 1948 originals, carefully overseen by her protégé and the present Greenbrier decorator, Carlton Varney. Varney maintains a store in the shopping gallery of the hotel.

Some things have hardly altered at all here over the years. The rooms are still enormous, the deluxe quarters bigger than some city apartments. Ladies still wear their prettiest dresses, and gentlemen don coats and ties for dinner; waiters, wine stewards, and busboys still hover while musicians play sweet music to aid the digestion.

But time has brought some changes. Guests can choose to dine in the Tavern Room, amid brass lanterns and equestrian prints, where there is a modern open kitchen and a less formal ambience than in the main dining room, or visit Sam Snead's at the recently renovated Golf Club, and watch sports or, later at night, listen to the music of today at Slammin' Sammy's.

These days, instead of tripping the light fantastic, many guests are likely to be working out in the light and airy Greenbrier Spa, which was doubled in size and completely renovated in 2001. It offers aerobics classes and state-of-the-art exercise equipment that would amaze the belles and beaus of old. Special spa programs still feature soaks in the famous mineral waters, but they now include delicious massages, facials, and beauty treatments as well. The Greenbrier Clinic, founded in 1948, has long specialized in diagnostic medicine and offers a two-day examination program, the ultimate vacation checkup.

Other additions to the program include a Falconry Academy and white-water rafting on nearby rivers.

The economics of hotel keeping have also demanded the addition of meeting rooms and a conference center, and nowadays it is likely to be conventioneers rather than plantation owners, dukes and earls, and tycoons who come to call. All are still treated royally, however.

Profiled against the mountains, the dark red brick façade, pillared portico, and white cupola of the Homestead bespeak Virginia gentility, and the interior reinforces that impression. This is also a large hotel, boasting over 500 rooms and its own maze of corridors and meeting quarters. The 22-foot-high, 211-foot-long, pillared-and-chandeliered Great Hall is impressive, yet on the whole the atmosphere at the Homestead is understated and gracious compared with the splash of the Greenbrier.

George Washington, Thomas Jefferson, and Alexander Hamilton all were among the early visitors seeking the curative powers of the 104-degree waters at Hot Springs. In 1766, one Thomas Bullitt built the first hotel here, supposedly in self-defense against the spate of uninvited guests at his home. The spa building was added in 1892. All but the original spa, casino, and cottages were destroyed by a fire in 1901, when the present hotel was begun. The trademark tower went up in 1929.

The hotel quickly attracted its own list of the socially elite, Mrs. Cornelius Vanderbilt and the Duke and Duchess of Windsor among them. The mahogany-paneled Washington Library is filled with memorabilia and photographs of famous visitors to the resort, including Henry Ford, Thomas Edison, John D. Rockefeller Sr., and 13 former presidents. Woodrow Wilson spent a portion of his honeymoon here.

If there is less feeling of overwhelming space indoors, there is more sense of the mountains outdoors at the Homestead. They envelop the hotel grounds, beckoning for a brisk walk on 100 miles of wooded paths wending uphill for splendid views. The proximity of the hills inspired the opening of one of the South's first ski areas here in 1959.

Golf is another special point of Homestead pride. They boast that the first tee of the Homestead's course, laid out in 1892, is the nation's oldest in continuous use, and the Cascades course is considered one of the country's top mountain courses.

Shoppers will be pleased by the browsing possibilities, which include Cottage Row, developed from a former colony of guest cottages, and 11 elegant shops along the Tower Corridor, part of the hotel's recent renovation. You can also walk into the tiny town of Hot Springs for more shops or a Sam-Wedge at Sam Snead's Tavern. Snead was long the resident pro at the Homestead.

The Pinehurst Company, which has renovated other classic resorts such as Pinehurst in North Carolina, took over the Homestead in 1993, and an ongoing multimillion-dollar renovation was undertaken, keeping the heritage but tastefully redecorating guest rooms and all the public spaces of the hotel, and adding conference facilities. Part of the aim is to attract younger patrons with facilities such as a sports bar, a year-round children's program, a golf school, snow tubing, and a halfpipe slope reserved for snowboarders—decided changes from the sedate old days.

It is pleasant to see young families with children all dressed up for dinner, with little ones beaming as they take a turn on the dance floor with Mom or Dad.

But some traditions endure. Around four o'clock at both hotels, everyone still gathers indoors for teatime. At the Greenbrier, you help yourself to refreshments and garden views in the opulent upstairs lobby. In the Great Hall at the Homestead, a pianist serenades, and as soon as you settle into one of the big wing chairs, a formally attired waiter or crisply aproned waitress magically appears with your personal tray, set with china teacups, dainty sandwiches, and sweets.

How to choose which hotel to visit? Try both. These tradition-rich resorts are a kind of never-never land in today's world, a return to more genteel times. The Greenbrier calls it "life as it should be." Yes, the tab is steep—but once in a while shouldn't everyone have a taste of gracious living?

Area Codes: West Virginia, 304; Virginia, 540

DRIVING DIRECTIONS White Sulphur Springs is off Route 60, just east of Lewisburg, West Virginia. Hot Springs, Virginia, is about an hour to the northeast. To drive from D.C. to the Greenbrier, take I-66 west to I-81 south. At Lexington, pick up I-64 west to first exit for White Sulphur Springs, and follow U.S. 60 for two miles to entrance. The approximate distance from D.C. is 250 miles. To The Homestead: Follow directions above to I-81 south. At Mount Crawford, take Route 257 to Route 42 to Goshen, then Route 39 west to Warm Springs and U.S. 220 south to Hot Springs. The approximate distance from D.C. is 220 miles.

PUBLIC TRANSPORTATION Amtrak serves White Sulphur Springs, West Virginia, and Clifton Forge, Virginia. Air service goes into Ingalls Field, 20 minutes from The Homestead, and several airlines serve both Lewisburg, West Virginia (about 15 minutes from Greenbrier), and Roanoke, Virginia (about 90 minutes from either hotel). Connecting limousine service is offered to both hotels from both airports. Check the hotels for current transportation schedules.

ACCOMMODATIONS AND INFORMATION *The Greenbrier,* White Sulphur Springs, WV 24986, (304) 536-1110 or (800) 624-6070, EE, MAP; www.greenbrier.com • *The Homestead,* Hot Springs, VA 24445, (540) 839-1776 or (800) 336-5771, EE, MAP or CP; www.the homestead.com. Highest rates are in effect at both resorts from April through October. Ask about special theme weekends and sports package plans.

Maps

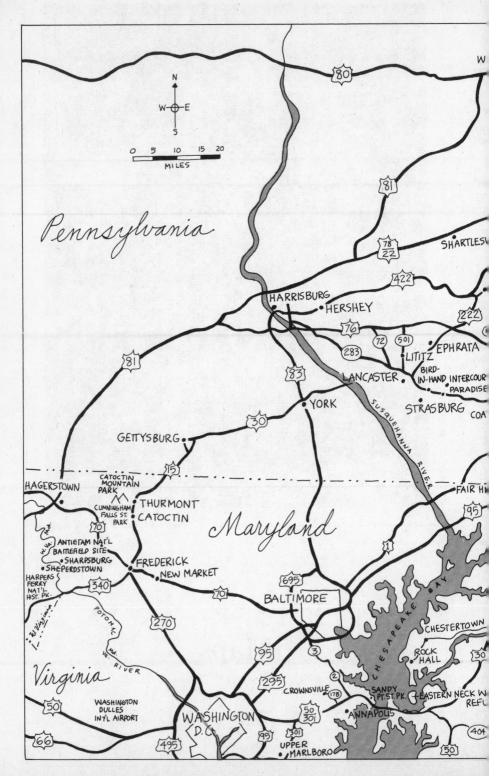

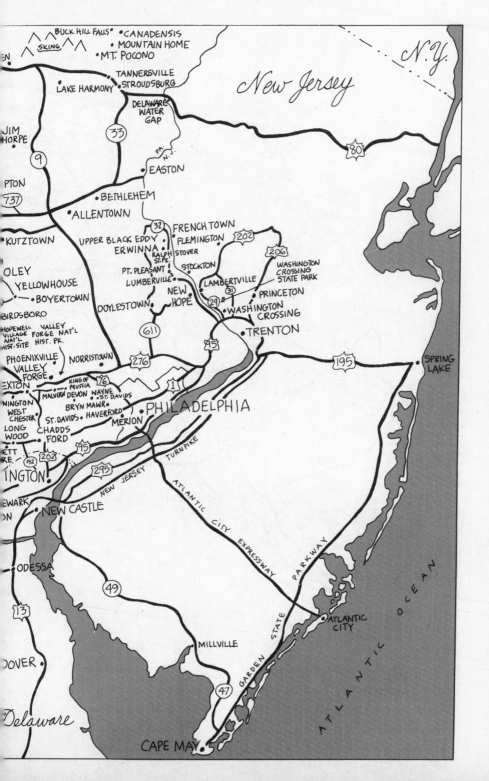

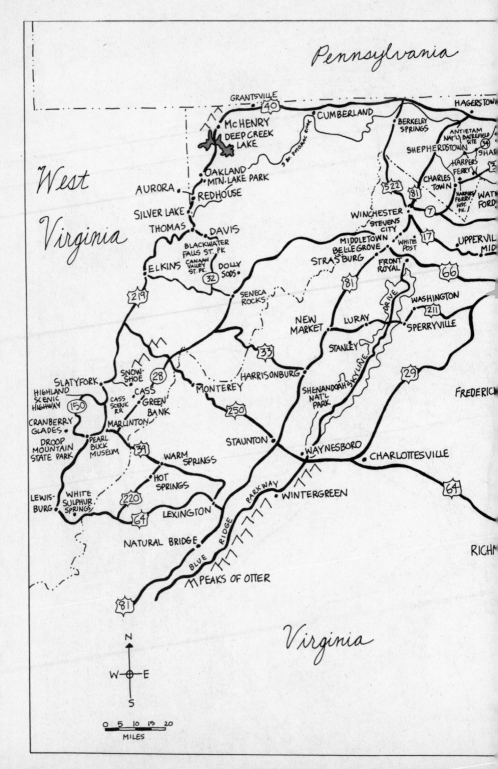

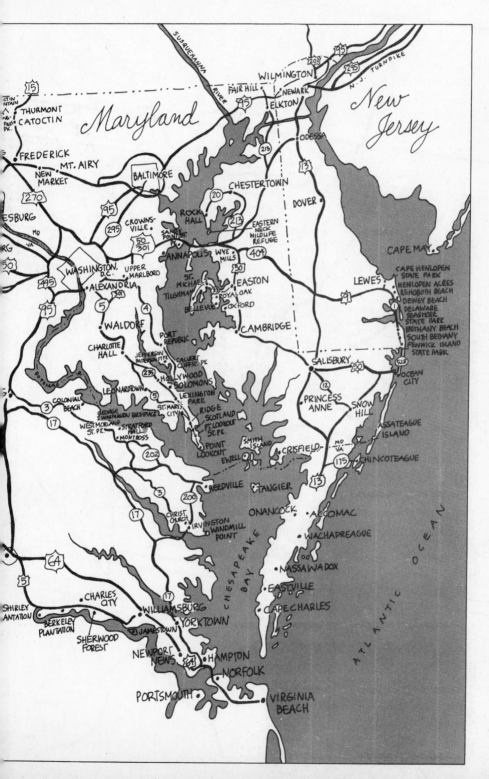

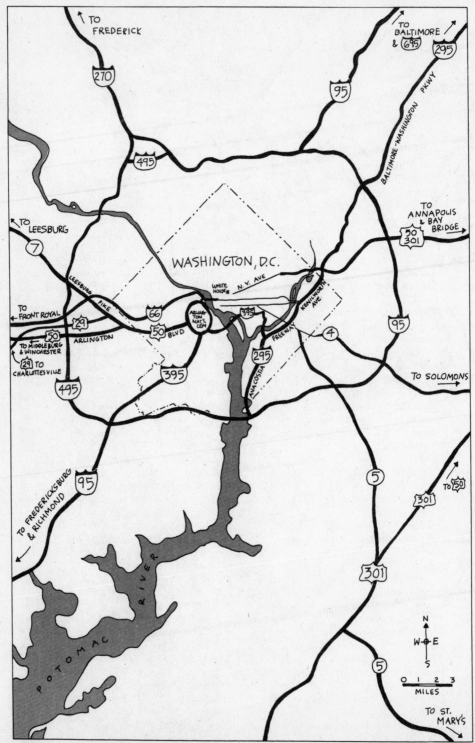

GENERAL INDEX

CATEGORY INDEX